T0382618

Green Retreats

Green Retreats presents a lively and beautifully illustrated account of eighteenth-century women in their gardens, in the context of the larger history of their retirement from the world – whether willed or enforced – and of their engagement with the literature of gardening. Beginning with a survey of cultural representations of the woman in the garden, Stephen Bending goes on to tell the stories, through their letters, diaries and journals, of some extraordinary eighteenth-century women, including Elizabeth Montagu and the Bluestocking circle, the gardening neighbours Lady Caroline Holland and Lady Mary Coke, and Henrietta Knight, Lady Luxborough, renowned for her scandalous withdrawal from the social world. The emphasis on how gardens were used, as well as designed, allows the reader to rethink the place of women in the eighteenth century, and understand what was at stake for those who stepped beyond the flower garden and created their own landscapes.

STEPHEN BENDING is a senior lecturer in English at the University of Southampton.

Green Retreats

Women, Gardens and Eighteenth-Century Culture

STEPHEN BENDING

CAMBRIDGE
UNIVERSITY PRESS

CAMBRIDGE
UNIVERSITY PRESS

University Printing House, Cambridge CB2 8BS, United Kingdom

One Liberty Plaza, 20th Floor, New York, NY 10006, USA

477 Williamstown Road, Port Melbourne, VIC 3207, Australia

314-321, 3rd Floor, Plot 3, Splendor Forum, Jasola District Centre, New Delhi - 110025, India

79 Anson Road, #06-04/06, Singapore 079906

Cambridge University Press is part of the University of Cambridge.

It furthers the University's mission by disseminating knowledge in the pursuit of education, learning and research at the highest international levels of excellence.

www.cambridge.org
Information on this title: www.cambridge.org/9781107040021

First published 2013

A catalogue record for this publication is available from the British Library

Library of Congress Cataloging in Publication data
Bending, Stephen.
Green retreats : women, gardens, and eighteenth-century culture / Stephen Bending.
   pages   cm
Includes bibliographical references and index.
ISBN 978-1-107-04002-1 (hardback)
1. Women gardeners – Great Britain – Biography.   2. Gardeners – Great Britain – Biography.   3. Gardening – Great Britain – History – 18th century.   4. Women gardeners – Great Britain – Correspondence.   5. Gardeners – Great Britain – Correspondence.   6. Women – Great Britain – Social conditions – 18th century.
I. Title.
SB469.9.B46   2013
635.082 – dc23   2013005956

ISBN 978-1-107-04002-1 Hardback

This book is for my parents – two quite different gardeners; and in memory of Kevin Sharpe – a great friend, and a great loss.

Contents

Illustrations

Acknowledgements

In a 1997 job interview, after giving a well-worn presentation on eighteenth-century gardens and politics, I was asked by Cora Kaplan, 'Where are the women?' Fifteen years later I've come up with an answer of sorts, and to reach it I have been aided by many. At Southampton, Stephen Bygrave, Gillian Dow, Clare Hanson, John McGavin, and Peter Middleton; to Sujala Singh and Aashish Singh Dasmahapatra I owe especial thanks; Linda Bree and my two Cambridge readers offered some extraordinarily detailed and generous suggestions and support; to them I must add Jennie Batchelor, Rachel Crawford, Margot Finn, Cora Kaplan, Larry Klein, Karen O'Brien, Annie Richardson, and Michael Symes. My thanks also to St Gabriel's School which was kind enough to give me access to Sandleford Priory. Over the years I have been aided immensely by a number of institutions. Along with leave from the Humanities Faculty at Southampton and from the AHRC, research fellowships from the Huntington Library and the Leverhulme Trust have played a crucial role in the completion of this project, not only allowing me time to do the research but sustaining a sense that such research was valued.

Introduction

Gardens are places of pleasure and of punishment; they are places to read, to dance, to work, to laugh, to study, to labour, and to rest; they are places of horticultural competence and of happy amateurism; they are places to imagine, to make, to own and to visit; they are places which speak of elsewhere and places which signify home; they are places of retirement and of ostentation, they are places of transgression, of meditation, of excitement, boredom, seduction, luxury, and suicide. All but the last are the subject of this book.[1]

This, then, is a book about gardens; but more than that it is a book about eighteenth-century women and the gardens they created, inhabited, and imagined. It starts from the assumption that the shaping of physical space is the shaping also of identity, and that gardens are microcosms, speaking of and reacting to a world beyond themselves. It starts also with an anecdote. In the summer of 1761 Sarah Lennox could be found in the hay fields of Holland Park: dressed in her finest clothes, and with one eye on the turnpike road, she was a shepherdess in search of a prince (Figure 1). This was no pastoral daydream, however, for the prince in question was the newly crowned George III and for a time – with the aid of her pastoral trappings – it seemed that she might succeed in becoming the queen of England.[2] Ten years later, disgraced by an extra-marital affair and by the scandal of divorce, she had swapped the landscape of pastoral for a landscape of disgrace.[3] Where before she had been a beautiful shepherdess waiting for her handsome prince, now she was a penitent waiting for absolution; and where once she had inhabited the splendid gardens of Holland Park, now, wearing plain clothes and a doleful expression, she was banished to an old manor house and country obscurity in the recesses of her brother's estate at Goodwood. Forced by her family to exchange the pastoral for the penitential, Sarah Lennox traversed the extremes of how her society imagined a woman in a garden; at each extreme she knew only too well the conventions, the expectations, and the costs.

If this language of pastoral romance and shameful retirement, of shepherdesses, piety, and penitents, of old manor houses and Edenic gardens seems the fanciful stuff of fiction, the staple of poetic effusions, and in short

1

Figure 1 **Palemon and Lavinia, 1780 (engraved by John Raphael Smith; painting by William Lawrenson). ©The Trustees of the British Museum (2010,7081.2227)**
Ostensibly an illustration of Thomson's pastoral lovers in *The Seasons*, the image was popularly thought to represent George III and Sarah Lennox. Holland House is recognisable in the background to the right.

a 'literary' world we should be careful to distinguish from lived experience, in the course of this book I will be arguing instead that such literary models were never far from the leisured elite, that they were amongst the first, and most powerful, associations to come to mind, and that when we look to the gardens created by women in the eighteenth century, the languages of retirement and disgrace, of pastoral, piety, and penitence are fundamental to the ways in which they imagined themselves and were in turn imagined by others. As Roy Strong notes: 'Actual gardens never quite shed their relationship to a rich literary inheritance. Such concepts would have been part of the furniture of the mind of any educated viewer of both actual and imaginary gardens.'[4]

It is as well to be clear about what kind of garden I have in mind here, and what kind of women. Along with the traditional kitchen gardens, fruit gardens, and flower gardens that take centre stage in the horticulturalist Philip Miller's long-running *Gardeners and Florists Dictionary* (first published 1724), the eighteenth century saw the burgeoning of town gardens and the increasing popularity of public pleasure gardens in London and other large cities.[5] It is not, however, kitchen gardens or fruit gardens, public pleasure gardens or town gardens that form the focus of this book; instead, it is the large-scale landscape gardens which came to be associated with an English style. By the middle of the eighteenth century that style had developed into various forms – in his influential *Observations on Modern Gardening* of 1770, Thomas Whately suggested the categories of ornamented farm, park, riding, and pleasure garden; other writers offered alternative divisions and distinctions – but with the need for large areas of land, and a concomitantly large income, one factor that held them together was that these gardens were beyond the reach of most. A focus on women who created such gardens inevitably means that this book is concerned with an educated, leisured, wealthy, and relatively tight-knit female elite; but this small group of women offer us an extraordinary density of writing about gardens which, while public in some sense, were nevertheless recognized as a private venture, as an image of their owner, as an opportunity to articulate one's identity, and as a place in which, and on which, one would be judged.

Even amongst this group of elite women, female experience can all too often disappear within estate papers and the 'shared' records of married life, or be misleadingly confined to the flower and kitchen garden. However, where sustained personal records do survive, large-scale gardens in the country clearly offered quite distinct opportunities both for female owners and for female visitors. As a private space visited by the public, as a public space shaped by a private individual, as a space in which one might very often be alone, and as a landscape designed to look beyond, and to resist domestic containment with its far-reaching views and a vision of large-scale change, the landscape garden was addressed by eighteenth-century women owners and women visitors with a sustained and particular intensity.

Part of the reason to write of gardens when in the country was that – unlike the town, with its more disparate, and more often indoor, pleasures and fascinations – the country offered fewer distractions; and part of the reason to write of the *landscape* garden was that it offered elite women a peculiarly dense, suggestive, at times contradictory, but undoubtedly nuanced means of writing about themselves. The gardening women I offer in this book are chosen because they have left to us a sustained record of their thoughts and actions and aspirations, but chosen, too, because they had an acute sense of what, and how, the garden could mean.

One of the most powerful aspects of the garden in the eighteenth century is that it allowed men and women, those who owned and those who merely visited, to claim its rich cultural resources as their own. In this they were aided by a great wealth of religious, literary, and practical writing that made the garden as much a metaphorical as a physical space. Gardens are not of course unique as spaces of solitude or retirement, of display or of ostentation.[6] They are, however, the locus for a recognisable complex of interconnected activities and concerns which range from solitude to sociability, from planning to planting, from politics to pleasure, and they carry a cultural freight on which individuals draw, or in which they can find themselves implicated and embroiled.

Tom Williamson has rightly argued that a stress on the literary has misled us in the past into a false account of eighteenth-century garden design by emphasising what was written over what actually happened on the ground. My concern is rather different; for, while Williamson's careful work brilliantly traces the physical layout of a garden, its changing appearance, and its broad social significance, that is only one part of its existence: as Williamson is also keenly aware, its significance lies at least as much in what is brought to it by an individual as in what is physically present. To put women back into garden history we should be less concerned with those narratives of innovations in design that have always championed the work of men, and we should turn instead to the sources in which women actually appear and to the cultures on which they drew.[7] We should turn, that is, to the letters, journals, and diaries, to the fiction and to the poetry in which women's gardens continue to have their existence. The world of letters and of cultural imagination was not just some literary exercise for women who gardened; rather it was a crucial part of the way in which they engaged with a world beyond their apparent rural seclusion. Indeed, if they have been largely omitted from narratives of garden history, women who gardened nevertheless confronted and were forced to engage with some of the central cultural narratives with which eighteenth-century society sought to understand itself.[8] Moreover, when we turn to the accounts of gardening left to us by eighteenth-century women, passive acceptance of gender roles and the cultural narratives that support them is far from universal. Rather, gardens are recognised as the opportunity for a self-fashioning engagement with cultural norms and narratives, a space in which the disparate agenda of eighteenth-century culture would inevitably have to be confronted.[9]

As an activity, gardening confronts the individual with both their influence over, and their place within, the world. Many of the documents left to us by amateur gardeners may appear to address little more than the vagaries of the weather, but even in this they imply the delight of seeing things grow and the disappointments of decay. Gardeners, that is, invest their hopes in plants that can all too easily wither under the external influences of the elements, diseases and pests, or from the gardener's own inattention or indifference. It is not that such experiences necessarily lead to reflection on one's place in the world, but they certainly provide the occasion for such reflection, and many women who gardened in the eighteenth century took that opportunity.

The eighteenth century provided a range of easily available models for such meditation and their interest lies not least in how the individual might engage with those conventions, embrace or resist them, question or deny them. Thus, for example, seemingly endless poems and essays celebrate the joys of country life, the advantages of retirement, or the pious opportunities offered by garden solitude; but if such writing could be turned to account for the individual's acts of self-fashioning, so too could it be wielded to reinforce eighteenth-century cultural norms of gender and class. In many cases such encomia could in principle at least be claimed by both men and women, and the garden could offer a shared space for labours at once physical and intellectual, moral and emotional. In important ways this is just what the idea of the garden did offer, both to men and to women; but it also allowed for a breaking down of those apparently shared interests along gender as well as class lines, and it was aided in this by a great mass of writing that claimed the garden as its subject while addressing issues spreading well beyond the cultivation of trees and flowers. When Sarah Lennox turned from pastoral romance to take up the role of penitential recluse after her ill-fated elopement with Lord William Gordon, both she and her family recognised, and then went on to reproduce, conventions to be found in popular magazines, in novels, and in moral tales. Her shift from pastoral to penitential was certainly physical in its geography, but it was also literary in that it repeated and reinforced the narratives her culture told itself, about itself, and literary too in that those narratives were articulated in terms of the complex language of retirement.

What is important here is that popular tales of seduction in gardens, of retirement to gardens, and of punishment in gardens, could jostle alongside biblical accounts of Eden, encomia on the joys of rural solitude, or classical tales of delightful retreat. At different moments each might be drawn upon to justify a way of life or a momentary experience, but each might also become a means for others to judge the individual against a claimed social norm and its inequalities. Notably, while in popular fiction and poetry men might be figured as melancholic recluses in the wilder parts of the countryside, or praised in poems for inactive leisure after public labours, it was women who were regularly punished with a lonely life in a garden that could give them no pleasure but only remind them of their loss.

For men who wished to do nothing but read there was a ready Roman inheritance; for men who wished to do nothing at all, that inheritance was conveniently refashioned by the likes of John Pomfret in his hugely popular celebration of retired sociability, *The Choice*.[10] Indeed, for the eighteenth-century man of leisure, myths of male retirement offered numerous justifications, and the figure of the man in the garden could be used to claim intellectual rigour, proper ease after political labours, or the innocent (and not so innocent) pleasures of quiet sociability away from the ambitions and corruptions of court and city. The creation or habitation of a garden offered a bulwark against accusations of being vulgar, or lazy, or dull: to garden was to create a work of art, to transform the physical world into the intellectual world of pastoral, to demonstrate one's distance from boorish rusticity, even to assert one's sense of national responsibility.

In the much repeated claim of Francis Bacon, gardening is an innocent pleasure; and its innocence is derived in part from its association with the intellectual, spiritual, and moral claims of retreat. For women, however, something far less comfortable is frequently at work, and that lack of comfort is acutely related to the problematic language of retirement with which eighteenth-century women had inevitably to engage. Certainly, in assuming the role of the penitential recluse in her plain clothes and obscure situation, Sarah Lennox adopted a set of retirement conventions wholly gendered in their assumptions about her misbehaviour, her necessary regret, and her equally necessary punishment. When her contemporary Henrietta Knight was thought to have had an affair with the Rev. John Dalton, the young parson still went on to modest success as a dramatist and writer of sermons, but Knight was immured in country obscurity for the rest of her life.[11] Poetry, piety, and literary tales could offer aspirational models for women who took to gardening on a large scale, but conversely they all too often reiterated and reinforced cultural expectations that could leave women alone in their gardens, that could taunt them with unattainable aspirations, and that as a result could damn them to disappointment, to disillusionment, and to a depressing sense of failure.

It is women's response to the clash of cultural narratives, traditions, and agenda surrounding the gardens in which they found themselves which offers us such a rich resource when we try to understand the place of the woman in the garden and the place of the garden in eighteenth-century culture. My aim is not to argue that when women created landscapes their actions and experiences were wholly different from those of men; it is, however, to argue that those experiences could be crucially different because of the gendered accounts of retirement received by both men and women. Often widowed, divorced, separated, or unmarried, women gardeners tended to be social and economic anomalies of a kind. As female landowners, such women confronted not only the dominant structures of landowning but the ideological freight which had built up around it. More than this, gardening signalled a peculiar kind of cultural agenda that distinguished it even from landowning: when it came to farming and estate management, landed women, like men, would inevitably use the services of local farmers, stewards, and overseers; when they gardened on a large scale their involvement was likely to be much more personal, and crucially, so too was their public identification with the landscape that they had created. Indeed, women who created landscape gardens inevitably engaged with the eighteenth century's understandings of women's place in the world, their relationship with the public sphere, with domestic space, with piety, luxury, retirement, and fame: if we turn to women's gardens, that is, those gardens turn us back to the larger culture of which they and their creators were a part.

When women gardened, then, they entered a conversation with both men and women, a conversation at once public and private, and a conversation which turned perhaps most frequently on the subject of retirement. However, while retirement for men was routinely inflected by a ready stock of classical examples, and justified with the easiest of nods to Horace, or Pliny, or Cincinnatus, for women such classical models were deemed of little relevance.[12] Thus, while men and women might share the same physical location, their sense of retirement might be quite different. What follows this introduction is an attempt first to identify the ideas and assumptions upon which such different experiences might draw, and second, to identify how the languages of retirement and gardening are played out in individual cases. Before we reach these case studies and the language of retirement with which they are so intimately entwined, however, I want to use the following pages to set out some contexts in which women and their gardens might most usefully be placed. Those contexts can be broken down into the following interrelated areas: a modern garden historiography still influenced by the eighteenth century's own insistence on design and innovation; conventionally gendered accounts of men and women's place in the garden; and women's robust responses to that gendered rhetoric of gardening which equates men with design, with education, and with intellect, but women with piety, domesticity, and sexuality.

My argument then is twofold: first, that far more women gardened on a large scale than most garden histories assume; and second that in gardening these women not only confronted their culture's assumptions about class and gender, but that these confrontations broaden our understanding of eighteenth-century gender politics as a whole.

With that in mind, this book recognises women's gardens – like men's – as an imagined quite as much as a physical space; and to make sense of that imagined space we must turn to the cultural languages in which that imagining was articulated, complete with their conflicting narratives and often quite divergent agendas.

The genius of the place / The place of genius

One of the founding myths of the eighteenth-century landscape garden is that it was the creation and the domain of men. Following the lead of eighteenth-century writers, modern historiography of the landscape garden has remained predominantly male in outlook and interests; it has placed at its centre the idea of male genius and the conceit of the male designer transforming a female Nature; and thus – with its fascination for design and for narratives of formal change – to read eighteenth-century garden history is predominantly to read a story of men. Characteristically, the names of professional designers from Charles Bridgeman (1690–1738) and William Kent (1685–1748) to Lancelot 'Capability' Brown (1716–83) and Humphry Repton (1752–1818) are used to articulate a series of 'breakthroughs' in design, all leading towards the 'natural' style of the late eighteenth century; to these professionals are usually added a handful of 'gentleman amateurs', including the likes of Charles Hamilton (1704–86) at Painshill, the banker Henry Hoare (1705–85) at Stourhead and the poet William Shenstone (1714–63) at the Leasowes. Equally, and despite the large number of gardens being created or remade throughout the century, the same few sites tend to recur in garden histories, whether those histories were written in the late eighteenth or the early twenty-first century.

A conventional account of changes in eighteenth-century garden design would run something like this: early in the century influential writers, including Sir Richard Steele and Alexander Pope started to reject the French and Dutch styles of gardening which had been popular since the Restoration and the Glorious Revolution (Charles II introducing the one, William and Mary introducing the other). They championed the removal of clipped hedges, parterres, and geometrical layouts, and in their place advocated a style of gardening that mirrored and drew into its bounds the natural beauties of the landscape. Thus, while the great Dutch topographical artists Jan Kip and Leonard Knyff's illustrations for *Britannia Illustrata* in the early decades of the century recorded the huge French-style geometrical layout of Badminton in Gloucestershire (Figure 2) or the careful topiary and parterres of Southwick in Hampshire, by the 1740s and 1750s it was the great show gardens of Stowe and Stourhead (Figure 3) which were in fashion, by the 1770s and 1780s it was the innumerable works of Capability Brown and his followers which were spreading across the land, and by the time that Jane Austen was writing her early novels, Brown's designs were in turn being adapted to a more domestic form by his self-styled successor, Humphry Repton.[13]

Whether we are told that the landscape garden is the apotheosis of 'natural' design, the culmination of an 'English' tradition, a site for personal engagement with nature, a killing ground for elite gift exchange, or a space asserting class solidarity, an emphasis on design and innovation has tended to cement the association between large-scale gardens and men.[14] In part, this is the doing of Horace Walpole (1717–97) who claimed in the middle of the eighteenth century that the landscape garden was a new and peculiarly English invention made possible only by the power of the landowning gentleman.[15] For Walpole, such gardens were the product of liberty and the aesthetic result of a political constitution that upheld the rights of the property-owning individual: his history of gardens is a history of inevitable progression towards 'Nature', but that account of the 'natural' is quite as much about politics, economics, and empire as it is about trees and fields and things that grow.

Not least thanks to Walpole, it became an eighteenth-century commonplace to associate the landscape garden with a kind of freedom Englishmen

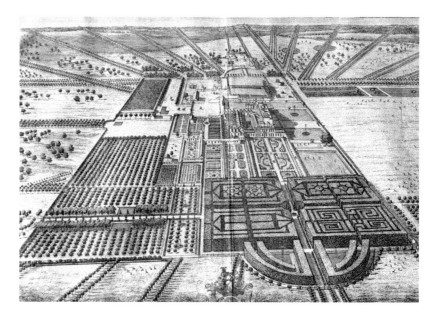

Figure 2 Badminton, Gloucestershire, from *Britannia Illustrata* (1708/9)
With its high clipped hedges and radiating avenues, Badminton's French-style gardens
became increasingly unfashionable by the mid-eighteenth century. Kip and Knyff's
image is conventional in entitling Badminton the seat of Henry Duke of Beaufort, but
it was the Duchess (1630–1715) who was largely responsible for the gardens, amassing
one of the largest collections of exotics in the country.

thought only they could know; but we should also be aware that this style
of gardening made its appearance in a century which saw an increasing
emphasis on property rights and a legal system which, while adopting a
rhetoric of individual liberty, was in fact removing many of the traditional
rights of the poor. In this sense, we should recognise landscape gardens
not only as aesthetic objects but as a metaphor for the power of the ruling
class and its legal system. The appearance of landscape gardens was made
possible in part by the removal of public rights of way, the enclosure of
common land, the rise of a wage economy, and an increasing rejection of
a manorial system which had asserted not only the rights but the duties
of the landowner.[16] Over the course of the seventeenth and eighteenth
centuries, the distance between those with property and those without
grew ever greater: we should be wary, therefore, of over-adulatory claims
for the glory that is the English garden and wary also of garden histories that repeat the self-serving rhetoric of an eighteenth-century male
elite.

Figure 3 View across the lake to the Pantheon, Stourhead, Wiltshire
Situated between London and Bath, Henry Hoare's Stourhead was one of the great
show gardens of the century. Maria Rishton wrote to Frances Burney in 1773 'I never
saw anything prettier in my Life'; John Wesley agreed but disapproved of the temples
and statues 'because I cannot admire the images of devils, and we know the gods of the
heathens are but devils; [and] because I defy all mankind to reconcile statues with
nudities, either to common sense or common decency'.

   While in the broadest of terms the narrative of formal change in garden
design I have just outlined remains helpful, in recent years garden historians
have sought to complicate the picture in a number of important ways.
Thanks to the work of Tom Williamson – with his careful emphasis on
when and where changes actually took place on the ground – it is much
less easy to assume a gradual transition from the 'unnatural' to the 'natural',
from the 'formal' to the 'informal'. As Williamson argues: not only did the
'formal' garden remain important at many sites well into the later eighteenth
century, but the early eighteenth-century garden can only be viewed as a
precursor of the Brownian style in the most cursory of ways and must
be understood in terms of its own precedents and in the context of its
contemporary social and political concerns rather than of those imposed
several generations later.[17] Similarly, historians are beginning to redress the
absence of the less-than-glamorous kitchen garden, the limited appearance

of the flower garden, and the only recently-studied town garden – all forms which tend to be associated with the domestic, and the first two, at least, predominantly with women.[18]

What stands to change our understanding of eighteenth-century gardens the most, however, is the new emphasis on reception and use. John Dixon Hunt has argued that until the late eighteenth century there was a common recognition that the garden necessarily used artifice in order to represent nature; that with the rise of 'natural' gardening in Europe, at least, the well-understood distinction between objects and representation all too easily collapses into an apparently undifferentiated 'nature'; and that accounts of the garden which lose sight of representation's role in design have predominated over the last two centuries.[19] Reiterating in the world of garden history what has been argued also in cultural geography and art history, Hunt stresses the relation between the garden and what is beyond it, and stresses also, therefore, the need to separate out the merging and conflicting accounts of nature with which gardens inevitably operate.[20]

As Hunt suggests, accounts of nature must necessarily be accounts of the cultural frames of reference and the modes of understanding necessary to articulate an individual's place in the world: if gardens are a knowing account of their relation with the world beyond, accounts of gardens are at least as much an image of that larger world. Distinct, perhaps, from any other art forms, the construction of the garden potentially placed man, or woman, within a physical statement of how he or she understood their place in the world, geographically, temporally, morally, and spiritually. It is also the case, of course, that the individual garden visitor – or owner – might be cheerily oblivious to most of these claims, inhabiting instead, for example, a world of fashion, class interests, or social competition. This brings us in turn to what Hunt has termed the 'afterlife' of gardens, that is, to the *use* of gardens by individuals, rather than a focus wholly on design.[21] It is the range of responses to the garden – by owners and by others – that is now being recognised in critical and historical writing, and which has moved garden history away – in part at least – from earlier obsessions with design, designers, and the recovery of design intentions which might somehow determine and solidify meaning.[22]

That there can be a fundamental mismatch between the intentions of designers and owners and the experiences of individual visitors has of course long been recognised – not least because there are frequently very different stakes at play and because individuals bring with them their own account of the world – but Hunt's term 'afterlife' points usefully to the need to take account of the variety of ways in which individuals might respond

Figure 4 The Flower Garden, Osterley Park, Middlesex
Sarah Child's recently-restored flower garden at Osterley, with its fashionably irregular flower beds and Robert Adam conservatory for exotics was developed from the mid-1760s. Conveniently close to London, Osterley was bought by the powerful banking family as a suitable country venue with which to impress clients.

to a designed object.[23] Such variety of response is not of course unique to gardens (though the range of responses may be); nor does it need to come *after* the designer's work is done.[24] As numerous accounts of garden-making suggest, conflicting responses to gardens, even as they are being made – which, with gardens, is almost continually the case – is inevitable and also inevitably an account of culture. In those sources where the traces of use remain, the role and significance of women becomes much harder to ignore. So too does the recognition that eighteenth-century accounts of 'nature' are constantly gendered and that women's 'nature' is as much the subject of garden writing as the physical landscape itself.

Even in older histories of garden design, it is not, of course, that women are said to have no place in gardens, but that their place is characterised as domestic, as private rather than public, as devotional rather than political, and so on. Above all, women are repeatedly associated with the small-scale and easily moralised endeavour of the flower garden (Figure 4). In some respects of course this holds an important truth. In general, with marriage came the transfer of property from the father to the husband and with it control of the estate, so that women were far more rarely landowners than men; and while the park and estate were properly considered the domain of men, the neatly defined, and confined, space of the flower garden was more usually assumed as the proper place for women. Lady Caroline Damer was nothing if not conventional in the gendered assumptions she made about large-scale landscape design on the one hand, and flower gardens on the other, when she wrote to her friend Lady Caroline Dawson in Ireland in 1785, 'I conclude Lord Carlow is very busy with his improvements at Dawson Court, but have you got a flower garden in order? That is such a pleasure at this time of the year, and so easily done if you delight in it yourself.'[25] All too often, when women appear in garden histories, they do so very much in Damer's terms and are set within the confines of the flower garden, associated with the respectable science of botany, or at best offered as quirky exceptions in a male-dominated world of large-scale landscape design.

As Mark Laird has shown, flower gardens formed an integral part of many pleasure gardens by the second half of the century, and they were increasingly associated with domesticity and femininity.[26] Some women, however, gardened on an altogether different scale, creating their own land-scaped estates either by buying in a designer like Brown or – more often than histories of the landscape garden suggest – designing for themselves or with their partners and taking an active and sometimes physical role in the creation of their landscapes.

Women landowners were hardly the norm in the eighteenth century, but they were far from unheard of; similarly, while women who created landscape gardens might be thought unusual, they were not thought of as startling oddities. As Arthur Young's scattered references to women garden-ers at the end of our period suggest, whether married or single, they are routinely mentioned in contemporary sources without the urge to remark further upon their gender. In his account of the recent landscaping at Snet-tisham Hall in Norfolk, for example – 'the seat of Nicholas Styleman' – it is Mrs Styleman who is responsible for the design and who has 'formed some exceeding pretty plantations; particularly those upon a stream, which she calls *New-bridge* and *Catherine's island*'. According to Young the stream

is managed with true taste; naturally it is only a ditch, but where this lady has improved it, it is a winding stream of clear water, and the greatest ornament of her plantations . . . The stream is yet more beautiful in the other plantation, called *Catherine's-island*; for it forms five little woody islands, with cool, shady, and sequestered walks about it, in a taste that does great honour to this most ingenious lady's fancy.[27]

However, for all that this may suggest a world of gardening free from gender distinctions (though note here a striking emphasis on the domestic, the small scale, and the fanciful), women in fact confronted quite different problems from men when they took to gardening on a large scale.

Shaping women's gardens

If we ask who shapes gardens, one answer is that it is the designer. But beyond their physical form, gardens are also shaped by their use, and the use of eighteenth-century women's gardens is frequently shaped also by conceptions of femininity. The brief account of garden history I have just given should make clear the successful insistence of recent work on recognising the garden as an ideological as well as a geographical location. With the fascination that history has demonstrated for great men and great designs, however, it has spent less time asking if women can be neatly subsumed within such accounts of class, taste, and politics, and has often ignored them because they were not the originators of a garden's design. Certainly there is a tendency in older garden histories to lose interest in the great gardening widows of the eighteenth century, or to see them only as maintaining the work of their now-dead husbands (as, for example, with the Duchess of Marlborough at Blenheim in Oxfordshire, or Lady Peterborough at Bevois Mount in Southampton).[28]

Part of the problem with traditional garden history, then, has been the listing of 'greats' and the assumptions on which that operates. For the significance of the English landscape garden lies not only in its major innovators and master practitioners but in the depths to which it penetrated eighteenth-century culture, the importance it was given as a national art, and the emotional significance with which it was invested by individuals. We take nothing away from 'great' men by arguing that gardens offer us rather more to think about; and if the insistence on great works and great designers effectively relegates women to the margins, we must look elsewhere for their presence in the garden.

What I also want to get away from is some notion that eighteenth-century women gardeners simply fit into traditional narratives but in a less interesting way because they do not appear at the forefront of innovation. Elizabeth Montagu's Sandleford Priory in Berkshire appears as little more than a footnote, or as the opportunity for an amusing aside, in the histories of its designer, 'Capability' Brown. Dominating the salon culture of late eighteenth-century London, however, Montagu was hardly a footnote, nor was she alone amongst women in recognising and drawing upon the garden's wealth of meanings. Indeed Sandleford was not only a major element of

Montagu's correspondence for half a century, but it played a crucial role in the self-fashioning of a woman acutely aware of her own public identity.

Montagu's attempt to fashion her garden as an account of herself raises another crucial issue. If the language of great works and great men tends to exclude women from its vision, that exclusion is made possible by shifting the act of labour from the physical to the intellectual: in this, women landowners could certainly share, and Montagu along with other elite women who chose to represent themselves in terms of retirement, solitude, and garden-making, inevitably relied upon acts of labour from which they chose to distance themselves. Claims of solitude or pastoral pleasure necessarily exist in the context of this labour and in the company of large numbers of people. It is not that labour is absent, rather, that elite status is dependent upon labour and dependent too upon an account of labour which makes it at once visible and invisible.

The majority of women in gardens (whether flower gardens, kitchen gardens, or landscape gardens) were not of course leisured ladies, but labourers; they were also, on the whole, illiterate. The effect of this last is particularly powerful as it confronts us with the limits of the historical record made by and in the image of the elite. In a large estate the position of gardener was inevitably filled by a man, but as Twigs Way notes, the 'monotonous but intricate work' of weeding and cleaning a large garden had long been the preserve of women, and often of single women.[29] Status, wealth, leisure, the ability to write, and the privileging of certain kinds of historical record all combine to curtail the traces of these women in the garden.

Estate papers, personal letters, and visual images all record the presence of working women in gardens; but they are rarely given a voice and often not even a name. On moving to Notting Hill in the 1760s, Lady Mary Coke found both that the gravel court was filled with weeds and that her gardener thought weeding beneath him (as, apparently, was gardening). Characteristically, Coke's response was to start the weeding herself, but she then also hired 'a Woman to come tomorrow that it may not look like an uninhabitable Place'.[30] If Coke knew any more of this woman it was not of enough importance to figure in a letter, and so she remains no more than 'a woman'.

At Montagu's Sandleford Priory, that same distancing of anonymous labour can also be found, even in the letters of a woman famously concerned to project a vision of her humanitarian credentials. In the summer of 1786 thirty three women and girls were at work in the pleasure grounds of Sandleford. In June of that year Montagu wrote to her friend Elizabeth Carter: 'The nightingales have not yet ceased to give their evening Song, but for some mornings, with less melody, I had sounds still more affecting to the human heart, the voice of mirth & joy from 33 Women & girls who were weeding & picking up stones in ye pleasure grounds. They laugh'd & sung incessantly.' A month later this same group of female workers appeared in a letter to another close friend, Elizabeth Vesey:

I now inhabit [my new dressing room] with great pleasure: each window of the Bow presents a most delightful pastoral scene, which was yesterday rendered more gay by 33 Women & girls singing while they were weeding & picking up stones from a place where there had been some building. My Nymphs were not such as the Poets describe the Arcadian Shepherds to have been, nor was there much of harmony in their tunes, or elegance in the lays they sung, but the tones of joy & gladness are ever touching to ye human heart, & mine sympathised in their chearfulness.[31]

While this tells us much about the propensity to frame – quite literally here – the countryside as pastoral, it does so by marginalising and making labour anonymous; thirty three women and girls may appear to be the centre of this sentimental scene, but – in true sentimental style – they ultimately focus attention on the benevolence and sympathy of their landowning employer. Any, or all, of these weeding-women might be replaced and the picture from the window would remain the same.

Even where we find quite detailed accounts of women working in gardens, as for example in the estate papers of Wotton under Wood in Buckinghamshire (an estate closely linked to Stowe, and owned by a junior member of the same family), the information such records provide is distinctly circumscribed. At Wotton (Figure 5), where a landscape garden was being created from the mid-eighteenth century onwards, women appear in the estate papers most noticeably once the main structures of the garden had been created, and in particular once the high-maintenance gravel paths – which would all too quickly be blemished by weeds – had been properly established. The form of the Wotton estate papers is telling in itself in that the record of payments is kept in two quite different forms, one as neatly-bound account books, the other a mass of individual vouchers recording individual payments. While women are almost uniformly absent from the account books they appear with regularity in the individual vouchers once the major work on the garden had been completed. What these carefully-folded vouchers confirm, and the account book does not, is that working-class women played an important role in maintaining and sustaining the gardens of the great. At Wotton, soon after the new layout had been established by 'Capability' Brown, Ann Tabby '& Co' were paid 'for

Figure 5 The Warrells, Wotton, Buckinghamshire
'Capability' Brown's naturalistic lake at Wotton replaced an earlier geometric design and required the sophisticated hydraulic engineering for which he was famous. Large numbers of weeding women were required to keep the gardens in order, especially the high-maintenance gravel paths.

weeding the Graville from the Menerserey Door to the Grotto Island' and 'for weeding the Graville from the Door at the Long Island to the Pirtar wall', while Ann Shepherd was paid 'for weeding the Graville from the head of the warrells [the lake] to Nepthons Bridge' (11 April 1767). Families like the Guntrips made the garden a major part of their income for decades: Edward Guntrip was employed to create many of the garden's hard and soft features (from planting and levelling turf, to making new gravel walks); and, like Ann Shepherd, Elizabeth Guntrip received regular payments (as on 27 June 1767) for 'weeding the Graville walk from Nepthon's Bridge to the head of the warrells' (clearly a problem area). By the 1790s, the expanding Guntrip family were all at work on the gardens, with Edward Junior, Sarah, Sarah Junior, and Mary all cleaning and weeding the gravel walks. In September 1791 they were joined by Hanna Lowe and Mary Mole who (with six men) were 'Working in the South Garden & Plantation & Fishen – and Workin in the For Court & making Borders round the frunt of the house for Flowers and Cuttin of the turf in Ditto pleace & taking up flowring Srubs upon the Grotto & throwing the Earth of Ditto and working with the Plumbers' (12 September 1791).[32]

Such examples of women working in gardens can of course be multiplied but their traces in eighteenth-century archives tend to reaffirm the vision of a landowning elite by mediating or suppressing the sight and sound of labour, by accounting for it as economic but otherwise uninteresting, or by offering it as a sentimentalised reflection of the landowner's benevolence.

One exception would be Mary Leapor's 'Crumble Hall' (1751). A rare country-house poem written by a working servant, Leapor's 'Crumble Hall' offers us an experience of the garden as glimpses from doorways and rooftops. Leapor wrote the poem after being dismissed from her job as a cook at Edgcote house (apparently for spending too much time reading), and gives her reader a detailed description of the estate and its inhabitants. Soon after Leapor's dismissal the gardens at Edgcote were remodelled in the new style and her poem ends with a lament that the once-familiar landscape has been uprooted in favour of 'modern whim'. With its delighted description of the old gardens, 'Crumble Hall' claims for its author an aesthetic appreciation of the landscape; tellingly, however, her narrator, Mira, remains confined within the working world of the house and its kitchen garden. Mira may momentarily see from the rooftop the 'gay prospect' of 'Meads, fields, and groves in beauteous order', but she is immediately plunged back into the 'nether world' of the kitchens. In 'Crumble Hall', social hierarchy, household structures, education, and even garden design, combine to exclude servants from the leisured visions of pastoral. Leapor may claim that vision for herself, but her poem recognises that, in this, she is exceptional.

Estate papers and the records of the elite would seem to affirm that sense of exceptionality, but in doing so they also highlight the gaps, absences, and occlusions which make a landowning vision possible. Tantalisingly, however, when we confront other apparently 'exceptional' cases – as with the letters of the governess Ellen Weeton with which I end this volume – they offer us a glimpse of just how much might be shared by women from quite different classes when drawing on their experience of the garden as an account of themselves.

Above the trifling Amusements of Ladies

One of the tensions for the garden throughout the eighteenth century was that while it was frequently claimed as a place of meditation, it was also recognised as unnecessary and perhaps, in its physicality, even a distraction from meditation. As the Earl of Shaftesbury had written in his *Philosophical Regimen* (a work not published till long after his death, but contemplated, no doubt, in one of his several town or country houses):

What are gardens, what are houses of show? – What are those the children make? What are dirt-pies? Or where lies the difference? In the matter or in the minds thus employed? Is it not the same ardour and passion? The same eagerness and concern? The same falling out and in? Angry, and friends again, in humour and out of humour... What is a rattle? – a figure, colours, noise? And what are other noises? What are other figures and colours? – a coach, liveries, parterre and knolls? Cascades, *jetts d'eau*? – How many rattles?[33]

However much the garden might be claimed for inward experience and the unworldly, it always also invites its inhabitant to experience the pleasures of the physical and the sensual. That dilemma was of course shared by both men and women, but it is women in particular who were associated with garden meditation, and women, too, who had to confront perhaps more obviously than men that sense of the garden not only as a private space of meditation but also as a demonstration of the false and dangerous delights of society.

As David Coffin and Sylvia Bowerbank have both demonstrated, the link between women's gardens and a form of domestic spirituality is insisted upon by numerous garden writers of the eighteenth century, both male and female, and in their insistence such sources invite us to reiterate the limited significance of women.[34] Indeed, if we turn to a work which has become pivotal in the debate about the 'newness' of the English landscape garden – Stephen Switzer's *Ichnographia Rustica* – we can see how fully established those conventions were by the early decades of the century.

Switzer's *Ichnographia Rustica* has an extended publishing history: the first volume appeared as *The Nobleman, Gentleman, and Gardener's Recreation* in 1715; a three-volume edition appeared in 1718 and a revised edition (used here) in 1741–2. Offering one of the first histories of English gardening, Switzer's text – with its emphasis on the value of modern gardening – provides us valuable insights into the state of garden theory and practice at the beginning of our period and it has come to play an important role in the debate about the originality and progress of the 'English landscape garden'.[35] Trained at Brompton nursery under the most famous gardeners of their day, George London and Henry Wise, Switzer (1682–1745) had first-hand experience of some of the major garden-making ventures of the century's early decades and indeed – with its detailed discussion of gardens from Hampton Court to Castle Howard – the *Ichnographia* has remained one of the founding texts for those histories of gardening which emphasise theory and design. The limits of such an emphasis become apparent, however, when we look to Switzer for women and their gardens.

As part of his survey on the current state of English gardening, Switzer includes, the 'Lives or Memoirs of the most eminent virtuosos in Gardening', listing around seventy important figures and the gardens they created. Amongst them are to be found only three women (and a fourth in a later aside): both the way in which they are represented to us, and the subsequent mining of Switzer's work for information on design and theory tell us much about a garden history which has remained predominantly male.

Switzer's eminently aristocratic women, the Duchess of Bedford (1580–1627), the Duchess of Beaufort (1630–1715), and the Countess of Lindsey (1645–1719), all gardened on an impressive scale, but alongside their horticultural prowess his main concern is to stress their domestic and spiritual virtues and to align them not with design but with flowers and with the specifics of horticultural plantation. Certainly he was in no way unusual, for example, in associating the women he names either with exotics and piety (Beaufort) or with a practical participation (Lindsey) which 'has something in it that looks supernatural'.[36] Indeed, the appearance of these women is heralded by a historical turn to the close association between women and flowers stretching back to the classical world. Noting first, 'The inextricable mazes and Forest-work Hangings wrought by the *Phrygian* and *Tyrian* Dames' which he links to their particular delight in 'Woody and Flow'ry Scenes' (vol. 1, p. 71), then the flower festivals or Floralia of Roman women, and finally Cleopatra's well-known love of flowers, he then turns to his contemporaries. With only the briefest mention of the Duchess of Bedford, Switzer gives especial praise to the Dowager Duchess of Beaufort, who, 'spent in her garden at Badminton those moments which many other ladies devote to the tiresome pleasures of the town . . . Her servants assured us that excepting the time of her Devotion, at which she was a constant attendant, gardening took up two thirds of her time.' He then continues, 'What a Progress she made in Exoticks, and how much of her Time she virtuously and busily employed in her Garden, is easily observable from the Thousands of those foreign Plants (by her as it were made familiar to this Clime) there regimented together, and kept in a wonderful deal of Health, Order, and Decency' (vol. 1, p. 72). It is not simply that women are linked with the exotic, and with exotic flowers in particular, but also that what is emphasised here is the domestication both of the plants and of the duchess herself, with the insistence on the good housekeeping of a woman who herself insists on health, order, and decency. Even the Duchess's interest in botany, and her patronage of scientists, is aligned with the arts of the virtuoso and with 'Botanick Amusements' (vol. 1, p. 73).

Of Lindsey (formerly Lady Elizabeth Pope, married to Robert 3rd Earl of Lindsey) and the large-scale planting on the family's Lincolnshire estates at Grimsthorpe he writes: 'This Lady was reputed to be a continual Attendant and Supervisor of her Works, without any regard to the rigid Inclemency of the Winter-season; and not only so, but also in the Measuring and Laying out the Distances of her Rows of Trees, she was actually employed with Rule, Line, &c.' But having established what may seem a worryingly practical and even mathematical understanding of gardening on Lindsey's part, he quickly continues, 'When Men are observ'd to busie themselves in this diverting and useful Employ, 'tis no more than what is from them expected; but when by the Fair and Delicate Sex, it has something in it that looks supernatural, something so much above the trifling Amusements of Ladies, that it is apt to fill the Minds of the Virtuous with Admiration' (vol. 1, pp. 73–4). In praising Lindsey's oddity, Switzer asserts – just as he had with the Duchess of Beaufort – that more usual association between women and the frivolous luxuries of city pleasures; and having nodded at the retirement poetry of Catherine Phillips – with its equally conventional dichotomy between rural contemplation and the 'glitt'ring World' – he turns to politics, to the public, and to the gardens of William and Mary.

For Switzer, the gardens of William and Mary – especially as designed by his mentors London and Wise – represent the zenith of garden art. Certainly he puts particular emphasis on Mary (another active – and innocent – gardener) and then on the continuation of this work (notably at Kensington) by Queen Anne; but, having offered this tradition of royal and aristocratic female patronage of gardens, he then turns to the professional and aristocratic men (from London and Wise at Hampton Court to the Earl of Carlisle at Castle Howard) whose work, he claims, epitomises the English style.[37] It is Castle Howard (another of the estates on which Switzer himself worked) that represents, 'the highest pitch that Natural and Polite Gard'ning can possibly ever arrive at' (vol. 1, p. 87), and it is this tradition, the tradition of the professional and of the gentleman designer – so insisted upon by Switzer – that has largely been followed ever since. The trajectory he traces, of progress towards the 'natural', has dominated the majority of garden writing ever since, and with it has come that easy acceptance of women's place being safely within the domestic economy and moral shelter of the flower garden.

In making the link between women and flower gardens Switzer was hardly alone: numerous guides offered women practical advice on the cultivation of flowers both native and exotic. In 1717, for example, with his *Lady's Recreation, or, The Third and Last Part of Gardening Improv'd*, Charles Evelyn compounded the connection by publishing a work predominantly on flower gardens and greenhouses and by assuming that this was naturally the domain of women.[38] In the introduction to the volume he wrote (in words close to Switzer),

As the curious Part of *Gardening* in general, has been always an Amusement chosen by the greatest of Men, for the unbending of their Thoughts, and to retire from the World; so the Management of the Flower Garden in particular, is oftentimes the Diversion of the Ladies, where the Gardens are not very extensive, and the Inspection thereof doth not take up too much of their Time.[39]

Praising the Duchess Dowager of Beaufort, as Switzer too had done, for a 'Soul above her Title, [and] Sense beyond what is common in her Sex', he offers her to his readers as the country's greatest example of 'Female Horti-culture' (p. 1). The exemplary woman gardener, with her careful (and natu-ral) attention to detail and her self-cultivated moral vigour is a trope which would find itself repeated throughout the century, and it is the flower gar-den, perhaps more than any other kind, to which writers would repeatedly return both as a fit place, and convenient metaphor, for female domesticity and moral worth.

In the middle of the century, James Hervey published what was to become a much-read collection of moral essays on an imaginary flower garden, *Reflections on a Flower Garden in a Letter to a Lady*.[40] When the poet William Mason described a flower garden based on his own design at Nuneham, in the fourth book of *The English Garden* (1782) a poem otherwise relentlessly political, he chose to moralise, sentimentalise, and to use that garden as the setting for a story of love and moral rectitude.[41] And in the same decade as Mason's poem appeared, we find the following in a collection of essays pitched squarely at the female reader:

A bed of tulips, a border of pinks, the jessamine and woodbine, not only regale my senses, but, by a secret finger, seem to point to the power who made them. Lessons of the finest morality may be conveyed by such lovely monitors. For my part, I know not a single flower that is less abounding in moral instruction, than in beauty and sweetness.[42]

Here, in *Letters to Honoria and Marianne* (1784), the moral usefulness of the garden appears in the context of a work written for a clearly middle-class female audience as a form of conduct book for polite society. Moral exercises become part of the conduct appropriate to well-brought-up young ladies. The work as a whole consists of a series of short essays on such subjects as taste, marriage, conversation, the folly of face-painting, pride, dissipation, retirement, reading romances, virtuous sorrow, particularity, friendship, choice of subjects in conversation, dress, and so on. Towards the end of the second volume we find a letter entitled 'On the Cultivation of Flowers', and here we are told:

> As it is a most convincing proof of a just and uncorrupted taste, to prefer the works of God to those of man, I am never more delighted than when I see my Honoria and Marianne busied in the cultivation of flowers. What lessons of morality are conveyed by such lovely monitors! – I often think, they abound no less in moral instruction, than in beauty and sweetness; which is, in truth, the very perfection of elegance: – they seem equally calculated to convey instruction and delight. How deplorably stupid, then, is that opinion of many people (who even set up for persons of *taste*), when they look upon them as *trifles*, utterly unworthy their notice! (Letter XXIX)

As the letter continues, the beauty of flowers, their delicate and fragile nature, and their inevitable decay are conventionally moralised. Honoria and Marianne are finally advised, 'There is, undoubtedly, the closest affinity between a proper cultivation of a flower-garden, and the right discipline of the human mind'. The industry and diligence needed to weed a garden 'will naturally suggest to a thoughtful person, how much more necessary it is, to exert the same diligence in rooting from our minds its various follies, vices, and prejudices'. Here, then, the flower garden is insistently equated with women, with a private female sphere set apart from the public world, and – in the context of the other letters – with a culturally defined range of respectable actions and attitudes.[43]

The power of this image, of cultivation at once physical and moral, becomes even more apparent when we turn from inevitably moralising conduct books to women's private letters. For here, too, that merging of physical and moral weeds comes naturally to mind. To take but three examples from many, in 1753 Lady Mary Wortley Montagu wrote from Italy to her daughter:

> I have now lived almost seven years in a stricter retirement than yours in the Isle of Bute, and can assure you, I have never had half an hour heavy on my hands, for want of something to do. Whoever will cultivate their own mind, will find full employment. Every virtue does not only require great care in the planting, but as much daily solicitude in cherishing, as exotic fruits and flowers. The vices and passions (which I am afraid are the natural product of the soil) demand perpetual weeding.[44]

Of a young woman being sent to a French nunnery in 1783 Elizabeth Carter would write:

I am persuaded there are many fair flowers in her disposition which will grow up and flourish with proper cultivation; but they have been sadly overrun with weeds, though I hope the present system will root them out.[45]

While at the end of the century, Judith Ussher wrote to a friend in July 1796 of her recent bout of depression:

When walking a few days ago in a garden, a lily attracted my attention; then how did the thought sink deep into my soul, that the soul that appears with acceptance in the presence of the Most High, must be clad in garments as pure and white as that lovely flower. How did I, and do I, fear I shall never attain to the being clothed with these unspotted robes.[46]

Ussher's response to the lily takes a particularly enthusiastic turn, but like Montagu and Carter before her she registers that sense of the flower garden inviting – almost demanding – a demonstration of moral or pious meditation. Indeed – as *Honoria and Marianne* suggests – the *idea* of the flower garden as a moral site becomes hard to disentangle from the physical flower garden in the social world: one is always, it seems, in both.

Fresh as the Verdure of her grassy Bed

Haunting these flower gardens of idealised domesticity and moral virtue, however, is an altogether different account of femininity; indeed it is not too much to say that these accounts of happy domestic morality are constructed from, and offered as a buttress against, a far more dangerous, transgressive, and unsettling account of natural female behaviour which aligns women with the city, with sexuality, and with the unchecked desires of a dangerously corrupting world of luxury. That point could hardly be more starkly made than in Mary and Matthew Darly's satirical image of 1777 entitled, 'The Flower Garden' (Figure 6), one of a series of caricatures of outlandish wigs.[47] With its immediate object of attack the increasingly large and elaborate hairstyles that had become fashionable in the 1770s, the print's use of a flower garden on top of the sophisticated city lady's hair addresses also the century's concerns about nature, proportion, luxury, usefulness, fashion, desire, and sexual morality. Setting high fashion against the old-fashioned (the hairstyle is very much of the mode, the geometric flower garden is not), and in depicting a male servant tending the garden rather than the woman imagined in *Honoria and Marianne*, it makes the flower garden's moral usefulness a thing of fantasy in the context of city fashion; it nods at natural

THE FLOWER GARDEN.

Figure 6 'The Flower Garden' (engraved by Matthew and Mary Darly) 1777.
Courtesy of The Lewis Walpole Library, Yale University
One of a series of engravings by the Darlys in the 1770s satirising over-sized wigs and
the fashionable women who wore them. The design of the garden is traditional, but the
rotunda with winged Mercury (top left) is distinctly showy.

female behaviour while signalling its absence, and conversely it suggests that self-display, an obsession with fashion, and the lack of proportion are naturally female; and, in insisting on the falsity of this feminine display and aligning that falsity with the city, it offers the ghost of domesticity and the quiet of retreat. We might also say that in signalling women's self-recognition as objects of desire, it emphasises that other crucial account of women in gardens, which is of sexuality and of ungoverned desires, and we might note that the statue of Mercury on top of the flower garden's rotunda suggests the usual associations with commerce (and thus fashion) but also stands to hint at least at the eighteenth-century's cure for venereal disease. What is at stake here is the nature of nature itself, not least the nature of female nature, and the gendering of nature as female: what holds together 'The Flower Garden' and *Honoria and Marianne* is, then, the clear recognition – overt in the former, silently but no less insistently asserted in the latter – that women must be cultivated, governed, controlled, if their naturally conflicting desires are to be socially contained.

Beyond the garden, the eighteenth century had a ready language for women's apparently contradictory natures and culture's equally contradictory expectations of female behaviour. In the garden, such dichotomies were signalled perhaps most easily by the use of statues of Venus and Diana. As both David Coffin and Wendy Frith have noted, Venus – the goddess of love and the goddess of gardens – makes a regular and significant appearance in landscapes designed by men.[48] Distinct from Diana, the goddess of virginity and the hunt, Venus signals both the sacred and the erotic charges claimed by the garden; she signals also the problematic position in which women – real rather than merely symbolic – were also placed by a culture which imagined the garden – and femininity – as at once domestic and decadent, pious and permissive. Focussing on Castle Howard in Yorkshire, and West Wycombe in Buckinghamshire, Frith has explored two eighteenth-century gardens in which Venus was to play a particularly symbolic role and has demonstrated how discourses of sexuality are played out in Ray Wood at Castle Howard, and, most notoriously perhaps, in the Temple of Venus and its associated structures at West Wycombe. In the former, the figure of Venus is balanced by the appearance of Diana, the erotic is placed in conversation with the virginal, and, at least in a poem by Anne, Lady Irwin (the daughter of the garden's creator), which offers to interpret the landscape, the two are claimed to be reconciled by marriage, by family, and by dynastic inheritance. At West Wycombe things are rather different, for it was here that Sir Francis Dashwood constructed a group of blatantly erotic garden structures, the foremost of which was a Temple of Venus, set upon a

Figure 7 **The Temple of Venus, West Wycombe, Buckinghamshire**
The reconstructed Temple of Venus and Venus' Parlour, replete with suitably
anatomical orifice and mound.

mound, complete with 'Venus's parlour', reached through an oval doorway,
and only the garden's most overt of gestures towards female genitalia and
an available sexuality (Figure 7). Around the estate were further invitations
to indulge in the natural pleasures of sex. Moreover, where Castle Howard
might balance the dangers of sexuality with the figure of a chaste Diana and
thus invite its visitor to construct an account of female sexuality safely contained within marriage, at West Wycombe, the goddess of virginity and the
hunt is replaced by Bacchus, the god of wine and libidinal excess. Stories of
the landscape being laid out in the form of a reclining female nude seem less
certain, but what is undoubtedly the case is that Dashwood's insistent sex-
ualising of his landscape is only the most obvious example of that easy turn
to a language of nature which aligns women with sexuality, with availability,
and with submission to male desires.[49]

The use of statues of Venus or Diana should of course alert us to
those other physical signifiers of femininity in the garden. At Stowe, for
example, the Lady's Temple (Figure 8) celebrates the domestic virtues of

Figure 8 The Elysian Fields, Stowe, Buckinghamshire
The emblematic, and politically charged, view from the Temple of Ancient Virtue
across the 'River Styx' to the Temple of British Worthies; the Lady's Temple (now
renamed the Queen's Temple) is visible on the far left.

needlework, shell-work, music, and painting, but is also separated by only a
thin band of trees from the famous – and distinctly manly – political satire
made up of the Temple of Ancient Virtue, the Temple of Modern Virtue
(built as a ruin), the Temple of British Worthies, and the headless statue
of Robert Walpole.[50] As numerous commentators have noted, the relation
between the temples and the headless statue tells a tale of modern corruption (notably under Walpole), of ancient ideals (the Temple of Ancient
Virtue contained statues of Lycurgus, Socrates, Homer, and Epaminondas,
all suitably inscribed) and of a distinctly Whig history of progress signalled
by the carefully chosen busts of poets, politicians, monarchs, and merchants
set into the Temple of British Worthies.[51] That satire, and the insistently
readable relation between structures and inscriptions, has made Stowe one
of the foremost examples of the 'emblematic' garden, and it is this political iconography which remains the garden's best-known feature; but Stowe
also offered itself as a 'garden of love', a garden which, much like West
Wycombe, contained temples celebrating Venus and venereal pleasures,
offered lascivious poetry and painted scenes of love-making, and which –
just as West Wycombe – assumed a classically-educated male audience while
imagining a sexually available femininity. Thus, while the Lady's Temple,
like the flower garden, offered a space for domestic femininity to be celebrated, alongside this contained space of domestic feminine enactment

Figure 9 The Temple of Venus, Stowe
In its modern guise the temple looks much more innocent than its original design; the
voyeuristic ceiling-paintings of naked women and the smutty poetry are no longer in
evidence but were recorded in detail in the various mid-century guidebooks to Stowe.

was a far more pervasive account of femininity as sexually permissive or
submissive.

In the Temple of Venus (Figure 9) – complete with Francesco Sleter's
ceiling painting of a nude Venus and distinctly lascivious, indeed voyeuristic,
scenes from *The Faerie Queene* – but perhaps most notoriously in the Latin
inscriptions to be found in St. Augustine's Cave, Stowe offered its male
visitors a series of titillating scenes. Of the numerous poems in the latter,
and along with the claim that 'In what we call the Loins, they say, / The Devil
bears the greatest sway', visitors were confronted with a Latin poem on the
swelling 'fleshly Members' of monks and invited to imagine with the poet
the vision of an enticingly naked 'maid':

Fresh as the Verdure of her grassy Bed,
Reclin'd in Posture half-supine, she lay,
A World of Beauties did her Form display:
Her Face, her Neck divine, her Bosom too,
With all their Charms were open to my View.
Her heaving Globes no sooner struck my Eye,
But strait the Flames thro' all my Vitals fly.[52]

This turn to the erotic could hardly be lost on visitors. Certainly in Thomas Cogan's novel *John Buncle, Junior* (1776) – much of which is set at Stowe – the stark contrast between sophisticated political rhetoric and predatory male desire becomes an opportunity to dramatise the sudden shifts of which the garden was capable and the radically different sense of space that it might create for male and female visitors. In Cogan's novel, a mixed group of visitors take the tour of Stowe, stopping at each of the temples, and engaging in conversations duly prompted by each of the garden structures (a practice both assumed and enabled by numerous guidebooks, and by the likes of William Gilpin's early work, *A Dialogue on the Gardens at Stowe* of 1748). On reaching the Cave of St. Augustine, Buncle notes the inscriptions 'in imitation of the old monkish rhimes', but is dismayed when he discovers their obscenity. 'Without affecting the prude', he writes, 'I must acknowledge that I felt myself both disappointed and disgusted when I entered this cave'. While there may be room for obscenity in the temple of Venus or Dido's cave, this spot 'naturally conveys to the mind . . . the ideas of a happy retirement, and a pious poverty' (vol. 2, pp. 17–19). Buncle is relieved that the inscriptions are at least in Latin and apparently therefore beyond the capacity of 'chaste eyes', but in the following letter, entitled 'Learned Ladies', this very issue is emphasised as Fanny, a new member of the party, asks for a translation of the inscriptions. One member of the party, the rakish Charles, 'was in a mood for cross purposes, and instead of giving their literal meaning, he translated as follows; *Diem perdidi*, "we have been losing time, Fanny"' and continues with a series of sexually rendered translations which Buncle confirms and which Fanny finds less than amusing: 'She immediately began to expatiate upon the tyranny of our sex, who purposely keep as much knowledge as possible to themselves, in order to triumph over her's' (vol. 2, pp. 30–1). The use of Latin inscriptions, which Henrietta Knight would find such a problem at Barrells, assumes and even appears to demand a submissive role for women in this fictional account of Stowe. Lady Mary Wortley Montagu, whom Fanny summons to the defence of female learning, was no doubt right in characterising her own learning of Latin as a Promethean act of transgression.[53]

Stowe, like some of the other great show gardens, was in fact well provided with guidebooks for such tourists as Fanny; very much products of polite culture, such guides – with their translations of Latin quotations – provided another form of entry into the landscape of the patrician elite and one which largely circumvented the exclusions of gender.[54] However, the combination of casual male erotics, limited female learning, double standards of propriety, and gendering of power relations is, I would suggest, central to women's experience of the garden in the eighteenth century.[55]

In the face of such pressures, even the flower garden could become a difficult space. When, in 1791, Mary Morgan visited the flower garden at Blenheim, she recorded an experience not of moral cultivation but of wariness because its distance from the house, and its associations with sensuality, made it seem a dangerous space for a lone woman:

> whilst the beaux pursued their walk, I explored the flower garden. I was in some degree of trepidation, till I had got out of it and approached near the house, for the distance from it is very great; and as there is a number of parties walking, it had rather an appearance of singularity for a female to be seen by herself, in a secluded part of the garden... It put me in mind of an eastern harem, where every female displays the utmost of her charms, in hopes of attracting the attention of the sultan. Thus these favourites of the hour open their beautiful eyes, and expand their delicate leaves, to attract the notice of the god of day.[56]

Morgan's uneasiness characteristically signals the need for moral expression when confronted by the garden's erotic potential, and signals too that the garden is a space in which women are on display. This is not to argue that women who found themselves in gardens necessarily defined themselves in such terms; but it is to argue that we should attune ourselves to the pervasiveness of such language and its influence on women's self-representation, whether that self-representation drew on the language of piety or botany, philosophy or fashion.

Women shaping gardens

So far we have been exploring those mainstream accounts of eighteenth-century gardens which align women either with pious domesticated femininity or with a passive sexual availability; but women were far from silent in their responses to such naturalising of the gender divide. As Frith's analysis of the notoriously sexualised gardens at West Wycombe suggests, claims about sexual behaviour, its naturalness, and the gendered assumptions about desire and submission loom large in eighteenth-century gardens; in turn, that raises the question of how women might respond in the face of such an apparently insistent discourse. The fictional account of reception in *John Buncle, Junior* is one kind of answer, but Lady Irwin at Castle Howard was far from alone in her attempt to resist careless male erotics and to claim the resources of the garden as her own. Moreover, while physical structures can be seductive (not least to modern critics) in their attempt to dominate the meaning of the landscape and to tell a particular kind of story, they can also leave untold the rather different stories of use, and in particular of use by women. That is, for all its seductive power, iconography should in fact alert us to its own limits and to the limits of an iconographical approach to garden history: an emphasis on statues of goddesses and assumptions about the importance of iconography invite us to assume the influence of designers and their intended meanings rather than to explore responses or to recognise that designers' intentions can always be evaded or ignored.

In a garden one can literally look the other way; indeed one need hardly look at all. When Lady Caroline Dawson attempted to recall all the York-shire gardens she had visited in July 1781, she found they had become indistinguishable: in a letter to Lady Louisa Stuart she wrote,

But to go back to my tour. I must tell you, after Lord Exeter's, the next place we proceeded to was the Duke of Kingston's, which I admired almost as much . . . The next was the Duke of Newcastle's, but I don't know why I should describe places you have probably seen when you was in Yorkshire, and indeed I could not describe them very accurately, for we were in such a hurry we hardly saw any of them with comfort, as they all lie close together, and four is rather too many to see in one day and get to a good inn to sleep at besides, so at the Duke of Portland's we only saw the garden and plantations, and the same I think at the Duke of Norfolk's, but, as I said before, I regret I did not give you an account at the time, as I have almost forgot which was which in the number we saw.[57]

So much for iconography. Much harder to evade were those far more per-vasive, normalised, indeed naturalised, accounts of women and gardens which – like the myths of Venus and Diana – invite assumptions about female virtue, female sexuality, female intellect, and their relation to the natural. Women's letters, for example, in which they describe their own or others' gardens, spend little time on statues of Venus, or temples of love; as my case studies will demonstrate, however, they are acutely aware of the languages of sexuality, the normalising fantasies of rakish masculinity and of passive or permissive femininity, and acutely aware also that when writing of themselves and of gardens, they must respond to, resist, or articulate themselves in relation to these ubiquitous assumptions. That is, while the traditional sources of garden history tend to reiterate an equally traditional gender politics, women's letters and journals in fact record a far more boisterous, challenging, and intellectually varied range of possibilities.

Though boisterous would hardly be the word, we can see something of this in the gardening life of Frances Seymour, Lady Hertford (later the Duchess of Somerset). Hertford (1699–1754) is perhaps best known now as the woman to whom James Thomson dedicated 'Spring' in his four-part poem, *The Seasons*, where she appears – convenient to Thomson's larger agenda – as a figure of natural domesticity and connubial bliss. Hertford, however, was quite capable of speaking for herself, of fashioning her own image, and if that image reiterated some of Thomson's claims, we can nevertheless see how the stuff of gardening might help in the construction of a voice more nearly her own.[58] Hertford's careful discussion of female retirement in letters to her friend the Duchess of Pomfret will appear in a later chapter; here, however, we can fruitfully turn to a poem she wrote in response to one by Lady Mary Wortley Montagu on the character of Lord Bathurst.

In 1739 the Hertfords had bought Bathurst's old estate of Riskins in Buckinghamshire (also known as Richkings, or Richings, and later renamed Percy Lodge). Bathurst had poured huge resources into the gardens and by the 1720s Riskins had become a favourite meeting place for Alexander Pope, the politician Henry Bolingbroke, and their close circle of friends.[59] An early example of a *ferme ornée*, Riskins was also championed by Stephen Switzer in his *Ichnographia Rustica* (a plan of Riskins appears in the 1742 edition). For Switzer, Riskins represented a Roman ideal in its merger of the productive and the ornamental; Pope, too, delighted in the irregular beauty and the old-fashioned hospitality of what he referred to as Bathurst's 'extravagante bergerie'; but by 1735 – for all the initial enthusiasm – Bathurst had largely lost interest and turned his attention instead to his huge estate at Cirencester.

On taking up residence at Riskins in 1739 Hertford sent her friend a series of detailed descriptions of the gardens and admitted in a letter of 1742: 'I begin to fear that the air of Richkings is whimsically infectious; for its former owner had scarcely more projects than my lord and myself find continually springing up in our minds about improvements there.'[60] Nevertheless, Hertford was keen to stress her difference from Bathurst, and in particular to separate the whimsy of design from an account of herself as the true possessor of the garden.[61] Her poem on Bathurst appeared as a part of this correspondence with Pomfret, a correspondence which had already established Hertford's quite insistent identification with a life of spiritual and domestic retirement.[62] It is that insistence on retirement, but on retirement as use, as activity, as spiritual engagement with the creation, which Hertford also uses to mark out her own sense of the garden from that of its original designer.

The poem begins conventionally enough: Bathurst, the great man, has designed the garden as a place of retreat, 'Of Love and Gaiety the destin'd seat', where maids of honour can pleasurably rove, while statesmen 'might forget the nation's cares, / And find a refuge from perplex'd affairs'. Men are aligned with public life, Bathurst himself with wide-ranging interests, with political endeavours, and with the genius of design, while women flit amongst the gloomy groves enjoying sensual pleasures. But this all-too-recognisable account of gender politics in the garden is swiftly followed by the quite decisive assertion of Hertford's ownership once the estate has changed hands, and with it the subordination of male design to female use. Thus, Hertford writes,

For such he form'd the well-contrived design;
Nor knew that Fate (perverse) had mark'd it mine.
Amazing turn! – could human eyes foresee
That Bathurst planted, schem'd, and built, for me?

But she then goes on to align Bathurst, rather than women, with the loss of proportion and with endless desires (a neat reversal of the strategy used in the Darlys' coiffured 'Flower Garden'): his energetic and apparently manly urge to design is aligned not with sober seriousness, but with a flighty, pleasure-seeking desire ('Yet, to perfection when his work arriv'd, / His fanc'y tir'd of all his art contriv'd'); and his notion that this small garden ('Within a pale of scarce two miles confin'd') could be in any way suitable for a great man in retirement is laughed off as a piece of foolishness, a failure to know himself, a failure to be content. Setting the great man against the domestic woman she returns to her refrain of ownership:

Again I ask, could human eye foresee
That such a one should plant and build for me?
For me! Whom Nature soberly design'd
With nothing striking in my face or mind:
Just fitted for a plain domestic life, –
A tender parent, and contented wife.

Insisting that – unlike Bathurst's fantasy of wits and politicians, of modern nymphs 'dancing on the green' – this is a garden of retirement truly understood, the poem concludes with an elaboration on the pleasures of the natural world when one has given up public life. Thus, in a poem which apparently accepts the dignity, seriousness, and significance of male public life and private study – all instantiated in the designing and desiring of a garden as a place of retreat – Hertford repeatedly undercuts those claims by aligning Bathurst's *creation* of the garden with the temporary pleasures of the chase, but her *use* of the garden with contentment (conventionally enough figured as domestic and spiritual, to be sure), with a sense of self-knowledge, and finally (as a poem written to Pomfret) with the reconfirmation of female friendship.

Hertford's emphasis on male and female desire in, and use of, the garden springs not least from her acute awareness of the gendering of retirement. I opened this chapter with the tale of Sarah Lennox, but as Hertford's poem suggests, Lennox is only one of many women who chose, or was required, to articulate a sense of self in terms of conflicting accounts of retirement, of social and spiritual submission, of natural domesticity. Certainly Hertford's claims for the garden are set within confines we might recognise from the likes of Switzer or Aubrey at the beginning of the century, but her poem should also alert us to the ready use of gardens in ways not sanctioned by designers and not simply defined by men. Thus, for example, while in *John Buncle, Junior*'s account of Stowe we saw how garden structures might be used to dramatise female exclusion and the opportunities of male dominance, we might set alongside it not only Hertford but, from a quite different perspective, Frances Sheridan Lefanu's account of visiting the garden of the famous travel writer, Philip Thicknesse, in Bath.

Writing to her sister in 1786, Lefanu described Thicknesse's garden at The Hermitage in some detail: remarking on the garden's various sentimental structures and invitations to think sad thoughts (notably with the repeatedly carved Miltonic inscription, 'il penseroso'), the 'grotto' in which Thicknesse buried his daughter, a memorial to Chatterton and another to a favoured travelling companion, Lefanu's careful description of a garden is also a record of her friends' experiences and of their resistance to its intended designs.[63] At the daughter's grave a quotation from Pope's poem on a female suicide is drily questioned ("What tho' no Sacred Earth allow thee room, etc etc' but as Miss Thicknesse did not destroy herself I can not say I thought the selection judicious'); Thicknesse 'and a party of ladies walking past with as much unconcern as they look on any other garden ornament' is duly noted; and after yet another 'il penseroso' inscription, this time to the travelling companion who turns out to be a monkey called Jacko, and whose fine qualities are praised above those of dogs (or as Thicknesse has had it inscribed on the monument 'Those sons of Bitches'), things rather fall apart. The scene

quite got the better of [her companion] Mrs Paterson's gravity and the young Ladies caught the laugh – as Thicknesse was still in sight I was fearful of giving offence and scolded and remonstrated in vain . . . finding all attempts to bring them to order were in vain I escaped into the nearest field to avoid being included in the censure I thought they would meet for a conduct so contrary to all ideas of sentiment, and at the same time to indulge a good laugh which I had suppress'd with great difficulty.

Lefanu's anecdote should alert us to those moments when the kind of conduct-book gender divides of *Honoria and Marianne* fail to be maintained, as here when Thicknesse's invitation to sentimental emotion is met with laughter born of intellectual self-confidence but which is also only possible, perhaps, because of Thicknesse's relatively lowly social status and what was, by all accounts, a rather pompous public persona. As a statement of Lefanu's surefooted sentimental and aesthetic judgement the anecdote could hardly be clearer; but the telling of this tale in a letter to her sister is also about something else. It is about the recognition of the garden as a place of peculiar freedoms and as the opportunity for the performance of female friendship and the assertion of a feminine sociability. Crucially, then, what is being constructed both here and in Hertford's poem on Riskins is an imagined space which recognises itself to be in competition with other forms of gendered space both urban and rural. Taken in conjunction, what Hertford and Lefanu's accounts should make most apparent is that the garden is a place of conversation, whether one is an owner or a visitor, whether one is in the country or in the city, whether one is female or male; and that conversation is as much about the construction of sociable identities and about conflicting imagined spaces as it is about any slavish subservience to the imperatives of design.

Women, gardens, and retirement

Hertford's poem about Riskins was written of an estate shared with her family, and while a husband and wife's engagement in the stuff of garden design was perhaps the norm, women commissioned, developed, maintained, and enjoyed gardens with very little need for the designing presence of men. It is these women who are the main focus of this book, and my choice of them is made in the belief that things were different for women. Drawing on the wealth of sources and genres which take the garden as their subject – and particularly on women's correspondence both with men and with women – I aim to demonstrate what some of those differences were, but it is also important to recognise the range of experiences and rhetorical manoeuvres which might be shared by women and men alike; or at least by women and men who were alike, in terms of class, wealth, and often education. Certainly, in concentrating on women, on their gardens, and on the idea of retirement, I am not suggesting an experience wholly separate from that of men, or indeed articulated in wholly different terms; I am, however, arguing that the gendered language of gardens and retirement offered peculiar problems to women in gardens, to women who gardened, and to women who wrote of gardens.

Focussing on the garden as a place of retirement also helps us to collapse unhelpful distinctions between physical geography, literature, and cultural 'meaning'. Assuming the importance of use, of the active construction and inhabiting of space, helps to free us from garden history's obsession with innovation and design, a history in which women tend to disappear from view. If one looks to the design of women's landscape gardens it is tempting, for example, to suggest that they contained fewer inscriptions and political pointers than those of men; it is also tempting to argue that when women's gardens addressed an audience that audience tended to be private rather than public (whatever value such a distinction might hold). In truth, however, I have been unable to discover – and will be unable to offer my reader – some neat account of how women's gardens looked different from men's. What I can do is suggest what might be different for those who did the looking and for those who – in gardening – offered themselves to be looked at. Thus, while I will sketch out the physical forms of gardens created by Elizabeth Montagu at Sandleford Priory in Berkshire and Henrietta Knight at Barrells in Warwickshire, by Lady Mary Coke at Notting Hill and by her neighbour Lady Caroline Holland at Holland Park, my concern is with spaces which must constantly be constructed and reconstructed by owners and by others, spaces which change in shape and significance as they confront and negotiate alternative evaluations, representations, and needs.

To reconstruct such imagined space we must turn to the cultural languages in which that imagining was articulated, complete with their conflicting narratives and often quite divergent agenda. While it was undoubtedly possible for men and women to share some of these accounts of the garden and of retirement, there were powerful cultural narratives with which women alone had to grapple and with which both men and women had been schooled from an early age. Notably, women's letters and journals, poetry and fiction repeatedly turn to the idea, and to the value of the garden: gardens visited, imagined or made; gardens as places of pleasure or of danger; gardens as punishment and gardens as reward. In this they offer an experience of the garden often quite different from those apparently normative accounts of masculine genius and feminine domesticity so often reiterated by garden history. Repeatedly placed within conflicting paradigms – from the temptress of *Paradise Lost* to the intellectual retreat of Astell's *Serious Proposal*, from the penitent (and not so penitent) recluse of Elizabeth Rowe's fictional letters to the ideal woman of *The Spectator* and *The Tatler* – the problem for women gardeners, we might say, was the abundance of culturally important roles they might choose to embrace, or into which they might be pushed. To put that another way, we might also say that in gardening women were confronted with the problem of trying to do retirement by the book.

To support such claims, this book is broken into two parts. In the first half I map out the eighteenth-century's problematic engagement with the idea of female retirement as it appears in both literary and private writing, from novels and poetry to pious tracts, practical guides and personal correspondence. My purpose is to sketch out a range of narratives and allusions with which one might construct an account of oneself in a garden; but it is also therefore to argue that gardens are made from what one brings in to them; that physical location is an invitation to construct psychological space; and that space is something over which one has only partial control. By offering these alternative and overlapping modes of retirement, I want to map out an apparently shared language but also to explore why accounts of solitude and retirement, of piety, pleasure, and penitence, offer such difficult and yet appealing models for women to embrace.

Such abstractions, however, can hardly be lived and female retirement is inevitably enmeshed in, a part of, and generated out of, the social world from which it claims to be distinct. Thus, while it is important to sketch out that range of discourses which look to, or draw upon, the idea of the garden and the place of retirement, in the second half of this book I turn to individual lives and individual gardens. Drawing in particular on private letters and journals, these case studies range from gardens commissioned by women (Sandleford), to those created with husbands (Holland Park), and gardens created predominantly alone (Notting Hill and Barrells). As my combination of married, widowed, and single women suggests, in adopting the category of women gardeners I am not suggesting a world of activity wholly separate or disengaged from men. I am, however, attempting to redress the balance in male-orientated garden histories, both by reiterating that women gardened on a large scale – with and without men – and by taking seriously their gardening activities, their possible motivations, and the attempt to fashion an account of oneself with the aid of a garden.

The case studies I offer in this book are held together by the survival of a sustained record of use by owners and by others, by a sustained interest in the problem of female retirement, and by a recognition that gardens offer us something more to think about than varying arrangements of trees and flowers, of open spaces and walled enclosures. As case studies, these examples are not chosen as generally representative of women gardeners, neither do they reiterate the eighteenth century's own insistence on the flower garden as the fit domain of women. If botany, too, seems strangely absent here, it is absent not least because its emphasis tends to reiterate that gendered eighteenth-century rhetoric of female accomplishments and, in so doing, to underplay the more complex relations women might have with their gardens and with the self-fashioning that those gardens might allow.[64]

Finally, then, these case studies are an attempt to explore some of the ways in which accounts of cultivated self-awareness, of pleasure, and of punishment, might be fragmented and entangled by individual desires, understandings, and expectations. The very ubiquity of myths, narratives, and traditions surrounding the garden was what in part enabled women to imagine and shape both their lives as individuals and their place in society; but as I will demonstrate, those same myths and traditions could be cripplingly detrimental, and the weight of a literary culture's expectations could be crushing. The gardening lives of Montagu and of Knight, of Holland and of Coke offer us an acute sense of the challenges faced by the woman in the garden and offer us also, therefore, peculiarly dense accounts of retirement as an act of self-fashioning and of the garden as a space in which to imagine oneself. It is some of those self-fashioned selves that this book tries to reconstruct from the shared sources and individual utterances of literature and letters, guidebooks, and garden design. Such sources inevitably have an agenda and push their readers in particular directions: turning to women who landscaped – and wrote – on a grand scale, mine have pushed me to the language of retirement and to that problematic space created by the conflation of the physical and imagined, of the social and the solitary, created, that is, by the garden.

PART I

1 | 'Gladly I leave the town': retirement

In the summer of 1747 George Oxenden, Charles Fielding, and Edward Coke leapt the fence of Lady Gray's estate at Denhill, Kent, and rode their horses through the newly created garden. Tearing up the lawn, scattering all before them, and riding through the previously tranquil bower and grove in pursuit of a hare, the riders' explosion of rural sports in a widow's country retreat was only one of the more physical demonstrations of competing accounts of cultural space in the eighteenth-century countryside. The episode was celebrated in a poem by Nicholas Hardinge, entitled *The Denhilliad*, in which Hester Gray (1685–1781) appears a figure of innocent retirement, and her daughter – fearing for her shell-work vase – as the image of domestic sensibility.[1] If the poem's sympathies are ostensibly with the women, its mock-heroic tone inevitably undercuts the seriousness of this violation of female space, and Hardinge relies upon and reiterates some of the more prevalent stereotypes of the woman in the landscape. In the *Denhilliad*, peace, tranquillity, innocence, sentiment, retirement, and gardening are aligned with a form of femininity unable to defend itself against a world of raucous, rustic masculine action; but while the men are made to look like rustic buffoons, the poem also laughs at the seriousness of the women's attachment to their garden, and avoids aligning itself too neatly with the importance of retreat. Acknowledging that a substantial garden has been created by Lady Gray, the poem also insistently feminises and eroticises that garden, and stresses not only the pity, but the delight, to be felt from delicate structures and soft borders being violated by men.

Representations of country life undoubtedly offer us such divisive extremes of action and retirement, of opposing male and female modes of inhabiting space. However, the purpose of this chapter and the next – while recognising the power and the contemporary attractions of such binary oppositions – is to explore the elisions and contradictions which are also central to eighteenth-century understandings and experiences of retired life. To understand female retirement we should not divorce it from its male counterparts, neither should we think in terms of neat oppositions. When we confront eighteenth-century retirement, that is, we inevitably confront also alternative constructions of space and the ways in which such constructions overlay, elide, and frequently clash with one another. We also confront the interrelation between literature and lived experience and the mismatch between the imaginative spaces opened up by poetry and the social spaces one might inhabit as an individual in the country. Literary texts play two important roles here: one, as the production and articulation of cultural norms in the public sphere; the other as the far more intimate stuff of personal debate and self-fashioning. They invite us to explore how individuals might use literary traditions and cultural constructions in the organisation and understanding of their own lives; but they also invite us to recognise that, for women living in the country, retirement is both a physical location and an ideologically constructed and imagined space inevitably in dialogue or competition with other forms of space. Even as one looks to geographically similar locations, male and female retirement – but also retirement as experienced by individual women – can be entirely different because the power relations inherent in gender difference and social status mean that the world is mapped in fundamentally different ways.

In the following chapter I'll be exploring the more troublesome side of being alone, which, one way or another, tends to be linked with selfish desires and which equates retirement with forms of disgrace, but here two fundamental points are worth stressing. The first is that the language of country retirement is class-based and only possible for those with the wealth to create leisure – without that, life outside of towns and cities is simply living and labouring in the country. The second is that in all of these accounts we need to recognise two quite different models of retirement. One is in theory permanent (though not necessarily the result of age in the way that we would recognise today) and the other is seasonal and cyclical. Both, however, have classical origins, and both make claims about the values of a country life. The seasonal model – close in many ways to the lives described by Horace and Pliny – assumes retirement is itself cyclical and part of a life which moves between the country and the city. In Britain, that tended to mean the country in the summer and the city in the winter; but what makes the term of interest is not least that even in this merely seasonal account, the term carries with it the loss of urban sociability and at least the notion that – as *not the city* – the country requires a different – and in some ways better – mode of behaviour.

We can begin with that widely-circulated account of country life which appears to offer it as an ideal model for men and women alike. In what remains the most detailed and compelling study to date, Maren-Sofie Røstvig has argued that from the late seventeenth to the mid-eighteenth century there was a relatively widespread, and comfortable, model of

Horatian retirement on which the individual could draw.[2] In the English tradition one would point to John Pomfret (1667–1702), but also to Abraham Cowley (1618–67), Matthew Prior (1664–1721), to Alexander Pope (1688–1744), and later to William Cowper (1731–1800), in all of whom, however tempered by realism, the idea of quiet retirement is offered as the only sensible response to the frivolity and false values of modern urban or courtly life. In perhaps the most famous passage from *The Choice* (1700), Pomfret paraphrases Horace's Satire 2:6 when he writes,

Near some fair Town I'd have a private Seat,
Built Uniform, not little, nor too great:
Better, if on a rising Ground it stood,
Fields on this side, on that a Neighb'ring Wood.
It shou'd within no others Things contain,
But what are Useful, Necessary, Plain:
Methinks, 'tis Nauseous, and I'd ne'er endure
The needless Pomp of gawdy Furniture:
A little garden, grateful to the Eye,
And a cool rivulet run Murmuring by:
On whose delicious Banks a stately Row
Of shady Lymes, or Sycamores, shou'd grow.
At th'end of which a silent Study plac'd,
Shou'd with the Noblest Authors there be grac'd.[3]

While most of Pomfret's poetry drifted quickly from view, *The Choice* was hugely popular throughout the century. Noting that popularity, Samuel Johnson suggested the reason for this was that it appealed in particular to the middling sort, to 'that class of readers, who without vanity or criticism seek only their own amusement. His *Choice* exhibits a system of life adapted to common notions and equal to common expectations; such a state as affords plenty and tranquillity, without exclusion of intellectual pleasures'.[4]

Taking up the story where Røstvig left off, John Sitter has argued that after about 1750 this ideal of cheerful retirement is replaced by the language of retreat and by a flight into solitude: while earlier eighteenth-century poetry of retirement might be characterised by the socially engaged epistle, later eighteenth-century poetry retreats into soliloquy and lyric. That seems right; but while I too will be concerned with poetry in this chapter, I want to explore it from another direction: Røstvig traces changing literary accounts of retirement across the centuries, Sitter points to a flight into retreat from society in mid-century poetry, but what is striking in the letters and journals of many women who live out or think about retirement is the acute awareness of the term's multivalences, or, more starkly, of its irreconcilable oppositions. Sitter suggests that in mid-century poetry, 'Again and again, the feminine image is used as a focus for withdrawal, a symbol of retreat from the harsh world of traditionally male history', and Margaret Anne Doody has suggested in turn that, 'Women poets are, of course, much less happy at using feminine images as foci of withdrawal . . . [and] were often most successful when figuring their disenchantments and reactions to the socio-political state of things through non-human beings'.[5] Rather than trying to re-map the chronology of a poetic tradition, however, I want to establish instead the terms that remain in play – if one judges by the use of quotation, for later eighteenth-century readers, for example, Cowley is as current as Cowper, and Pope, Prior, and Pomfret continue to be read for what they say about retirement rather than what they say about the 1660s, the 1720s, or the 1760s. Johnson's friend Anna Williams was far from alone in writing retirement poetry in the mode of Pomfret's *The Choice*,[6] and women's letters frequently draw on the works of Matthew Prior, of Edward Young, and so on when they address the question of retirement (Abraham Cowley was a favourite of Elizabeth Montagu; Mary Coke turned to Alexander Pope; and in prose, allusion to *The Spectator* was endless). However, if that suggests a world easily available to both men and to women, the purpose of this chapter is to explore why that is not quite so; and the answers I will be suggesting are concerned with solitude, with domesticity, and with just what it is one might be retiring from, and to.

As the widespread quotation of Pomfret across the eighteenth century makes plain, the model of domestic ease in the country clearly held attractions for men and women alike and its influence is hard to overstate. We see it appearing not only in the endless repetition of quite a small number of quotations but as prose reinterpretations in fiction and essays – indeed one of the striking features of prose writing is its ready use of poetry as a touchstone for the pleasures of retirement. At the other end of the century from Pomfret, for example, the heiress in Charlotte Lennox's 1790 novel *Euphemia* loses her wealth, moves to a small place in country, is snubbed by nouveau riche neighbours, but (in an echo of *Candide*'s final lines) is happy because 'we worked, we read, we dressed our little garden – all was peace, friendship, and mutual complacency'.[7] In 1790, too, Dorothy Wordsworth would write to her friend Jane Pollard, 'I have every reason my dear Jane to be satisfied with my present situation; I have two kind Friends with whom I live in that retirement, which before I enjoyed I knew I should relish. I have leisure to read; work; walk and do what I please in short I have every cause to be contented and happy';[8] and amongst women novelists Frances Burney, Sarah Scott, and Hannah More all provide us with further examples, while Henry Fielding's Mr Wilson is only one of the more famous versions of this ideal offered by male writers of fiction.

In essays the image appears with equal ubiquity, as, for example, in 'Thoughts on Retirement. By a Lady' (1787):

Retirement affords innumerable pleasures which we wilfully overlook, and fix our thoughts on those things that are out of our reach, which appear desirable for no other reason but that they are so. We are blind to the noblest productions of nature, and with a stupid insensibility, admire not her greatest beauties; in vain the earth is dressed in all her gaudy colours, and calls forth every charm to delight us; we pass them unnoticed in the pursuit of fancied pleasures, and neglect the real – only because they are in our power, or rather, our minds are too little and contracted to relish what is truly great . . .

In short, would you be happy in retirement? Do nothing your conscience can reproach you with; be virtuous yourself, and be intimate with none that are not so; do to others as you would be done by; and live in such a pious exemplary manner, as to be able to meet death without fear.[9]

Several points are worth noting here. One is that when the rhetoric of poetry is transformed into prose it demonstrates the essential blandness, indeed banality, of such aspirations; another is that in terms of concrete advice it has almost nothing to offer; a third is that, in this example at least, what advice there is could be equally applied to life in town; a fourth is that it makes plain the link between retirement and desire, or retirement as the possible end of desire; and – connected to this last – a fifth is that it entirely avoids the powerfully gendered assumptions about retirement to which I now want to turn.

Pomfret's *Choice* is again helpful here, not least because of its stress on *choice*. For all that its opening lines suggest a life of 'blissful Ease and Satisfaction' which may be shared by men and women alike, the poem moves very rapidly to a world of male fantasy and to a retreat which is as much from wives and families as it is from the corruptions of modern society. Pomfret would have about him good company, good wine, good books, and a convenient mistress in the neighbouring village. Women in this vision of happy retirement may lay claim to good sense, prudence, humour, and courage, but they nevertheless play the role of local love interest or figure as the spectre of the unwelcome wife: their own choices – and indeed their frequent lack of choice – were likely to put them in a quite different place. That the poem was popular with both men and women would surely seem problematic were it not for that eighteenth-century habit of selective – decontextualising – quotation and the apparently endless urge to rewrite.[10] The *Choice* was of course itself a rewriting not only of Horace, but of that more recent – and more risqué – tradition of Cavalier retirement poetry; in turn it would be rewritten in a voice less gender specific and without the troublesome desires of the flesh; but arguably it was also rewritten in another form, by Joseph Addison, in *The Spectator.*

Amongst the most ubiquitous images of a woman's life in the country as at once retired from, and engaged with, a world beyond, was to appear in the endlessly republished *Spectator.* As numerous critics have now argued, while part of the agenda of *The Spectator* was a feminisation of culture, a further part was the stabilisation of 'femininity' itself within the confines of what has come to be known as the 'domestic sphere'.[11] While much of this account of the domestic is linked with the interior space of houses, and with the tea-table conversation of a metropolitan middling sort, it also operated by offering the country life as an ideal against which to set the hurry and bustle of such metropolitan living. In *The Spectator* no. 15 (Saturday 17 March 1711), Addison asserts that true happiness 'is of a retired Nature, and an Enemy to Pomp and Noise; it arises, in the first place, from the Enjoyment of one's self; and, in the next, from the Friendship and Conversation of a few select Companions. It loves Shade and Solitude, and naturally haunts Groves and Fountains, Fields and Meadows.' Against this account is set the false happiness of those who live fashionable town lives, those who love 'to be in a Crowd, and to draw the eyes of the World' upon them. To reaffirm his point Addison then offers us the figure of Aurelia:

Aurelia, though a Woman of great Quality, delights in the Privacy of a Country Life, and passes away a great part of her Time in her own Walks and Gardens. Her husband, who is her Bosom Friend, and Companion in her Solitude, has been in Love with her ever since he knew her. They both abound with good Sense, consummate Virtue, and a mutual Esteem; and are a perpetual Entertainment to one another. Their Family is under so regular an Oeconomy, in its Hours of Devotion and Repast, employment and Diversion, that it looks like a little Common-wealth within it self. They often go into Company, that they may return with the greater Delight to one another; and sometimes live in Town, not to enjoy it so properly as to grow weary of it, that they may renew in themselves the Relish of a Country Life. By this means they are happy in each other, beloved by their Children, adored by their Servants, and are become the Envy, or rather the Delight, of all that know them.

As Røstvig notes this use of Aurelia is heavily influenced by Abraham Cowley's mid-seventeenth-century essays, but with a particularly eighteenth-century agenda: 'Addison turns his attention to the vanity of women in an attempt to induce more rational and sensible attitudes, and it is to achieve this end that he exploits the *beatus ille* terminology to point out the contrast between the virtuous Aurelia and those unhappy females who are 'smitten with everything that is showy and superficial'. In foregrounding and making iconic the figure of the woman in the garden, Addison certainly appears to offer us the lone woman in country contemplation as an alternative, perhaps an antidote, to that easy correlation between fine ladies and city fashions; but in placing around her not only her husband – the companion in her solitude – but servants, children, and like-minded neighbours, he also aims to temper the unsettling potential of solitude as an occasion for anti-social self-concern.[12] In Addison's essay, then, the image of a woman in a garden is a metaphor for the ideal world; but like all ideals, it comes with its own agenda. If it stresses the importance of self, and the independence of a self that does not require an audience, it takes care to subsume this within the larger structure of domestic life.[13] It also highlights one of the more problematic terms associated with life away from the city: solitude.

Sweet Solitude, thou placid Queen

As Addison's essay makes clear, in solitude one need not be alone; in the *Spectator* at least, it signifies the absence of the city and the public world, while also assuming the presence of companionate marriage and family life. Formulated in this way, the term is effectively indistinguishable from retirement; however, it is worth taking a brief excursion into the language of solitude because where distinctions arise, they tend to make plain the rather less comfortable potential of the two terms. In the case of Addison, for example, we might understand the stress on sociable solitude as itself an indication that there are other – less sociable – kinds. Indeed, what this account of sociable solitude should alert us to is the fractures and ambiguities in the language of solitude and retirement which make an easy idyll of country life far less stable than it may appear, and, notably for us, far from easily inhabited by women who find themselves less than companionably alone in the country.

Part of the problem when confronting either retirement or solitude is indeed their close synonymy; and it is a problem because the apparent synonymy is as often an opposition. In 1772 an article in the *Town and Country Magazine* entitled 'Retirement and Solitude distinguished' confidently stated that,

There is a difference between retirement and solitude; the first may be social, and filled up with the endearments of life; the other can scarcely be so: we carry with us into retirement the affections of nature; but we drop them in solitude. In the one, we fly from the incumbrance, in the other, from the delights of society. (p. 192)

As frequently, however – and as Addison's *Spectator* essay suggests – the cultural charge of the two terms might be neatly, and completely, reversed. At the heart of this is a cultural uncertainty – one might even say confusion – over the value of solitude or retirement however defined, not just in opposition to each other, but as defined in themselves; or rather, in their inability to be defined in or by themselves. Both terms, that is, assume the presence of a public world quite as much as they assume its absence; both are essentially public in their accounts of private life and in their constant awareness of a world they claim to have left behind. In this sense, more important than an individual adjudication is the *attempt* to adjudicate; that is, there is a perceived need for a distinction to exist, and that distinction turns upon the problematic nature of sociability, the equally problematic nature of solitary self-regard, and the place of the individual in relation to them both.

Some examples will help here. The cultural anxiety about solitude of course has a long tradition, from Aristotle's *Politics* onwards, and in the broadest of terms solitude is at once a problem because it apparently rejects mankind's necessary sociability and yet is itself necessary in order to provide the individual with the reserves needed to participate in that otherwise endless social engagement;[14] but as we have seen this can also be framed conversely with society recognised as thoughtless, indeed vacuous, and solitude offering an opportunity for the only sensible alternative, which is the contemplation of God and nature.[15]

In the European tradition, Michel de Montaigne's late sixteenth-century essay on 'Solitude' remained perhaps the most influential account of solitude as an opportunity for self-improvement and self-sufficiency but also crucially as a temporary expedient the value of which was to be determined by one's return to society; it was a stance largely repeated in perhaps the best-known English essay on the theme, Abraham Cowley's 'Of Solitude' (1668), and it is echoed in essays and poems throughout the century. If we return to the anonymous lady's 'Thoughts on Retirement', for example, we find the following:

Those people who cannot be happy in solitude, would not be so in a crowd, since it is from their own minds, and not from any outward cause, that their uneasiness springs. Miserable is that wretch who is obliged to seek for happiness from others, and has nothing within himself to amuse him. So capricious is the human mind, that it is always dissatisfied with its destiny: thus those who are confined to towns and cities, dream of nothing but flowery meads and purling streams; while the person whose fate is to live always in retirement, can propose to himself no pleasure abstracted from noise and hurry. But were either to exchange their situation, they would still repine.

This emphasis on self and on self-sufficiency is important because it sets itself against the sociability of the city and becomes a means of judging – and finding wanting – the individual's need for company; and while the quotation recognises what it terms the capriciousness of the human mind, it nevertheless damns the individual who is over-reliant on sociability. More than this, it also recognises the restlessness and placelessness of human desire; or, to put that another way, the location of desire in the elsewhere and the other. In this sense, a country idyll is striking for nothing so much as its ability to be both aspirational and unattainable. It is this very dilemma that many leisured women in the country had to confront. In confronting it they also confronted the self-expectation, and the wider cultural expectation, that they should limit and control the desire for something beyond their situation. It is this dilemma, too, which forms a central concern of solitude poetry.

There are of course numerous poems on solitude to which the eighteenth-century reader might turn; many, inevitably, would be hard to distinguish in any useful way from a poetry of retirement, and most are striking for nothing so much as a desire to follow conventions. Thomas Tickell's apostrophe to 'Solitude' in 'On the Prospect of Peace, A Poem' (1713) was particularly popular, and by the end of the century it was joined by Hannah More's 1773 poem, 'Sweet Solitude, thou placid Queen', as one of the most quoted and anthologised renderings of the theme (though her letters and journals record a much more problematic engagement with the experience).[16] The tradition is of course much longer, with quotation from Milton and Pope, Cowley and Cowper, playing a particularly notable role as a shorthand justification for its pleasures.[17] At the beginning of the eighteenth century, however, we can turn to Mary Lee, Lady Chudleigh's *Solitude* of 1703 to provide us both with an outline of some of the major themes to which women poets would return over the following decades, and with an indication of the issues which might present themselves to women alone in the country.

The opening lines of Chudleigh's poem are striking for their rapid departure from Horace's ode, not only in their insistence on the meditative life rather than Horace's cultivation of paternal lands, but also in their use of a construction which allows for the inclusion of women – Horace's 'Happy the man, who, remote from business, after the manner of the ancient race of mortals, cultivates his paternal lands with his own oxen, disengaged from every kind of usury' becomes Chudleigh's,

Happy are they who when alone
Can with themselves converse;
Who to their Thoughts are so familiar grown,
That with Delight in some obscure Recess,
They cou'd with silent Joy think all their Hours away,
And still think on, till the confining Clay
Fall off, and nothing's left behind
Of drossy Earth, nothing to clog the Mind,
Or hinder its Ascent to those bright Forms above.[18]

If this looks like a departure from Horace, it is of course very close to Cowley's essay on Solitude, a work which echoes through the letters of so many when they write of their retired lives. However, what is also important here is the characteristic shift to the city. Chudleigh's poem is notable for avoiding the easy merger of retirement with the pastoral, but characteristically of much retirement poetry, most of the poem is about the absence of solitude rather than the experience of it; indeed solitude becomes the unspoken which is to be set against the sociability of the city and its crowds.

But few, ah! few are for Retirement fit;
But few the Joys of Solitude can taste;
The most with Horror fly from it,
And rather chuse in Crouds their Time to waste (ll.22–25)

The crucial point about solitude, then, is that for all its aspirational appeal, it can only be for the special few; and thus while poetry may offer solitude as an ideal, the rhetoric of solitude holds within it the accusation that an inability to enjoy it is a form of moral failure. This insistence on self-sufficiency is not peculiar to Chudleigh – as Joshua Scodel has argued of a quite different poet, Dryden's influential translation of Horace in the 1680s is equally determined to stress the individual's independence from society – but it represents a challenge for those who are alone even as it offers the potential of solace.[19]

There are further complications too. Much writing about retirement seamlessly merges the countryside with the moral and makes much of the delight to be gained from a rather abstract, or at least vaguely sketched, world of rivers, trees, and fields. Chudleigh's poem is unusual in that while it merges solitude with retirement, retirement is not then merged with the pastoral and its pleasures. This should highlight for us another important aspect of retirement and solitude poetry which is to do with how the two terms are geographically located. It would be tempting to offer a generalised formulation arguing that while solitude can be represented as placeless, retirement more frequently inhabits and enjoys a physical space. And arguably it is worth making this kind of statement in order to highlight its inadequacies in particular instances. Where such a statement most immediately falls down, of course, is precisely in the willingness of solitude poetry to provide for itself a pastoral setting.

But we should also recognise the reverse of this locating of solitude in the pastoral world. In Henry Fielding's *Tom Jones*, the Man of the Hill voices an alternative, but also wholly conventional, position when he tells Tom that,

I hastened, therefore, back to London, the best retirement of either grief or shame, unless for persons of a very public character; for here you have the advantage of solitude without its disadvantages, since you may be alone and in company at the same time; and while you walk or sit unobserved, noise, hurry, and a constant succession of objects entertain the mind, and prevent the spirits from preying on themselves, or rather on grief or shame, which are the most unwholesome diet in the world.[20]

Grief and shame are the stuff of the following chapter, but the change of location for solitude is important because it makes plain the further ideological freight so often attached to the country. For Fielding's misanthrope, city solitude is an essentially secular experience; in Chudleigh's poem, and in so many other accounts of retreat (whether framed as solitude or retirement), the country is a place for pious reflection on the works of God and on one's place in the larger Creation. It is also more than this, for if the sociable solitude of the country is framed as feminine, domestic, and quiet, with the abstraction of country life into a pastoral idyll an ostensibly physical location is ultimately framed in terms of absence: the unreal nature of the pastoral setting highlights the absence of a social world. In this sense, the pastoral mode, so closely associated both with retirement and with community, is another form of complication, and one which produces problems when elided with the physical location of owned landscapes that might as easily be framed as rustic, rural, georgic, or merely vulgar.

One of those problems is location itself, or at least the sense of location, because for all its physical specificity (this place and no other place), the experience of location remains doggedly relational (this place rather than that place). In terms of pastoral, location is important both because inhabiting the country need not signal any kind of pastoral experience at all, and because it can invite a powerful engagement with pastoral's various forms and expectations. To unpack that further, we might say that pastoral invites one to see oneself, to situate oneself imaginatively in a location, and therefore to affect the perceived space one occupies. In turn, that raises the question of what happens when an imaginative form confronts its imagined location, when women find themselves where 'pastoral' is supposed to happen. In one sense of course it's not there, and cannot be there – with a physical move to the country the projection of the idyllic onto the countryside is necessarily projected yet further away and remains tantalisingly beyond reach – but that doesn't preclude an awareness of its absence or the attempt to create it as an experience. It also does not resolve the problem of just what pastoral might be.

So far I have been gesturing towards an account of pastoral as both idyll and absence, but pastoral contains and invites a range of conflicting possibilities. The most obvious of these may indeed be the fantasy of untroubled happiness, but this in itself is complicated by pastoral's other possibilities, from its articulation of a sense of loss to its equally powerful ability to engender and to become an object of desire; from its tales of aristocratic sophistication in peasant guise to its dramas of female sexuality and female power in the huge and for a time hugely popular romance epics and pastourelles of the seventeenth century.

William Empson famously referred to pastoral as the process of 'putting the complex into the simple' and identified pastoral as any text which contrasts a simpler life imagined to exist in the past with the complexity of the modern age; in this account the pastoral mode is the articulation of longing, the desire for simplicity, innocence, sensuous pleasure, and freedom from death and mutability.[21] Such desires remain powerfully current in the eighteenth century, but we also need to address more particular aspects of pastoral in order to understand what it might offer leisured women in the country.

In the high literary forms of the Renaissance, the justification of the pastoral mode and of retirement was the state of otium, an escape from business and worry, whether public or private, and an opportunity to cultivate true happiness: it was the ability to link leisure both with intellectual activity and with true happiness which was to prove one of pastoral's major attractions, but which, for Renaissance writers, was also to establish it as a mode only available to the cultural elite. A further aspect of this essentially meditative tradition was that pastoral was imagined as primarily transformative: Shakespeare's pastoral romances are characteristic in offering pastoral locations as places of transformation, but characteristic too in assuming a return to the city once that transformation has taken place. Similarly, in Milton's early poetry pastoral locations have the power to affect the individual, and his first collection of poems (1645) did much to develop an English tradition of pastoral writing which, like 'L'Allegro' and 'Il Penseroso', acknowledged the rural environment's ability both to inspire pleasure and nurture melancholy.

Alongside this tradition of landscape aesthetics, however, appears another quite distinct transformation of pastoral writing in the sixteenth and seventeenth century, which we might variously term pastoral epic or romance, which would include elements of Torquato Tasso, Edmund Spenser, Giovanni Guarini, and Madame de Scudery (amongst many others), and which would place a distinctly sexualised heroine centre-stage.[22] In Spenser's *Faerie Queene*, Pastorella and Serena are both objects of desire and innocently (or, when whisked off by the Blatant Beast, perhaps not so innocently) desiring; in Scudery's mid-seventeenth-century romances (which continued to be read well into the eighteenth century), heroines spend decades at once revelling in and suffering for the power afforded them as objects of male desire. Such pastoral romance held out the country as a land of love and of innocent, unconsummated, but powerful sexuality.

Another account of pastoral, then, is that it offers an engagement with female sexuality which can be culturally endorsed because it sets that sexuality in a fantasy context and in doing so resists its more destabilising potential. In this sense we might say that pastoral romance promises an ideal form of reading for eighteenth-century women because it endlessly avoids sexual consummation and offers instead a fantasy of pleasure. However, as a location which leisured women had been schooled to think of in terms of excitement, desire, and love, for the majority the country's most striking feature was likely to be the way in which it failed to be those things. Conversely, therefore, we might also say that when thoughts of pastoral take place in a country location they stand to be deeply disruptive, both because they may signal the imagining of a better state, and because that better state not only acknowledges female sexuality, but – at least in the form of the pastoral epic – implicitly gives to women a power beyond the merely domestic and quotidian. The issue here is not that we adjudicate between these two contradictory accounts of pastoral; rather, that both remain powerfully potential.

That sense of conflicting potentials brings us to one more definition of pastoral, and perhaps the most useful. As Paul Alpers has argued, rather than characterising pastoral in terms of a location, a set of trappings, or a sense of loss, we might understand it instead as the articulation of contradictory positions of resistance and acceptance. For Alpers, pastoral has always been 'concerned with various human separations and their implications'. Set in opposition to the heroic (with its urge to overcome and to conclude), pastoral is an exploration of 'things disparate or ironically related, and yet at the same time does not imply that disparities or conflicts are fully resolved'.[23] That formulation surely offers a powerful model for the appeal of pastoral to women in the country. Rather than idle fantasy and the dressing-up box – those overly-quick caricatures of Marie-Antoinette and her hameau – pastoral explores a suspension between states; and if it concerns itself with acceptance, it is acceptance of the unresolved.

By the time Chudleigh's poem was published in 1703, the composition of what we might term formal pastoral was undoubtedly on the decline; but if poets were less willing to offer what might seem an increasingly irrelevant world of shepherdesses and their crooks, the imaginative potential of pastoral remained strong; and while Samuel Johnson famously dismissed Milton's *Lycidas* as 'pastoral, easy, vulgar, and therefore disgusting', and claimed that 'an intelligent reader . . . sickens at the mention of the crook, the pipe, the shet, and the kide', those comments misrepresent both the influence of Milton's pastoral poetry, and the willingness of the leisured classes to associate the country with visions of pastoral ease. What Johnson was actually objecting to, of course, was pastoral as mere trappings and outdated conventions; indeed as a deeply nostalgic writer, much of his work could itself be characterised as 'pastoral' in Empson's terms. Johnson's comments are misleading, then, because they fail to recognise the essential seriousness of pastoral, and fail to recognise, too, pastoral's abiding concern with a question he would himself pose in *Rasselas* (1759): how might one be happy in the face of restless and unending desire?

It's that question which makes pastoral so important to leisured women in the country, because pastoral invites them to think about the terms on which they might be happy. As a form of writing, the power of which lies in the ability to offer a language of longings and of limitations, pastoral also offers structures for thinking about desire and about the restraint of desire. Johnson, inevitably, had views on this too. As Patricia Meyer Spacks argues, 'The trouble with desire, from Johnson's point of view, is that we want the wrong things and want them too much . . . Desire's power, derived from the dangerous prevalence of imagination, depends on the human tendency to project into the future. To resist the power of the imagined future almost exceeds human capacity.'[24] Johnson's answer – at least for young women – is to remain busy: in his *Rambler* no. 85 needlework fends off idleness and thus restrains desire. One obvious inadequacy in that formulation, however, is that the restraint of desire inevitably remains a form of desire; indeed, as Judith Butler has argued, the articulation of 'desire is never renounced, but becomes preserved and reasserted in the very structure of renunciation'.[25]

While debates about the nature of desire turn frequently on conflicting ideas of loss and absence or of energy and purpose, and while those debates will inevitably continue because they are debates about the nature of the self, a strand of thinking runs through them – again, most powerfully articulated in recent years by Butler – that the relation between the self and desire is a simultaneous process of production and constraint.[26] That insight helps us to understand what might be at stake when women draw on the language of pastoral in order both to question and to make sense of their place in the world. In more concrete terms, it also helps us to understand the way in which leisured women's move to the country confronts them with an experience at once literal and metaphorical, and where the prevalence of pastoral means that – almost inevitably – they must confront its codes and expectations but also its contradictions and uncertainties. It is not just that the trappings of pastoral – despite Johnson's claims – come very quickly to mind for many women, rather, its appeal lies in something more profound, that is, in its ability to address the relations between different states, between one's desires and one's sense of self.

Looming large here is *Paradise Lost* and its account of human desire and the Fall, a myth which continues to echo through psychoanalytic musings from Freud to Butler and Lacan. Milton's constant reimagining of a state of innocence (in *Comus*, in *Paradise Lost*, in *Areopagitica*) should again alert us to the problem of what innocent desire might mean for women well-schooled in poetry and romance, and acutely aware of the conflicting expectations of women in rural retirement. In these terms, the nature of pastoral is no mere theoretical abstraction; rather, in embracing its pleasures or in feeling its sense of loss, in acknowledging the limits of fantasy and in accepting its appeal, women's confrontation of pastoral's disparate forms meant confronting also their sense of themselves in the world, their power, the inevitable curtailments of that power, and their willingness, or need, to embrace such limitations whether as piety, or duty, or self-control.

A case in point would be Anne Finch, Countess of Winchilsea's well-known 'Petition for an Absolute Retreat' (1713), a poem which characteristically merges retirement with solitude, solitude with sociability, and locates retreat in a countryside we might wish to align with what we know of the estate in Kent where she spent so much of her time, but which we could hardly reconstruct from the minimal geography the poem offers.[27] Indeed, the lack of geographical specificity is of central importance here: Finch's poem is located in a landscape that is mythic and symbolic rather than localised and quotidian. It offers recognisably pastoral conventions for its representation of an imagined countryside as edenic, as a place of easy plenitude. For Finch, 'those Windings and that Shade', repeated throughout the poem are an invitation to see beyond themselves, to see the larger creation in its smaller forms and therefore to see oneself (rivers invite one to think of eternity; ancient trees of old age and decay, and so on). In this we might say that for all its stress on the physical, Finch's poem shares much with Chudleigh's abstract solitude in that the former's insistent reading of the physical landscape as a set of signs effectively makes the physicality of the landscape disappear. The poems share something else as well, for like Chudleigh's poem, Finch's retreat – with its series of negatives – is characterised from the very beginning by a withdrawal from the public world which nevertheless makes that world a central concern of the poem; by the insistence that the lessons one is taught in such solitude are 'unutterable'; and by an equal insistence that the desire for absolute solitude (to be provided by '*indulgent* fate') is an unrealistic dream. Above all, what Chudleigh and Finch offer to their readers is a highly moralised (and abstracted) account of how to behave when alone, while insisting – as would Addison a few years later – that solitude is to be spent in company.

The staying power of these themes is surely striking: almost a hundred years after Chudleigh and Finch's poems appeared, Mary Robinson's 'Solitude' (1791) would adopt a recognisably similar position with its inability to leave behind the city from which it claims to retreat and in its account of a countryside which is fundamentally pastoral in its abstract longings and nebulous locations, but pastoral, too, in Alpers' terms, in articulating the sense of suspension between states.[28] Even in her earlier poetry – where the mismatch between pastoral solitude and a very public city life is less tantalising – Robinson makes plain the centrality of the city in the urge for solitude. The 'Letter to a friend on leaving Town' (published in *Poems*, 1775, after the best part of a year spent in the King's Bench Prison) follows a tradition established by Ben Jonson's *To Penshurst* of starting with a negative, an absence, in this case 'Gladly I leave the town . . .' and ending with 'Farewell . . . / Farewell . . . / Farewell'.[29] The subject of that absence and those farewells is inevitably the stuff of the city. Like 'Solitude', this is a poem aware of, and attuned to the town, while the apparently-praised country life is an oddly nebulous imagined space in which little appears to happen beyond the vague abstractions of peace, friendship, and virtue. We might say the same of 'Written on the outside of an Hermitage', with its stress on necessary virtues and the absence of vice; and in all of those poems we should recognise an account of solitude which in fact has little place for place. Retirement, solitude, and retreat work here as a topos, as the kind of imagined space that Cowper neatly distinguishes in the 'peasant's nest' episode of *The Task* when he points to the disjunction between an imagined rural solitude and the actual experience.[30] This is not to say – as Cowper would not say – that such imagined spaces have no value; it is, however, to ask what value that might be for women not poetically, but socially alone. What Robinson's pastoral poems make clear is that the experience of solitude is precisely poetic: they represent an exercise on a literary theme rather than the contemplation of that more complex world in which solitude might mean any number of things; they have the freedom to insist that solitude can be defined, and defined in terms congenial to one's own desires. Again, this is not to dismiss Robinson's or Chudleigh's or Finch's poems, nor is it to suggest that poetry is unimportant as an account of solitude and landscape: rather, it is to argue that their importance lies in the imagining of states of mind and possibilities which may be at once consciously present and practically absent for women who inhabit not poems but places, not abstracted pastorals but working estates.

Solitude poetry, then, has the potential to create an imagined space allowing freedoms which may be far less possible in a world outside of the literary; however, if it opens up possibilities it surely also distances them from the lived; and thus one further way of understanding the frequent poetic quotations in women's letters is not simply as the kind of shorthand I suggested earlier but also as something rather different, as an acknowledgement of the gap between an individual's experience of their own life and a world of poetic aspirations and possibilities: in Alpers' terms, an acknowledgement of 'things disparate or ironically related'. This holds true, I would argue, beyond the use of direct quotation – for the language of retirement and solitude is almost inevitably shadowed by a sense of absence, loss, the unattainable, or the anti-social. We should also recognise the reverse of this, however, in that while poetry may claim retirement as the unutterable, women's letters and journals written from the country are far less reticent and are striking for nothing so much as their readiness to engage with the conflicting models of retirement with which they found themselves presented.

Kiss me and be quiet

To understand how the imagined spaces of solitude and retirement might
be used and negotiated by those who find themselves alone we need to
move beyond those poetic accounts of female solitude explored so far and
turn to the many other ways in which female retirement might be framed.
The tradition of essays and poetry running from Prior to Pomfret, from
Cowley to Pope, and eventually to Cowper is regularly quoted by men and
women throughout the eighteenth century. Notably, however, at least in
the writings of those women who form the subject of this study, those
poets and essayists tend to be men. We might say that this is because male
poetry was generally given a higher cultural status in the eighteenth century,
but there is also something specific here which is to do with the nature of
retirement, where although it appears to be offered as an ideal free from
gender difference, in fact it tends to assume retirement from the masculine
activities of public life, while female retirement is, if anything, so normalised
as the domestic that it excites little remark. I will go on to complicate and
to an extent undermine that claim in a moment, but it remains, I think, a
useful position from which to start and one which we can support with the
aid of George, Lord Lyttelton's well-known 'Advice to a Lady' (1733):

Seek to be good, but aim not to be great:
A woman's noblest station is retreat;
Her fairest virtues fly from public sight,
Domestic worth, that shuns too strong a light.
To rougher man Ambition's task resign:
'Tis ours in senates or in courts to shine

Again we need to tease out just what 'retreat' might mean here, and we will
see the elisions and distinctions between solitude, retirement, and retreat as
they are used in women's letters and journals later in this chapter; but for now
it is important to register that neat and apparently unexceptionable elision
of retreat, domesticity, and femininity which – precisely because it denies
women a place in the world of public action – effectively excludes women
also from the high-status world of retirement after public endeavour.[31]
Writing to her husband in 1753, Elizabeth Montagu appeared to offer a very
similar account when describing the life of an old woman she had recently
visited: 'I dare say her pleasures were all of the domestic kind, her dairy and
poultry her care, her garden her amusement; perhaps to know no more, is
woman's highest honour and her praise'.[32] Perhaps; but it was not a model

she chose to adopt for herself. Neither did her cousin-in-law, Lady Mary Wortley Montagu, who summarised Lyttelton's poem thus: 'Be plain in dress, and sober in your diet, / In short, my deary, kiss me and be quiet'. In a moment I will go on to explore further male accounts of female retirement, but it is also important to recognise that what goes with Lyttelton's account of female retreat and male ambition is an alternative vision of retirement as masculine, political, and active.[33]

That vision was prominently on view throughout Britain. At Stowe, at Hagley, at Studley Royal, but in fact at any of the great estates where owners had time and inclination enough to develop their gardens, the public could see retirement on display. As Elizabeth Montagu wryly suggested in a letter of 1757, if sons were apprenticed to gardeners before going into the House of Commons, they would be better prepared for the retirement which would inevitably follow.[34] But beyond such practical pleasures, what these gardens had in common was their owners' access to a strong classical tradition of retirement which could justify the politician's retreat from the corruptions of public life and which could make retirement itself an active principle of patriotic virtue. In both France and England, Henry St. John, Viscount Bolingbroke – arch politician and arch-rival of Robert Walpole – would adopt exactly this role, and his cause would be championed by the most influential poet of the day, Alexander Pope; at Kingsgate in Kent, a politically disgraced Henry Holland would carve angry invectives into his fragile garden monuments; at Hagley, Lord Lyttelton's life of rural ease was justified by his eulogist James Thomson as that of the patriot statesman ready to save the nation from the corruption of those in power; and at Stowe, the Temples and the Grenvilles would follow Bolingbroke's lead and create perhaps the greatest show garden and political allegory of the eighteenth century. Moreover this language of male retirement from the public world need not be exclusively the domain of the politician: at Studley Royal, William Aislabie – removed from public office for his part in the South Sea Bubble – created another of the great show gardens of the century, using retirement and gardening to recuperate himself in the public eye; and at the Leasowes, the garden of the poet William Shenstone, retirement and gardening gave the poet a public status his poetry had largely failed to do.

We need not follow these stories in detail – though Bolingbroke and Shenstone, Lyttelton and Holland will appear again in later chapters – and this brief sketch of course hides the nuances of male retirement, but the classical language of retirement, and the ability to model oneself (or at the very least gesture towards) Horace and Pliny, Seneca and Cincinnatus gave men a high-status justification for retirement and gardening which was – rhetorically at least – unavailable to women. This is not in any way to argue that women were excluded from political life: late in the century we can of course turn to the celebrated example of the Duchess of Devonshire, but, more important still is the sheer volume of 'politics' in the letters of elite women writers throughout the century (thus the letters of Montagu, Holland, and Coke are brimful with political reportage and commentary). Equally, public claims could undoubtedly be made by women about their 'private' lives; but what is absent is that ability to justify the inactivity of retirement as a form of classical rigour after public service; for women, the virtues of retirement must be made on other grounds.[35]

At Hagley, Thomson's eulogy on Lord Lyttelton, in *The Seasons*, would turn at once upon his absence from office and his readiness to act for the national good.[36] Away from London, and placed in a landscape redolent of the classical Arcadia, Lyttelton (1709–73) can 'stray', 'wander', 'silent steal', or just sit, and all of these actions can be claimed as public zeal. Characteristically – and one might say conveniently – Lyttelton can,

> wander through the philosophic world;
> Where in bright train continual wonders rise
> Or to the curious or the pious eye.
> And oft, conducted by historic truth,
> You tread the long extent of backward time,
> Planning with warm benevolence of mind
> And honest zeal, unwarped by party-rage,
> Britannia's weal – how from the venal gulf
> To raise her virtue and her arts revive.
>
> *Spring*, ll. 926–931

Lyttelton's friend Elizabeth Montagu would have to work much harder to account for herself when sitting in a garden, and while she and other women might join with Lyttelton in the collective venture of landscape gardening as Britain's great contribution to the arts, Thomson's political justification of leisured inactivity did not extend to women. Instead, women appear in Thomson's poem in that alternative, complementary, but far less glamorous account of retirement, the domestic.

Only a few lines on from the passage above we are introduced to Lyttelton's first wife, Lucy (1717/18–47), and her appearance so soon after Thomson's vision of public zeal provides him with a useful transition to *Spring*'s closing lines on love, but crucially also allows Lyttelton his part in connubial retirement while distancing him from its feminising implications.

Switching his gaze from the public weal to Lucy, Hagley can be re-imagined as a private space in which the public man can take comfort after political labours:

Perhaps thy loved Lucinda shares thy walk,
With soul to thine attuned. Then Nature all
Wears to the lover's eye a look of love;
And all the tumult of a guilty world,
Tossed by ungenerous passions, sinks away.
Spring, ll. 936–940

Party rage, venal gulfs, and strenuous labours are replaced by the 'softening' influence of the 'tender heart' and 'animated peace':

And, as it pours its copious treasures forth
In varied converse, softening every theme,
You, frequent pausing turn, and from her eyes,
Where meekened sense and amiable grace
And lively sweetness dwell, enraptured drink
That nameless spirit of ethereal joy,
Inimitable happiness! which love
Alone bestows, and on a favoured few.
Spring, ll. 942–949

Here, then, Lyttelton's leisured retreat is offered as a form of feminisation; but it is immediately followed by a much-quoted passage on the 'bursting prospect spread immense around', and thus by a return to the easily politicised language of prospect poetry.

The apparent absence of such a political language for women should highlight for us still further an insistently domestic account of female retirement. Thomson compounded that emphasis on the soft domesticity of female retreat by dedicating *Spring* to Frances Seymour, Lady Hertford, and offering her as a model of unaffected grace and benevolence, as a woman fit to shine at court, but choosing to 'walk the plain / With innocence and meditation joined' (*Spring*, ll.5–10). It is compounded also, however, by Lyttelton's once-famous monody on the death of his wife.[37] Lyttelton had married Lucy Fortescue in 1742, and while she appears in his early love poetry, it was in the poem on her death, at 29, 'To the Memory of a Lady lately Deceased: A Monody' (1747) that she was to be not simply linked with Hagley, but figured as its genius loci, as much a part of nature as the groves, the rills, and the nightingales silenced by her death. Like Thomson,

Lyttelton takes an imaginative journey around Hagley, but whereas Thomson offers the garden as a site for political meditation and connubial delight, Lyttelton finds only the reminders of a lost past and of a bleak present: while Thomson claims a form of manliness in Lyttelton's political retirement, Lyttelton himself associates retirement, here at least, with the feminine and with Lucy's female virtues as they are figured in the domestic and spiritual harmony of her life. Lucy has shunned the public eye to follow the 'silent paths of wisdom', and 'banish'd every passion from her breast, / But those, the gentlest and the best' (ll.61–63). In retirement with Lyttelton she can share a delight in literature both classical and modern, she can be celebrated as a woman of 'more than manly sense' and 'more than female tenderness' (ll.145–147), and, within the Edenic confines of Hagley, the couple can be 'the happiest pair of human kind!' (l.252), but for all its pathos the poem traps Lucy in a conventionally gendered account of both femininity and retirement.[38] The championing of a silent retirement inevitably reflects on Lyttelton's own withdrawal from public life: we might ask if the silence of meditation undermines Lyttelton's own stance or feminises his position as a politician in retirement, as a man who does not speak. But as the brief gesture towards the public world makes clear – 'What pleasure now can pall'd ambition give? (l.235) – Lyttelton has an alternative. The 'Monody' allows Lyttelton to demonstrate the sentiment and fine feeling shared with his wife, but the larger context of the poem is a world in which men can return to the public arena. Thus, while the poem celebrates Lucy's virtues, it subordinates femininity to a private world of retirement that Lyttelton can leave but which Lucy could not.

Much of Lyttelton's account of Lucy is framed in terms familiar from Addison's *Spectator* paper; but for its emphasis on female piety modernised for the eighteenth century we can turn usefully to the *Tatler*, no. 42 (16 July 1709) and to the figure of Aspasia, said to be based on the charitable (and single) Lady Elizabeth Hastings:

Methinks, I now see her walking in her garden like our first parent, with unaffected charms, before beauty had spectators, and bearing celestial conscious virtue in her aspect. Her countenance is the lively picture of her mind, which is the seat of honour, truth, compassion, knowledge, and innocence ... In the midst of the most ample fortune, and veneration of all that behold and know her, without the least affectation, she consults retirement, the contemplation of her own being, and that supreme Power which bestowed it. Without the learning of schools, or knowledge of a long course of arguments, she goes on in a steady course of uninterrupted piety and virtue, and adds to the severity and privacy of the last age, all the freedom and ease of this. The language and mien of a court she is possessed of in the highest degree; but the simplicity and humble thoughts of a cottage are her more welcome entertainments. Aspasia is a female philosopher, who does not only live up to the resignation of the most retired lives of the ancient sages, but also to the schemes and plans which they thought beautiful, though inimitable.

Where the *Spectator* stresses the domestic and the secular, the *Tatler* stresses an equally conventional account of female retirement and piety. Virtuous but not learned, polished but pious, Aspasia's country retirement – like Lady Betty's own at Ledstone in Yorkshire – merges modern manners with charity, piety, and domestic economy. Veiled references aside, the life of Lady Betty Hastings (1682–1739) should itself alert us to another important model of female piety and retirement. Soon after her death from cancer in 1739 – having managed her own estate for nearly 40 years (and brought in the famous Charles Bridgeman to design the gardens), having hosted and given patronage to some of the leading theologians of her day, and having spent half of her £3000 income each year on charity – her life was celebrated in Thomas Barnard's, *An historical character relating to the holy and exemplary life of. . . Lady Elizabeth Hastings* (1742), just one of numerous publications in the eighteenth century celebrating female piety and offering it as a model for the modern ages.[39] Such accounts of eminent women tend by their nature to focus on aristocratic lives, but the insistence on piety and female retirement is of course far more widespread. Medieval and early modern accounts of female piety continued to circulate as did more recent works such as Alexander Pope's influential account of Martha Blount in his 'Epistle to a Lady' (1735), while the conventions of quiet piety and retreat are also to be found in works aimed squarely at the middling sort, the novel and the conduct book.[40] The figure of the female recluse, so popular in women's fiction of the late eighteenth century would be one example, but another is the anonymously published *Letters to Honoria and Marianne* of 1784 which merges the pious inflection of the *Tatler* with the more sociable retirement represented by the *Spectator* and in doing so suggests the ongoing debate not only about modern femininity but with it the relationship between the private self and the sociable world. Letter XXV, 'On Retirement' begins with the example of Mrs M – , whose low spirits are caused by her husband's determination to, 'carry her down to an estate of his in the wilds of Sussex, where she should be absolutely buried alive', and who believes that, 'death itself would be preferable to what is called a *country retirement*'. Countering that unreasonable position, and with it 'the *horror* of being alone', Honoria and Marianne are invited to embrace 'an opportunity of being acquainted with *yourselves!*' though with an important proviso:

Yet I would by no means have you turn recluse. – Life is the gift of heaven; and we are chiefly enjoying that blessing, when we are engaged in a *constant* course of humane and benevolent actions to our fellow-creatures.

So natural is the love of society to every human being, that we are too apt to look on even the retirement of a few hours as a very sad and irksome misfortune. But surely our situation would be much more disagreeable, to be perpetually disturbed with the insupportable conversation of people we *dislike* – (for very *few* we in reality *like*, deceive ourselves as we will) – therefore how much more happy are we, to be at liberty to pursue our own contemplations, to endeavour to know *ourselves*, and to adore in silence the works of our heavenly Maker!

Like Addison's *Spectator* before it, *Letters to Honoria and Marianne* parallels conflicting female responses to retirement with the eighteenth century's conflicting accounts of femininity and sociability. While the appearance of those themes in a pot-boiler like *Honoria and Marianne* is suggestive of their sheer ubiquity, nowhere was the alignment of femininity with both nature and artifice more influentially restated than in Rousseau's *La Nouvelle Héloise* (translated into English in 1761).[41] In Rousseau's pastoral fantasy of poor but happy peasants, homemade wine, and calm retirement from fashionable society, Eloisa's 'reading and study has given place to that of action': domestic action. Thus,

She formerly sought solitude and retirement, in order to indulge her reflections on the object of her passion; at present she has acquired new activity, by having formed new and different connections. She is not one of those indolent mothers of a family, who are contented to study their duty when they should discharge it . . . Her time for reading and study has given place to that of action. (III, 251)

Action here is domestic and maternal, and contemplation – so closely linked to solitude and retreat – is the contemplation only of one's domestic duties as the mother of children, and as the awed subject of a providential universe:

On every side she sees and adores the benevolent hand of providence; her children are her pledges committed by it to her care; she receives its gifts, in the produce of the earth; she sees her table covered by its bounty; she sleeps under its protection; she awakes in peace under its care; she is instructed by its chastisements, is made happy by its favours: all the benefits she reaps, all the blessings she enjoys, are so many different subjects for adoration and praise. If the attributes of the divinity are beyond her feeble sight, she sees in every part of the creation, the common father of mankind. (IV, 9)

At Clarens, Julie's garden is described as natural but it is kept this way by the combination of Julie, *and* by the practical estate management of her husband. If Clarens functions as the site in which Saint-Preux can leave behind the solitude of the Alps and the heightened emotion they engender in favour of calm reflection, it also functions, of course, to reduce women to their apparently biological limitations while claiming to celebrate their sensitivity to nature and their role as the markers and upholders of civilisation. As Eve Tavor Bannet has argued, 'It was precisely the affinity between the benevolent patriarchal ideals of England's male establishment and Rousseau's utopian fictions which made the latter such a convenient butt for British Egalitarians and Matriarchs';[42] it was in part for this reason also that Rousseau proved such a difficult figure for many eighteenth-century women, but especially for those who gardened. Notably, in the letters of the garden-obsessed Lennox sisters – and especially Caroline Fox (later Holland) – a Rousseauvian pleasure in the garden is both delightful and unsettling. Thus, for example, we find Caroline expressing a characteristic ambivalence in a letter of 8 October 1767 when she wrote, 'Rousseau is undoubtedly right in some things, but I have so bad an opinion of the man, and upon reflection think his writing so very dangerous, so very destructive of all principles hitherto held sacred both moral and religious, that I hate to think I could be drawn in for a time to admire him. To be sure his eloquence is great and very persuasive; but examine his principles, they are certainly bad and hurtful.'[43]

In one sense we might say that retirement in all of these accounts is essentially figurative, and merely stands in for another debate, but in the second half of this chapter I want to turn to alternative constructions of retirement not as the silent space of conventional gender politics but as a space in which to question and at times resist its merely domestic forms. In particular, while we can certainly point to the deeply conventional through- out the century, retirement in women's letters and diaries is such an active topic of conversation that it is effectively being re-imagined in ways which resist the conventional and which make retirement a space constantly to be constructed and negotiated.

Kept out of the road of sin

At least since the beginning of the century, and the writings of Mary Astell, women had been able to look to a model of female retirement as some form of learned feminist utopia which stressed at once the rejection of fashionable commercial society and the embrace of an inward meditation on self. In Astell's words,

You are therefore Ladies, invited into a place, where you shall suffer no other confinement, but to be kept out of the road of sin: You shall not be depriv'd of your Grandeur but only exchange the vain Pomps and Pageantry of the world, empty Titles and Forms of State, for the true and solid Greatness of being able to despise them. You will only quit the Chat of insignificant people for an ingenious Conversation; the froth of flashy Wit for real Wisdom; idle tales for instructive discourses . . . Happy Retreat! Which will be the introducing you into such a Paradise as your Mother Eve forfeited, where you shall feast on Pleasures, that do not like those of the World, disappoint your expectations, pall your Appetites, and by the disgust they give you put you on the fruitless search after new Delights, which when obtain'd are as empty as the former; but such as will make you truly happy now, and prepare you to be perfectly low hereafter. Here are no Serpents to deceive you, whilst you entertain your selves in these delicious Gardens. No Provocations will be given in this Amicable Society, but to Love and to good Works, which will afford such an entertaining employment, that you'll have as little inclination as leisure to pursue those Follies, which in the time of your ignorance pass'd with you under the name of love. (*A Serious Proposal to the Ladies* (1694–7))

In Astell's retired community, away from the snares of society, women would be 'kept out of the road of sin . . . the vain Pomps and Pageantry of the world, empty Titles and Forms of State' and would thus be able to concentrate not on 'those Follies, which in the time of your ignorance pass'd with you under the name of love' but instead on 'adorning their minds with useful knowledge'.[44] As these brief quotations from Astell suggest, retirement is always retirement from something, and that something inevitably takes the form of the city; but the city and its fashions are inflected in quite particular ways. Modern scholarship has rightly pointed to the significance of the *Serious Proposal* as a re-imagining both of female retirement and of its concomitant, the figure of the fashion-conscious socialite.[45] Indeed, what the models of retirement we have been discussing so far share is the need to set themselves against the commercial desires of fashionable society. Thus, just as they offer us the image of the learned woman, the pious woman, or the proper lady secure in her country retreat, so they offer us that retreat in reaction to another figure, the figure of the 'fine lady' with her fashionable city ways and her too close association with thoughtless consumerism and the evils of luxury.[46] These opposing yet intertwined accounts of femininity as at once morally ideal and morally deficient are far from peculiar to the language of retirement: as Vivien Jones has argued the distinction was used widely in the eighteenth century 'to help forge a precarious distinction between polite culture and the world of fashion and consumerism'.[47] What this highlights in turn is that female retirement – at least as an attempt to leave the world behind – is inevitably doomed because it can never leave behind the ways in which it is constructed by the world beyond itself and about which it inevitably speaks.

In Astell's case, female utopian retirement from the world offered the possibility of learning and meditation while still retaining one foot in the pleasures of the modern world. As Kathryn Sutherland has argued, 'The quality which for Astell distinguishes retirement is reflection, by which concept and word she encompasses the complexities of an act which is at the same time a withdrawal of female value from the market place and an engagement to trade on different terms'.[48] This is surely so, but it is also only part of the picture.

Astell's negotiations take place in the idealising space of literary publication, and while she assumes the elite status of the inhabitants of her retreat, and claims its separation from fashionable city ways, most well-to-do women would spend up to half of each year in a space already defined as retirement, but one far removed from the idealised aspirations of an all-female community. Elizabeth Montagu characterised the mode of life thus:

I believe the English are the only people now in the World who make a pretty equal division of their time between the Town & Country, & totally vary their mode of life with their place of residence. Some of the French people of fortune leave Paris in Summer for Villas in its Neighbourhood, but they do not seem to change their amusements. Gay Cotteries, good Suppers, & Cards seem to make up the sum of their pleasures there no less than in Paris itself. Those who have Seats in remote Provinces go to them but rarely, & usually stay only the time of the Vintage. The regular retirement to the Country in Summer, & return to the Capital in Winter, I suppose usual only here; but I think it adds much to the pleasantness of our lives. The gratefull viscissitude prevents the weariness of Solitude, or surfeit of society.[49]

This surely complicates for us the figure of the fine lady as the antithesis of the serious, meditative, and learned lady in retreat because in fact one might inhabit and indeed aspire to inhabit these different stances at different moments. Montagu – always alive to the pleasurable ironies of being a fine lady with a country estate – wrote of her own experience 'Next Sunday I quit the peaceful groves and hospitable roof of Bullstrode, for the noisy, turbulent city; my books and serious reflections are to be laid aside for the looking-glass and curling-irons, and from that time I am no longer a Pastorella, but propose to be as idle, as vain, and as impertinent as any one.'[50] The rather more earnest Catherine Talbot took a very similar stance after spending several months in the country with Dr Thomas Secker (later Archbishop of Canterbury). Talbot, who tends in her letters to refer to time in the country as solitude, wrote to their mutual friend Elizabeth Carter, 'I do love this solitude, and this leisure dearly well, though I do not make half the improvement of it that I might'. That sense that the leisured retirement of the country brings with it the expectation of improving oneself by study and meditation is undoubtedly characteristic of Talbot's letters, and indeed of many other writers, but so too is the following, written from the depths of the countryside: 'this day se'nnight I go [to] that idle place London, where, after the long solitude of this *paisible hameau*, I propose to spend four months in incessant talking, and all the variety of agreeable company I can hook myself into, without writing, or reading, or any of those kinds of things'.[51] That is, while the seasonal model of retirement might be characterised simply as a convenient terminology for conventional social behaviour, it nevertheless articulates a framework of solitude and sociability which invites the individual to address their changing desires, their sense of sociable purpose, and their moral value as an individual.[52] As we have already seen, there is a long poetic tradition which offers exactly this invitation to moral reflection, which links the country with the natural, the natural with the moral, and which sets both against the misguided but nevertheless pleasurable world of the city. But as even these brief quotations suggest, the rather less-public world of retirement writing in women's letters and journals introduces us to a more complicated sphere of experience which cannot separate retirement from the things it claims to leave behind, where the individual cannot align themself simply with the ideals of retirement poetry, and indeed where the lived experience of both retirement and social engagement cannot be neatly aligned with the abstractions of poetry, the moral injunctions of conduct literature, or the perceived pleasures of a single-sex community. Those complications can be seen in action if we return to Astell, or rather if we recognise why we might leave her behind.

That dead vacation from all present hopes and fears

As Rebecca D'Monté and Nicole Pohl's collection of essays on literary and historical female communities suggests, the idea of, indeed the creation of, all-female communities continued to hold a significant allure throughout the seventeenth and eighteenth centuries.[53] However, for all the appeal of the *Serious Proposal* or, later, the likes of Sarah Scott's *Millenium Hall* (1762) and Mary Hamilton's *Munster Village* (1778), the kind of all-female community most likely to appear in British women's letters and journals through much of the eighteenth century was not Astell's visionary account (or even Scott's own more practical attempt to construct a community at Hitcham in Berkshire); rather, it was the strangely fascinating world of the Catholic convent – always on the itinerary for women travelling in Europe, and always a subject arousing mixed feelings.[54] The explosion of gothic fiction at the end of the eighteenth century – and notably of course with Matthew Lewis' *The Monk* – highlights a fascination for the more lascivious possibilities of the convent, but the combined uneasiness and attraction with which convents are met by Protestant women has a much longer history. In some ways the Catholic Alexander Pope's 'Eloisa to Abelard' (1717) sets the tone for much of the writing to follow with its emphasis on interiority, romance, piety, and suffering, but what is striking about the appearance of the convent in women's letters and journals is the willingness, and perhaps the need, to think about it in relation to their own lives and that of other women they know.

Travelling on the Continent in 1716, Lady Mary Wortley Montagu articulated a wholly conventional response to convents when she recorded the melancholy she felt for women she can only describe as 'buried alive'. Half a century later, Elizabeth Carter would express similar views when she wrote to her friend Catherine Talbot that, 'the vicissitudes of the world much more naturally carry the thoughts to a sense of our dependence upon the divine protection, than that dead vacation from all present hopes and fears that stupefies the retirement of a convent'; and Hester Thrale, while wondering what better alternative there might be for the poor and the ugly, could not help but be shocked by the superstition, bullying, and ignorance that forced women into these isolating communities.[55] Such knee-jerk Protestantism was not the only response, however, and indeed reactions to this kind of female seclusion tended to turn also on the very uncertainties surrounding retirement and solitude, voluntary or unwilling isolation, that we have already encountered.

Writing on 16 September 1740 to her close friend Henrietta, Countess of Pomfret (1698–1761), Lady Hertford (later Duchess of Somerset, and the woman to whom Thomson dedicated *Spring*), thanks her for her descriptions of the various convents Pomfret has been visiting while travelling on the continent, and continues,

Your account of the nuns of the order of Santa Teresa gives me a very agreeable idea of their course of life. I have always entertained a notion that a monastic retirement

is a very happy situation, under many circumstances; and have thought it a pity that
our legislature have not provided some retreat of this nature for people who, either
through misfortunes or by the cast of their natural temper, might be led to wish for
such a refuge from the cares and hurry of the world. But then, I would not have it
in the power of any parent, brother, guardian, or relation whatsoever, to shut up
people against their inclinations; for retiring from a public life, and being torn from
it, are very different things, and likely to produce opposite effects.[56]

As a call to establish an all-female retreat in England (tempered by the usual
suspicion of Catholic institutions), Hertford's letter appears to recall and to
support the ideals of Astell's *Serious Proposal*; what complicates that claim,
however, is the much longer discussion both of convents and of solitude
in which the two women had been engaged.[57] A year earlier, Pomfret had
written to Hertford of meeting a young woman who had chosen to enter
a nunnery after an unfortunate love affair. A maid of honour in Genoa,
Teresa Giaccomini had fallen in love with a man below her station, was
banned from marrying him, and resolved therefore on a life of retirement.
Pomfret and Hertford's responses to the episode are valuable to us because
they demonstrate how closely such examples might be knitted in to a sense
of one's own place in the world, of one's experience of solitude, and of the
balance between the two. More than this, they point to the association so
frequently made not only between convents, piety, and solitude, but between
solitude, romance, and depression. In a letter of 23 September 1739, Pomfret
wrote to Hertford:

I could not forbear shedding a tear at her unhappy, irremediable mistake – that
retirement and thought would banish from her heart a passion that is often produced, and always fed, by them: indeed all the disorders of the mind are more
effectually dispersed, or laid asleep, by motion and variety, than by solitude and
meditation; for whenever pleasing thoughts are wanting, unpleasing ones will always
introduce themselves.[58]

From her own rather more comfortable retirement in Windsor Forest,
Hertford replied,

I do not wonder that you shed tears at the profession of the unhappy votress at
Genoa, since I could scarce restrain mine at the recital of her sufferings. I am afraid
solitude is not a cure for love; but I think the inclination to it a very natural effect
of that passion, when it is unsuccessful; it leave the mind in a state of languor and
melancholy that makes it shun society, and retire from mankind to indulge the idea
of what it ought most carefully to avoid, and which probably it would endeavour to
free itself from, were it not generally attended with a depression of spirits, that is to

the mind what fetters are to the body, and prevents it from using sufficient motion to put itself in a more easy situation.[59]

This alternative account of solitude as an opportunity not only for meditation but for depression acts as an important counterweight to those more cheering visions of moral self-sufficiency encountered so far. One context for Hertford's reply was her own ever-increasing retirement from the public world and a tendency towards 'lowness of spirits'.[60] One-time maids of honour, both Pomfret and Hertford had retired from public life on the death of Queen Caroline in 1737; but while Pomfret undertook the three-year period of travel which was the occasion of these letters, Hertford – already drawn to retired life in the country, in part, her biographer argues, because of the continuing hostility shown to her by her husband's family – became an increasingly reclusive figure, and especially so after the death of both her husband and son in the late 1740s. What is shared in these two women's response to the figure of Teresa Giaccomini is an insistence on the experience rather than the idealisation of solitude, even if – as Hertford's letter from 1740 suggests – the pull of that idealisation is quite strong. It is perhaps for this reason also that a quite different figure of solitary retirement becomes the object of Pomfret and Hertford's particular attention and admiration.

Whilst at Antwerp in the summer of 1744 Pomfret encountered the unusual figure of Mrs Blount, 'who lives a little out of the city, in a small but convenient house, moated round. To this she has a draw-bridge that pulls up every night'.[61] The daughter of Sir John Guise, and married into the Blount family (known to many for their association with Alexander Pope), Ann Blount's father had encouraged her to learn Spanish, Italian, and Latin. In her youth, she tells Pomfret, she had translated passages from Horace, and worked on her literary talent, now, however, she has burned all such works in order to follow a life of domestic duties. The one literary work she does offer to Pomfret is an autobiographical poem recalling this early literary talent but turning also on a vision of Phoebus exhorting her not to continue in 'manly works' like poetry and translation. Instead she should take up a 'housewife's wiser cares, / Mind well thy needle-work, and say thy pray'rs'. So she does. As Pomfret goes on to explain, after the death of her husband she is now retired 'to prepare for the next world, and she calls herself the *Solitaire*. Her dress is plain, and she never goes into company; but if any persons come to her, she receives them with the greatest apparent pleasure, and talks with such vivacity and variety of wit, that you would imagine she was still in the midst of the beau monde.'

In reply, Hertford offered the example of the Dowager Duchess of St Albans, living at Windsor and rarely moving beyond the confines of her 'delightful room', her chapel and her closet. Comparing her with Mrs Blount, she writes, 'I believe her pleasures in her solitude are more owing to the goodness of her heart than the attainments of her head, for she has none of the ingenious entertainments that Mrs. Blount finds in her retirement; and the part of the day which is not employed in her devotions, is generally passed in receiving visits, and talking of news'. Hertford continues, 'It has long been my fixed opinion, that, in the latter part of life, when the duty owing to a family no longer calls upon us to act on the public stage of life, it is not only more decent, but infinitely more eligible, to live in an absolute retirement'.[62]

These accounts of cheerful domestic piety are a recognisable enough ideal by now – though we should distinguish graceful retirement into old age and pious solitude from those other accounts offering retirement as an ideal at any point in life – but what is striking in Pomfret's account of Mrs Blount is the disagreement it creates among her companions:

The oddness of this lady's turn, and way of life, gave very different sentiments to our company. Some of us pitied her, and some of us pitied the world for losing her; but all wondered at her except myself, who really wonder no persons ever thought of secluding themselves in this manner before. To be weary of the hurry of the world at a certain age, for people of any degree of sense, is the most natural thing imaginable; and no longer to seek company when the dearest and best of company has left us, is equally conformable to a tender heart and strong understanding. But to shut one's self up irrevocably in a prison, to torment the body and try the constitution, because our minds are already too much distressed, is what I cannot so well comprehend; therefore I confess myself an admirer of Mrs. Blount's disposal of her remaining days. Nobody can say or imagine that she repents of a retirement, which her children and friends every day solicit her to leave, to her; but she rather seems to have been storing up entertainment for her guests, which she presents with as much readiness, and as great plenty, as if she expected to receive cent. per cent. for it, whereas few are able to return her half the real value.

For Pomfret, then, this is a powerful alternative to the convent's physical torment and mental distress, but it highlights for us another account of retirement of which we should be aware. Blount leads a comfortable life of seclusion – while retaining just enough of its sociable and material pleasures – but she has also made her remaining life the business of preparing for death, and this aspect of retirement, the pious rejection of worldly things, presents a powerful but potentially disturbing alternative to the more secular ideals of retirement as a comfortable life away from town.[63] In the case of

Lady Hertford her own increasingly spiritual solitude would effectively split her from the friend of her youth, Henrietta Knight, whose own enforced retirement at an early age was of quite a different order, but there was a still more radical form of spiritual retirement which challenged the very basis of property-owning retreat.

Inward retirement helps to show us ourselves

An influential member of Hertford and Pomfret's circle of friends was Elizabeth Rowe (1674–1737), a prolific author but also a famous recluse. Rowe's retirement from public life after the early death of her husband put her in the position of being at once retired and famous, and this, alongside such works as her *Letters Moral and Entertaining* and her numerous poems made her an object of much discussion amongst her friends.[64] Rowe's use of the garden as an image both of reward and punishment in her fiction is the subject of the following chapter, but most relevant here is her attitude towards the afterlife. Certainly in her fiction Rowe may reward her heroines with fine gardens, great houses, and six thousand a year, but this is repeatedly undercut by the knowledge – most clearly stated in her *Devout Exercises of the Heart in Meditation and Soliloquy, Prayer and Praise* but consistently present in the *Letters* – that all sublunary things, and nature itself, are at best troublesome delusions. In the first of the *Devout Exercises* (published posthumously in 1738), Rowe addresses the 'flowry Varieties of the Earth', the 'sparkling Glories of the Skies' and finds that their 'blandishments are vain . . . I would fain close my Eyes on all the various and lovely Appearances you present, and would open them on a brighter scene'.[65] More strikingly, in exercise XXVII, 'Breathing after God, and weary of the World', which turns on a quotation from James 4:4, she writes:

Vanish, ye terrestrial Scenes! fly away, ye vain Objects of Sense! I resign all those poor and limited Faculties by which you are enjoy'd; let me be insensible to all your Impressions, if they do not lead me to my God. Let *Chaos* come again, and the fair Face of Nature become an universal Blank: let her glowing Beauties all fade away, and those divine Characters she wears be effac'd, I shall yet be happy; the God of Nature, and the Original of all Beauty is my God.

What if the Sun were extinguish'd in the Skies, and all the etherial Lamps had burnt out their golden Flames, I shall dwell in Light and immortal Day, for my God will be ever with me. When the Groves shall no more renew their Verdure, nor the Fields and Vallies boast any longer their Flowry Pride; when all these lower Heavens, and this Earth are mingled in universal Ruin, and these material Images of things are no more; I shall see new Regions of Beauty and Pleasure for ever opening themselves in the divine Essence with all their original Glories . . .

. . . Bring my Soul out of Prison; I am straiten'd; the whole Creation is too narrow for me; I sicken at this Confinement, and groan and pant for Liberty . . .

. . . The Friendship of this World is Enmity with God.

Even the editor of the *Devout Exercises*, Isaac Watts, found Rowe's more rapturous moments uncomfortable, but the strain of thinking which rejects *all* earthly things, from wealth, status, and property to the physical creation itself remains uncomfortably present in Christian spiritual writing of the eighteenth century and is always available as a riposte to the more comfortable platitudes of country retirement.[66]

Notably in the letters of low-church Christian women, 'retirement' figures as a withdrawal from company in order to commune with God, but that retirement need have no particular location and certainly did not require the complex paraphernalia of a country estate. Thus, for example, in the generation after Rowe, we can look to Lady Darcy Brisbane Maxwell's diary entry of 1772 where retirement is synonymous with prayer: 'When I rose this morning, I felt my soul rather languid; but, after breakfast, inclined to retirement and secret prayer. Enjoyed a good time at the throne of grace'.

A more extreme version of this (and indeed a version edited to suggest that extreme) would be the Quaker Mary Waring's diary, recording her religious life in the 1790s.[67] Waring (1760–1805), whose diary only begins after her sudden conversion, is, as her editor notes, striking for the frequency of her private retirements; and, as he goes on to write, 'There is reason to believe that retirement is one mode pointed out by the good Shepherd, to wean the tenderly visited person from associates who would impede their advancement in the way of the cross; and to induce them to let their affections centre in spiritual gratifications, and permanent treasures: and much is it to be desired that such as at times feel the gentle attractions of heavenly love, thus "to sit alone, and keep silence," would yield to the salutary intimation'.[68] In Waring's diaries, retirement is those moments which can be grasped in between the otherwise unremitting requirements of domestic management and family responsibility in a Godalming household. Thus, we find her writing in January 1793, 'My time fully occupied in attending my dear sister: and, though I have no suitable time for retirement, yet have frequently felt the tendering influence of truth on my mind while thus engaged'. More frequently, however, she was able to find these moments of retreat within her household, as an entry from September the previous year suggests: 'a portion of each [day] has been spent in retirement, and, I may with gratitude acknowledge, that in these solitary sittings, I have felt the over-shadowing of the Divine wing, to my great refreshment and encouragement; yet I also retain a humbling sense of my manifold weaknesses.' It would be tempting, of course, to argue that here we have an entirely different usage of retirement which has little to do with the lives of well-to-do women in the countryside and which stresses the insignificance of location except insofar as that location is a withdrawal from company. However, we have already seen how the figure of solitude – stripped of pastoral trappings – could be used to similar effect in Chudleigh's 'Solitude', and indeed these diaries of the later eighteenth century share other assumptions with their precursors.

In a diary written by Waring's contemporary, Elizabeth Ussher (*c.* 1772–96), we find her arguing in 1795 that, 'To those who find religion a real good, retirement is delightful, as it enables us without interruption to seek for peace, and to enjoy the greatest privilege, – communion with *Him* who condescends to be the friend of sinners, and rejoices over them to do them good'. In 1771 Margaret Hoare Woods (d.1821) claims that, 'Inward retirement helps to show us ourselves; the weakness and poverty of our situation, and the necessity of receiving strength and consolation from Him, who can remove all difficulties'.[69] But for all of these writers retirement is inevitably still constructed as a move away from an otherwise embracing sociability. In Margaret Althans' letter of advice to her brothers, along with a recommendation to 'save your pocket money' and to 'despise not the poor' comes the advice to, 'Love retirement, and be more fond of being alone, than of letting your tongue run in company'.[70] Even in Waring's diary, that clash between pleasurable sociability and inwardness that so marks the language of retirement we have been exploring so far is powerfully present, as we find in an entry from August 1791 fearing that she has 'given way too much to a roving disposition to-day, which I feel wrong, and Oh how have I desired, in this my retirement, to be enabled to mount a little upward above this low and lowering world; to shake myself from the dust of this earth, and feel my mind renewedly strengthened to press forward, laying aside every weight and burden!' This last surely captures both the desire to leave the world entirely behind that we found in Rowe's *Devout Exercises* and that sense of a pleasurable but dangerous entrapment in worldly sociability. And in fact it would be wrong to represent Rowe's writing simply in terms of the *Devout Exercises* not least because her far more popular *Letters Moral and Entertaining* retain and explore that desire for a world of pastoral pleasure. Thus, while we are undoubtedly confronted by a different intellectual context and by a language which mainstream Anglicanism would find uncomfortably enthusiastic, both forms share assumptions about the importance of interiority and self improvement, the necessity of looking beyond the physical, and the dangers of sociability and worldly ties however consuming they may be. They share something else as well: with the turn to, and reliance upon, interiority comes a sense of weakness, failure, and anxiety which has the potential to make solitude *and* sociability uncomfortable and uncertain spaces.

The mild majesty of private life

At this point we may appear to have come a long way from John Pomfret's *The Choice*, but the division between the secular and spiritual need not be that extreme. When we turn to the correspondence of Elizabeth Carter (1717–1806), for example, we find a sustained attempt to address the relationship between solitude and sociability, the spiritual and the secular, in the lives of two of her close friends, Elizabeth Montagu and Catherine Talbot (1721–70).[71] Montagu's use of, and relationship with, retirement will be dealt with more extensively in a later chapter. Here, however, we should just note the characteristic playfulness in the construction of her own self-image when she wrote to Lord Lyttelton in 1765:

Ladies of gallantry in their old age grow perfect saints, and can live in hermittages, occupied with the works of repentance, and enthusiastick visions of a happier state to which they think the fervour of their devotion will peculiarly entitle them. As in my youth I have not been a Sinner, I have no hopes of growing a Saint in my old age. With the hopes of a Christian, & the temper of a philosopher, I hope to pass gently through the vale of years.[72]

This light-hearted dismissal of religious enthusiasm – and with it the likes of Mrs Blount, Lady Hertford, and Elizabeth Rowe – is characteristically dense in its manoeuvres: Montagu's ladies of gallantry turning perfect saints may be an echo of Pope's prudes in *The Rape of the Lock*, but her twin appeal to philosophy and Christianity is also an attempt to negotiate a position which could encompass both a famously urban sociability allowing an overt display of her huge wealth, and a rural retirement which stressed charity, piety, domesticity, and privacy. With far less financial backing behind her, with no pretensions to being a London hostess, and repeatedly defining herself in opposition to the figure of the 'fine lady', Carter was undoubtedly aware of the possible disjunction between the two friends' experiences of retirement. Indeed, in her correspondence with Montagu one striking difference between the two women's accounts of spiritual reverie brought on by the contemplation of nature is that Montagu's tend to be rehearsed from within her own garden while Carter – living in Deal, with only a small house and garden – can be carried off into the wider universe by looking at a wayside flower. One consequence of this is that the letters of the two women must work hard to create an account of retirement able to negotiate their quite different social status, their shared love of London sociability, and their differing needs for, and experiences of, solitary retirement.

In her 1768 translation of Epictetus, Carter would include the stoic's essay on solitude with its insistence on self-sufficiency, its rejection of solitude as a lonely state (because of self-knowledge and the ability to 'bear our own company'), and its accompanying claims of inner peace in the face of adversity.[73] With its further insistence on the suppression of desire ('Totally repress your Desire, for some time, that you may at length use it according to Reason') and on the need to serve others ('When you eat, be of service to those who eat with you; when you drink, to those who drink with you. Be of Service to them, by giving way to all, yielding to them, bearing with them . . .'), the stoicism of Epictetus appears to merge itself seamlessly with one account of eighteenth-century femininity (as domesticity) while setting itself against another (of ungoverned desire).[74] But this is not straightfor- wardly Carter's own stance.[75] Certainly, she may share with Epictetus a belief that contentment in solitude is gained 'by God, through reason', but where Epictetus turns to philosophy in the face of shipwreck, fire, envy, grief, and love, Carter's correspondence repeatedly turns to an understand- ing of the less-than-stoic, of the pleasures of sociability, of the need for company, of the supports of friendship, and of the power of one's longings and desires. In this, as Karen O'Brien's account of Carter has demonstrated, Carter expresses a view shared by her Bluestocking friends Catherine Talbot and Elizabeth Montagu, and heavily influenced by the writings of Joseph Butler, that while it must be subordinate to conscience, self-love, and self- regard are an inevitable and necessary part of human nature'. According to O'Brien, human nature for the Bluestockings 'is judiciously self-regarding yet naturally sociable and self-reflectively ethical in orientation', and the concomitant of this is that solitary retirement and a regard only for the afterlife represents a wrong turn.[76] When her own small garden was ruined by storms, Carter wrote to her friend Elizabeth Vesey of the buffeting winds,

I could forgive all this violence to my dress if the tempest would but spare my poor little garden, which is almost torn up by the roots; and, to the great mortification of my orderly spirits, the leaves and flowers are scattered into rags and litter: this distresses me more than such a trifle ought, but you have no idea how I love my garden.[77]

Similarly, in Carter's correspondence with Catherine Talbot, when they turn to the problem of solitude, their focus most frequently falls upon the practicalities of a retirement intertwined with active, and often city based, sociability. We have already seen how Talbot's desires might shift between the quiet meditation which seems only imaginable in a country – even a pastoral – setting and the more energetic sociability of London; but she could as easily find herself questioning the value of solitude, writing to Carter in June 1751: 'I begin to have less regard for solitude than I used to have in theory, as I do not find I can improve it so as to do or think any thing that is worth doing or thinking. It is at the worst a pleasant state of idleness and indolence when one has fair fields to range in, sweet fresh air to breathe, and books of one sort or other.'[78] For both women, these shifting locations of pleasure and duty – of desires to be embraced or repressed – are central to their accounts of themselves and of retirement.[79]

On reading Montfaucon's *French Antiquities* in the autumn of 1751, Talbot wrote to Carter that such tales of heroic action left her feeling 'sick of all human greatness and activity'; Carter's reply, that there is 'no other refuge from the horrors of history but in the mild majesty of private life', may sound like an acceptance of female domesticity in retirement (of the kind that we saw Lyttelton recommend to women), but it is not a rejection of the sociability made possible by public life (and so much associated with the salons of their friends Montagu and Vesey), neither is it a rejection of the moral value of that sociability.[80] As O'Brien argues, 'Talbot was at one with Carter and Montagu . . . in her belief that a cheerful, sociable life diversified by innocent indulgences was in accordance with God's will . . .'.[81] Writing from the hubbub of fashionable Piccadilly in 1751, Talbot asks forgiveness for not having written sooner, and then continues,

My excuse is nothing but mere *wicked racketing*, as you very justly call it; and wicked it really is, for nothing, I believe, so effectually corrupts the heart and depraves the understanding. The thing itself, *racketing*, is a bad thing, by which I mean, not only going to public places, not only consuming life in idle visits and dress, but merely the being out upon whatever succession of plausible pretences, perpetually out all day and every day. This is my case; I have not time to reflect upon a line I read, or consider the line I write, or indulge one remembrance of past times, or carry on one train of useful thought, so much am I taken up with the ordinary and due civilities of life. What can one do? I have not been at one public place; I have seen a card-table but twice; I never go to bear-gardens or auctions; and yet my poor head is as giddy and as empty as if I whirled through the whole round of impertinence. Yet I cannot wish the number of people I love and esteem less, nor can I refuse to be with them while it is in my power; but glad I shall be when I get into the peace and freedom of the country.[82]

This figuring of city life as wicked racketing and the country as peace and freedom is of course wholly conventional, but once again it is important to register the fluidity of these rhetorical ploys and their repeated reversals. Thus, while we might draw on an account of pastoral as an urban longing for the moral simplicity of the country, the expression of that longing is hardly a rejection of the city; rather it becomes necessary because the speaker has not left the city and its pleasures behind. Insisting that one must constantly adjudicate between disparate desires, Talbot and Carter's letters offer us once again that suspension between states which Alpers' suggests is the true articulation of pastoral. In these terms, we should accept both the seriousness and the self-deprecation in Talbot's moral evaluation of her London life, but with this the need to find a justification for its pleasures. Carter offers two. The first is linked to that seasonal account of retirement and to its use as a space for learning and self-reflection (six months of each year spent in studious retirement mean the world could rightly claim the other six and would benefit from her example). The second – related – turns to the need for moral action in the public world. Noting that the likes of Hercules and Theseus had clubs for knocking people on the head, and suggesting that Talbot (and thus any woman) would make very awkward use of such things, she argues that neither of these heroes achieved their designs 'by spending their whole lives in retirement'.[83] That is, while violent male heroics may be outside the female realm, heroic action is not. Rather, as the following passage from Talbot's essays makes clear, moral courage may be more necessary in society than in untested moralising in solitude:

The Joys of Society are, of all others most mixed with Pain. Yet where all are perfect, and where all are happy, how sublime must they be! Alas my great, my continual Failure is in social Duties! Why? Because I am almost continually in Society. In Solitude, one has nothing to do, but to cherish good and pleasing Dispositions. In Society, at every unguarded Moment, bad and painful ones break out, and fill one with Shame, Remorse, and Vexation.[84]

Characteristically, however, Talbot also records in a letter to Carter an experience of solitude at least as shameful, and far removed from the easy cultivation of a pleasing disposition:

How insignificant do I feel myself! how poor a nothing! The languor attendant on a slight fever has taken away all my superfluous spirits, and I see myself in a true light, honest indeed, and well meaning, but wonderfully useless. While one goes on in a daily routine of employments, one is apt to think the time filled up in an exemplary manner. But what have I been doing since I came here? giving trouble and reading idle books to while away the hours of prescribed solitude. Sometimes I fancy solitude and leisure is all my mind wants to expand a pair of eagle's wings, and soar away nobody knows whither. How gladly would I embrace wearisomeness, lowness, pain itself, could I but find my mind improve by them.[85]

What emerges, then, is a form of active Christian duty which must inevitably temper any account of either solitude *or* sociability as the most morally admirable position. What is most notable in the correspondence, however, is that these exchanges continue throughout their friendship and the justifications for sociability rather than solitude – and vice versa – are offered from both sides. Thus, a year after the above exchange, Talbot would write to Carter, 'The love of retirement seems to grow upon you. But it ought not. The use of retirement is to fit us for moving more reasonably, more beneficially in the world. And mixing in the world is of use to rub off the rust . . . which the best and noblest minds will contract in too long a retirement.'[86] Both women are, then, working towards an account of life which finds moral justification for something that feels like a guilty pleasure, and both need to be reminded of that goal. What this tells us once again is that the relationship between retirement and a physical location is inevitably far from stable; what it also tells us is that retirement is constantly being (re)imagined as a space in which one's desires and one's sense of self can be addressed.

The land of friendship

As both Talbot and Carter agreed, 'of all solitudes a solitude in London is the worst'; to be in town, without one's friend, is to be in 'the most forlorn and joyless of all deserts' – but it is in town also that one can be most fully social.[87] That dilemma returns us to the beginning of this chapter and to the nature of sociable solitude.[88] For Addison, as for Chudleigh, country solitude could be a crowded place; but it is important not to miss the fundamentals here: when writing from the country women in retirement (however defined) are always writing to absent friends and in some sense about their separation – many express not happy domestic sociability but an experience of isolation.[89] Carter, for example, wrote that while Samuel

Johnson called London the land of ideas, 'I call it the land of friendship',[90] and she certainly valued those periods in her life that gave access to the kind of intellectual and emotional exchanges so readily available in London's salon and visiting culture.[91]

Though a deliberate misrepresentation, we have already seen how Catherine Talbot constructed her London self as too busy, too frivolous, and too scattered for serious thought; we have seen Elizabeth Montagu do much the same with her youthful claim to abandon the studies of retirement in order to be as idle, as vain, and as impertinent as any one; and as Mary Lepel, Lady Hervey (1700–68), wrote more earnestly from Chevenings (the vast country estate of the Stanhopes, in Kent) to her close friend the Rev. Morris:

> 'tis the retirement of the country that allows me time to write you so long a letter: in London, what with the necessary business of my family, the commissions I have to execute from abroad, and the many people who, at all hours of the day, are dropping in upon me, I have scarcely a moment to myself.[92]

What complicates this neat division between London sociability and country solitude, however, is letter-writing itself. Life in London undoubtedly allowed a form of physical sociability and conversation less possible when dispersed across the countryside, and as an imagined space London is frequently constructed as the site of endless interactions and possibilities; but letter-writing could create its own imagined spaces, and if those letters frequently contained the spectral figure of the city and of absent intimacy, they were also by their nature a means of resisting solitude and of reclaiming sociability. As Clare Brant has argued in her study of eighteenth-century letters,

> writers who describe their letters as conversational often follow it with an evocation of the recipient's presence . . . the conversational idiom is tied to a fantasy that the addressee will surmount absence . . . Initially, correspondence seems to dematerialise bodies, that is, letters substitute for the person of a writer who would have a physical presence in conversation. Eighteenth-century writers' liking for tropes of voice through the image of conversation can be seen as a way of dealing with the body's imperfect disappearance in letters.[93]

We can see all of these moves at work in the letters of women writing from the country, and with it the urge physically to situate that imagined presence in the sociable space of the garden. Thus, Lady Hertford, like many women, expressed the wish that her friends could be with her when out in her garden, and would conjure up that lost sociability in the act of imagining. Writing to Lady Pomfret from her estate at Marlborough, she told her friend,

When I am sitting near the cascade, upon a favourite seat, by the side of a little wilderness of flowering shrubs, I cannot help thinking (or almost saying) to myself, 'Lady Pomfret would like this shade.' How happy it would make me, if I could place you there in reality, as often as I do in imagination. No longer ago than last night, after having read over your letter there, which contains your journal from Rome to Bologna, I fell into so deep a reverie on your passage amongst the Appenines, that I almost thought I saw every beautiful landscape you have described, and was ready to mistake the sheep-bells on the neighbouring down, for those of the little chapels you mentioned.[94]

London may be the land of friendship, as Carter suggests, but sociability can construct and inhabit alternative spaces; and while retirement may be figured as a welcome absence of the city, it may be figured as its unwelcome absence at the same time. The act of letter-writing inevitably mirrors that dilemma – a demonstration of sociability driven by its loss. Carter, too, was not averse to recording her sense of absence and presence in the garden, writing to Elizabeth Vesey of her stay with Mrs Cosnan at Wingham, in October 1784, 'we passed many hours in the garden, or sitting on a bench at the end of the grove, near a sweet stream, soothed by the gentle fall of water over a little cascade, and we never returned to the house till the sun had shed his last rays on the extremity of a dark walk of thick trees. I often secretly, and sometimes openly, wished for you'.[95] More positively, however, we might argue that this palpable sense of community in absence found in so many women's letters from, and discussions of, retirement represents an alternative to the more troublesome model of the Catholic convent or the largely impractical ideals of an all-female retreat. Instead, the idealised space of an all-female community in retirement is inhabited not as the physical location imagined by Astell, or made concrete by religious institutions, rather it is experienced in the interchange of letters between women from quite different locations in the countryside.

What complicates this in turn is the heavy ideological freight running through the traditions and languages of retirement, a freight which must be confronted (one way or another) by women alone in the country or separated from their friends. Thus, while on the one hand retirement need have no direct correlation with a particular locality, on the other a striking feature of letters written from the country is the overwhelming sense of its cultural codes and expectations, of the requirement not simply to behave but to think, feel, and represent oneself in quite particular ways. This is not to say that individual letters have nothing to tell us about their author's experience of retirement; it is, however, to argue that the representation of that experience is structured by (well-recognised) convention.[96]

Notably widespread in its influence as a model of female writing in retirement was the posthumous appearance of Madame de Sévigné's letters (in both French and English) from the early to mid-eighteenth century. Having read Sévigné in 1726, Lady Mary Wortley Montagu (1689–1762) claimed in a letter to her sister Lady Mar that her own would outdo them forty years hence.[97] In rather less time than that she had changed her mind entirely – about Sévigné rather than herself – and wrote to her daughter Lady Bute in 1754, 'How many readers and admirers has Madame de Sevigny, who only gives us, in a lively manner and fashionable Phrases, mean sentiments, vulgar Prejudices, and endless repetitions! Sometimes the tittle tattle of a fine lady, sometimes that of an old Nurse, allwaies tittle tattle.'[98] The change of opinion aside, Lady Mary was right to point to Sévigné's influence on English women letter writers. Certainly Sévigné was a ready foundation for Sarah Lennox's fantasy of country life when she wrote to her sister in 1778,

in most of my imaginary dreams of the happiest state in life I always represent myself a husband, wife and children living in a pretty country house, with just neighbours enough to make them enjoy Madame Sevigne's pleasure of being rid of them, and friends enough to draw them from home now and then; but the chief part of their life being spent . . . busy with education, and amused with reading in a family way in common in the evening – I must not forget a little planting and improvements, just to keep one out a good deal and make one fancy one has a great deal of business which enlivens one.[99]

Tittle tattle or not, one reason for the popularity of Sévigné's letters was that they provided a model of intimate sociability which seemed to avoid the pitfalls of writing about oneself. Early in Pomfret's European travels, Hertford – another confessed admirer of Sévigné – wrote to her friend,

what return can I make for the most agreeable letters in the world, but a dry account of a life spent in solitude, and too uniform to afford any entertainment in the repetition? My greatest amusements would be none to you at second-hand. The trees I planted some years ago in my garden, though they now afford me a delightful shade (under which I pass many solitary hours), have no beauties that will appear upon paper, unless a pen like that of Mr. Pope should describe them.[100]

As we will see, Lady Mary Coke would make similar apologies, but, like Hertford, she would continue to write. Indeed, perhaps the most striking convention of letters written from the country (though one must exclude Elizabeth Montagu from this claim) is their perceived need to apologise.[101] That apology is for a lack of news about the society from which one is absent, but it is also for writing about oneself. Just as with the language of solitude, the need to apologise for writing of one's thoughts is closely linked to the absence of society being perceived as some kind of failing: there is a language which allows for and valorises certain modes of female thought in private (primarily devotional), there is too a notion that women can and should write social news, but when they turn to other subjects – including themselves – then they must make an apology, even in private letters to friends. Here, then, solitude and the inability to write of society require apology because they mark the distance from an attribute of sociability, gendered as female, which means little more than a superficial account of society news. The need to apologise comes from writing about something more serious, which is themself. It is not that the lone reverie or meditation are to be disapproved, but there is undoubtedly a sense of awkwardness in making this the subject of a letter; and as Hertford's letter suggests, while an account of one's garden, or of one's reading, can do some of the work of sociability, there remains a sense that writing of self is not enough.[102]

A solitude like this is not displeasing

Sévigné's letters offered to English women in the country a highly-regarded example of a lone woman making the solitary sociable, and doing so by merging local and national events with reflections on friendship and solitude which claimed significance beyond the experience of the individual. Precisely because they are letters and because they are published – they offer a model of retirement which is at once public and private, domestic and philosophical. That is, they allow a form of public self-fashioning which – with its carefully cultivated image of retired religious interiority – can resist and renegotiate the collapse of femininity into the near-silent domesticity of the *Spectator* and the *Tatler*. What they also did was reinforce a deeply ambiguous sense of solitude.

Like the *Spectator* and the *Tatler*, Sévigné's letters undoubtedly stress the pleasure of retirement, but a further aspect is her awareness that retirement can be isolating and lonely. In a letter from Livry of March 1671, Sévigné (1626–96) wrote to her daughter:

I pretend to be here in Solitude, and to make a little Trappe of this Retirement. I intend to pray...to fast...and more especially, to be excessively dull, out of a Regard to Religion. But, my Dear, what I shall acquit myself of much better than all this, will be to think on you; I have not yet ceased to do it, since I arrived here; and no longer able to contain all my Sentiments. I am writing to you at the End of the little dark Alley, which is so much your Favourite; and sitting upon the mossy Seat where I have so often seen you reposing your self. But where is it, alas! that I have not seen you in these Shades! There is no Nook nor Corner in the House, or in the Oratory, in the Gardens, or in the neighbouring Fields, where I have not seen you; no Place that does not bring something relating to you to my Remembrance; and in whatsoever Manner it be, it pierces my Soul. I see you; you are present with me; I think, and repeat over ever thing in my Thoughts . . . in vain I look for the dear Child I love with so much Passion; she is removed two hundred Leagues from me; I have her no more; I weep, without the Power to restrain my Tears.[103]

Repeatedly in Sévigné's letters the following phrasing occurs, 'A solitude like this is not displeasing', or 'Be not uneasy about my solitude, I do not dislike it', which – with their oddly negative constructions – neatly encapsulate the conflicting charges of the term, a recognition of the wavering public acceptance of its value, and an understanding that country obscurity can be, quite simply, dull.[104] Moreover, while Sévigné's retirement seems to offer a model of self-expression to women alone in the country, or in Elizabeth Montagu's case a counterweight to her fashionable city persona, her conventional stress on the pleasure of solitude can act quite differently and offer an example of happy pious domesticity in striking contrast to one's own sense of country isolation. The lonely gardening retirement of Henrietta Knight, Lady Luxborough, and of Lady Mary Coke will be explored in later chapters, but we can end this one by turning to the experience of Lady Mary Wortley Montagu and her letters from Italy in the 1740s and 1750s.

Lady Mary's changing opinion of Sévigné tells us much about the perceived problems of writing from solitude, and it tells us something also about her own experience of solitude in Italy in the middle years of the century. As both of her major biographers have argued, Montagu's letters provide a carefully crafted account of herself which chooses to omit the awkward and the uncomfortable in order to avoid direct misrepresentation. A prominent aspect of this self-image centres on the uncertain pleasures of solitude. Isobel Grundy has noted that while Montagu frequently mentions her solitude while in Italy, she was not entirely alone: that solitude included a cook, a maid, further servants, and the visits of whist-playing monks, the local priest, and a rather fractious collection of nobility and gentry. Nevertheless, as Grundy argues, 'she *felt* alone'.[105]

One means of combating that feeling was to turn to gardening, which she did with great energy, claiming it was 'certainly the next amusement to reading'. Moreover, unlike reading, gardening allowed solitude to be

refigured as bucolic and pastoral even as the life she describes comes close
in its regularity to the rigours of the convent:

I generally rise at six, and as soon as I have breakfasted put my selfe at the head of
my Weeder Women, and work with them until nine. I then inspect my Dairy and
take a Turn amongst my Poultry . . . At 11 o'clock I retire to my Books. I dare not
indulge my selfe in that pleasure above an hour. At 12 I constantly dine, and sleep
after dinner till about 3. I then send for some of my old Priests and either play at
picquet or Whist till tis cool enough to go out. One Evening I walk in my Wood
where I often Sup, take the air on Horseback the next, and go on the Water the
third.[106]

Lady Mary's descriptions of her gardens clearly record a sense of delight –
excitement even – both in the act of gardening and in the experience of the
garden as a place of pleasurable ease. In the summer of 1753, she wrote to
her daughter,

I am really as fond of my garden as a young author of his first play, when it has been
well received by the town, and can no more forbear teasing my acquaintance for their
approbation: though I gave you a long account of it lately, I must tell you, that I have
made two little terrasses, raised twelve steps each, at the end of my great walk; they
are just finished, and a great addition to the beauty of my garden . . . I have mixed
in my espaliers as many rose and jessamin trees as I can cram in; and in the squares
designed for the use of the kitchen, have avoided putting any thing disagreeable
either to sight or smell, having another garden below for cabbage, onions, garlick.
All the walks are garnished with beds of flowers, beside the parterres, which are for
a more distinguished sort. I have neither brick nor stone walls: all my fence is a high
hedge, mingled with trees; but fruit is so plenty in this country, nobody thinks it
worth stealing. Gardening is certainly the next amusement to reading; and as my
sight will now permit me little of that, I am glad to form a taste that can give me
so much employment, and be the plaything of my age, now my pen and needle are
almost useless to me.[107]

Characteristically, however, these descriptions of pleasure and retirement
also come in the context of wanting to know news from home and regretting
that one has so few correspondents; they also come in the context of a very
recognisable set of conventions which merge moral and physical cultivation,
which recall and dismiss courtly life in favour of retreat, which attempt to
re-imagine for women the troublesome space of the monastery or convent,
and which express the need both to apologise for and defend one's own
solitary condition. Writing to her daughter about the education of women,
Lady Mary figures her granddaughters as 'a sort of lay nuns' who may well

end up living in quiet retirement. And, echoing Sévigné's claims of a not
displeasing solitude, she then offers the following mixture of advice and
self-justification:

> I know by experience, it is in the power of study not only to make solitude tolerable,
> but agreeable. I have now lived almost seven years in a stricter retirement than yours
> on the Isle of Bute, and I can assure you, I have never had half an hour heavy on my
> hands, for want of something to do. Whoever will cultivate their own mind, will
> find full employment. Every virtue does not only require great care in the planting,
> but as much daily solicitude in cherishing, as exotic fruits and flowers. The vices
> and the passions (which I am afraid are the natural product of the soil) demand
> perpetual weeding.

Turning to the misguided breeding up of women to mere accomplishments,
and to men's self-styled monopoly of learning, she then continues,

> I could add a great deal on this subject, but I am not now endeavouring to remove
> the prejudices of mankind; my only design is, to point out to my grand-daughters
> the method of being contented with that retreat, to which unforeseen circumstances
> may oblige them, and which is perhaps preferable to all the show of public life. It
> has always been my inclination. Lady Stafford (who knew me better than any body
> else in the world . . .) used to tell me my true vocation was a monastery; and I now
> find, by experience, more sincere pleasure with my books and garden, than all the
> flutter of a court could give me. (6 March 1753)

Lady Mary's letter is perhaps unusual (though not for her) in the density
of those conventions and allusions explored throughout this chapter but it
is also wholly characteristic of the range of tropes and ploys felt necessary
by women alone in the country. That is, claims of retirement are part of a
larger rhetorical strategy in letter-writing – a useful means of representing
oneself but one which inevitably draws on, and is itself a form of, convention. This is not to say that the experience of pleasurable retirement
is not felt, rather that it may be constructed and held on to in the face
of less appealing circumstances. In Lady Mary's case, those circumstances
included the ongoing outrages of Count Palazzi with his constant demands
for money, his property scams and barefaced lies which combined to make
Montagu's retirement in Gottolengo and Lovere more enforced and less voluntary than letters to her daughter and sister suggest.[108] Certainly then, we
need to understand this retirement in terms of what it hides, but we should
also recognise the value of the topos for a woman cut off from her own
society and unable to return: we should not, then, dismiss the language of
retirement as merely rhetorical or even as misleading, rather, that language

gives Montagu a way of claiming enjoyment of a life which was certainly framed by others as imprisonment.[109]

My aim in this chapter has been to establish some of the key models of thought about retirement and solitude in order to suggest the complications for lived experience, perhaps the biggest complication being how the individual can place themself in relation to a set of social and moral norms, conventions, and platitudes constantly at variance with themself. We should recognise from the outset, that is, that several models of retirement were available to eighteenth-century women; that the focus of retirement is inevitably on the social world it claims to have left behind; and that in such social concerns, these various models of female retirement tend not to agree.

As we have seen, a central problem when confronting literary retirement is the unstable relation between the expectations of location and the destabilising effects of desire. The wide range of retirements and solitudes explored so far suggests the difficulty of aligning one's thoughts and feelings with a conventional morality of retirement – wherever located – because the conventional is multiple and contradictory and because location locates so little. Certainly we can identify a mainstream tradition of retirement which figures it as both pastoral and admirable, but what the troubled language of solitude helps us to see is how fragile this is, because the cultural anxieties – or at the very least uncertainties – around the term mean that values are constantly being reversed and questioned. Thus, solitude is all too often merged with, or to be found in a poem about, retirement, and when retirement is offered as a theme its chief benefit is frequently characterised in terms of the opportunities it offers for solitude. Equally, while we may attempt to tease apart the two terms only to see them collapse back into each other, this should not blind us to the quite different charges they may at times carry: just as both terms claim separation from society even as that society is their object, so individuals' accounts of their absence from society are aware of the accounts and claims of other forms of solitude, retirement, and retreat.

One purpose of my case studies is to explore the ways in which individuals turn to modes of expression which may allow them to challenge the disapproving or silencing moral rhetoric of modesty, temperance, moderation, and piety or the equally disapproving rhetoric of fashion, frivolity, and thoughtless ennui. As Lady Mary's letters suggest, women must constantly decide where to draw the line, but must also then justify where they have drawn it. As modern readers, in turn, we need to hear the echoes and alternative meanings whenever these terms occur because this is exactly what eighteenth-century women had to negotiate for themselves: poetry may offer solitude as an ideal aspiration, and pastoral repeatedly assumes the pleasures of retirement, but women's letters suggest a rather less satisfactory experience, where the visualising frame of pastoral idyll can drop away to leave the rustic and boorish, where solitude can highlight one's failure to live up to its high ideals, and where solitary retirement can mean pleasure, or punishment. Punishment is the subject of the chapter which follows.

2 | 'No way qualified for retirement': disgrace

My sad Soul,
Has form'd a dismal melancholy Scene,
Such a Retreat as I wou'd wish to find

(Nicholas Rowe, The Fair
Penitent, 1703)

In Addison's *Spectator* (of 1711), the ideal woman lives a life of quiet but admirable retirement in the country; her name is Aurelia. In *The Weekly Journal or British Gazette* (1720) the 'innocently Guilty' Aurelia is seduced and abandoned by a faithless lover, retires to a neighbouring wood where, weakened by lack of food, she watches her child's death and subsequent disfigurement by worms and vermin. Saved by a charitable country lady, she lives on as 'a Melancholly Example of Injur'd Virtue, and a fair Landmark for other Maids to steer clear of the dangerous Rocks and Quicksands on which she so unhappily Split'.[1] The choice of name may of course be no more than a coincidence, and the easy turn to the names of romance is nothing if not conventional; but what may also be a nod towards the mother of Julius Caesar, and to an ideal of matriarchal behaviour, should alert us once again to what is at stake when women are placed in a landscape which can speak of innocence and of sexuality, of piety, of punishment and of shame.[2]

Domestic pleasure and pious retreat was the subject of my last chapter, but as we saw, even these visions of piety and ease carried the spectre of transgression, failure, and disgrace, and it is this alternative vision of the country, and the peculiar place of the garden, which is the subject of this chapter. My aim is to establish the ubiquity of this alternative account of the country and the range of genres in which retirement and transgression appear throughout the century; to establish the close ties between pastoral romance and transgression in the imagination of the country; to argue, along the way, that while critics have used the novel to chart the decline of romance, it remains powerfully alive in women's letters and in the imagination of rural space; and to demonstrate that models of disgrace and punishment are part of the mainstream cultural imagination of retirement quite as much as those more cheery idylls of country pleasure outlined in the previous chapter.

So far we have been exploring ways in which a woman's life in a country estate might be figured as various forms of retirement; in this chapter we move also to some of the ways in which the highly charged site of the garden brings its own problems and possibilities for female retreat. Notably, as a pre-eminent meeting point of nature and culture, the garden highlights the gendered divisions central to eighteenth-century society's understanding of itself. More than houses, but crucially adjacent to houses, gardens invite the individual to cultivate both surroundings and self, but also to set the self within larger cultural narratives, whether they be of Eden, Paradise, and the Fall, of desire, temptation, and punishment. This is not of course to argue that gardens are uniquely the domain of self-fashioning, but the contrasting and eliding discourses explored in these opening chapters bring such questions of self-cultivation and self-representation to the fore. In many respects one might make quite similar claims for houses – and for women, particularly the house interior – where they depart, perhaps, is in the unique relationship between garden and 'nature', a relationship in which working with nature and with natural forms is about creativity but also about Creation.[3] In this sense, inhabiting a garden invites the individual to think of herself in relation to the natural order where interior decoration and architecture invite that individual to think of social order. Both, certainly, are *about* culture, and both invite reflection on cultivation; but the garden's territory is always shared ground, and it is shared with something over which one only has limited control.

The garden, then, is a liminal space which invites analogies with Eden and with the biblical wilderness, which can be styled as a paradise but also therefore as a place of temptation. For women, in a way that need not be the case for men, this is inevitably also a sexualised space; and in the pages which follow I will be exploring women writers' acute awareness of the garden as at once an unregulated and a highly stylised space, a space heavily freighted with its culture's ideological contradictions.[4] In particular, I will argue that scandal and punishment, alongside the eroticisation of women's landscapes, is central to eighteenth-century accounts of women and gardens and something with which women who gardened inevitably had to contend.[5]

From early in the eighteenth century the theme of country retirement had been used by a number of women novelists in order to narrate the lives of 'fallen' women.[6] In the novels of Eliza Haywood, in popular fiction and in scandal magazines, retirement and penury are, if not a punishment, at least the only options available to women who step outside patriarchal traditions and values. One further purpose of this chapter, then, is to explore the troubled engagement between retirement and disgrace: as we have seen, much writing about retirement seeks to offer it as a positive model of retirement from corruption. But by turning to the tradition of women's fiction which places women in country retirement telling their stories, I will argue that for all that the country and retirement is claimed as a place of resistance, and a challenge to the false morality of society, it is also inevitably about failure in the public world, and the interest of such narratives lies not only in what these women do in dull country obscurity, but what they did to get themselves there in the first place; in this sense, the experience of the garden is the experience of what one cannot leave behind.

A resource against the tedium of life

In Charlotte Smith's 1788 novel, *Emmeline, the orphan of the castle*, the eponymous heroine finds herself the guest of the Demoiselle de St. Alpin at a gloomy and antiquated chateau. The Demoiselle, 'with no other relations than her brother and her nephews, whom she was seldom likely to see', had become a keen gardener and a collector of plants: 'Detached from the world ... she found in this innocent and amusing pursuit a resource against the tedium of life.'[7] This two-edged celebration of gardening should remind us of Sévigné's ambiguous claims for the pleasures of solitude; and notably, while Smith's heroine can enjoy with her host the sublime landscape in which the garden is set, neither garden nor the 'magnificent scenery' beyond is enough to satisfy the longings of her heart. Emmeline, still 300 pages from a romantic conclusion, is not yet ready to resolve her desires into the constrained gardening domesticity of her host. Gardening may be a resource against the tedium of life, but the very different responses of Smith's two women should alert us to the range of ways in which the garden acts as a moral test for women who find themselves alone. Emmeline's urge to leave the garden is acceptable because her desires lead her to marriage; and if the Demoiselle's decision to stay in her garden suggests retirement is the curtailment of desire, that retirement is in fact offered as the proper reshaping and refocusing of desire as an acceptance of powerfully pervasive gender norms and expectations.

The Demoiselle's retirement is, then, an opportunity for the domestic socialisation of self, for a recognition of one's weakness and limits within the Creation, and for an acceptance of the natural order; but, if the lone woman in the garden repeatedly appears as an account of pious domesticity, she is as frequently accompanied by an apparently quite different kind of woman, a woman whose self-interested city pleasures leave her with a horror of being alone, and whose reaction to the garden underlines her departure from the natural order. Thus, in Soame Jenyns', *The Modern Fine Lady* (1751), we meet the dissolute Harriet who must mend both fortune and reputation with an unwelcome marriage to a dull country squire: 'forc'd to quit the Town' in exchange for a 'lonely seat' she 'starts and trembles at the sight of Trees', and finds her country estate no more than 'The doleful Prison where for ever She / But not, alas! her griefs, must buried be'. Half a century later, fine ladies continue to be appalled by the country: when, in *The Female Gamester: or, the Pupil of Fashion* (1796), the foolish Lady Fortescue is confronted by a garden she spends most of her time ostentatiously 'dying of ennui'.[8] Fear of trees, and boredom in beautiful gardens make easy targets for satire, and the figure of the fine lady in the garden proved a powerful image of misguided desire; but the potential dangers of taking one's fashionable city ways into the country, the dangers, too, of failing to be content with what should make one content, proved far less easily resolved for many women writing from the country.

In the words of Elizabeth Montagu, country life could all too easily be 'sedentary, solitary, lazy and dull'.[9] And as Anne Dewes admitted, one must sometimes try hard to claim an experience one did not quite feel: after returning to the country in 1736 Dewes wrote to her friend Catherine, Lady Throckmorton, 'Do not be so cruel as to imagine I don't feel very sensibly the leaving my agreeable friends in London; but perhaps I brag of the pleasures of my solitude more to show my philosophy than the great joy they give me, for nothing alone can be very delightful'.[10] What Dewes' letter makes clear is a sense of anxiety that one might not live up to literary ideals, or, conversely, that finding the country dull signals a moral weakness: just as with Madame de Sévigné, the spectre of dullness and of loneliness appears with extraordinary regularity in women's letters, even if only as part of a claim for its absence.

Faced with life away from town, faced also, therefore, with the potential boredom of the country, one answer was to turn to the language of pastoral romance. In the previous chapter we saw how pastoral might be co-opted to support forms of female piety, but pastoral romance could offer something rather different. Madame de Sévigné's and Madame de Maintenon's letters certainly offered women a model when writing of solitude, and the poetry and prose of the last chapter could certainly support women in their experience of country life. But this was far from all that was available to them: at least as prevalent in women's letters written from the country is that world of romantic pastoral pleasures to be found in Spenser and

Milton, in Ariosto and in Tasso, in *Amadis de Gaul*, *Orlando Furioso*, and in *Clelia*. Catherine Talbot was hardly unusual in writing to Elizabeth Carter of the delight she took in reading Salomon Gessner's pastoral epic *La Mort d'Abel* (1758) while ensconced in her country retreat. Lady Louisa Stuart's urge to enjoy the country as pastoral retirement is equally characteristic: writing from the great house at Luton, she told Lady Caroline Dawson of how uncomfortable it felt after the pleasures of a little country cottage,

> Now I must indulge myself in talking a little of my beloved Yorkshire... you have no idea... how compleatly uncomfortable I feel in this great house, after being so much the contrary in our dear little clean, neat cottage at Wharncliff, where we really lived in quite a pastoral manner. I never think of it but as the abode of peace and content, for it is exactly the retirement you sometimes see described in a romance, where travellers driven in by a storm find a happy family and a place that they think a paradise. 'Tis true we are quite solitary and quiet enough here, but it is with a mixture of melancholy and stateliness, while there we seemed to be in a retreat from all care and anxiety, just what poets are always talking of, though I never saw their descriptions realised before. I doubt you will laugh at my style of admiration and delight, but I will defy you and go on. I could scribble for three hours upon the beauty of that place.[11]

One version of pastoral, then, is that wholly ubiquitous urge to frame one's stay in the country in terms of literary models, to lay claim to the experience of placid delights, and to enjoy romantic visions of beautiful landscapes divorced from the social realities of everyday life. This account of pastoral may have little to do with those visions of pious meditation mapped out in the previous chapter, but we should also distinguish it from a rather more problematic romance form.

As the following brief examples will suggest, pastoral romance had the potential to place women in the foreground of their own landscapes, landscapes in which lowly gardeners may secretly be yearning princes, and in which dull country lawyers could be transformed into elegant swains. Retirement as an imagined world of romance is the stuff of Constantia Grierson's witty poetic epistle 'To Miss Laetitia Van Lewen... at a Country Assize', where Grierson (1705–32) feigns shock at a world turned upside down when her friend writes from the country of all the 'belles and beaux that there appear' and of the 'gilded coaches, such as glitter here'. Instead, she insists, such beaux can be no more than young attorneys, and that for all the fantasies of a 'romantic brain', they too will soon be boring with their loud voices, legal jargon, and empty heads. Insisting on the dullness of the country, on a world of old maids in earnest conversation about possets and poultices, and of gentleman with no more conversation that 'what horse won the last race', Grierson invites her friend to give up such misguided pastoral romanticising of the country and return to the city. In the companion piece, 'To the Same, on the Same Occasion', that championing of city pleasures is in turn complicated as the poetic voice is more clearly aligned with a slightly dubious city culture, and with hints of 'the lovely Damon' languishing in town and awaiting the return of his belle. The tone of both poems is certainly light-hearted, but it nevertheless points to that pleasurable language of pastoral fantasy to which one might easily turn and which one might turn to most especially in the face of those country pursuits from which it seems so far removed. In Grierson's poems the neat dichotomy of country and city is complicated because neither is offered as the safely and obviously moral space, but, as she demonstrates, what causes the uncertainty in part is the ubiquitous language of pastoral romance surrounding and misrepresenting gender relations.[12] Moreover, as Grierson's poems suggest – and this is fundamental to pastoral romance – placing women in pastoral landscapes inevitably brings a sexual charge into these spaces.

Two decades after Grierson's death we can turn to what is now one of the best-known uses of such misplaced romance, Charlotte Lennox's satirical novel *The Female Quixote* (1752). It has become conventional to read Lennox's novel as a demonstration of romance's fall from favour in the face of the novel's new realism, and certainly the novel works to that end by insisting that its heroine, Arabella, must give up the delusions of romance in order to become a properly socialised wife. It has also been recognised, however, that Arabella's world of romance offers a fantasy of female power which is ultimately removed by the return to convention.[13]

The novel begins with the beautiful and wealthy heroine growing up within the secluded confines of a country estate, with a garden made natural by art, the 'Epitome of Arcadia', a landscape of 'artless and simple Beauties' (vol. 1, p. 2), and with a library full of romances bought by her mother to 'soften a Solitude which she found very disagreeable' (vol. 1, p. 4). While Arabella's father has chosen a self-imposed retirement after a fall from political grace, for Arabella confinement to the solitude of the country is enforced: French romances (in bad English translations) are a means of combating the dullness of retirement, of re-imagining the landscape, and crucially of injecting into that landscape a drama of adventure and of excitement in which the heroine plays the lead:

The surprising Adventures with which [Romances] were filled, proved a most pleasing Entertainment to a young Lady, who was wholly secluded from the World; who had no other Diversion, but ranging like a Nymph through Gardens, or, to say better, the Woods and Lawns in which she was so inclosed . . .

. . . supposing Romances were real Pictures of life, from them she drew all her Notions and Expectations. By them she was taught to believe, that Love was the ruling Principle of the World . . . and that it caused all the Happiness and Miseries of life. (vol. 1, p. 5)

The joke in Lennox's novel is that of a woman taking the conventions of romance for reality but also of taking those conventions – and the desires they embody – into the real world. The punishment for Arabella's transgression is no more than damp clothes and a didactic interview. What danger there is becomes apparent when the fantasies of pastoral romance move from rural landscapes to the complexities of public life: the seclusion of a landscape in which one might flit like a nymph may have allowed Arabella's misprision but her isolation is also a form of protection. Thus, the landscape in which we first find Arabella is not incidental; rather, romance is linked to a secluded country estate and to a landscape of retirement because it is here that such things seem possible; but equally, that uncertainty about the landscape – 'Gardens, or, to say better . . . Woods and Lawns' – and the reimagining of a garden as wild nature, is an invitation to misinterpret the space one inhabits. Arabella's landscape is 'romantic', but part of that romantic charge is that it invites thoughts of adventure which may be chivalric, sexual, or both. Arabella must learn to leave romance behind, certainly; but she must also reform her imagined landscapes, she must move from the dangerous wilderness of Aurelia in *The British Gazette* to the more comfortable, and the more safely domestic, garden of Aurelia in *The Spectator*.

The *Female Quixote* points to the dangers of long French romances, but what I have more loosely termed the language of pastoral romance hardly goes away. At most, it shifts its ground. Arabella's obsession with romance may be dismissed as part of her misguided desire for self-determination, but that act of mapping pastoral romance onto the modern world is to be found throughout the century. Notably, in journals, in collections of didactic tales, in conduct literature, and of course in pastoral poetry, the choice of names from pastoral romance is almost so conventional as to become invisible, but it nevertheless has a powerful effect both on the imagination of rural space and on the individual's experience of that space. Thus, while French romances may have gone out of fashion by the mid-eighteenth century in the way that Lennox's novel has been used to suggest, pastoral romance had certainly not: Richard Hurd's mid-eighteenth-century exploration, and championing, of medieval English and Italian romances in *Letters on Chivalry and Romance* (1762) should give us some sense of this, and of course with the emergence of what would become known as gothic fiction in the final decades of the century, romance conventions were once again to the fore.

Long before this gothic turn, however, women's letters from the country demonstrate that urge to transform their lives – if only momentarily – into a pastoral romance. Lennox was hardly alone in warning of the dangers of romance nor of linking romance with retirement; late in the century there is of course Austen's tour de force parody of gothic romance in *Northanger Abbey* (first drafted 1798–9; published 1818), but didactic essays appeared with regularity throughout the second half of the century. In the preface to the English translation of *La Nouvelle Eloisa* (1761), and in phrases which should by now be familiar, Rousseau writes:

In Retirement, the want of Occupation obliges those who have no Resources in themselves, to have Recourse to Books of Amusement. Romances are more read in the provincial Towns than at Paris, in Towns less than in the Country, and there they make the deepest Impression: The Reason is plain.

    Now it happens unfortunately that the Books which might amuse, instruct, and console the People in Retirement, who are unhappy only in their own Imagination, are generally calculated to make them still more dissatisfied with their Situation. People of Rank and Fashion are the sole Personages of all our Romances. The refined Taste of great Cities, court maxims, and Epicurean Morality; these are their Precepts, these their Lessons of Instruction. The colouring of their false Virtues tarnishes the real one. Polite manners are substituted for real Duties, fine Sentiments for good Actions, and virtuous Simplicity is deemed Want of Breeding.[14]

For Rousseau all of this leads inevitably to the destruction of rural society, and to a rural gentry who – disgusted with their country lives – move to the city, only to die in 'Misery and Dishonour'. Similarly, Anne Grant warns in her *Letters from the Mountains* (1807) that the reading of romances damages women's ability to enjoy retirement and warns also of 'a restless desire to be seen and admired, kindled by the surprising adventure of heroines, the wonderful events which the admiration excited by their beauty produces, and the splendid destiny which generally awaits them. It is this that makes young people so impatient of peace and retirement, so sick of the plain realities of common life'.[15] And true to form, the author of *Honoria and Marianne* warns the two girls:

The subject I am censuring, is a fondness for what are generally called Romances; as the Clelias, the Cassandras, and the Amadis de Gauls, &c. of the last century. I am convinced, a woman, who gives herself up to the reading this sort of entertainment, will have her head full of nothing but enchantments, battles, wounds, challenges, amours, torments, complaints, and abundance of stuff and impossibilities, which never did, and never can exist, in common life.

A lady, who is an advocate for this kind of reading, will very gravely tell you, it is of no sort of consequence, and quite immaterial, whether the heroes of romance were real, or imaginary. According to this absurd tenet, a footman, or the meanest groom in the stable, may be as great a hero as a prince, since it depends upon the imagination only. The fatal consequence of this principle is very obvious. (pp. 20–21)

The moral tale which inevitably follows is a rather more dangerous version of *The Female Quixote*, in which a young woman – her head full of the heroes and heroines of Spanish, French, and Italian romances, of Amadis de Gaul, Clelia, Felixmarte, Orlando Furioso, and the Knight of the Burning Sword – mistakes the new postillion for a prince, runs away with him to be married at Gretna Green, and only discovers too late that her prince is a common felon, twice tried at the Old Bailey and once shipwrecked on return from transportation. Notwithstanding the kind of warnings in Grant and *Honoria and Marianne*, and indeed the growing denunciation of French romances as the century progressed, that urge to imagine oneself as the heroine of a pastoral romance was widespread: knights, maidens, white palfreys, and ancient castles appear prominently in women's personal letters throughout the century. In the 1720s the circle of friends centred on Lady Hertford – and including Henrietta Knight and Elizabeth Rowe – would circulate poetic epistles in which they appeared as the heroines of romantic pastoral dalliances. At the beginning of the 1740s we have already seen how willingly a youthful Elizabeth Montagu styled herself as Spenser's Pastorella. Later that decade, and with no need for a landscape garden, Montagu's close friend Elizabeth Carter would write to Catherine Talbot of a visit to Enfield:

I had a great curiosity to ramble a little about the country, but was discouraged from this adventurous attempt by fearful accounts of straggling damsels being picked up by errant knights, and carried to enchanted castles, so that I did not venture beyond the garden, a range much too small for the extent of my genius.[16]

And in the 1780s, Lady Craven (1750–1828) would write from her travels through Europe,

I saw many chateaux, which from the singular towers, their only ornaments, my fancy might have represented heralds, giants, or dwarfs, issuing forth to enquire what bewildered heroine came so near – mais hélas – I did not see one preux chevalier, nor any thing about these ancient structures that could make me imagine they belonged to gentlemen, much less to noble warriors – Besides I was gravely seated in a comfortable coach, varnished and gilt, instead of being on a white palfrey.[17]

Just as Lennox's heroine uses romance conventions to place herself at the centre of her own drama, so women in the country might imagine themselves as the subject of their own pastoral romance. In such moments, the tone is almost always light-hearted or ironic, but the lure of a fantasy landscape which might replace quotidian realities is surely striking, indeed the need for irony underlines the desire even as the impossibility of that desire is acknowledged, and thus while these gestures have an obviously ironic charge in their implicit recognition of a more quotidian reality, they nevertheless signal the desire for something more.

In the 1720s, the urge to style oneself as a romantic shepherdess would, in part, cause the banishment of Henrietta Knight to an obscure estate in the Midlands, but the letters and poems which caused her downfall were only part of a much larger – and more threatening – tradition of pastoral romance. That is, there is another strand of romance in which the dangers of transgression are far more real and where a pastoralised landscape is not only the site of danger and transgression, but the circumstance that allows that transgression. In Lennox's mid-century novel, any hint of sexual threat is limited, but it appears as far more real and dangerous in the poetry and drama of the 1700s and 1710s, in that burst of female fiction that appeared in the 1720s, and in the use of pastoral romance to tell tales of sexual transgression which continued throughout the eighteenth century in novels, in poetry, and in the periodical press.

I will divert myself in my Gardens

Where Constantia Grierson's poems take pleasure in, and warn against, single women's pastoral fantasies of romantic adventure, the self-taught poet Mary Masters (*c.* 1694–*c.* 1771) uses the garden of a country estate to lure a woman towards marriage. In the rather elaborately entitled poem, 'Sent to a young Lady in Town, who had vow'd to die a Maid, in Answer to a Letter, where, in a Copy of Verses, she signify'd her Resolution, and desired an Account of the House and its Situation, in which a new married

Lady of her acquaintance was settled. Wrote suddenly at the request of her Correspondent in a very sultry Day', Masters teases a woman who has vowed not to marry by revelling in the pleasures of a garden, 'With Flow'rs and Fruits of various kind; / Where gravell'd Walks and Beds of green, / Diversify the Sylvan Scene', and concludes:

Come then and see this lovely Seat,
So healthful, happy, and compleat:
Or tell me, from Description now,
Would you not break an idle Vow,
For such a Seat, in such a Shade,
And own the Vow was rashly made?[18]

The poem, only slightly longer than its title, is a humorous example of how the country estate with its garden is recognised as something other than a site for meditation and instead as pastoral fantasy become real; it recognises, that is, the rather different world of the marriage market and social bargaining which, much later, finds a faint echo in Elizabeth Bennett's claim to have fallen in love with Darcy when she first saw Pemberley. However, the romantic lure of the country estate need not include assumptions of marriage. In the last chapter we saw how the vision of retirement in *The Choice* included a pliable mistress in a nearby village, and while in Pomfret's poem the mistress remains part of an absent dream, the sexual freedom enabled by retirement to a country estate was hardly lost on eighteenth-century writers.

Late in the 1710s Mary Hearne published two novels in close succession, *The Lover's Week, or, The Six Days Adventures of Philander and Amaryllis,* and *The Female Deserter. A Novel.* Both tell the tales of unmarried lovers; both use retirement as the opportunity for illicit passion and as the site from which to tell the tale of that passion. In *The Lover's Week,* a pleasant country retreat is sexualised as a place in which to hide from prying eyes. Here, Amaryllis – who has rejected the advances of an Earl – takes shelter in the country with her lover Phillander, who in turn draws on the language of retreat from society in order to avoid that society's moral censure.[19] With its happy ending, the tale is hardly conventional but it highlights that alternative account of country pleasures which have little to do with pious meditation. In the novel which followed soon after, a vision of retirement as sexual freedom is less easily maintained, but the importance of retirement from society as the occasion for sexual pleasure remains central to the narrative. At the opening of *The Female Deserter* the heroine writes to her friend Emilia, 'cease to blame me for quitting the noisy Impertinence of the Town'.

But if we expect this to be followed by a journey to the conventional world of pastoral retreat and its pious pleasures we are mistaken; instead, the town is rejected in order to 'enjoy a pleasing Solitude with the Man, whose Company alone is sufficient to make all Places entertaining'.[20] Far from expecting to see him all the time, she contents herself in his absence to enjoy the pleasure of their idyllic country cottage, and writes, 'I will ... divert myself in my Gardens, which are extremely neat, or with a Lady whose Company is very agreeable, and her Circumstances differ but little from my own'. The lady's circumstances differ little in that they are both kept women, kept not least from prying eyes, in a country estate with a garden which must provide their amusement. What is of note here, also, is a set of tropes which can be found throughout the eighteenth century, not least of which is that of the fallen woman telling the tale of her misfortune (or otherwise) from within the gardens of a secluded country estate. In Hearne's narrative this takes the form first of Calista telling of her amour with Torismond; and then of Calista's servant, Isabella, telling of her love for Polydor. In the former, Torismond drugs Calista with sleeping pills and engineers a situation which gives her little choice but to stay with him in a place of retirement; but if this retirement is initially enforced, Calista finally claims her time with Torismond is spent, 'in a far greater Tranquillity than I once thought could have been enjoyed in this life' (p. 106). In the latter tale, Isabella and her lover resolve a misunderstanding by walking in the garden and talking of love. When asked by her father, 'what Chat we could find to keep us so long out, we told him, we had been admiring the handy Works of Nature, and the Delicacy of the several Walks we had gone through' (pp. 47–8). With the language of pious reverie a convenient mask for amorous encounters, with seduction leading to a sudden retreat to the country, and with tale after tale of intrigue unfolding in the conversation of two women in a summer house which shields them from the prying ears of servants, Hearne's gardens offer freedom of female conversation, criminal and otherwise.

One further convention that should not be lost on us – and which is shared with those women letter-writers who might style themselves as Pastorella or Sylvia, as a damsel or a shepherdess – is the use of names drawn from a generalised but potent world of romance. Like Hearne's use of the garden, these names are not simply a convention, they are a convention which allows freedoms not otherwise possible and which enable authors to address modern sexuality in a heightened yet 'realist' form acceptable for mainstream publication. This tradition of pastoral romance, and in particular this use of the garden as a site for sexual quite as much as pious encounters remains central to the cultural construction of the country retreat throughout the eighteenth century. It is important that we hear its echoes alongside those of a now better-known tradition of pious pleasures.

We can see the continuing currency of this towards the end of the century, for example, if we turn to a series of stories in a single edition of *The Berwick Museum, or, Monthly Literary Intelligencer* of 1785. The challenge to any easy assumptions about pastoral pleasure is first underlined in a tale entitled, 'The Artful wanton. A Tale from Life', which tells the story of Mr Townly, duped by the scheming Maria Lovegold into maintaining her as a kept woman. The crucial deception takes place – inevitably – in a garden ('she stept into the garden, where she walked with a disconsolate air, as if bewailing the loss of her virginity'), and the narrative begins with a warning that, 'In this enlightened and sceptical age, the disguise of religion, even in the softer sex, has ceased to deceive its most pious professors. But an air of pastoral simplicity has still the power of imposing on the soundest minds' (vol. 2, pp. 147–51).

Later in the same volume – and in the space of only two pages – the journal moves from an essay entitled, 'Character of a Lady of Rank or Fashion', to a second, entitled 'The Indiscreet Argument'. In the first we are offered that all too familiar figure of the fashionable city lady inhabiting a world turned upside down; a woman who, 'short as life is, has more time upon her hands than she knows what to do with', who makes her morning visits in the afternoon and who can never be fully awake except when night has fallen and when fashionable society can share its mindless laughter and scandal. Set against this vision of fashionable female vacuity in the city is the briefest sketch of those right-thinking women, 'who are convinced that no rank or station exempts a woman from the practices of domestic virtue; who can be gay without affectation ... and pity the fools that are ashamed of being loving wives and tender mothers' (vol. 2, pp. 365–6). Set against it also, however, is the tale which follows immediately after: while the first essay offers us a world we know, with the fashionable city lady set against a female piety and domesticity the shorthand for which is most often retreat, this second tale takes us to an altogether different part of the country.

In 'The Indiscreet Argument' a young couple retire swiftly after their private marriage, 'to experience the sweets of the honey-moon, secluded from the noise and bustle of town, at an old family mansion, situated upon the borders of the new forest in Hampshire'.[21] The sweets of this retirement are only loosely domestic: 'free from the intrusions of ceremonious visitors, or the prying eyes of impertinent curiosity',

Every room in the old mansion had witnessed their enjoyments. Not a family picture, bust, or Chinese mandarine, but if endowed with speech, could have given evidence of their chaste caresses.

Having exhausted the house, the couple move outdoors where soon the birds, 'in every recess, summer-house, and alcove in the garden, had been spectators, and cheered the happy pair in amorous song'. Exhausting the confines of the garden too, they step into the forest. Here, Frederick's 'contemplation upon the wisdom and beauty of providence' is both occasioned and directed by the sight of copulating squirrels and, like the house and the garden, the forest too becomes a site of nuptial pleasures. What interrupts those pleasures is the appearance of a gang of gypsies ready to 'take their share of the conversation' but finally driven off by an irate Frederick. Exposed, the couple return home, and 'seating themselves upon a sopha, the argument which had been commenced in the forest was completely finished in the drawing room' (vol. 2, pp. 366–7). This movement from house to garden to forest reiterates that link so often made between natural landscapes and 'natural' desires, but whereas Frederick and Fulvia's desires are sanctioned by 'nuptial rights' more often it is their absence which drives the narrative and which can make the garden and the park beyond such dangerous spaces.

A place of penance and mortification

The quotation with which I began this chapter comes from Nicholas Rowe's hugely popular 1702 play, *The Fair Penitent* (published 1703), in which the heroine, Calista, seduced by the faithless Lothario, can see no future except in the shameful solitude of retreat. This vision of retirement as punishment and shame highlights for us another powerful vision of the woman in the landscape and one which echoes throughout the century (not least because of the play's own longevity).[22] *The Fair Penitent* opens in the gardens of a Genoese palace, and it is in these gardens that we hear in close succession of the heroine's impending marriage to one man and her seduction by another. With its focus on the moral dilemma of Calista, the play articulates an experience of the domestic as little more than imprisonment and of retirement as no more than a fantasy. For Calista, the condition of women is to be, 'Thro ev'ry state of Life the Slaves of Man', first under the control of a 'rigid Father' who 'dictates to our Wills' and then of the 'Tyrant Husband' who 'holds Domestick Bus'ness and Devotion / All we are capable to know, and shuts us, / Like Cloyster'd Ideots, from all the World's Acquaintance, / And all the Joys of Freedom' (Act II, scene 1). It is after her infidelity becomes public that Calista turns to a vision of rural retreat:

Calista: My sad Soul,
Has form'd a dismal melancholy Scene,
Such a Retreat as I wou'd wish to find;
An unfrequented Vale, o'er-grown with Trees
Mossie and old, within whose lonesome Shade,
Ravens, and Birds ill omen'd, only dwell;
No sound to break the Silence, but a Brook
That bubbling wind's among the Weeds: no Mark
Of any Human Shape that had been there,
Unless a Skeleton of some poor Wretch,
Who had long since, like me, by Love undone,
Sought that sad Place out to despair and die in.
. . .
There I fain wou'd hide me,
From the base World, from Malice, and from Shame.

Instead of this melancholy retreat, however, Calista ultimately chooses death, as though she recognises that the romantic, Miltonic inflection of her own vision is not finally possible. The resolve 'Never to live with publick Loss of Honour', or to 'bear the Insolence / Of each affected She that tells my Story, / And blesses her good Stars that she is virtuous', may lead to a fantasy of retirement as escape in which the language of melancholic rural beauty holds out a tantalising glimpse of release from suffering; but the world from which one wishes to escape can never be left behind, for it underwrites the very notion of retreat. Retirement may seem an escape from the public and its cruel moralising, but Calista's guilty sense of self – tied to a public world she can no longer inhabit – means that this can only be an escape into further punishment. This language of escape, punishment, hiding, suffering, guilt, and shame, made so apparent in *The Fair Penitent*, is a crucial counterbalance to those more optimistic visions of female retirement with which we are now familiar and found itself repeated not only in the endless revivals of Rowe's play, but in poetry and novels throughout the century.

In Calista's case the seduction and loss of honour takes place in an urban landscape of Genoa, but in numerous poems and works of fiction it is the pleasure garden and its wider landscape that becomes both the site of seduction and the place of punishment after that seduction. In Jane

Brereton's poem, 'Verses on the loss of a Friend' (1709) the speed at which the landscape is transformed from one of happy solitude to a place of despair is nothing if not striking. The poem begins in the most conventional of fashions ('Ah! happy Solitude, thrice blest the Day! / When in thy Shades I pass'd my Hours away; / Exempt from Cares, retir'd from public Noise, / Nought to prevent, or interrupt my Joys') and soon moves on to elaborate the pastoral pleasures of the Flintshire landscape, where, 'all that's fair, that's beautiful, or sweet, / The Lilly, Rose, and purple Vi'let meet, / And seem enamell'd round my happy Feet'. Reading books by the river, revelling in the bird-song, and sharing 'near this beloved retreat' a friendship which 'made my Joys compleat', Flintshire becomes the garden of Eden, but like Eden it is soon to be lost:

So well we lov'd, so faithful and so true,
That mutual were the Joys and Pains we knew.
Thus liv'd we, like our early Parents, free
From Fears or Cares, in sweet Simplicity:
Till by a most unhappy turn of Fate,
We lost our Eden, our contented State,
For Love the false seducing Serpent play'd,
And soon beguil'd the fond believing Maid.

Like the imagined paradise of a pastoral romance, the myth of Eden – so quickly conjured as a frame of reference – contains within it the dangerous potential of sexual desire and the figure of the seduced, guilty woman. In Brereton's poem it is prefigured also by Philomela, the nightingale, who 'Tunes her solemn Strains' and 'Of *Tereus*, still she mournfully complains'. This overlaying of classical and Christian myths of rape and seduction should alert us once again to the kinds of landscapes women – rather than men – may inhabit, and the ready habit of eighteenth-century culture to imagine the landscape as a place of seduction and of punishment after seduction. The call of the nightingale – so prominent in accounts of evening landscapes, and so much a signal of their sensual pleasures – remains an oddly troublesome reminder of more dangerous possibilities. In Brereton's poem, 'left to share a Grief I could not aid', the poet leaves the landscape, cast out of her Eden and mourning a lost friend. Here, a tale of seduction and loss is told at second hand, but many more are expressed as the confessional voice of the suffering woman.

In Nicholas Rowe's *The Fair Penitent* we are offered imagined retirement as something close to Milton's melancholic 'Il Penseroso', and as a precursor also to Pope's 'Eloisa to Abelard'; in Brereton's poem sexual desire destroys the retired pleasures of female friendship; what poem and play share, however, is an insistence on retirement as a site of female shame, and while in these two examples retreat inhabits quite distinct accounts of wild nature, in the 1720s seduction narratives of Eliza Haywood (*c.* 1693–1756) and in the moral tales of Elizabeth Rowe it is the more specifically cultivated space of the garden that plays a particularly insistent role.[23]

In Haywood's late *Epistles* female desire is often framed as a misguided lurch towards fashionable pleasure, but in her novels of the 1720s and 1730s, Haywood addresses the far more problematic account of female desire as unregulated, transgressive, and dangerous; like her contemporary Mary Hearne, who uses the garden as a site for sexual transgression and of solitude after that transgression, in Haywood's early fiction solitude – as the loss of society – may be liberty or punishment.[24] Using a now recognisable trope, Haywood's *The Double Marriage* (1726) opens with a secretly married woman going to an obscure country estate to meet her lover, out of sight of her father; in *The Injur'd Husband* (1723) Montamour must resist the temptations of her wayward lover, Beauclair, when he confronts her in the nunnery gardens; and in *Love-Letters on all Occasions* (1730) Elismondo loses her virtue to Theano in the garden. Even in her mid-century novels, the dangers of the garden appear, as, for example, in *Life's Progress through the Passions* (1748), where Natura is confronted with the dilemma of meeting two sisters – one the abbess and the other a nun – in the same convent garden, and at the same time (he runs away). That Haywood chose the garden of a convent on more than one occasion is only a further, and pointed, reminder that easy assumptions about female piety and the active capacity of the garden to reinforce or guarantee that piety are built on uncertain ground. Moreover, the drama this allows – of stepping from the nunnery into the garden – highlights a dilemma (or at least a challenge) faced by any woman who steps into the culturally shifting ground of the garden: once outside the surveillance and regulation of the chapel and cloister, female piety finds itself in competition with other social uses which make the garden a far less safe space. The convent may be a place of imprisonment, but its garden offers potential liberty – liberty from surveillance, liberty from moral convention, and liberty from gender norms. As it would later for Richardson in both *Pamela* and *Clarissa*, it is this potential for liberty that makes the garden such a potent symbol in Haywood's novels, whether it be attached to a religious institution or a private home, and we can see this most clearly in one of the best known of her early novels, *The British Recluse* (1722).[25]

With its double narrative, paired tales of seduction, and repeated move-ments between the city and the country, *The British Recluse* is a novel acutely aware of space and of the opportunities that differently inhabited spaces enable and curtail. Underpinned by that notion of a country–city divide, where the city is linked with fashionable and fine ladies, and where the country is both an imagined place of innocence and a real place of dan-ger, the novel tells of two women, one Cleomira, or the British Recluse, the other Belinda, who first hears Cleomira's tale and then tells her own. What joins them is not only the telling of two tales of seduction, nor even the revelation that both women have been seduced by the same man (known to one as Lysander, to the other as Courtal, but in reality the notorious Bel-lamy); they are joined also by their experience of an unregulated passion, and by the imaginative spaces through which they move. The novel begins in the city and ends in the country, but the dual narratives and constantly shifting locations deny us an easy sense of how those cultural spaces should be valued and what they should denote. Notably, although the novel ends with the two women's decision to retire to the country, they tell their tales from within the city boarding house which has enabled Cleomira to live as a recluse. That image of the city as a place of obscurity and anonymity con-tinues to be used throughout the century – both in fiction and in women's letters – but its importance for us here is that it raises the question of why these unlucky women finally choose a country retirement rather than that city retreat which has served the Recluse so well. To answer that question we need to turn to the shifting valences of country, city, and garden that Haywood employs throughout the novel.

Haywood certainly offers us that most conventional account of a country–city divide, which associates the city with falsity and fashion and the country with innocence and tranquillity; but she offers us any number of alterna-tives as well, and she offers them with an acute awareness of the desires which may lie behind these different articulations of space. Born to par-ents who 'had both been from their Infancy accustom'd to a Court, and had Spirits far above their Circumstances, which made them unable to endure the Thoughts either of a Retirement, or appearing in Publick with an Equipage any way inferior to what those of the same Rank maintain'd' (p. 14), Cleomira is aligned not simply with the courtly, but with that prob-lematic figure, the fine lady. Forced, on the death of her father, to take up residence in the country with her mother, the two women's accounts of the country and the city could not be further apart. While her mother, 'entirely throwing off the *fine Lady* began to practice the meer *Country gentlewoman*', Cleomira experiences this sudden change as being 'like present Death'

(p. 15) and her reaction to country life is wholly in keeping with those other fine ladies we have already met: 'the passionate Fondness I express'd for the Town Diversions, and Disdain of a Country Life, confirm'd her, that it was absolutely necessary at once to prevent the Dangers she imagin'd threatened me' (pp. 15–16). And of her release from this country oblivion to attend the London ball that leads to her downfall, she writes, 'Never was any Prisoner, who long had languish'd in a Dungeon, more rejoic'd to see the open Air, than I to find my self once more in Court' (p. 17).

Here, then, country life is the loss of pleasure, but also the loss of liberty; at best it offers a world of domestic ease. As part of a retrospective narrative, Cleomira's rhetoric may be intended to underline the error of her reaction to the country and the good sense of her mother's decision, but Haywood offers nothing to suggest such a life would be anything but dull; and what complicates this further is that the country can hardly be aligned with the mother's vision either. The choice to 'play the good housewife' in the country (p. 16), if not simply a mother's whim in the way that Cleomira first imagines, is also a fantasy, and a dangerous one. Certainly Cleomira is offered the chance to marry a sensible country gentleman, and thus to settle into a vision of the country, and of herself, close to the *Spectator's* Aurelia; certainly, also, her undoing comes swiftly after her rejection of such dull domesticity; but Haywood hardly offers us domestic obscurity as a satisfactory account of life, and this is the only kind of security the country seems able to afford. When Cleomira rejects it, the country is scarcely a place of safety. As we soon discover, outside of unwelcome domestic oblivion, the country offers little protection for a daughter and is instead both the occasion and the location of her downfall.

The immediate cause of Cleomira's misfortune comes when she makes an ill-fated but much wished for return to town to attend a ball; there she meets the duplicitous Lysander (Bellamy) and falls instantly and passionately in love. It is back in the country, however, that the dangerous potential of this passion is played out. Ironically, given her mother's belief that the court is 'a Place too dangerous for a young Woman to continue in', it is the country, with its looser surveillance and less regulated spaces, which provides Cleomira with a liberty far more dangerous. On visiting their country neighbours, the Marvirs, Cleomira's mother is distracted by Mr Marvir only for Cleomira to be taken into the garden by his wife, where, inevitably, Lysander is waiting in the arbour. What follows is a classic scene of Haywardian seduction. With Cleomira's sentimental body unable to resist the advances of her lover, Lysander kneels before her, and 'interpreting my Disorders in his Favour, he took me in his Arms, all blushing – trembling, and incapable of Defence, and laying his Head upon my panting Bosom, seem'd to breath out all his Soul in fervent Tenderness'. Thus, the hour they spend in the garden 'was past in nothing but offending and forgiving'.

The final seduction, and Cleomira's undoing, takes place within a chamber at Marvir's country house – where she has fled from her mother – but this first garden seduction establishes the terms on which Cleomira's sexual fall is to be judged. And of course fall is the appropriate word here because this garden is a reminder of Eden, of innocent sexuality, and of the loss of that innocence ('Never was any so form'd to *Charm*, and to *Betray* – never was such foul Deceit, Hypocrisy, and Villainy, couch'd in such seeming Sweetness, Softness, and Sincerity', p. 42). This language of innocence, temptation, and deception set within a garden gives Cleomira's situation a significance beyond the merely personal, and if, like Eve, she is to be condemned for succumbing to temptation, it is her male lover who appears as the deceiving serpent. The metaphysical framework created by the garden scene may reinforce a sympathy for Cleomira in the face of male deception; but the significance of the garden remains pointedly and unsettlingly diverse because its apparent resources can be drawn on to radically different ends at one and the same time. As Haywood's narrative demonstrates, the garden provides the stage for a psychological drama about desire and moral choice, but it also invites confusion between a shared location and a shared experience of space. During this scene of seduction the couple inhabit the same physical location – they could hardly be closer – but as Cleomira soon discovers this is not the imagined meeting of souls to be found in a garden of love. Instead, the couple's construction and inhabitation of the garden is radically and dangerously different. For the libertine in the garden, this space provides an opportunity for seduction, but that seduction makes use not simply of a secluded situation but of a powerful invitation to align erotic with natural desire. For the woman who may succumb to this invitation, however, there remains not least that narrative of Paradise lost, with its warning that gardens contain serpents, that with temptation comes punishment, and that the consequences of erotic desire are not equal.

For all their physical proximity, then, Lysander and Cleomira are not in the same garden, and it is this uneasy combination of location and dislocation that is central not only to Haywood's narrative but to how we should understand the garden as a space. Certainly the sense of space as constructed and contested is played out repeatedly in Haywood's novel. In the parallel narrative of Belinda, seduction once again takes place in the garden and the less regulated landscape beyond. Here, it is finally thwarted by the appearance of the sensible, but uninspiring Mr Worthy. Worthy, who looks like the conventionally ideal man, is not ideal because he is not desired; and when Belinda describes him, she describes also her sense of the life she would lead in the country:

I felt no Hopes, no Fears, no Wishes, no Impatience, nor knew what 'twas to be made uneasy or transported. When I saw Worthy . . . I was well enough pleas'd, indeed, but when I saw him not I was the same; in fine, every thing was indifferent to me, and had this Insensibility continu'd I had liv'd one of the most contented Women in the World. (p. 91)

Despite – or perhaps because of – her country education, Belinda (like Cleomira before her) rejects the *Spectator*'s vision of the woman in the garden: not only is country life with a sensible man imagined as domestic rather than romantic, but the supposed contentment of the domestic is equated only with indifference. Again, we might say that this is the voice of a misguided woman, and certainly against this account Belinda defines her desires as 'wild passion', as an infection which will inevitably lead to 'Shame, Remorse, Confusion, and Despair' (p. 96); but it nevertheless offers a critique of those easy visions of female retirement for which *The Spectator*'s Aurelia has been my shorthand, and suggests instead that the happiness of country domesticity may only be the happiness of stupefaction.

Just as Lysander had led Cleomira into a secluded landscape, so (as Courtal) he leads Belinda through the garden and further away from the house. Just as Cleomira had imagined a shared landscape of love, so Belinda imagines a garden of Eden and the possibility of innocent desire:

we were wandered, insensibly, perhaps, to either of us, at least to me, I am sure it was so, a great Distance from the House, and into the thickest and most obscure part of the Wood . . . Never was a Night more delectable, more aiding to a Lover's Wishes! The arching Trees form'd a Canopy over our Heads, while through the gently shaking Boughs soft Breezes play'd in lulling Murmurings, and fann'd us with delicious Gales; a thousand Nightingales sung amorous Ditties, and the billing Doves coo'd out their tender Transports – every Thing was soothing – every Thing inspiring! the very Soul of Love seem'd to inform the Place, and reign throughout the whole . . .

. . . methought, we sat with all the Sweets of Nature blooming round us, like the first happy Pair while blest with Innocence, they knew not Shame, nor Fear. (p. 112)

This landscape of seduction is described in terms we can recognise from the conventions of romance and from fantasies of pastoral pleasure; but alongside the cooing doves, the amorous ditties of a thousand nightingales are once again a signal of danger and only a more obvious warning that the turn to a fantasy landscape of pastoral romance holds real dangers for women. As Belinda registers ('perhaps, to *either* of us, at least to *me*'), she and her lover may once again inhabit different spaces: for both, this is an erotic landscape of love, for both nature seems to invite the consummation of desire; but when Belinda turns to the garden of Eden she turns to a dangerous – indeed impossible – fantasy. Belinda envisages Paradise before the fall, ignores the nightingales' warning that she has entered instead a landscape of erotic violence, and thus finds, too late, that the serpent has already entered the garden. Haywood's novel insistently repeats this movement between imagined landscapes, and if this tells us of their danger it also tells us of their inevitability.

At the very moment when Belinda's faculties are overpowered, her limbs are trembling, and her tongue faltering, Worthy appears, and drives Courtal away: this may be deliverance from the dangers of a fantasy landscape, but it is quickly followed by Belinda's recognition that she has now entered a landscape of shame. Soon after she has been saved by Worthy she hears that he has been murdered by Courtal and her sense of responsibility for his death drives her further into the country and further into obscurity. Staying with a cousin 'about eight Miles farther in the Country', Belinda's movement mirrors the instructions of Mr and Mrs Marvir that the pregnant Cleomira must 'go into the Country till I was deliver'd of my Burthen' (p. 58). This trajectory of ever-greater obscurity as one moves further into the country, and the repeated association between obscurity and shame, leaves us with a problem, however, when we confront the two women's final retirement to a place in the country, seventy miles from London.

At the end of the novel – indeed in only the final ten lines – the narrator tells of Cleomira and Belinda's decision to retire to the country:

in a short time, both their Resolutions of abandoning the World continuing, the RECLUSE and she took a House about seventy Miles distant from London, where they still live in a perfect Tranquility, happy in the real Friendship of each other, despising the uncertain Pleasures; and free from all the Hurries and Disquiets which attend the Gaieties of the Town. And where a solitary Life is the effect of Choice, it certainly yields more solid Comfort, than all the public Diversions which those who are the greatest Pursuers of them can find. (pp. 137–8)

That claim for the happiness of solitude when based on choice is wholly conventional; but equally conventional is an account of retirement couched in terms of absent city pleasures, an account close to those poetic celebrations of solitude with which we have already met, accounts which can say much of what has been left behind but little of substance about current pleasures.

Moreover we should also ask what kind of choice is actually involved: what we seem to be offered is tranquillity based on true female friendship, but the choice to retire is driven by the women's perceived absence of alternatives, and tranquillity is derived from reminding oneself of where one is not. It may be that we are offered here a neat Butlerian demonstration of subjection producing its own form of pleasure, and desire certainly resurfaces in this structure of renunciation; but such sudden claims of 'solid Comfort' do little to address the inequality of gender codes which drive these women into obscurity, or to challenge that earlier account of contentment as mere resignation to insensibility.

For all that the narrator invites us to read Cleomira and Belinda's retirement as a happy ending the whole structure of Haywood's novel resists such easy conclusions, and resists them in particular through its insistence on the shifting and contested construction of imagined space. In the novel's final lines we hear of country retreat as tranquil, happy, comfortable; and yet nowhere else in the novel can such a static and uncontested account of space be achieved. Instead, we are repeatedly shown how space is psychologically constructed from the interaction between physical location, competing cultural agenda, and individual desire. In Haywood's novel we can say little of the design of a garden, the shape of a house, or even of a geographical location which is not London; what we are presented with instead is a wealth of interrelations and of cultural cues which construct an individual's sense of space; and crucial to that construction is the sense of self that the individual carries with them, their history, their emotions, their desires, but also their awareness of how they will be figured, placed, and constructed by others.

Thus, we can take such claims of happiness at face value if we wish, but what Haywood has left us with is a far more problematic account of retirement which includes the shifting landscapes of pleasure and shame, of dullness and delight, and where an individual's claim of contentment may still be viewed as punishment by the world from which they have retired. In the last chapter we saw how Mary Astell used the image of female retirement to champion female learning and to resist those accounts of love which might distract women from their intellectual potential; what is so striking about Haywood's account of retirement in the *British Recluse*, however, is that the two women are unable to leave love and its consequences behind. Early in the novel Cleomira speaks of a grief beyond consolation, and in reply, Belinda too claims a misfortune which cannot be forgotten:

To forget the Misfortunes I lament (reply'd Belinda) wou'd be, perhaps, a greater Ill than any I yet have known – 'tis my Desire always to remember them, and nothing sure can so well enable me to do it with Patience, as the Knowledge that so many excellent Qualities, as you appear to be Mistress of, cannot be exempt from Calamities . . . Believe me Madam (continu'd she, weeping still more) were you acquainted with the History of this Wretch you see before you, you wou'd allow that as none like me has ever suffer'd, so also none ever has like me deserv'd to suffer. (p. 10)

Apart from setting up what will be the crucial mirrored circumstances of the two women, this exchange stands in stark contrast to the glibness of the novel's happy ending. What complicates any claim for perfect tranquillity is the desire 'always to *remember*', the belief that grief can be of a kind which may not admit relief (repeated later with 'her Griefs were indeed past Remedy'), and that powerful set of assumptions about retirement which invite – and at times insist upon – pious resignation, but insist also that retirement after sexual misconduct is rightly a form of punishment. At the end of her tale, Cleomira concludes, 'Thus, Madam, have I given you a faithful Account of the Causes which induc'd me to this Retirement; and I believe, you will own that they are such as merit no less than my whole Life's Contrition'; and on hearing this, Belinda 'cou'd not disapprove the Justice of her Lamentations or the Resolution she had taken of concealing herself' (p. 89). This, then, is what Cleomira will carry with her into her newly-found retirement, while Belinda ends the account of herself by admitting, 'I confess I am weak enough to retain still in my Soul a secret Tenderness for this unworthy Man; and that not the Knowledge of his unexampled Perfidy and Inhumanity to you . . . nor the Miseries he has brought on my self, can bring me to consider him as I ought. Tho' I resolve never to see him more, I neither can forget, nor remember him, as a Woman govern'd by Reason wou'd do.' We hear nothing otherwise until the narrator's sudden claim of contentment in the novel's final lines.

What then of this final tranquil retreat and a return to the country instead of the anonymity of a London boarding house? The two women enter their vaguely located retirement with a shared trajectory of grief and uneasy longing, with a sense of misery which must inevitably be reconstructed in a retreat made necessary by guilt and explicitly linked with living death: Cleomira abandons her attempts at suicide, but 'as *Lysander* believ'd me dead, I was willing every Body else shou'd do so too'. Until that final page, the novel is consistent in assuming the need for contrition for the rest of one's life: retreat to the country may be ameliorating, but it remains a form of self-punishment where punishment is imagined as the loss of society, and where retirement may offer the hope of being obscured, but where that hope itself acknowledges the dominating power of the public view.

In Haywood's novel, the urge for retirement may, then, be driven by this awareness of how one will be seen – and judged – by others; but it is perhaps driven also by one further fantasy. In abandoning a boarding house which appears to have offered anonymity, obscurity, and in short, retreat, the women are finally located in yet another pastoral idyll, an idyll which has no more substance than those other shifting fantasies of pleasure and desire which have proved so dangerous throughout the novel. *The British Recluse* does much, then, to offer us the country estate, the garden and the forest as places of excitement and danger, but very little to imagine it as a place of tranquil retreat – it turns in the most cursory of ways to conventional platitudes of retirement which can do little to efface that idea of the country as a place of romance, seduction, and intrigue, shielded from the prying eyes of the public or the surveillance of the family, but also as a place of punishment, shame, and disgrace. Mary Astell imagines retreat as an attack on patriarchal complacency; Haywood's *British Recluse* ends with a retreat akin to banishment from a society in which men continue to dominate and enforce sexual double standards.

What beauteous scenes can please a guilty mind?

Any garden may remind of us Eden, but Eden reminds us of temptation, transgression, and loss. If it is Milton's Eden, it also reminds us of the weakness of women, the dangers of sexuality, and of who is to blame for the loss of happiness. While Haywood leaves us with the possibility of happy – if nebulous – retirement, her close contemporary Elizabeth Rowe (1674–1737) moves the psychological action into these retired spaces, and here, while country idylls abound, the potential for retirement to be a place of shameful punishment and an occasion for unwelcome reflection is left in no doubt.

Between 1728 and 1733 Rowe produced a series of *Letters Moral and Entertaining*, in which the garden as a place of rural retirement played a crucial role. Written in the years directly following the death of her young husband, written also from a self-imposed retirement in Frome, the *Letters* is a miscellany of short stories, mostly focussed on the lives of women, all with a steady confidence in the life hereafter, and all with Rowe's Christian morality carefully spelled out.[26] More, perhaps, than in Haywood's tales, the idea of the garden plays a crucial role in Rowe's vision of retirement. The sign of wealth, it also signals nature, and acts here – as so often – to naturalise and make acceptable such wealth as may otherwise prove embarrassing to claims of pious reverie. Throughout the *Letters*, Rowe offers us the traditional dilemmas of untested retirement versus active morality, and of sublunary pleasure versus the real pleasures of the afterlife. Thus, while in the second of the 'Letters to the Author By Another Hand' the correspondent dismisses retirement to pastoral pleasures as a 'cowardly flight' (whereas the truly heroic act is to despise the world 'in the midst of its dazzling temptations'), in the letter which follows the garden to which one might retire offers a strangely satisfying allure:

> You will be surprised to find, that at a time when health is declining, I should be planting trees, and laying out walks, as if I thought I had two or three hundred years to enjoy them. I need not assure you, I have no such expectations; but it gives me an innocent delight to form these sylvan scenes in an irregular manner, and with a secret art to imitate nature in her negligent appearance.
>
> I have no giants in yew, nor tigers or birds in holly; but instead of them, firs and pines, that grow just as nature designed them; and so intermixed with woodbines, syringas, and other flowery shrubs, that in a few months they will be a perfect wilderness of sweets.
>
> The satisfaction I take in this undertaking, makes me often fancy I am not sincere in my thoughts of soon leaving it: I am as busy in my garden, and as much surfeited with the Grande Monde, as ever Dioclesian was.

Enjoyable and innocent, this fast-growing garden avoids the trap of worldly concerns by setting itself in opposition to fashion and its misguided obsessions, but the frail rhetorical manoeuvre which allows that happy state must constantly be reasserted. In the *Letters*, that is, it is important for Rowe to offer us the figure of the fashionable city lady failing to inhabit pastoral space. The representation of that failure is an implicit warning for those well-to-do women who find themselves living in retirement (and such implicit criticisms were certainly not lost on Lady Hertford); but it is also a means of distinguishing one's own desires from their more troublesome implications. Certainly in Rowe's own correspondence (some of which would appear in the *Letters Moral and Entertaining*), the lure of earthly pleasures and the knowledge of their dangers remains ever present.[27] In a letter to Lady Hertford, for example, Rowe writes,

> I am not surprised to find your Ladyship diverting yourself with the scenes of low Life in the print you are copying. While Fields & Cottages seem to be the Abodes of Innocence & Peace, I must own that Scenes of Grandeur & Art please me better, but then

'tis only in Speculation & at a Distance for without pretending my self more Philosophical than I really am I should chuse to be again confin'd in the Peaceful Shade
of some remote Wilderness rather than to the Hurry of the Most Splendid Court.[28]

That imaginative movement between splendid courts and peaceful shades,
and indeed the glamorous lure of a courtly grandeur one cannot quite let
be, is characteristic of Rowe's public and private letters, but characteristic
also of much writing which takes retirement as its theme. Inherent, then, to
Rowe's tales of retirement is the ambiguity of Rowe's own stance and in the
case studies which follow these opening chapters we will see that ambiguity
being repeated by the younger generation of Bluestockings in Rowe's circle.
Notably, Rowe's complex of ideas about wealth, rank, retirement, and virtue
would be read by, admired by, but also criticised by the likes of Elizabeth
Carter, Elizabeth Montagu, and Catherine Talbot: at issue for all of them –
though from quite different backgrounds, and living in quite different forms
of retirement – is one's place within, and after the destruction of, the
Creation.

    Johnson rather sententiously referred to Rowe's tales as 'the ornaments of
romance in the decorations of religion'. More helpfully, Rowe's editor (and
brother-in-law) Theophilus Rowe, noted that the design

is, by fictitious examples of the most generous benevolence and heroic virtue,
to allure the reader to the practice of every thing that ennobles human nature,
and benefits the world; and by just and lively images of the sharp remorse and
real misery that attend the false and unworthy satisfactions of vice, to warn the
young and unthinking from being seduced by the enchanting name of pleasure, to
inevitable ruin.[29]

Amongst many other things what both accounts miss is Rowe's acute recognition that the place of rural retirement in women's lives is necessarily fluid
and ambiguous. While the garden appears in many of her stories as a place
of meditation, it is far from a stable ideal. Instead, Rowe's stories are constructed so as to question an easy reliance on retirement and meditation as
models for female behaviour. And while Rowe may well be aware of, and
responding to, the traditions of female retirement explored in the previous chapter, the Letters allow her to move beyond this and to question the
motives and meanings of retirement in the wider context of the society from
which it claims to be divorced. In Rowe's stories we are never allowed to
forget what has brought these women to their rural retirements and what
has made meditation so central to their lives.

    In a series of epistolary tales, Rowe is able to cover a range of opportu-
nities and predicaments facing what we might recognise as contemporary

individuals in a broadly pastoral-romance setting. If we can always be certain that her narratives will end with the bad being punished and the good being lavishly rewarded, what marks Rowe's tales out is her willingness to address the issue of temptation, and if not to sympathise with, at least to give voices to, those who are tempted. It is this insistence on the need to make choices and the difficulty of those choices that gives to the landscapes in which she places her heroes and heroines their moral uncertainty. The constant movement between rural retreat, garden, and wild nature (but also the difficulty of distinguishing between them at times) points to the constantly shifting space of retirement: for Rowe – as for Haywood – the nature of the space one inhabits must constantly be confronted. Figures who fail to think in such terms, or who miscomprehend the space constructed around them, are inevitably put in danger.

In some of Rowe's tales the garden undoubtedly seems to offer a happy merging of property, politeness and Christian faith. When the virtuous Rosalinda runs away from home to avoid a loveless marriage to a man both Catholic and foreign, she is rewarded not only with the ideal partner and time for Christian meditation and good works, but with her husband's vast estate and his 6000 pounds a year (Part III, Letter II). Similarly, in Leticia's letter to Emilia, when she includes a poem on the joys of solitude, she notes that it is inscribed to a Mrs M——, 'a person of strict piety, though she does not turn recluse and live in a grotto, but converses freely with the polite world, and keeps an unblemished character in it' (Part II, Letter VII). But for each of these happy examples, rooted as they are in 'nature' and religion, we are offered at least as many where solitude and rural retirement denote punishment and shame. Iris, writing from her country retreat, insists:

I pursue the pleasures of the world, at the same time that I know them to be fleeting and worthless. I distract myself about the opinion of the public, though I despise the injustice of its censures...

... I am uneasy with my faults, without correcting them; and in love with my duty, without practising it. I act contrary to my highest reason, and turn rebel to the authority of my own judgment.

After this account of me, you will not wonder that I retire as much as I can from noise and hurry; though no shade is gloomy enough to hide my folly from my eyes, nor any retreat calm enough to lull my passions.

(Part I, 'Letters to the Author, by another Hand', Letter VI)

When, in the group of letters entitled *Letters to Cleora*, a correspondent writes in conventional support of 'such a retreat as disengages the mind from those interests and passions which mankind generally pursue' and which 'must leave a person in perfect and unenvied repose', that eulogy is introduced with the acknowledgement that 'Nothing is, perhaps, more terrible to the imagination than an absolute solitude'. While the latter is implicitly mistaken, Rowe's tales nevertheless recognise, and dramatise, the fear of being cut off from society, the fear of being alone with one's thoughts. Iris, at least, ends her letter with the hope that religion and the grace of God will assist her in her struggle and make her solitude more bearable. In the tale of Aurelia, however – who has fallen in love with a married man and been banished to the wilderness of an obscure estate with her beautiful but illegitimate child – retirement simply reaffirms her suffering:

And still I love this worthless man: were I penitent, could I resolve on a reformation, this leisure and retirement would be a blessing, an advantage to me; but I am obstinate in guilt, while I despair of happiness in this world or the next. 'Till I came hither, my hours were spent in frolic and g[a]iety; a constant series of diversions shortened the days, and gave wings to the jovial hours, which now have leaden feet, and, burdened with grief, lag heavily along. No sort of reflection gives me joy; whether I look backwards or forwards, all is darkness and confusion; I am no way qualified for retirement: books are my aversion; thinking is my horror; I am weary of living, and afraid to die. (Part III, Letter XV)

The tale of Aurelia, as told by Polydore in a letter to Alonzo, runs the gamut of possible responses to the landscape in which Aurelia is found. Quickly rejecting 'country diversions, or any kind of rural sports', Polydore's pleasures are 'confined to the charming shades and gardens' of his friend's estate. Citing the *Spectator* as he wanders 'from rising hills to winding vales, through flowery lawns to leafy woods', he finds even the cawing of the rooks 'a kind of natural prayer to that Being who supplies the wants of his whole creation' and is soon 'inspired with a pleasing gratitude to the beneficent Father of the universe'. When he comes across a beautiful child with a basket of flowers (the daughter of Aurelia), his imagination shifts smoothly to the world of romance as he hopes she is 'one of the fairy race, or some pretty phantom that haunted the grove!' It shifts again, however, as he sees the 'adjacent house, belonging to this reverend avenue' in which he finds Aurelia, and which looks 'more like a dormitory for the dead, than an habitation for the living . . . more like the mansions of despair, than a retreat for a lady of pleasure'. As Polydore walks through the landscape and moves from his own world of easy and elegant retirement to the ruins and 'detested solitude' of Aurelia's life, he also traverses both the physical and moral extremes of the garden, from the wonders of the Creation and God's beneficence to a landscape of disgrace and social ruin. If this is a recognisable, and in its way quite conventional movement, we should still note in Rowe's story the speed and ease with which one frame of reference is replaced by another, one set of cues lead to another. We should note also – as in Haywood's narratives – Rowe's insistence on alternative but coexisting experiences of space. With little at stake, Polydore can enjoy the shifting literary pleasures of a rural landscape in which he is merely a visitor; as the inhabitant of a self-made solitude, trapped by her own sense of guilt, and by her inability to repent, the experience for Aurelia is quite different.

It may be merely coincidental that Rowe chose for this tale the name used by Addison in the *Spectator* when describing his exemplary woman in her garden; what it highlights, however, is Rowe's insistence that garden retirement holds no absolute moral worth: it may be the occasion for satisfying thoughts of another life, it may appear to offer a supportive moral space, but ultimately there is nothing there, it is a place of absence, a space to be filled by one's self, by the choices one makes in society and in relation to the afterlife. For this reason, Rowe's gardens (like those of Haywood) can be both places of seduction and places of punishment after that seduction. When Sylvia runs to the country to avoid her passion for the married Compte de R——, she claims that, 'the retirement of the country, and serious reflection, soon freed me from the tumultuous effects of a guilty passion', but when the Compte comes to visit, finds her in the garden, and must himself run away from a reciprocal passion, it is the signal for Sylvia to fall into a fever from which she is saved only by bending her thoughts to heavenly rather than earthly delights (Part I, Letter III, & Part II, Letter V). When Amoret confesses to Mrs—— (Part I, Letter V), 'I am not that modest innocent person you believe me' and describes her seduction by Sebastian, she records also her flight to the country and its failure to offer respite from the sense of shame:

I have no refuge from the insults of the world, but solitude, and thither the thoughts of my guilt and infamy pursue me; the country shades, the seats of tranquillity and peace, afford me no relief...

What beauteous scenes can please a guilty mind?

For Amoret, flight to the solitude of a country retreat, and the desire to forget oneself in the beauty of the garden, are confounded and undone by the guilt she carries with her into those spaces: 'Where shall I seek for peace, when I am at variance with myself...?' Pastoral pleasures are rightly the preserve of the virtuous and the error of Rowe's fallen heroines is to mistake physical location for a spiritual space which can only be constructed by the virtuous. In the *Letters Moral and Entertaining* the figure of the lone woman in the garden is, then, a corollary to, and image of, a self-concern which is not social, and in this sense – whether Rowe turns knowingly to *The Spectator* or not – they are set in direct opposition to Addison's vision of sociable solitude. Worse than this, the powerful cultural associations of the garden as Eden, as Paradise, as a place of pious delight are shown to be as damaging as they are apparently enabling: the literary language of pleasure with which Polydore can play, those all-too-insistent accounts of the garden as innocent and easy, reinforce for Amoret, as for Aurelia, a painful sense of distance from their delights.

In her various tales, then, Rowe develops that female voice of despair found also in Haywood; but while Rowe offers a peculiarly sustained account of the absence of pastoral and the experience of disgrace, these landscapes of shame, punishment, unwelcome reflection, and the tantalising sense that the garden might offer something more, continue to appear throughout the century. Certainly we can trace the continuance of a poetic tradition which sets unruly or thwarted sexual desire in landscapes characterised by their failure to be comfortably pastoral. In Ann Yearsley's 1787 poem, 'Lucy, A Tale for the Ladies', for example, we can recognise a familiar trajectory from pastoral romance to melancholic solitude.[30] A reader of romances, Lucy 'gently sighs, / When weak impatient Werter dies'; chaste but unfortunate, she cannot marry her true love Lelius (because he is too poor) and is forced by her father to wed the vulgar Cymon, 'A stupid money-loving man'. Confined to 'a Gothic mansion rude, / Built in the breast of Solitude', and to a life in which 'They silent sit; he sinks to sleep, / Leaving the choice – to think, or weep', Lucy's dull domestic retirement is broken by the discovery that Lelius, now rich, is her new neighbour. Unaware of their earlier relationship, Cymon leaves them to the platonic pleasures of each other's company, but with talk of scandal in the neighbourhood, with neither able to settle upon platonic ideals, Lelius withdraws to die of a broken heart; Lucy – though much more slowly – does the same. Close in theme to Rowe's tales, the poem moves between different imagined landscapes, and like the tale of Aurelia in Rowe's *Letters*, from pastoral pleasure to melancholic despair. As with Rowe, crucial here is the recognition that sexuality transforms the experience of landscape and unsettles easy accounts of pleasurable retreat. Romance may be dismissed as the misguided sentimentalism of Werther, but it is replaced only by domestic oblivion: instead of the happy retirement we find in Addison and Steele, the domestic is not simply dull, it is painfully dull. Solitude is the occasion 'to think, or weep'; love, born in pastoral romance, leads to scandal, to shame, and to death.

Tales of retirement as disgrace, with their insistence on an uncomfortably close association between solitude and shame, continue to haunt the imaginations of women writing from the country or imagining life alone. We could trace this tradition further in poems by Mary Robinson in the 1770s and 1780s, and in Charlotte Smith's sonnet of the 1790s 'To Solitude' (which assumes many of the same tropes). In the periodical press we could note the tale of fine ladies in the *Female Tatler* (number 56) who delight in scandal but who must disappear to small country estates to be cured of mysterious abdominal swellings; or we could turn to *The New Pleasant Instructor*'s 1781 story of the unmarried Henrietta and her lover Stanley. When Stanley dies, his family throws her out of her house, she is persecuted for his debts and though her father takes pity on her and supports her, 'The babe on the breast he put out to nurse, and sent the boy into the country with his mother, where they lived in the greatest retirement. But say, ye tender-hearted, how wretched must not her life be, with opulence exchanged with penury, honour for shame, and hope for despair!'[31] More important, however, is to recognise that sexual transgression is on the one hand an extreme example of a much broader fear of social disgrace and failure; and on the other that a stress on the eroticism of female sexuality, female weakness, and female disgrace remains powerfully present in accounts of lone women in retirement.

Intertwined with these two quite different concerns is the language of melancholy, and it is to the framing of melancholy as both a pleasurable aesthetic and a form of painfully debilitating depression that we should next turn. As we will see in the case studies which follow – and notably in the letters of one of Rowe's literary friends, Henrietta Knight, Lady Luxborough – ideas of pious retreat, of the happy hermitage, of Paradise regained, offer uncomfortable models for those women who experienced retirement not as sociable retreat, but as lonely isolation. Melancholy is crucial to such experiences of retirement, because, like the garden itself, it proffers a tantalising but often unattainable image of pleasure.

Thinking is my horror

For Elizabeth Rowe's lonely and unrepentant women, punishment takes the form of retirement, and retirement is synonymous with melancholy. In a stark analysis of her situation Iris states: 'my melancholy proceeds from the irregularity of my affections; love, vanity, distrust, and repentance, conspire to rack me' ('Letters to the Author by Another Hand', Letter V); but as Rowe recognises, melancholy can encompass peculiarly disparate experiences. In her tale of the suffering Aurelia, for example, Rowe characteristically emphasises the striking disjunction between experiences of landscape, with the peripatetic Polydore anticipating the pleasures of melancholic gloom while Aurelia – trapped and isolated within a landscape from which she cannot depart – experiences something much more threatening. That disjunction highlights for us the dual aspect of Rowe's tales but also of melancholy itself: like Polydore, the reader is offered the literary pleasure of melancholy at one remove, but for the recluse the experience may be one of overwhelming debilitation. In Rowe's poetry that same uneasy shift between pastoral pleasures and melancholic despair is also evident; as her biographer has argued, tales of pleasurable retreat sit uncomfortably with Rowe's personal melancholia in later life and with those poems which take despair as their theme.[32]

Like any number of eighteenth-century writers, we should acknowledge the influence and echoes of Milton's *l'Allegro* and *Il Penseroso* in such later accounts of pleasurable and melancholic rural landscapes. The source of such staples of eighteenth-century landscape description as 'Bosom'd High in Tufted Trees' and 'storied Windows richly dight, / Casting a dimm religious light', Milton's poems offered a powerful exploration of nature as a source of creativity while also inviting its readers to revel in the sensuousness of its forms; but a turn to this originary pair (or at least the duality's most influential statement) should not blind us to the current needs of authors or what might sustain an ongoing ambivalence. Moreover, while Milton may celebrate rural melancholy, and recognise its close relation to pastoral pleasure, *Il Penseroso* hardly allows for melancholy's more debilitating forms, and this almost too-readily-available account of melancholic retreat and its imaginative delight not only needs to be distinguished from the fear of thought, and the despair so often voiced by the likes of Rowe's lonely recluses, but also recognised as itself a potentially debilitating vision of unattainable rural pleasure. For this latter vision, while Milton certainly echoes through the poetry and prose of eighteenth-century writing on the pleasures of retirement, it is perhaps William Cowper's poetry which most clearly articulates an account of debilitating retreat and of the inability of retirement to offer release from the kind of incapacitating low spirits we might now recognise as depression.

For Maren-Sofie Røstvig, Cowper's poem, 'Retirement' (1782), represents a last – and rather late – gasp of the retirement theme in eighteenth-century poetry. Close to *The Task* in many ways, 'Retirement' offers a recognisable attack on those in the city who dream of country retirement, on vulgar 'cits' living two miles from town, and on the great politician who thinks retirement is the answer but who is over-quickly bored. Less a rehearsal of previous retirement *literature*, Cowper's poem registers the social practice of retirement and its popularity in the preceding decades.[33] It also recognises the threat of retirement for the melancholic: 'Absence of occupation is not rest, / A mind quite vacant is a mind distress'd' ('Retirement', ll.623–4). Solitude may be admirable, but only if it is that social solitude we have already seen championed by earlier writers. In the absence of such sociability the space of retirement must be filled one way or another.[34] For the Cowper of the 1780s such retirement should be turned to account as an opportunity to contemplate God's works and one's place in the Christian scheme of things; but there remains the anxiety of spiritual failure, the fear that the nothingness of retirement will be filled by the weakness of unfulfillable desires; and the recognition that the much-vaunted pleasures of rural landscape can proffer nothing to support the melancholic mind. In Cowper's poem, then, retirement is a vacancy but a vacancy which invites responses based on cultural expectations; and the garden – so often the site of Cowper's reveries on retreat – is to be understood both as empty and as framed.

In Rowe's fictional tale of Polydore and Aurelia, crucial to melancholic pleasure is the ability – literally – to walk away, and indeed pleasurably melancholic interludes frequently assume movement through a landscape; by contrast, accounts of melancholic depression register the sense of entrapment in a landscape which merely reiterates the sense of failure and loss. Another of Cowper's poems from the same period makes this uncomfortable ambivalence its central theme. In 'The Shrubbery, Written in a Time of Affliction' (*Poems* 1782), Cowper offers dual visions of rural retreat, one the elusive world of Miltonic melancholy and pious reverie, the other a reiteration of melancholic low spirits made worse by the knowledge of a pleasurable alternative:

Oh happy shades! To me unblest,
　Friendly to peace, but not to me,
How ill the scene that offers rest,
　And heart that cannot rest, agree!

. . .

The saint or moralist should tread
　This moss-grown alley, musing slow,
They seek like me the secret shade,
　But not like me, to nourish woe.

Me fruitful scenes and prospect waste,
   Alike admonish not to roam,
These tell me of enjoyments past,
   And those of sorrows yet to come.

              (ll. 1–4, 17–24)

This dramatising of alternative but coexisting states, of pleasure felt by its absence, is characteristic of Cowper's uncertainty about retirement, but characteristic also of a much larger tradition of writing about melancholy, retirement, and depression, a tradition articulated not least in the letters of women writing from, and of, the country.

In Rowe's tales the failure to experience retirement as pastoral pleasure is an inevitable result of sexual misdeeds. But we can also trace a strand of writing – by women quite untainted by the kind of sexual transgressions used by Rowe to articulate the danger of misguided desires – where the experience of isolation in the country, the experience indeed of dullness, is aligned with low spirits, with something close to modern accounts of depression, and, as it is for Rowe's anti-heroines, with a sense of shame and punishment. Such experiences of retirement are in part the subject of the case studies which follow these opening chapters, but we can usefully turn to one of Rowe's circle for an example of what might be at stake.

The danger of experiencing retirement as dullness is that it can be framed by others – but more damagingly by oneself – as a spiritual failure, as a failure of self-sufficiency, as both a demonstration of, and a punishment for, the failure to live up to domestic ideals. Close to Rowe's circle of friends, Elizabeth Carter is characteristically articulate about the challenges of self-cultivation and the dangers of dullness when confronted by the solitude of country life.[35] In Carter's case, letters to friends demonstrate an acute awareness of literary melancholy (which she rehearses in the appropriate location of the ruin, the wood, and so on) and alarm in the face of low spirits which offer nothing pleasurable and from which no comfort can be found even with the knowledge of literary pleasures. Thus, she recognises that the enjoyment of country solitude is frequently haunted by a sense of failure, but for Carter it comes too with an acute awareness that country retirement can engender something more dangerous than mere boredom, that it risks – and perpetuates even – a kind of melancholic depression against which one has to struggle. This experience of melancholic retirement needs to be set alongside, and to some extent tempers, Carter's more theoretical accounts of theology and her championing of private virtue mapped out by Karen O'Brien and Harriet Guest. It is not that such accounts are in bad faith, rather – as both Guest and O'Brien insist – that for Carter they must jostle along with other less admirable but inherently human experiences and desires.[36]

By the mid-eighteenth century the pleasure of melancholy in the garden – and most especially that melancholy engendered by the ruin in the landscape – was a well-established, indeed wholly conventional, theme. Numerous historical and theoretical works on garden design nod dutifully at Milton and point to melancholy as one of the many pleasurable emotions which could be experienced in the changing scenes of the landscape garden.[37] An ardent traveller at times, Carter is undoubtedly aware of this and in her visits to some of the great show gardens of the eighteenth century she records a suitably fashionable response. Thus, for example, the ruins of Fountains Abbey and the park at Studley Royal offer 'sublime entertainment' and an opportunity to demonstrate one's melancholic abilities. Carter writes of the park:

It is surely very beautiful in its own singular style, but looks like the retreat of solitude and silence. I never saw any place which appeared to me so perfectly the abode of melancholy. She meets one in every walk, and

> ' – -round her throws
> A death like silence, and a dread repose,
> Deepens the murmur of the falling floods,
> And breathes a browner horror o'er the woods.'

The whole scenery is however admirably adapted to the solemn ruins of Fountain Abbey, which stands in the centre of it.[38]

Along with lines from *Il Penseroso*, the 'browner horror' of Pope's 'Eloisa to Abelard' provides a stock phrase for melancholic pleasure, and one apparently stripped here of any sense of female yearning or suffering that a quotation from Pope's poem might imply. But for all Carter's ability to inhabit such spaces of melancholic pleasure when experiencing a garden as a visitor, her letters show an acute awareness of melancholy's more threatening forms. In the garden of her former friend Mrs. Gambier, Carter can enjoy – to some degree – the melancholic pleasure of remembering a dead friend when walking in her now deserted garden, and thus she writes,

I indulged a melancholy propensity to walk over the garden in which I had so often accompanied her, and amidst the variety of thoughts with which this circumstance filled my mind, I could not help feeling a tender concern at seeing a place in which she took so much delight, neglected and in ruins, and the myrtles and roses, which were still in bloom, almost covered with weeds. A moment's recollection could tell me, all this was nothing to her; but I know not how it is, instead of accompanying our departed friends in their happier state, our minds are perpetually endeavouring to keep up their connection with our own, and in great kindness we invite them back from the unfading blooms of paradise, to a participation of mortal roses with all their thorns.[39]

But when faced with illness and low spirits, knowledge of the literary is of little help, and to Carter it is clear that it is to society rather than solitude that one should turn. Away from show gardens, and in spaces with a more personal resonance, that is, Carter registers her own less pleasurable experience of melancholic low spirits. Thus, we find her agreeing with her friend Elizabeth Vesey (and implicitly with their friend Elizabeth Rowe) that, 'what affords a sublime entertainment to the wanderer of the world, has a very different effect on the poor imprisoned recluse'. In the case of their close friend the heiress Mary Sharpe, with 'a mind naturally prone to languor and low spirits', Carter admires the melancholic beauties of her deeply forested estate at South Lodge ('admirably adapted to raise the imagination to sublime enthusiasm, and to soften the heart by poetic melancholy'), but for this very reason, 'I think she will find it a great relief to her spirits, and an improvement to her train of life, to turn her eyes upon the gay prospect of cultivated fields, the whistling of the honest ploughman, and the prattling of the cheerful reapers, instead of constantly indulging melancholy thoughts under her venerable oak trees' (Figure 2.1).[40] This normalising of a Miltonic literary trope – with its switch from gloomy oaks to honest ploughmen and cheerful reapers – highlights the pervasive influence of literary models but should alert us again to those moments where the literary fails to offer support.

Troubled by headaches, and by her bouts of low spirits, Carter was an acute recorder of her own states of mind. Momentarily cheered by the thought of Elizabeth Montagu's return to England in the autumn of 1776 she wrote to her friend, 'I am such a poor wretch that I am fit for nothing but to sit down and sleep, or sit down and cry, or do any other idle or foolish thing; in consequence of the languor succeeding two days bad head ache, much increased by a good deal of unavoidable exertion. In the midst of all this depression however, my heart rejoices in the near prospect of your return to England . . .',[41] and integral to these accounts of low spirits is the language of melancholic landscape explored so far. Even here Carter can adopt an arch tone about low spirits and play with the idea of sentimental melancholy as she does in a letter to Montagu of August 1759, where she writes from a town house in Bristol,

I am at present quite in the temper of a peevish fretful child, who has quarrelled with all its play-fellows, and is crying for the moon. The thing I wish for, is just as

Figure 2.1 South Lodge, Enfield (engraved by Charles Warren) *c.* 1800
Designed by William Pitt the Elder in the late 1740s, and praised by Thomas Whately,
South Lodge became the home of Mary Sharpe in the 1780s. While its heavily-wooded
landscape was much admired, Sharpe's friends thought its melancholic gloom
unsuitable for a woman in low spirits.

much out of my reach; not that I can tell, if it was ever so near, I might put it to any
use, but still I should be glad to have it my power [*sic*]. You cannot tell what I mean,
nor I either; but I do verily believe that I mean something, and that if I was not half
asleep, I should be able to find it out. I wish I was reclined beneath one of your trees
at Sandleford; the garden within my view does not suit the situation of my thoughts;
it would be absolute disgrace to the figure of elegant and sentimental melancholy,
if one was to squat down upon an artichoke or a cabbage. My disposition requires
some poetical shade, some soft twilight sky, the faint whisper of dying breezes,
and the murmur of a sleepy stream. O dear, O dear! I do protest that I am not
in love, which I think quite necessary to mention, because by what I have read
in a book, this description seems wonderfully like it, but indeed that is not the
case; so far is true, that my present odd disposition arises from the struggle of a
philosophical head, against the fooleries and idle refinements of too sensible a heart,
and the fermentation of these two opposite principles, has produced the neutral
composition of nonsense with which you have been so plentifully regaled.[42]

Striking in this account, however, is the merging of those tropes encountered
throughout this chapter: the anxiety of personal desire and the realisation
that others will frame female desire as romance; the inability to express such
desire without the aid of a literary model, but with this the sense that such
models are themselves inadequate; and the longing for a garden which might
release one from low spirits and incompatible urges. Faced with depression

rather than literary melancholy, Carter once again argues for sociability rather than solitude. On hearing of Montagu's fatigue and low spirits in the winter of 1776, she wrote to her: 'I am glad . . . that you are to come to town, where your spirits will be more likely to be relieved . . . than in the solitude of the country. To a vacant heart and cheerful disposition, the soft melancholy of autumnal scenes is a very pleasing repose; but the view of faded woods and falling leaves, is not a good remedy for the depression of grief.'[43]

In the summer of 1783 Carter wrote again to Montagu of her own small garden's failure to lift her out of depression: 'I am still very low and spiritless, but hope to get about the world again in a few days. My poor little garden droops for the assistance of its mistress, one of whose great delights it is; and all my goods and chattels are in a litter and confusion very grievous to the orderly spirit of an ancient gentlewoman.'[44] That mirroring of the garden and the mind finds its echo of course in Cowper, and as in Cowper's poems, it registers the failure of the garden to lift the spirits when they are low; it also reiterates for us that other aspect of the melancholic garden, which is its close association with guilt and shame. At the beginning of this chapter, we encountered the figure of the fine lady, the fashionable lady, the lady bored and unable to encounter the natural world as she should: that same figure surely haunts these accounts of low spirits because it marks the same perceived failure of self-sufficiency, the same failure to inhabit the space of the happy domestic woman in the quiet of the country. Here, melancholic landscapes emerge from the experience of retirement not as sociable retreat, but as lonely isolation; and, as it does in Rowe's tales, guilt is formed by a sense of irreconcilable desires, formed by something close, also, to Cowper's damaging knowledge of pleasures one cannot attain and of dutiful resignation one fails to achieve.

Without virtue for a companion, retirement must be dismal

In the imagined landscapes of disgrace I have mapped out in this chapter, the space of retirement is inhabited by unfulfilled desire, by longing and by shame, where that sense of shame arises in part from the cultural freight retirement imposes. If that freight is 'literary' it is hardly confined to the literary world, rather it offers models and meanings for women who found themselves alone in the country and in particular for women touched by the stigma of scandal. Not least, female retirement was viewed as both a testing ground and a punishment, and the nature of such retirement was the stuff of public judgement. In 1800 a debate took place in the House of Lords concerning a bill on adultery and the support for seduced women abandoned by their lovers. At the centre of that debate was the need for such women to repent and the circumstances in which they might best do so; while one side argued that the lover should be forced to marry the woman, the other countered by asking what incentive for repentance this might offer. Attacking the bill, Lord Mulgrave argued that, 'it would deprive women of all hopes of being restored to some degree of society by a life of exemplary conduct and repentance; that it would drive them to prostitution or desperation, while it would encourage the seducer to proceed in his guilty career, as he would no longer be bound in honour to marry the woman whom he had separated from all the enjoyments of life'. In reply, Lord Grenville, 'wondered the Noble Lord should contend that there was no path to repentance but the arms of the adulterer, and no inducement to morality but a continuation of her crimes: he thought solitude the best place for repentance, and where they would meet more true respect, if their conduct merited it, than by dashing away in the circles of gaiety and dissipation'.[45] A year earlier, during the divorce proceedings of Henry Ricketts and Lady Elisabeth Lambert, the House was told that after the latter's infidelity, 'She now led a penitent and exemplary life in retirement, where she wished to throw from her an odium to which she was not entitled.'[46] At the end of our period, the rhetoric recorded in these parliamentary debates represent only the most public demonstration of the century's views on retirement and disgrace.[47]

In the middle of the century, Lady Mary Wortley Montagu drew on this same set of expectations when she wrote to her husband (in 1747) of their relation, Isabella, the Dowager Duchess of Manchester. In 1743 Isabella had married Edward Hussey, an Irishman thought of in London society as a mere adventurer. Hussey was in fact wealthy in his own right, with extensive Irish properties, but the popular image of the Duchess being duped by a poor but handsome fortune-hunter made her the subject of widespread satire.[48] Faced with this public notoriety Lady Mary concluded, 'I think the Duchess of Manchester's silence is the most reasonable part of her conduct; complainers are seldom pitied, and boasters are seldom believed. Her retirement is, in my opinion, no proof either of her happiness or discontent, since her appearance in the world can never be pleasing to her.'[49] Earlier in the same decade her cousin-in-law, the young Elizabeth Montagu, had taken a rather firmer view. In 1741 she wrote to her friend Anne Donnellan,

Poor Miss Y——, to what misery has she devolved the rest of her life to comply with the pride, avarice, and a still worse passion of the man who might have made her his honourable wife! I suppose she intends to hide herself from the world for ever; but without virtue for a companion, retirement must be dismal. Her disregard of reputation is affected, and is seen through, by her mentioning the world's opinion when she pretends to despise it. Conscience is the private watch over our actions; it will blush in the dark, and blame bad actions though hid in silence.[50]

Half a century later, Elizabeth Montagu in turn would receive a letter from Elizabeth Carter which, while softer in its tone, reiterated those same assumptions about retirement, repentance, and the private atonement for public shame:

All do not fall indeed in the same manner as poor Mrs.——, for all have not the same strong passions. But gambling, extravagance, neglect of domestic order . . . are equal disqualifications for all serious attention to the duties of an accountable life . . . I had hoped that retirement, reflexion, and the gentle and compassionate care and admonitions of the tender friend, to whom it was said this unfortunate young woman had fled, might have brought her to repentance, and intitled her to the forgiveness of a merciful and all-gracious God, and to the reconciliation of her family, and in time to the comforts of private society, though her faulty conduct would exclude her from the world; but into what is called the world no true penitent would ever have the effrontery to try to enter; but alas! all these hopes are now done away with, and she must for life hide herself.[51]

In this language of retirement and disgrace, that is, we are not simply confronting a literary game; rather, the 'literary' has real consequences for an imagined life: as we will see in the case studies which now follow, poetry, piety, and literary tales could all offer aspirational models for women who took to gardening on a large scale, but conversely they could all too often reiterate and reinforce cultural expectations that could leave women alone in their gardens, that could taunt them with unattainable aspirations, and that, as a result, could damn them to disappointment, to disillusionment, and to a depressing sense of failure.

PART II

3 | Bluestocking gardens:

Elizabeth Montagu at Sandleford

> When I am sitting in my garden, I can add myself to the whole map of created beings. I consider some insects feeding on a flower which like them was call'd forth by the rising sun, & whose race & task of life will end with its decline. My imagination can travel on, till it gets to those planets whose revolution round the sun is many years in accomplishing . . . My hopes, fears, desires, interests, are all lost in the vast ocean of infinity & Eternity. Dare I find fault with the form or fashion of any thing that relates to me in the presence of him before whom all modes & forms pass away, & to whose duration all the systems of Worlds beyond World, & Suns beyond suns, are more transient than the flowers of our parterres are to us. From these thoughts I draw a philosophick peace & tranquillity for what atom in this stupendous system shall presume to find fault with its place & destination.
>
> Elizabeth Montagu to the Earl of Bath, Sandleford, 8 August 1762[1]

Drawing on the wealth of Elizabeth Montagu's manuscript correspondence from the 1740s to the end of the century, this chapter explores the place of the garden and the role of retirement in the life of one of the eighteenth century's most public of women. The vast bulk of Montagu's manuscript letters are now housed in the Huntington Library, and it is on these manuscripts that I focus in particular. While many of Montagu's letters have appeared in print – notably in collections of the early nineteenth and turn of the twentieth century – those printed collections are inevitably partial and often misleading as to Montagu's range of interests and daily concerns. Notably, they tend to play down accounts of the garden in favour of Bluestocking sociability and literary interests; and crucially – though perhaps inevitably – they tend to elide Montagu's frequent, but telling, repetitions.

A focus on retirement may itself seem an oddity in that Montagu – the 'Queen of the Blues' – has so long been associated with the sociability and literary culture of London, rather than with a life in the country that in her own words could be, 'Sedentary, solitary, lazy and dull'; but like most fashionable eighteenth-century women, Montagu (1718–1800) spent up to half of each year not in London, but at her country estates, and the way in which she represented that time away from London is a crucial part of her identification with, and resistance to, the title of a 'fine lady'. That term, and the problems it posed for Montagu (Figure 3.1), formed a ready subject of banter throughout her correspondence with Elizabeth Carter, but the figure would appear also in one of the three dialogues Montagu wrote for her friend George, Lord Lyttelton's *Dialogues of the Dead* (1760). Here, her fine lady, Mrs. Modish, refuses Death on the grounds that she is engaged to 'the Play on Mondays, Balls on Tuesdays, the Opera on Saturdays, and to Card-assemblies the rest of the week, for two months to come' and wonders if 'the Elysian Fields may be less detestable than the *country* in our world'.[2] Modish is undoubtedly part of Montagu's attempt to distance herself from this troublesome account of fashionable femininity and city sociability; so too was the sustained account of country life she offered to her friends in letters spanning the second half of the century.

In her voluminous correspondence of the 1760s, Montagu regularly represented her country life in terms of the philosophical contemplation, Christian resignation, and sense of personal insignificance suggested by my opening quotation. Without a larger context it may be tempting to assume that we understand Montagu's position, and it might also be tempting to think no further of it than as a conventional piece of moralising on an equally conventional and conservative subject.[3] Certainly we can find similar meditative journeys throughout the century. At the end of our period, Ann Radcliffe's sentimental heroines move effortlessly from the beauties of nature to thoughts of their creator.[4] A decade earlier Rousseau would offer a strikingly similar account to Montagu's in his *Solitary Walker*.[5] In Anne Penny's play, *The Birth-Day* (1780), Lady Haylem reads the poetry of William Mason and thinks of the Creator while in her garden.[6] In the *Lady's Magazine* of 1759–60 Oliver Goldsmith had already offered much the same scene.[7] Amongst Montagu's near contemporaries we can find similar gestures in the poets James Thomson and Mark Akenside;[8] in the generation of writers before Montagu, her influential friend Elizabeth Rowe would repeatedly insist on that same movement from the local to the universal, from the Creation to the Creator; and Rowe in turn reiterated a meditative gesture popularised by the likes of John Tillotson's sermons and given its structure in the English tradition not least by the influential physico-theologists John Ray and Thomas Burnet.[9]

Alongside this we should recognise that other tradition which stretched back much further and was potentially at least even more radical in its rejection of the world because it rejected not merely the fashionable world, but the entire world. This tradition, one of pious female retirement, with its

Figure 3.1 Portrait of Elizabeth Montagu (engraved by Charles Townley; portrait by Frances Reynolds) 1784
By the mid-1780s, Montagu (dressed here in clothes suggestive of pastoral) had commissioned Capability Brown to redesign the landscape of her estate at Sandleford in Berkshire and work was well under way.

roots in medieval mysticism, and, uncomfortably for many Protestants, in the culture of Catholicism, continued not only to thrive in the eighteenth century, but – as we saw in the figure of Elizabeth Rowe – also to exert a strong influence on members of Montagu's Bluestocking circle. What the gesture towards traditions occludes, however, is how an apparently recognisable manoeuvre and a shared topos might be used by an individual as an act of self-fashioning. Thus, while we can in some ways equate my opening quotation with the merely conventional, it is important to recognise how Montagu uses it and in particular how she positions herself as an intellectual, a landowner, and a woman of wealth. To take an extreme example, if we set Montagu's retired reverie alongside a passage from the spiritual diary of Margaret Althans, we find the latter writing on 1 May 1783:

I have again exchanged the noise and hurry of the city, for my beloved retreat in the country, where I hope to be favored with the Lord's presence, and to be again happy in the company of a most dear friend. May the Lord sanctify our meeting, and may we one day meet in Heaven, to part no more. How beautiful the face of nature appears. The gay landscape around me declares the mighty works of God, and that, from winter barrenness, his power can create new life. Shall I then doubt his power in raising my dead soul to life, or in forming my body anew, after it has slept in the dust?[10]

The language of retirement is undoubtedly shared with Montagu (and with those writers explored in my earlier chapters); the movement from the local detail of a beautiful landscape to an awareness of God is shared also; but where Montagu highlights her own thought processes, her sense of place in the creation, and indeed the possibility that she might question that place ('Dare I find fault . . . what atom . . . shall presume to find fault'), Althans, a servant living in the east of London, turns to a language of low-church spiritual enthusiasm notably absent from Montagu's letters, and to an account of writing which also helps us to understand the crucial differences in an apparently shared spiritual venture. Of her urge to continue these spiritual diaries, Althans writes,

Satan tries to sift me as wheat, but Jesus has prayed for me; my trust is in him, therefore I shall not be overcome. The enemy has been touching upon the old string – That I am a mere hypocrite, that my Diary is all deceit and the flights of imagination, that I write from a motive of ostentation, which will only sink me deeper in guilt, and add to my condemnation, and that therefore I had better destroy it, and not leave it as a witness against myself. But to thee, Oh my God, who knowest the secrets of all hearts, I can appeal; that my motives for beginning and continuing this Diary, are my own edification, and that I may more distinctly admire thy goodness to such an unworthy wretch. When it has answered these ends, my friends may inter it with me, in my coffin. But I trust no temptation shall prevail with me to omit writing.

These claims and concerns are also, of course, quite traditional and fol-low an established pattern in the writing and use of spiritual diaries of the eighteenth century; but what they also highlight for us is the quite distinct difference of purpose in a letter from a wealthy woman choosing to repre-sent her garden meditations to another. That is, while we can align aspects of Montagu's gestures in my opening quotation with a set of recognisable conventions – and it is important to acknowledge what she shared with women (and men) writing from quite different situations – we also need to ask why she chose to represent herself in this way, and why the garden at Sandleford was so frequently the occasion for that self-representation. Cru-cially, Montagu's letters – though they appear to offer something rhetorically similar to Althans in their claims of self-revelation and analysis and in their movement from Creation to Creator – are quite different in their acute awareness of audience and in the insistence of the publicly-oriented per-sona they engineer. In part this is to do with Montagu's own religious stance: there is no sign of Satan in Montagu's letters, and – as Karen O'Brien has argued of the Bluestockings – confronting the creation leads less to doubts about the afterlife than to resignation to one's lot on earth.[11] In part it is also to do with an acceptable mode of public writing about religion (in this case to friends) which the *Critical Review*, at least, found wanting in the publication of Althans' diaries.[12] But it is less the specifics of a theological position with which I am concerned here than with the ways in which this kind of manoeuvre is used by Montagu as an act of self-fashioning, and a self-fashioning acutely aware of alternative constructions of her identity.

For most of her life Montagu was associated with a spectacular city culture and indeed even associated herself at times with the 'fine lady' of *The Spectator* (a work she claimed to have copied out in its entirety as a child).[13] As we saw in an earlier chapter, Addison's idealised image of the woman in the garden was itself a reaction against a kind of fashionable sociability in the city all too easily equated with women, luxury, and vanity. Haunting the idealised gardens of domestic bliss and learned independence, however, the image of the 'fine lady' was a particular problem for Montagu. Even before the building of the 'great house' in Portman Square – which she began in 1777 and which soon became famous for the splendour of its elaborate interiors – Montagu's enormous wealth, combined with her studied insistence on the intellectual sociability of the French-style salon, had made her both a figure of admiration and a target of satire. Letters from acquaintances were certainly not above offering a double-edged account of her London life, acknowledging the splendour while hinting at the vanity of fine ladies.

Mary Delaney, in particular, was something of a critic, writing to Mary Port of a visit to Montagu's Hill Street house in January 1775 that she 'Was dazzled with the brilliancy of her assembly. It was a moderate one, they said, but infinitely *too numerous* for *my senses*. My eyesight grew dimmer, my ears more dunny, my tongue faultered, my heart palpitated, and a few moments convinced me that the fine world was *no longer* a place for me, tho' I met with encouragement eno' from beaus and belles, who gathered about me like so many gay birds about an *owl*, but my wisdom prevailed for once over my vanity!'[14] After Montagu's summer travels in the same year, Delaney returned to the subject of Montagu's perceived vanity in a letter to Frances Boscawen, and Boscawen's reply in turn (with its fear that Montagu will return from France *tout à fait gatée*, 'utterly spoilt') reiterates that troublesome sense of immodesty, Frenchified manners, and vanity despite – or even perhaps because of – real talents:

The sketch you gave me of Madame *de* Montagu n'est que trop ressemblante, and much I *fear* that she will *never* be Mrs. Montagu an English woman again! I wish she would learn by heart her friend, Mrs. Chapone's Chapter of Simplicity, wch surely is a better thing than egotism or boasting, or affectation of any kind; but how *little temptation* has she to *affect* any thing, when she has *such* natural endowments! but so it is, and I own I apprendend qu'elle reviendra de ces courses *tout à fait gatée*.[15]

Montagu's implicit response to such accusations can be seen in a letter from the following year to the far more sympathetic Leonard Smelt. Recently returned from another summer in France, she wrote:

From a gay Parisian Dame visiting the Beau Monde . . . I am at once metamorphosed into a plain Country Farmeress. I have the same love for my pigs, pride in my pottatoes, solicitude for my Poultry, care of my Wheat, attention to my barley, & application to the regulation of the dairy as formerly . . . I believe my Friends at Paris would be amazed & scandalized at the joy I feel in this way of life, for they have not any taste of rural pleasures. A French Lady told me, she thought the English Women not so happy as the French [because] they were obliged to spend part of the year in the Country. I combated her opinion, but found it was impossible to make her comprehend the pleasures of a morning or evening walk, the delight of animating the industry, or relieving the little wants of a district, or the dignity of that independence which we all feel in retirement.[16]

The urge to distance herself from sophisticated Parisian women is clear; so too is the need to align herself with the productivity, even the domesticity, of the country, with a sense of usefulness, and with the powerful language of retirement. Repeatedly linked with the dangers of immodest metropolitan sociability and implicitly therefore with the loss of quiet domestic worth, however, Montagu's claims to conventional feminine virtues could certainly seem weak. Notably, for example, all of Addison's assumptions about solitude, domestic life, companionate marriage, and the virtues of retirement over the city were problematic for Montagu. Until the death of her husband in 1775, she was in what she would admit at times was a loveless marriage, and, after the death of a son at the age of two, never had another child. The coal mines, the huge disposable income, the penchant for expensive diamonds, and the very public identification with sociable metropolitan culture, all distanced Montagu from that supposedly comfortable model of Addisonian retirement. However, against Addison's model of Aurelia as the ideal figure of the woman in the garden, Montagu's letters could – and did – draw on a wide range of other models of retreat in order to shape and justify her position, and these included not only the likes of Astell's *Serious Proposal* but Tasso, Ariosto and Spenser, Milton, Elizabeth Rowe, and indeed the Bluestocking circle of friends that included both her sister and Sarah Fielding. Her correspondence raises important questions about the individual's engagement with literary and cultural models of retreat, and invites us to consider the ways in which those models might be set against each other, be of limited value, or even prove to be a form of obstacle. Of course Montagu's letters do not give us access to some unmediated account of consciousness in the garden (however much she might claim this in the rhetoric of her correspondence), but we can use them to explore how she chose to represent herself and her experience of the garden to others.

Characteristic of Montagu's letters is the fluidity with which they move from one model to another in order to articulate a position for her; but the choice of model at any moment is not without its restrictions and costs. The questions I pose in this chapter are how does Montagu position herself both physically and ideologically when away from the town, what role does retirement play in her life, and what does this tell us about the overlapping but not entirely synonymous worlds of gardens and retirement in the eighteenth century?

I do not want a fine garden

To make sense of how Montagu situated herself in retirement, we should begin by recognising the position of Sandleford in relation to the other

Figure 3.2 Sandleford Priory, Berkshire
The new octagon room (centre) and (to the right) the converted chapel, designed by
James Wyatt, with fashionably gothic exterior and classical interiors. At Montagu's
request the fan light (far right of old chapel) was added to allow a full view of the arch
of trees stretching towards the great house meadow. From here, the gardens still retain
their extensive southern views into Hampshire.

spaces she occupied throughout the year and indeed throughout her life.
Like many well-to-do women, Montagu's early life had included extended
stays at the great estates of friends and neighbours (the Duchess of Portland's
vast gardens at Bulstrode, for example, would be of particular significance
in her early life); but with her marriage in 1742 to Edward Montagu (a
grandson of the first Earl of Sandwich), she gained access to a new set of
spaces which she could more clearly call her own. In addition to continental
travel, regular visits to Bath, and particularly to Tunbridge Wells (with its
pleasurable 'mixture of retirement and lonely solitude, with the resort of
company at other hours'), marriage brought to Montagu the coal-mining
estates at Denton and Carville near Newcastle, and the country estate at
Sandleford in Berkshire; the death of her husband brought the opportunity
to build the famously sociable (and expensive) new house in Portman Square
but also to remodel Sandleford in the latest style (Figure 3.2).[17] Throughout
her letters, these different locations offered Montagu the chance to construct
different imagined spaces and different accounts of herself. Away from the

city, and though it is not uniformly so (for she writes at times – especially early in her married life – of retirement in the north), the northern estates with their hugely productive coal mines tend to figure in Montagu's letters in terms of business rather than pleasure, of labour rather than retirement, of the vulgar rather than the pastoral: certainly she was not above caricaturing her new northern neighbours with the claim that their 'conversation always turns upon money' and that 'the moment you name a man you are told what he is, the losses he has had, or the profit he has made by Coal mines', even as those coal mines made her, in her own words, 'very rich'.[18] Conversely, and more than anywhere else, Sandleford offered the opportunity to feel, and to write of, retirement.

I began this chapter with a letter from Montagu to the Earl of Bath, but I could as well have begun with a letter to George, Lord Lyttelton which (though less certainly dated) is one of a number in which Montagu repeats – often word for word – the ideas and even the phrasing of her correspondence with the other great landowner. The repetition reminds us to be careful of any assumptions we may wish to make about letters being 'authentic' or confessional, but conversely it also suggests the importance to Montagu of representing herself in this way to close, but also aristocratically distinguished, male friends.[19] In the letter to Lord Lyttelton – as with the letter to the Earl of Bath – Montagu writes once again of absent friends and then continues,

If I sit on some contemplative bench on a summers day, I know that I soon throw myself, and all the circumstances that belong to me, into the vast Ocean of Animal life . . . and in so large a company all that is personal is lost . . . humbled without being mortified I acquiesce in the general laws, and determine to enjoy my short day of Being like the Animals about me.
(Elizabeth Montagu to Lord Lyttelton, *c.* 1760–2 (MO1407))[20]

Writing from rural Sandleford, Montagu offers Lyttelton a classic rehearsal of garden meditation. Here, then, Montagu's garden signals both its own and Montagu's limited significance in the greater scheme of things. As she moves from the local and the specific to the general and the universal, her particular location appears to lose its significance in favour of the absent and the elsewhere. In this, Montagu highlights one of the central ambiguities of the garden as a place of Christian meditation, and an ambiguity that further complicates our understanding of retirement. On the one hand, that is, we find a Christian tradition that looked to the Garden of Eden and almost unfailingly to Book IV of Milton's *Paradise Lost* in order to justify an owned space in which to meditate. On the other we find that equally Christian tradition associated with Isaac ('And Isaac went out to meditate in the field at the eventide', *Genesis* 24: 63) that rejects the man-made garden for the countryside of God's creation.[21] In this latter view, of course, one doesn't need a garden at all, and relying on such man-made objects demonstrates not piety but a willingness to grasp the things of this world rather than the next. In support of this latter view, we might turn to a letter to the Earl of Bath in 1764, in which Montagu asserts, 'I do not want a fine garden, a beautiful park, a rich prospect to amuse me ... I want not Stewart, Adams, or Brown, to build me a palace, or lay a County into a garden for me'.[22] According to Montagu, the bench on which she rests leads her to a loss of 'all that is personal' and allows her to forget the social world that has given her importance. But such independence is tenuous, for not only is this statement made in the context of a letter which (quite characteristically) laments the absence of close friends when in the country; but in stressing her ability to amuse herself in solitude, Montagu quietly conjures up, in order to resist, that image of city ladies, with their fashionable ennui and their lack of mental resources.

Read in this way Montagu's rejection of 'fine gardens' appears as a rejection also of her own status as a 'fine lady', a rejection of all-too-fashionable displays of wealth, power, and status. But if this stance seems to dismiss the garden as unnecessary to an understanding of the creation – one can as well meditate on a leaf, a bee, or a bird – Montagu's apparent rejection of the garden is surely complicated by the very bench on which she sits: the bench may provide the opportunity for a reverie that moves her beyond the social world and its false values, but it remains a signifier of the private property, the wealth, and the leisure on which her own meditative opportunities also rest. Notably, for example, while her close friend Elizabeth Carter could write to her of the divine when she had seen a wild flower on the roadside or when looking out to sea, Montagu repeatedly chose to represent herself sitting within her own estate and on a bench marked out as the place for contemplation. Indeed, her position seems to be complicated further by her decision a decade later – and only a few weeks after her husband's death – to open negotiations with James Stuart, James Wyatt, and Lancelot Brown to create a great house in London and to landscape and rebuild Sandleford in the latest style.[23] We might of course argue quite simply that people have a right to change their minds; more fruitfully, however, we might also ask why Montagu chose to represent herself in quite different ways at different moments, what place the garden held in her imagination, and just what it is that she rejected while sitting on her contemplative bench. My aim, then, is not to claim that Montagu is some kind of hypocrite who buys a fashionable landscape as soon as the inconvenience of a husband is over; nor is it to insist on two opposing accounts of the garden as either meditative or vainglorious; rather, I want to move beyond those binaries to suggest a more complex world of meanings engendered by and articulated from within the garden, to trace out the changing significance of retirement and the places both garden and retirement occupy in the thoughts and feelings of Montagu and the cultures she inhabits.

The negative pleasures of solitude

In 1751 Elizabeth Montagu wrote to her husband Edward, 'When one is very young and full of the hopes of inexperience, one looks forward from pleasure to pleasure; a few years more make us see tranquillity with as great eagerness. I can even bid the "mute silence hist along," and love the negative pleasures of solitude.'[24] That stress on solitude, and the framing of solitude in terms of absence, should remind us of the mid-century reappearance of Sévigné's letters and of the way in which the widowed Frenchwoman characteristically merged claims for pleasure with the rhetoric of loss. Just as Sévigné might write, 'I am perfectly contented with the profound solitude we live in here: The park is much more beautiful than you ever saw it, and my little trees now cast a delightful shade . . . ', or, 'Do not be under apprehension of my growing weary of solitude . . . I am tolerably happy in my temper, that can suit itself to, and be pleased with, any thing', or 'is not this solitude very proper for a person who should think of herself, and either is, or would be a Christian?', or 'there is nothing but you that I prefer to the melancholy, tranquil retreat, I here enjoy', so Montagu would write, 'I came to this place without any company to drive away l'ennui. But l'ennui has been too proud or too generous to insult a poor defenceless Woman in her solitary garden', or 'I assure you I preserve all my vivacity and good spirits, though I am deep embosomed in tranquillity', or 'Five months are to pass, before I return to the land of the living, but I can amuse myself in the regions of the dead; if it rains so that I cannot walk in the garden, Virgil will carry me into the Elysian fields, or Milton into Paradise'.[25] And throughout Montagu's letters – to her husband, but also to friends of quite different kinds – not only is retirement repeatedly figured as solitude, but that account of solitude persistently vacillates between pleasure and loss, tranquillity and loneliness, friendship and its absence.

For Montagu, then, retirement represents, and can be represented as, quite different experiences at different moments in her life and even at

different times of the year. In one sense we can understand the move to the
country as part of the seasonal order of things, whereby (in wealthy and
fashionable circles, at least) one moves from the city in the winter to the
country in the summer; and in this respect, all that may be at issue is how one
occupies one's time and the exchanging of city for country pleasures. But
this ignores the often quite vexed question of how long one must spend in
the country and the company one keeps; it also slides over the way in which
retirement, by the very nature of the term, is inevitably retirement *from*
something; it is always about absence; and if such retirement is claimed as a
place of contentment, it nevertheless carries an awareness of its alternative
and of the attractions of that alternative.

In Montagu's case, at least in the years before her husband's death, life
in the country was at times something of a forced retirement, with her
husband often elsewhere but insisting she go to the country rather than stay
in London. Thus, in a letter to Gilbert West from Sandleford, late in the
summer of 1755, she wrote,

I do not find that Mr. Montagu intends going sooner [than the meeting of Parlia-
ment]. He is never in a hurry to change place; for my own part I am thoroughly
tired of the country, and should be glad to leave it . . . but as I can endure this sort
of life without being out of humour or out of spirits, I shall acquiesce very quietly. Perhaps you will think this arises from stupid insensibility; but I assure you, I
have a lively and tender self-love, very sensible to what regards my pleasure; but as
Mr. Montagu has an undoubted right to choose what place he shall be in, I feel it
most fit and proper to sit here to listen to the winter's wind all day, and the hooting
of owls all the evening. I have lately acquired the constant society of a screech-owl,
who has taken up its residence under my dressing room window, and utters such a
number of melancholy notes, I have been tempted to ask it, whether it stays in the
country against its inclination.[26]

Raising the spectre of loneliness even as she records her enjoyment of the
country life becomes a characteristic trope of Montagu's correspondence. In
a letter to her husband, written from Sandleford, 28 June 1757, for example,
we find her writing: 'I passd the whole day in the garden, sometimes reading
& sometimes walking, & the fresh air revived me . . . One cannot feel a want
of Company when the whole creation is so animated, I grieve to think how
fast this fine season fades away & gives place to wind, rain, snow, & the
various horrors of winter.'[27]

These shifting claims of solitude both as contentment and as the lonely
absence of sociability continue throughout Montagu's letters, and so we
find her writing to Lord Lyttelton in the summer of 1764 of retirement at
Sandleford:

This place as your Lordship knows, has not had its capabilities improved by the great Mr Brown, but the season of the year, & happy condition of the weather, render it delightfull. I have been here a week in perfect solitude & undisturbed content... I have continually wish'd for the company of some of my best friends, but for the great World, the gay World, the wise World, or the witty World, I have not wish'd. All that the ample Dome of Ranelagh contains in the evening, all the briliant croud at the morning drawing room I regret not... These two last evenings have been so warm I have ventured into ye grove, & when I hear the tête à tête of two nightingales their voices so exactly match'd, & their sweet responsive notes I think they have the advantage of such a solitary bird as I am. But in the great Aviary of human society birds are so ill paired, they must not complain who sit in their cage alone.[28]

In these letters to friends – themselves an attempt to generate community out of absence – Montagu insists quite as much on solitude as she does on the imaginative flights of piety any garden bench may allow. Indeed, much of the letter in which Montagu's bench appears is taken up with her absence from Tunbridge Wells and from the pleasure of the Earl of Bath's company, with meditations on faith, and with the inadequacy of female education which leads to ill-practised 'accomplishments' and false desires rather than to the usefulness and contentment Montagu's own meditations would appear to demonstrate. If we add to this Montagu's keen awareness of the traditions of pastoral romance with their adulated heroines and subservient lovers, her shaken faith after several deaths in her family and particularly after the death of her son, a husband at once energetically agnostic and prone to self-absorption, this figuring of herself as a solitary Christian woman in retirement marks a more complex and less self-satisfied Elizabeth Montagu than my opening quotation may at first suggest. It is to Montagu's awareness of the choices she makes in her self-representation as a woman in retirement that I now want to turn.

Thinking more like a Poet than a coal owner

It is a truism of eighteenth-century aesthetics that the layering of literary allusion – quite as much as forms of physical geography – is vital to the individual's experience of land as landscape. As Montagu wrote in a letter to Lord Lyttelton in 1760, 'One enjoys with a spirit of enthusiasm a fine park; imagination assists, fiction embellishes, and our pleasure is of the poetick kind.'[29] In Montagu's case such pleasures come also with an acute awareness of audience, of the shifting registers required by different aspects of one's life and to be articulated in the different spaces one inhabits. A letter to her husband in the summer of 1764 is characteristic, for example, in its movement from the pleasures of fine weather, to the song of the nightingales at Sandleford, to Milton's claim that the birds please silence with their song; it is characteristic also, however, in its shift of register with the comment, 'But I am thinking more like a Poet than a coal owner' and the sudden change from Sandleford's pastoral pleasures to the detailed business of coal mines and the north estates.[30] What is of interest in Montagu's letters is the fluidity with which she is able to move from one frame of reference to another and the purpose those changes of reference might serve. Writing to the Earl of Bath in 1762, and immersed in the business of agriculture on her estate, she chooses to style herself initially as a 'mere farmeress' in rural Berkshire. What follows, however, is a rapid movement of literary allusion from the 'beans and bacon' of Horace's farmer, to Milton's 'joint tenants of the shade', to brief nods at characters in plays by Dryden and the Duke of Buckingham, all of which suggest a rather different kind of identification, one which is clearly generated out of the fashionable literary knowledge of the town, and which marks a crucial distance between Montagu and her farming neighbours.[31] Indeed, what establishes Montagu as a woman in fashionable retirement is precisely that she will leave the country again and return to the metropolitan world of literature and high society; or, conversely, that she takes the town with her when she goes to the country. This last formulation, of course, is an account of pastoral, and it is the strategies of pastoral that play perhaps the most significant role in Montagu's account of herself as a woman in rural retirement.

When we look to the earliest-surviving Montagu letters, written in her early twenties before she was married (and thus in fact still Elizabeth Robinson), the language of pastoral comes easily to the fore, and she repeatedly styles herself as 'Pastorella' when she finds herself alone in the country. In the spring of 1741 we find her writing quite typically, 'Like a true Pastorella, I sat me down the other morning in a bed of violets and primroses worthy of a place in Arcadia.'[32] In one sense, this is just a conventional way of speaking about the rural, but it is worth asking ourselves just what the attraction of pastoral might be by the mid-eighteenth century for a woman who seems to have set her sights on a good (that is, a wealthy) marriage, and on a shining career in metropolitan society. For a start, in referring to herself as Pastorella Montagu signals a quite particular strand of pastoral writing. Her model here is Spenser's heroine in Book Six of *The Faerie Queene*, and as models go it is far from unambiguous. On the one hand Pastorella is a figure signifying simple faith set in rural obscurity. On the other, she is herself a figure of temptation for Spenser's Sir Calidore, and the narrative in which she is placed means that she is sexually threatened, rescued by knights, and carried through strange lands in three-canto adventures. Pastoral romance, that is, makes the countryside a place of seduction, excitement, and action; it is a model that places a beautiful woman at the centre of attention and moves her from rural obscurity to a life of adventure.[33] We can recognise in this the kind of escapist fantasy that Ros Ballaster, Deborah Ross, and others have mapped out in their accounts of early women's fiction; but we should also recognise Montagu's own playfulness in her self-image.[34] Even in her early letters, it was not a model to which she aspired on a full-time basis. Writing from her close friend the Duchess of Portland's vast country estate, Bulstrode, in December 1741, she remarked:

Next Sunday I quit the peaceful groves and hospitable roof of Bullstrode, for the noisy, turbulent city; my books and serious reflections are to be laid aside for the looking-glass and curling-irons, and from that time I am no longer a Pastorella, but propose to be as idle, as vain, and as impertinent as any one.[35]

This easy movement from pastoral delight and earnest meditation to the pursuits of a fine lady in fashionable society seems to have been characteristic of Montagu throughout her life. It is also characteristic of pastoral itself. As Frank Kermode has noted, 'the first condition of pastoral is that it is an urban product' and one created for a largely urban audience.[36] It would be a mistake, then, to assume a disjunction between country pleasures and city high life, because pastoral has always been the product of a city rather than a country perspective. If it offers a world of meditative ease and delight, it does so from the perspective of those who find it absent in their city lives. We can see something of this at work in the letter to the Earl of Bath with which I began this pastoral excursion. Recalling the year 1741, in which she was sent to the country to avoid the smallpox that was to disfigure her sister Sarah, Montagu tells Bath, 'I am to go to Sandleford quite alone, and shall live there quite a lone for some time'. Then, thinking back to her youth, she continues,

I had a foolish vanity which persuaded me I was made for the World, and I wish'd it had been made for me: But by the Accident of my sister's having the small pox I was sent to a farm house for some days with only my books to amuse me, and I found myself so happy, as soon as my Anxiety for my Sister was over, that I was persuaded the best resolution I could have taken for my own happiness, was never to have quitted that sort of life, in which I enjoy'd uninterrupted content, peace, liberty, and independency. I shall in some measure catch again the thread of these golden days in my retirement at Sandleford; but time and pass'd Afflictions have tarnish'd their lustre. The mind that has known no Sorrow, like the conscience that recollects no sin, has a tranquillity and an intrepidity that once lost can never be regain'd.[37]

Two things are worth noting here. The first is that this moment of confession, and the imagination of retirement, comes while Montagu is still in the throes of London sociability. The second is that when imagining her return to Sandleford, Montagu merges her sense of a complex present with a nostalgic appeal to the simplicity of the past. What she offers us, then, is a recognition that she has made a pastoral of her own life: if her youth was a golden age of peace, liberty, and independence, like all golden ages those things are now lost. Retirement, which would seem to offer their return, in fact confirms their absence.

Betty Rizzo has linked this early moment in Montagu's life with a rift between the sisters that was never wholly mended, and this gives us a further perspective on Montagu's account of herself in retirement.[38] According to Rizzo, much of Montagu's motive for Christian charity whether in town or country was driven by her uneasy relationship with her sister, Sarah Scott (1720–95).[39] A key example of this for Rizzo is Montagu's relationship with Scott's experimental community of women living in retirement at Hitcham. Montagu certainly put up a substantial part of the money for the project, and in her letters to her sister she undoubtedly writes of how she looks forward to joining them. What Rizzo goes on to argue, however, is that it is hard to see her giving up a very public and very fashionable London life to be part of a female community on such a small scale; and of course ultimately she chose not to do so. In Rizzo's account of Hitcham we are presented with a Montagu who constructs a self-image in response to and with an acute awareness of her sister's powerful but resolutely unglamorous moral values.[40] For Rizzo, Montagu is to be aligned almost wholly with a showy London life: her high-profile charity – and presumably also the stance of Christian meditative recluse – can be explained as a form of sibling rivalry. Whether we agree with this as an adequate characterisation of Montagu or not, the sense of audience, and the need to control one's self-representation, is crucial. Certainly, once we understand Montagu's bench-bound musings as themselves both a form of pastoral and a reaction to pastoral romance, both a claim for Christian piety and a response to the piety of others, then a reading of them as unproblematically confessional becomes difficult to sustain. Instead, we are forced to recognise them – like pastoral itself – as a knowing mode of leisured self-representation which has its own agenda, which aims to resist the agenda of others, and which ultimately allows Montagu at once to embrace and reject her problematic identification with the figure of the 'fine lady'.

This world is not intended for a place of punishment

The problematic nature of retirement, and the place of it in Montagu's own life, formed one of her ongoing discussions with her close friend, the poet and translator, Elizabeth Carter. From very different backgrounds, and with a huge disparity of wealth and social connections, the two were certainly held together by their public and literary interests, but they were held together also by the way in which they developed a shared account of their disparate experience of retirement. Carter had made an early foray into the world of London publishing but chose to return home to her father's house in Deal, Kent, after only a short time.[41] She was a regular member of Montagu's literary circle in London, eventually renting her own house there during the summer season, but her sense of home was clearly in Kent and its countryside. Repeatedly in Carter's letters, London appears as a place of energetic if often irrational entertainment, of 'racketing', and of 'fine ladies' and their fashionable ways.[42] She characteristically constructs her own persona in opposition to such things, but places Montagu in a far more ambiguous role, and this leads to a sharp awareness of the differences between herself and Montagu for all that they share in terms of their literary interests. Thus, while Carter enjoys their mutual interest in gardens, and while her letters insist on a shared sensibility and on the close intimacies established by an imaginative engagement with the landscape – she cannot resist noting the disparity of scale between their two estates, writing in the spring of 1763:

My garden is absolutely *en friche*, but I hope before the end of the summer to see it blooming (or that somebody else will see it) with roses and jessamines; and I have very magnificently ordered a wall to be built for their security, which will cost more than if I was to contract for all the roses and jessamines in the country of Kent by the year. But then I have a cherry-tree with half dozen blossoms, and an apricot that never bears, and all this in a piece of ground at least as wide, and I think rather longer than your dressing-room, but of this last circumstance I will not be too positive.[43]

Equally, while she can write, like Montagu, that 'every striking view of nature is always accompanied' by 'sentiments of religion' and that as a result, 'we feel the inexpressible delight which arises from a consciousness, that our heart is in its best disposition, both with regard to the Supreme Being, and our friends', she also insists that retirement, in Montagu's life at least, must be a short-term pleasure rather than an end in itself.[44]

Montagu's delight in Sandleford after the exhausting sociability of London is continually met by Carter's insistence that such retirement should – and besides, in Montagu's fashionable world of fine ladies always would – be temporary (as Montagu wrote to her husband in the summer of 1764, 'People tell me I shall be melancholly all alone, but they dont know me, I might indeed be tired of a long retirement, but at short intervals absolute solitude is no evil, especially after being so long in ye hurry & bustle of London').[45]

It is with this awareness that Carter insistently offers a moral account of Montagu's post-urban 'sauntering' and of her 'spirited enjoyment of the first delightful days of independent solitude'. In a letter of July 1770 she wrote to Montagu:

The human mind, destined to the rough exercises of probationary life, is, from its very constitution, incapable of a long indulgence of that happy indolence, on which you were inclined to make a panegyric, which ceases to be happy, when it becomes no longer necessary, as a relaxation from the fatigues of active exertion. And so, my dear friend, as soon as you have reposed yourself sufficiently after the bustle of your journey, by so literally sauntering in your garden, you will fly from the torpor of indolence to your farm, and your coal-pits, and your studies, and the garden, instead of the whole day, will only engage its own share.[46]

If not every summer, this kind of exchange occurs with regularity throughout the Carter–Montagu correspondence, as does that other insistence between the two women that the garden is the place in which one might imaginatively cement relationships with absent friends (the letter above continues – again, quite characteristically – 'I very sensibly felt the kindness of your wishing me to partake your retirement; which, on your first transports, was certainly one of the highest instances of friendship that any one human creature could bestow on another. If my heart did not understand what you say about solitude and silence, I should be ashamed to own it belonged to me'). Conversely, however, Carter's account of retirement, and of the pleasures of pastoral fantasy, is also a means of recuperating Montagu's social – quite as much as her retired – life as a life of morality. In a letter of 1760, and in response to Montagu's yearning for solitude amid the tiresome sociability of Newcastle, Carter writes: 'In this fever of dissipation, it is no wonder your imagination should often cool itself in the retirement of a desart wood, or the hollow of a rock. Yet, as charming as your solitary scheme appears in mere speculation, it is to be hoped, for the good of the world, as well as your own, that you will never be able to put it in practice.'[47]

All of this is not to say that the idea of retirement did not constitute some kind of ideal, but it is an ideal to be recognised as partial, temporary, and perhaps most important, not suitable or even appropriate for the majority of women. Visiting her friend Mrs Vane in 1781, Carter recounts in a letter to Montagu how, after the death of her husband, Vane chose to live in retirement at her estate in County Durham. The parallel with Montagu, though unstated by Carter, is informative: like Montagu, Vane had landscaped her estate, and done so after the death of her husband; like Montagu too, Vane moved in exalted circles; but implicitly unlike Montagu, Vane's style of reclusive piety is 'of so sublime a style, that I always feel little and humbled whenever I am with her' and Carter remarks on the feeling of awkwardness when one returns, as one must, to 'common every day life'.[48] What follows from this, however, is an opportunity for Carter to justify Montagu's more active and social life. Replying to Montagu's letter from Sandleford in which she had claimed, 'The first week I was here I passd entirely in the garden',[49] Carter writes:

A state of such absolute sequestration from all the bustle of society, is certainly for a short time, a most delightful repose to the spirits; and it is no wonder that those who are capable of thinking like you, should consider it as one of the noblest and most eligible parts of our existence ...

But beings appointed to the rough exercises of mortal trial, are wisely destituted even of a capacity for the enjoyment of long holidays: and this contemplative elevation of soul, so soothing to our indolence, and so flattering to our pride, is too destructive to our active duties, to be long supported without that languor and vacuity which brings us back to the ordinary tasks of life, and to a sense of the weaknesses, and of the wants of our disordered nature, which we are too apt to forget during the independence of solitude, and the suspensions of action: a situation in which we shall be strongly tempted to conclude ourselves to be wise and virtuous, while there are no objects to mislead our reason, or excite our passions.[50]

Again, Carter points not merely to the seasonal movements of the well-to-do, but to the moral purpose of retirement as a means of regenerating one's spirits after the dissipations of city life. Equally, however, if we seem to have returned to the garden as Paradise regained, for Carter it is also a false Paradise precisely because one is no longer in society, and is therefore no longer tested: far from being an ideal, the garden can also be an abnegation of responsibility, a space that leads to confidence in one's moral virtues only because they are not being tested. Here, for all that Carter relishes Montagu's moments of ease, she turns to that other model of the garden, the garden as a place of luxury and delight, a place of seduction and moral decay.

Carter's steady insistence in her letters to Montagu that pious retirement is at once impressive, exalted, and misguided accounts also for her difficult relationship with perhaps the most famous female literary-religious recluse of the early eighteenth century, Elizabeth Rowe. Referred to by Carter's friend Catherine Talbot as 'our favourite', Rowe had by the mid-eighteenth century become something of an icon of pious writing, literary fame, and rural retirement. Certainly Rowe was a convenient figure to set against the more scurrilous reputations of an early generation of women writers, including Behn, Manley, and Haywood. Her much-admired poems on the death of her husband cemented her fame and her choice of retirement led to claims that she was a modern-day Eloise, but crucially, an Eloise without the damning taint of illicit love. It was for these reasons that Rowe became an important model for mid-century women of 'pious religious devotion and a new exaltation of married love'.[51]

As a model for Montagu's own retirement, however, Rowe presents some important problems. Strikingly, of course, as an icon of married love, Rowe offers a model in which the husband is notably absent, and, while he will undoubtedly be met in the next world, he does not have to be dealt with in this one.[52] Moreover, Rowe's choice of self-banishment from the social world was in itself a persistent worry even for her admirers. Endless but mostly ineffectual attempts were made to coax Rowe out of the obscure rural retirement she had forced upon herself after the early death of her husband. Talbot in particular seems to have shared Rowe's view that life was best spent waiting for death, but like Carter she also recognised that such an exalted model of pious seclusion was problematic for other women. Indeed, while efforts were made – most notably by Rowe's posthumous editor – to justify her rural obscurity as peculiarly appropriate to herself, Carter and Talbot repeatedly worried over it as a model for the vast majority of women for whom such ascetic seclusion could be little more than an irrelevance or a nostalgic ideal.[53] We should also recognise one further thing: more than anything, perhaps, Rowe's choice of life in Frome illustrated the apparent paradox that retirement could lead to public fame, that retreat from society could make one an object of fashionable attention, and thus that letters claiming a withdrawal from the world and a loss of self may have a distinctly public purpose.

My point here is not to damn Montagu for a perfectly conventional Christian elision of property and spirituality, ownership and the afterlife. Rather, it is to suggest once again the ways in which Montagu's position is itself defined by the culture from which she claims to depart. It is also to suggest that the problem lies in part with the language of gardens and with the conflicting cultural freight they are assumed to carry. As Rowe makes clear both in her fictional letters and in those to her friends, and as Carter reiterates in her letters to Montagu, retirement can all too easily mean the loss of moral rigour; and while there is a place for it, the real test is to hold on to one's religious virtue while in the fashionable world. Gardens then become at one and the same time a false paradise because they shield one from the struggle that is the true state of sublunary affairs, and a hint of paradise because they allow one to meditate upon and recognise one's state: in turn, Montagu's self-fashioning in the letters has to negotiate not only between these two accounts of pastoral, but between these and the alternatives spaces of the industrial north and the sociable city.[54]

We should not leave Rowe behind at this point, however, for her significance to Montagu extends beyond the quite mainstream championing of active virtue and the problematic nature of fame. If in her own life Rowe was drawn to the role of religious recluse, and resisted the importuning of her friends to join in their society, her writings offered a far more complex and unsettling range of models, motives, and meanings for female retirement. It is with these, I would suggest, that Montagu also engaged as she sat on her contemplative bench. Rowe's complex of ideas about wealth, rank, retirement, sexuality, and virtue, were read by, admired by, but also criticised by, the likes of Montagu, Carter, and Talbot in their own attempts to make sense of their place in the world.[55] Montagu was hardly in the position of Rowe's sexually endangered women, but this did not insulate her from those eroticised accounts of the woman in the garden so insisted upon by Rowe's *Letters*; and with Rowe in mind, we can explore further both the spoken and unspoken choices that Montagu may be making as she engages with those problematic questions of property and power, sexuality and religious belief, taste, fashion, and wealth.

Open your breast to him boldly

Rowe's *Devout Exercises* and the reclusiveness of her later life invite us to emphasise the religious aspect of her writing as an influence on the Bluestockings; but the *Letters Moral and Entertaining* are also vitally about gender in an eroticised landscape, and while Montagu cannot be aligned with Rowe's fallen women, she nevertheless had to engage with her own eroticised image in the imagined landscapes of men. During the 1760s Montagu was to develop close relationships both with George, Lord Lyttelton, the owner of the vast landscape gardens at Hagley in the West Midlands, and with the elderly but active Earl of Bath. Both men undoubtedly admired her intellect, vivacity, and talent; both men wrote letters that were overtly flirtatious. The result is that while Montagu had been fond of representing herself as the romantic shepherdess in the 1740s, by the 1760s she found that she was enmeshed and implicated in a gendered discourse of nature and gardens which insistently sexualised her even as she was recognised as a woman of intellect. Myers has argued that, 'the bluestockings resisted the erotic element, although they were aware of its importance to other members of their society. They particularly disliked conventional male "gallantry" in which women were treated in a flattering way as sex objects . . . the blue-stockings resisted the intrusion of eroticism into both their male and female friendships.'[56] Exchanges with Bath and Lyttelton suggest it was not always that neat. The Earl of Bath largely confined himself to claims that he was learning the coded language of flowers – with which Turkish women were said to seduce their lovers – and planning, 'when my Garden is come to perfection, to send you now & then, a Billet doux in a Nosegay';[57] but the insistent use of sexual allusion is most strikingly evident in the letters of Lord Lyttelton whose nickname for Montagu was the 'Madonna'. That title at once made Montagu a figure of secular adoration while playfully under-cutting this with its knowing overstatement, and it was frequently adopted by Lyttelton in his attempts to bring her to Hagley or when imagining her there in her absence. In the autumn of 1761 he wrote to Montagu,

I think our Prospect will be fine but, alas! in all that Prospect I have not one Glimpse of You. When will you come, and dance on my Lawns with the Graces, or sport on my Hills with the Muses, or meditate in my woods with the pensive Goddess of Wisdom? Every Day that I see my Park in Beauty draws from my heart a sigh of regret, that the Madonna does not inhabit it with us. Let your Mind at least come to us, and if your Heart should be of the Party, we will make it very welcome.[58]

This emphasis on Montagu as an ethereal and yet distinctly physical figure of desire in Lyttelton's landscape is made more apparent however in a letter of 1764. It begins with a poem in which he styles himself as Apollo hoping to join Montagu alone in the country and ends with his disappointment on finding 'The Dame had all the Muses round her' so that, 'his Project vain, / The Child of a Love-heated Brain, / He wisely dropt, and took his Lyre / Content to join the tunefull Choir'. If this seems fairly tame, what follows is a mini-compendium of classical rapes and seductions as Lyttelton busies himself with thoughts that are quite as much about Montagu's body as they are about her bodily well being:

As therefore, Madam, I am now under no apprehensions of hearing a Sad story of your being turn'd into a Laurel, to escape from the violence of this amorous Deity, or of your becoming the mother of a Second Phaeton, who by the Fire derived from both his Parents would set the World in a blaze, I have no other Inquietude about you than absence always gives me with regard to your Health. Don't you read too long under the shade of your Garden? Does not the Warmth of the Sun make you sometimes too forgetfull of the Coldness of the Wind? Pray, Madam, remember, it is recorded in the History of the Thracians, that a rape was committed by Boreas on a Lady of that Country. Don't imagine that he carried her off in a Whirlwind. No – he slily insinuated himself into her bosom under the favour of a warm Sun, which made her neglectfull to guard it against him with the necessary caution. Do you therefore be more carefull: but, if the mild and benignant Zephyrus should come and court you in your garden, open your breast to him boldly, and let him sport there as he does among the Lillies and Roses: he will do you no more harm than he does them.[59]

As we have seen, Montagu was not averse to playing with this language herself, even in 1760 writing to Lyttelton at Hagley that she was 'ready to step into the Chariot of Armida whenever you send it'; but she seems increasingly to have moved away from the romantic language of her youth in order to adopt a less dangerous account of her life in the country.[60] Those dangers were certainly apparent and were expounded on, as we have seen, in the fiction of Elizabeth Rowe as well as in more contemporary novels like Charlotte Lennox's *The Female Quixote*. They were also made apparent, however, in the real-life fate of a rather distant member of Montagu's social circle, Henrietta Knight, Lady Luxborough. Knight, who was on visiting terms with the Lytteltons at Hagley, was a close friend of Frances, Lady Hertford, who in turn was close to the friend of Montagu's teenage years, the Duchess of Portland, and to Elizabeth Rowe. A lively woman of letters, Knight had found herself effectively banished from society by an alleged affair with the poet John Dalton, an affair that it was claimed had been instigated by the interchange of romantic pastoral poems. Knight maintained her innocence, but she represented to the polite world a startling incident of elegant literary romance tumbling over into illicit passion and social disgrace (in this case banishment to a life in the Midlands), and was a living reminder that this elegant language of pastoral dalliance had fundamentally different risks and implications for men and women. We need not assume a causal connection to recognise what might be at stake for Montagu in this kind of language and why she might choose once again to style herself quite differently as a meditative woman on a contemplative bench.

This is not to say that Montagu wholly shook off the gendered language of aesthetics employed by Lyttelton and many of her male correspondents, nor that her use of that language always denoted resistance to its gendered stereotypes. She undoubtedly questioned the bastions of masculine authority when she wrote to Elizabeth Carter in 1782:

When a Wife, I was obedient because it was my duty, & being married to a Man of sense & integrity, obedience was not painful, or irksome, and in early youth a direction perhaps is necessary if the sphere of action is extensive; but it seems to me that a new Master, & new lessons, after one's opinions & habits were form'd, must be a little awkward, & with all due respect to ye superior Sex, I do not see how they can be necessary to a Woman unless she were to defend her Lands & tenements by Sword or gun. I know, that by Fees to Lawyers, I laid out 36:000 in a purchase of Land, with as good assurance of ye title; and by ye help architects, Masons &c, I have built as good a House in Portman Square; & am now, by ye assistance of ye celebrated Messrs Brown & Wyatt, embellishing Sandleford within doors, & without as successfully, as if I was Esquire instead of Madame. All that I have mention'd has been effected in little more than 5 years, few Gentlemen in ye Neighbourhood have done more.[61]

But she could also make wholly conventional connections between her own fading beauty and the beautifying of Sandleford: 'As fast as time wrinkles my forehead, I smooth the grounds about Sandleford . . . In a little while, I shall never see anything belonging to me that is not pretty, except when I behold myself in the looking glass.'[62] What complicates this latter, however, is that while the trope may be conventional it need hardly signal a sense of gendered oppression.[63] Thus, for example, in a letter to her sister Sarah Scott, written from Sandleford in the summer of 1778, Montagu refers to her newly landscaping estate as a 'pretty Country lass with green top knots of Oak & Elm, flowers in her bosom, fruit in her lap, her petticoat of ye finest green'.[64] Certainly we might say that this likens Sandleford to the pastoral self-image of the 'Pastorella' letters in the 1740s; and certainly we should take note of Montagu's feminising and eroticising of her own landscape. But what that gesture tells us is surely as much to do with wealth, with hierarchy, and with the dominating certainties of landowning as it is with some ubiquitous account of gendered subordination. Just as her landowning male friends might draw on the gendered erotics of landscape to articulate control over their estate, so Montagu offers us an example of how a woman, too, might discursively occupy that position of erotic power and in doing so also distance herself from being implicated, undermined by, or identified with its object. It is to the remodelling of Sandleford and to the apparently masculine territory of landscaping that we should now turn.

A lovely pastoral – a sweet Arcadian scene

Two weeks after the death of her husband, Montagu wrote to Elizabeth Carter, 'I may perhaps indulge myself with laying out two or three hundred a year in embellishing ye grounds, as ye money will keep the neighbourhood in better employment'.[65] The process of altering Sandleford had, however, already begun in a small way during Edward Montagu's lifetime. Letters from the 1750s suggest that there was a careful negotiation between Elizabeth and Edward over the design of the landscape. As one might expect, Edward played an important part in the improvements to his estate; as one might also expect, so did Elizabeth.

Acknowledging Elizabeth's importance in the designing of the garden, Edward wrote to her in 1756, 'I have this morning been looking over the trees wch were planted last winter very few of which are dead, I think there seems vacancies which ought to be fill'd up but of that you will be the best judge when you see them'; two days later he wrote to say that he had found a gardener 'who will follow yr instructions & I doubt not give you content'; a year later he was busy both with moving and with purchasing trees to 'thicken the Wood walks'; and five years later, in November 1762, he was still writing to Elizabeth of his gardening ventures and still acknowledging her influence:

I am still employ'd in my Work of opening up prospect, favour'd with the finest weather imaginable for my purpose, the bright sunshine set[t]ing of[f] our view to the Hills in it's greatest beauty, & enabling me to discern, & as far as I dare venture to remove whatever obstructs. I have been continually out with the Workmen giving them directions, & seeing them execute without doing more or less than I intend. In such kind of work as this one thing leads on to another, new improvements shew themselves, of wch no advantage could be made, unless one was upon the spot continually viewing & giving orders. Perhaps you and others when you come here may think there is room for more to be done, but I am not myself displeas'd at what is already done, & what remains may hereafter be completed.[66]

By 1765 there were plans to begin remodelling the house with the aid of Adam, and Elizabeth was already defining the landscape in contrast to the large-scale building programmes of her friends. Writing to Lord Lyttelton after his latest update on temple-building at Hagley, she claimed, 'I aim at nothing more than a pleasant retreat. I would soften retirement and enliven solitude'. Then, turning to a language we should by now recognise, she continued:

Nature has bestowd sweet & gentle charms upon [Sandleford]. The august is for the ambitious, the magnificent for the great, the chearfull, the soft, & the agreable, is fittest for a philosopher . . . The years are coming in which I must seek resources in a comfortable habitation neither quite out of the World nor in the midst of its tumult. Ladies of gallantry in their old age grow perfect saints, and can live in hermittages, occupied with the works of repentance, and enthusiastick visions of a happier state to which they think the fervour of their devotion will peculiarly entitle them. As in my youth I have not been a Sinner, I have no hopes of growing a Saint in my old age. With the hopes of a Christian, & the temper of a philosopher, I hope to pass gently through the vale of years.[67]

Setting the ambition and the magnificence of the great against the gentle cheerfulness of the philosopher, conjuring up saints and seduction, hermits and sinners, setting enthusiasm and gallantry against quiet Christianity, Montagu's account of Sandleford marks her acute awareness of the ways in which she might be positioned by her culture, and of the need to position herself in relation to it. Distinct from Rowe's sinners and saints, distinct too from her own urban identity, the Elizabeth Montagu of Sandleford, like her landscape, is quiet, domestic, and philosophical.

What is also important here is that before Edward Montagu's death Sandleford was in no way a 'public' or show garden (Figure 3.3). Although it was large and had extensive views (particularly south into Hampshire), it was hardly fashionable, consisting of an old walled garden and evergreen maze, a bowling green, a canal, fish ponds, and an orangery.[68] Montagu took great delight in a letter from her sister that told of the Duchess of Beaufort's impromptu visit to Sandleford in 1762 and her surprise on actually seeing it. Ignoring the warning of the local innkeeper that 'no body ever went to see it, & that it was by no means fine', and assuming that Montagu's city glamour would be extended to the country, the Duchess's tour of brick and gravel walks left her with nothing but 'a fine perspiration' and a sense of disappointment.[69] For a woman so concerned with her place in fashionable society, Montagu's delight in this tale may seem strange; what it makes apparent, however, is Montagu's use of Sandleford – and of her carefully cultivated image of retired religious interiority – as a necessary foil to the self-display of a fine lady in the metropolis.

The lack of show at Sandleford would seem to ground Montagu's claims to meditative seriousness and distance her from the vacuity of city fashion. It is for this reason too, perhaps, that so many of her letters to the Earl of Bath and Lord Lyttelton insist on the values of the landowner, settled in the country, and on the role of such landowners as the true representatives of British values; thus, in a passage she finally chose to delete from a letter to the Earl of Bath, Montagu attacked Lord and Lady Warwick, 'who live like Citizens in a little box eleven Months of the year, and just come to this noble Palace [Warwick Castle] to dress it up in the stile of Marybone gardens or Vauxhall, and yet expect one should respect them as the Heirs of a great family'.[70] By contrast, at least at this stage of her gardening career, Montagu insisted on the easiness and comfort of Sandleford as a place to

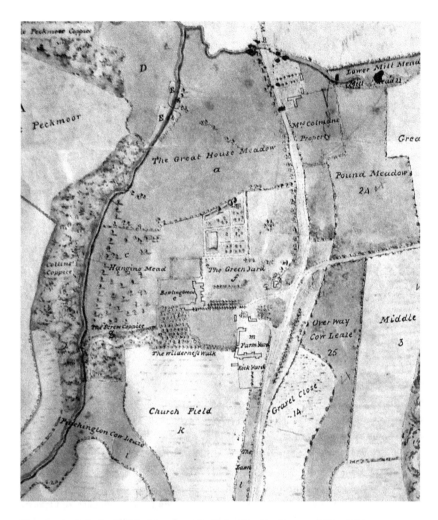

**Figure 3.3 A Survey of the Estate at Sandleford in the County of Berkshire
belonging to Mrs Montagu 1781 (detail). Courtesy of Berkshire Record Office
(BRO: D/ELM T19/2/13)**
The survey records the landscaping of Sandleford before Brown had developed the
park landscape and the chain of lakes. House (centre), with 'old-fashioned' elements
still visible, including the bowling green (directly east of the house), walled kitchen or
formal garden (to the immediate south west) with linear and rectangular ponds, and
wilderness walk (to the north); the lakes were developed along the stream in the eastern
valley (far left) in the 1780s and 1790s (note that north is to the bottom of the map).

dwell. Replying to Edward's letters of November 1762 detailing the latest
improvements, she wrote:

You are very good in consulting me about the Trees . . . I would chuse Sandleford for
my residence preferably to most of the fine places I have seen, as I would a chearfull,

easy, & good natured companion, to the greatest witt & brightest genius who had great faults and follies. Most fine places are either in remote Countries, or in great neighbourhoods, or have in themselves a kind of state inconsistent with the true comforts & pleasures of rural life.[71]

With the arrival of 'Capability' Brown, however, something different happened.[72] As the most famous landscape designer of his day, and as a man whose professional task was to recast working agricultural land as an aesthetic object of luxury and leisure, Montagu's choice of Brown inevitably signalled a statement about fashion, taste, and wealth. If earlier in her life Montagu used the garden at Sandleford to resist the title of 'fine lady', and to represent herself instead as a learned lady, a rational woman, and a good Christian, by the early 1780s Sandleford's gardens were being remodelled as the fashionable accessory of a very fine lady indeed. While in her letters Montagu still claimed Sandleford for solitude and meditation, the new design looked quite as much to the sociability of the city and to the tastes of a fashionable public. Montagu herself clearly made a distinction between the country and the city garden, writing of Portman Square in 1778:

I am now very busy about the Garden at my new House. Lord Harcourt has made a very pretty plan for it. I believe it will not be so stately as the garden of Semiramis, nor perhaps as that where ye *Sapient King with his fair spouse held dalliance*, but for these puny modern times it will be pretty well, & it will grow lawrels enough to crown Ld C[ornwallis?] when he returns from his American expedition, I shall give you a merry merry Vauxhall when my Trees & shrubs are in order. I assure you it will be a very pretty demi saison garden, in Winter, it will not afford such shelter from Storms as a Forrest of Pines; nor in Summer shade like ye Groves of Oaks of our Druids, but it will serve as umbrellas & fans for Beaux & Belles.[73]

At Portman Square the garden was envisaged as an outdoor room, a place of entertainment for Beaux and Belles, certainly, but a fitting venue also in which to celebrate the (hoped for) political and military successes of the American War. Set in the open landscapes of Berkshire, Sandleford was on an altogether different scale, but like the London garden it was to see increasing numbers of well-to-do visitors (Figure 3.4). With Samuel Lapidge and James Wyatt still at work in July 1786, Montagu wrote of the apparent tribulations this new show garden created, with 'No less than 5 Carriages full of fine folks were here yesterday to see ye place. I was happily taking ye air in my Whiskey'; three days later she wrote to Elizabeth Carter (and repeated the anecdote in a letter to her sister Sarah):

Figure 3.4 Sandleford from the western fields
The land west of the house was (and is) farmed fields, but was planted to suggest a park
landscape. The view is from a track leading to Wash Common, one of the many routes
taken by Montagu in her lightweight carriage, or 'whiskey'. Of the fashionable gothic
exterior (and Edward Montagu's interest in mathematics), the Dowager Countess
Gower wrote to Mrs Delany, 'We admire *Mountaskew*. Mr T. Pitt says ye owner of the
house deals in angles, from gratitude to ye memory of her dear spouse.'

Yesterday morning as I was returning from an airing in my Whiskey, my Servants
told me they saw 3 Carriages, & several Persons on horseback at my door, having
heard a larger party in the Neighbourhood of Winchester intended to come & see
the place, I veer'd round a Neighbouring Common till I heard ye Hall door was
clear of Carriages.[74]

The work on Sandleford – and its transformation into a minor tourist
attraction from which its owner must take flight – had begun with the
arrival of 'Capability' Brown in July 1781 (Figure 3.5). The broad outlines
of early progress at Sandleford have been recorded by Brown's biographers
Stroud, Hinde, and Turner, and in more detail by Sybil Wade and Rosemary
Baird.[75] As all have noted, Montagu was insistent that the project should
be achieved within the bounds of her annual income. Huge as this was, the
heavy spending on Portman Square both limited the outlay at Sandleford
and extended the period over which the gardens were laid out. She wrote to
Elizabeth Vesey of Brown's first visit:

Figure 3.5 Sandleford, Brown's Lake
With her great wealth, Montagu paid for improvements to Sandleford from her yearly income, but this lengthened the period of construction and the chain of lakes directly east of the house was still being developed in the mid-1790s.

Mr Brown sent hither ye beginning of last week one of his Ministers calld a Surveyor who has been & is still taking levels &c of the place, the end of ye week he did me the favour to call himself; he did not stay more than 24 hours, but indeed he had view'd the place before. He seems much pleased with it, & was extreamly good humourd & obliging. I told him I had sacrificed so largely to the City Demons, *Pomp* & *Vanity*, in Portman Square, I could offer but little to ye rural Deities. He seemd not displeased, but said, he wd make me a plan, & inform me what wd be ye expence of its execution; that I might execute ye whole, or part, of his scheme, as I pleased. He will call here again before the month of August expires, communicate his design, & then we shall go to work. It is pity the noble genius of Mr Brown should be restraind by ignoble considerations & circumstances, but you know, I have some low plebean sentiments which forbid my incurring debt, so his improvements must not go beyond what my cash will immediately answer. I shall begin by embellishing what lies under the view of my new room. It is great satisfaction to me, to find, that he thinks great improvement may be made at small expence.[76]

And to Elizabeth Carter she wrote the following month:

He has been here twice this summer, & his Surveyor has taken our dimensions levels &c, on these he made a plan of which I may execute a part or ye whole &c. He will contract at a certain sum for the plan fixd upon, so that I cannot be drawn in to a greater expence than I am aware of. The House in Portman Square having pretty well made my daily charge its daily bread, my purse is in a meagre condition, so my improvements here will not proceed very rapidly, or to great extent. Of all these circumstances I informd the great Mr Brown, & he was very polite on the occasion.[77]

With Brown's death in 1783, supervision of the work was taken over by Samuel Lapidge and then by William Eames. Alterations continued to be made well into the 1790s. With Eames at work on the gardens in the summer of 1790, the architect Joseph Bonomi required '280 yards of white Sattin . . . for the Window Curtains, & about 100 yards of white lutestring for ye Curtains for ye Octagon drawing Room'; by October Eames was required once again 'to hasten here as soon as he can, that we may begin our Water works'; by the end of October 1790 Montagu's nephew, Matthew (who was to inherit the estate on her death), heard news that,

Mr Eames . . . will require upwards of 30 Acres of land to make the addition of Water & pleasure ground, and as many acres belong to some persons near London, all operations must be suspended till they can be solicited for the sale – I fancy there will be no difficulty in obtaining it, but as the purchase, & the embellishment will be very costly, I have advised your Aunt to suspend her Operations till she has got thro' the toil, trouble & expence of her Great Room Garden, Walk, & Stuccoing . . . To this she is perfectly disposed, & therefore her works here this winter, still not exceed the bounds of charitable Employment to her old Men & Women, & the expence of Mr Eames's Agent to superintend them. I am happy to tell you that it is determined that the piece of Water before the House will be filled up; the Ground levelled 8 or ten feet, & the river inlarged so much in the bottom as to meet the Eye from the Windows, and amply compensate for the loss of the unnatural lake, which has had so many advocates. Mr Eames seems to have well imagined his plan for the valley. There are to be many Grass Walks, two sweet Meadows enclosed by the woods, & Sunk Fences so concealed as to admit of the sheep feeding on the banks of the River. There will [be] two Water falls, 6 feet high, & the Bridge at New Town will have a beautiful Effect from different parts of the Drive. Your Aunt desires you will not intimate that she delays her operations here, indeed was she prepared to begin them it wd be imprudent till she had finally settled all her bargains with the different freeholders to whom the Land belongs.

By 1792, however, negotiations remained incomplete and Montagu was still manoeuvring to buy the land that would allow her to create her new river.[78]

What is at stake in the creation of this sophisticated, complex, and long-term remodelling of the landscape at Sandleford can be seen if we turn from Montagu to her sister Sarah Scott's novel, *Millenium Hall*, with its attempt to claim the country house tradition for a retired female community. Published in 1762, the year in which we saw Montagu delight in Sandleford's lack of show, Scott's novel carefully raised the question of a professional designer like Brown only to insist that the beautiful landscaping around her utopian Hall had been designed instead by its female inhabitants. This rejection of Brown and the professional landscape designer signals a number of concerns. Most obviously it insists on the aesthetic ability of women in the largely masculine territory of architecture and estate management. However, it is also associated with a conservative strand of thinking amongst the landed elite that is suspicious of all 'professionals' and that sees the remodelling of the landscape by anyone other than the owner as a challenge to landowning dominance. What this points to in turn is that larger debate, running throughout the eighteenth century, between land and trade, between old money and the destabilising capital of an ever-aspiring middle class.

In offering her vision of self-sufficient benevolence and of sentimental organic community, Scott drew on the increasingly outdated language of moral economy, a language in which land was understood as a set of rights and responsibilities between owners and tenants, rather than as a commodity to be bought and sold by those with capital. If her novel is radical in its claims for a utopian female community, it is wholly conservative in its championing of those with landed wealth as the natural leaders of society.[79] Scott's problem was how to justify the financial inequality that meant the majority laboured for the leisure of the few: her answer was a 'benevolent' capitalism that claimed to merge moral with financial wealth and which justified ownership of a great estate on the grounds that it brought greater happiness to the worthy poor than the unchecked market economy of the city. In rejecting Brown and his like, Scott sought to reassert the moral responsibility of the landowner and to resist the increasing commodification of land as landscape signalled by the decision to buy a product from a professional designer. While she insisted that her landscape was tasteful in the modern style, she carefully distinguished that taste from the unrooted buying power of mere wealth.[80]

With much of her money coming from her northern mines, and on commissioning Brown in the early 1780s, Montagu's problem was that an outlay of capital purchased an aesthetic commodity that would speak to her peers of her leisure and her social status but not of her morality.[81] I have already suggested that Sandleford acted quite literally to ground Montagu's claims to moral responsibility. With the arrival of Brown such claims might seem tenuous, and we can see Montagu adopting two strategies to counter the threat of being caricatured as a woman of high fashion and of being associated merely with the commercial transactions of metropolitan life. The first was her insistence on playing the role of benevolent landowner, and in fact, despite claims that she was the target of Scott's satirical depiction of the foolishly fashionable and vain Lady Brumpton in *Millenium Hall*, Montagu put into practice many of the ideals of her sister's novel.[82] To this end, while at Sandleford she went out of her way to act charitably towards her poor neighbours, with schemes that ranged from buying pigs and cows for those with grazing rights, to the subsidised sale of her potatoes and the employment of indigent weavers as the labourers for Brown's earthworks.[83]

This first strategy supported Montagu's improvements with the claim that luxury was itself a moral good because, in the words of Alexander Pope, 'the poor are clothed, the hungry fed'; and indeed Montagu had already expressed such views when visiting the estates of her neighbours in the 1760s. In a letter to the hugely wealthy Earl of Bath in the summer of 1764, she wrote of the Berkshire countryside:

Nature is there so well featured & finely proportion'd, a little care & culture forms her to grace & beauty. It is for wealth & pride only to strike out rivers from dry & barren places, & make blooming gardens in a desart. Sometimes a noble fortune is exhausted in working these miracles, & when effected like other prodigies, they delight only at first sight. In a few years if there is not constant expence, they lapse into their former dreary state in a great degree, & look like the habitations of pride & poverty; an ill match'd pair, & whose particular deformities are much heighten'd by their conjunction. In these fine Countries a Gentleman of moderate fortune may afford to make his situation perfectly beautifull, the improvement of the verdure of his pastures is a gain to his farm, & tho to keep a place neat requires some hands, yet perhaps the parish taxes lessen'd by employing the poor, & the expence of planting &c is in some degree repaid to the family, and the Squire is more usefull to his neighbours by finding them employment, than he would by feeding them at his gate.[84]

Once Brown's plans were under way, the need to justify her own expenses in such terms became all the more apparent, and, writing in 1789 of her decision to continue the work, she informed her sister that:

[Mr Eames] is to finish what the great Brown had planned here. With oeconomy in my head, you will think it strange, perhaps, that I settled a scheme with ye said Mr Eames which will cost me eight guineas a Week to day labourers for some months to come, without reckoning ye expense of Trees for plantations & salary of a supervisor of ye business. However I hope you will not consider me as a Person who says one things, & means another, but while there are so many poor people, who in this time of high price of bread cannot get half employment, I will not Oeconomise in the article of Labour.[85]

With rather more than a moderate fortune (£7000 a year on the death of her husband, and set to rise), Montagu's second strategy was to develop that rhetoric of wealth and its proper use by insisting in her letters on the low-key nature of her plans and on Sandleford once again as a place of pastoral retirement rather than fashionable show. As early as 1781, just as she was to move her belongings from Hill Street to the new house in Portman Square, she wrote to Elizabeth Carter:

The great Mr Brown has sent me his plan for our improvements of the grounds which lye under our immediate view, & with very little expence it will form a sweet scene in the humble & simple character of pastoral. Few places have by Nature the sublime, & without it the epick makes a dull composition. All these improvements within & without doors will give me double pleasure when my dear Friend appears on ye scene.[86]

A year later, with Brown's work at Sandleford properly under way she reiterated that view:

He is forming it into a lovely pastoral – a sweet Arcadian scene. In not attempting more, he adapts his scheme to the character of the place and my purse. We shall not erect temples to the gods, build proud bridges over humble rivulets, or do any of the marvellous things suggested by caprice, and indulged by the wantonness of wealth.[87]

This insistence on pastoral – defined here in terms of an absence, in this case of luxury and ostentation – allowed Montagu to lay out hundreds of pounds a year on embellishing Sandleford while maintaining a sense of frugality and moral responsibility: in adapting to the character of the place and to Montagu's purse, Brown's landscape of retirement can be claimed as both natural and moral precisely because it rejects the novelties, whims, and reckless spending of a consumer culture. If we should be wary of such rhetoric, however, it is not least because this claim to simple and unassuming pastoral was also made by her friend Lord Lyttelton for his thousands of acres and expensive programme of garden building at Hagley. That is, in true pastoral style, Montagu and Lyttelton drew on the landscapes they had constructed to justify the naturalness of their own wealth and to distinguish their use of that wealth from the false aspirations of the vulgar rich and the world of fashionable show. What we should also recognise, however, is the acute awareness that such pastoral retirement is wholly reliant on the world it claims to shun. Long before she decided that Brown would remodel her place of retirement, Montagu recognised that the landscapes she inhabited were dependent upon the political state of the nation. In the autumn of 1753, while visiting the gardens of a Mrs Edwin near Cliefden, she described the scene on the upper reaches of the Thames and then imagined the river's journey on down to Greenwich. Noting the 'pastoral air of the place', she continued:

I will own that the river here, does not appear in such force and magnificence as near Greenwich, but where it gently glides through humble vallies, or fertilizes a little plain, it still keeps a character of nobility. Father Thames in a little valley, has the dignity of a great chief and statesman in retreat: we remember the invincible fleets he has sent forth, the commercial benefits he has procured to his country, the useful arts he has assisted, and the advantageous alliances he has made, uniting his city with every land from whence it can acquire benefit.[88]

While this largely glosses over the aggressive military strategy of Britain in support of its trade, Montagu was not blind to its implications.[89] Her problem, like that of many with one foot in land and the other in the city markets was the nature of Britain's imperial expansion. In 1761 she seemed to align herself squarely with the landed interest when she wrote to Benjamin Stillingfleet that, 'My ignoble soul hates the whole trade of War, & I could almost wish Old England had . . . lived like a gentleman farmer on his own lands than turn universal merchant.'[90] In a letter of 1762 to the Earl of Bath, however, that position is complicated. With the end of the Seven Years' War slowly coming into sight, and with the massive expansion of Britain's empire about to be confirmed, Montagu made a rather difficult distinction between war for domination, and war for mere wealth:

Self interest always had a great share in peoples actions, but it used to Act in a Mask, now it disdains disguise . . . Great Brittain would Monopolise the Commerce of Europe. Our Fleets would glory in being the most intrepid Pirates, and our Armies in being the most valiant Banditti in the World. Gain, success, riches, power, sanctify every thing . . . I must own I hope our late Success will give us a peace before the end of the Winter. War for dominion had something noble in it, when for liberty, nobler still, but all this murder for wealth is abominable.[91]

Characteristically attempting to distance her own life from a self-interested acquisition of wealth, what is at stake for Montagu can be seen in a letter written to her husband four months earlier about the power of the ministry and the King's ill health. In a move we can now recognise, she writes,

One of the principal benefits of a country life is to observe the system of divine wisdom & forget the foolish government of human affairs, & I have thought little of ministers in or out, but the health of the King is a subject of real concern. Under his government I shall hope to sit quietly under my own vine; & eat the fruit of my own fig trees, but one knows not what calamities might befall us if we had the misfortune to lose him, so I am anxious to hear how he does.[92]

At Sandleford Montagu may claim that she can ignore the world 'of ministers in or out', but she finds that she cannot ignore the government of the state on which her own retirement ultimately depends.[93] Three decades later, with another French war raging, the lure of Sandleford as a retreat from politics remained strong:

In the Society of London my attention was taken up with what was passing in the Civil, & moral World, & fierce Military exploits. Governments overturnd, Fortunes ruined, & brave men wounded & slain. Here, Mars & Bellona paleness & fear the Demons raging in Camps & Cities have no Dominion. We live under the protection of Pan, Sylvanus, Flora, Ceres, and Pomona. When I saunter in the Grove I hear the ring Dove cooing; if I drive out on the Commons in my Whisky the sky lark pours her melody round my head, should these softer delights, these sweeter pleasures be interrupted by the visit of some Country Neighbour, he only relates the process of his Hay Harvest. You will not blame me for preferring these & thee reclining on a Bench in the Grove, to sitting on the Velvet sopha in a Drawing room in London, where I heard tales of War, rumours of Wars, & relations of the horrid proceedings of the National Convention at Paris.

We have returned, then, to Montagu's choice of seat, and in doing so we can begin to see how her claims of pious meditation, abnegation of self, and a rejection of the fashionable world situate her not only in terms of place – her specific geographical location at Sandleford – but also in the ideological space which merges that geographical location with a complex series of debates about active virtue and pious retirement, about ownership and the afterlife, about retirement and fame. The problem, as always, is that – as a product of wealth and a sign of luxury – the garden is as much a site of fashion as of meditation, as much an assertion of property as an occasion for piety. Sitting quietly in a garden does not remove Montagu from the larger world she inhabits; retirement does not remove that world from her mind. Indeed, we might go further and argue that Montagu's repeated references to the English elite's peculiar love of the countryside is another means of securing the public status of a private situation. Of Count Bruhls' visit to Hagley she wrote to Lord Lyttelton in 1765:

I hope Count Bruhl was duly Sensible of the beauties of Hagley, tho' I think the English are the only people who have a true taste for the Country. The Germans love the sports that have the Air of war, and terribly invade the rights and liberties of the four footed Tenants of the Woods. The French men are become perfect fine Ladies, and pass their Summer evenings at a card table. Indeed I do not wonder that people who live in the land of slavery and Oppression should not love the Country. The neatness of our Cottages, and healthy well fed countenances of our common people give an Air of content and humble happiness which must rejoyce every humane spectator, but where the huts look rather like the dens of wild beasts than the habitations of Men, and pinching poverty has deform'd the human face and form, it is necessary to divert the mind by Artificial objects.[94]

Dismissing both German aggression and an otherwise much-loved French urban sophistication, Montagu places the quiet pleasures of Sandleford – and its owner – on the national stage. The apparent success of this mode of self-representation can be seen when we look to one of the most detailed accounts of a visit to Montagu's country estate, which appeared in Mary Morgan's *A Tour of Milford Haven, in the year 1791*, late in Montagu's life.[95] For Morgan (a friend of the Robinson family), Montagu's estate represents 'beauty blended with utility', the happy merging of house and garden (notably in the mirroring of arches in the old chapel and the grove), the absence of grandeur, and a demonstration of responsible landowning. Walking around the gardens, Morgan remarks not only on the beauty of the landscape, but also on the cleanliness and decency of the labourers. Discovering that (as in Scott's *Millenium Hall*), 'many of them had some great defect, occasioned by age, natural infirmity, or misfortune', but that Montagu, 'had so paired them, and fitted their employments to their several faculties, that the remaining sense of one served to supply the deficiency of the other', Morgan concludes:

The whole of this place suggested to me the idea of a Roman villa. There is every thing for use as well as beauty. The farm and the dairy are not omitted; they supply the family and table with all things necessary and delicate. In short, there is a style in every part of it, that bespeaks a superior degree of judgment. Nothing is gaudy or superfluous, yet nothing is wanting. Native genius, matured by observation upon what is simply elegant, has guided the hand of the amiable possessor of this enchanting place.

Upon viewing some fine houses, we are sometimes tempted to cry out with the wise man, 'All is vanity!' Many superb edifices eclipse their owners so much, that they seem the most insignificant things in them. But in every part of this you see the soul that animates the whole; yet no place appears half so agreeable, as when she is present. (p. 40)

However, if this suggests Montagu's successful acts of self-fashioning at Sandleford, we should note also Morgan's final comment on Montagu's public status, that when she is mentioned, 'many people enquire more about her feathered room than her book' (pp. 48–9). The persistent association between Montagu and the spectacular urban display of the great house in Portman Square is certainly countered by Morgan's vision of pastoral, classical retirement, but it is hardly removed.

My aim in this chapter has been to demonstrate a more complex experience of country retirement than Morgan's eulogy or Montagu's own claims of contemplative ease might suggest. Sandleford played a crucial part in Montagu's self-representation as a wealthy metropolitan woman who could be at once a 'fine lady' and a religious recluse, at once an icon of conspicuous consumption and display and a sober demonstration of financial prudence and charitable benevolence. By tracing the changing fortunes of Sandleford we can begin to understand the fluid meanings of the garden in the mid-eighteenth century and the place occupied by retirement in the imagination of Montagu and her friends. The web of discourses with which Montagu grapples inevitably extends well beyond those I have traced out here. My purpose, however, has been to pull at some of the threads stretching from a bench at Sandleford to the far reaches of the globe and beyond. Sitting on her garden bench, Montagu might claim to remove herself from 'her hopes, fears, desires, interests' and 'all the circumstances that belong to me', yet what her letters demonstrate is an acute awareness of the gendered politics of taste and of her place in a debate about charity, luxury, capital, the decline of moral economy, the emergence of empire, and the proper use of wealth.

4 | Neighbours in retreat:

Lady Mary Coke and the Hollands

> Poor Lady Mary Cooke cannot support the misfortunes of the Royal
> Family, and she is going abroad again. She cannot think of living in
> London, so while she is in England chooses to be retired in the
> country... As my sister Holland says, how little uneasiness she must have
> of her own to be able to make herself so unhappy about the Royal Family.
>
> Lady Louisa Conolly to the Duchess of Leinster, 14 January 1773

In 1773 the gardens of Lady Mary Coke (1727–1811) and Lady Caroline
Holland (1723–74) were parted by a lane no more than twenty feet wide.
Their experiences of the garden and their sense of retirement were parted
by far more.

Both women came from powerful aristocratic families, both had difficult
relationships with those families, both gardened and wrote of their gardens
with an unusual intensity. The daughter of John Campbell, 2nd Duke of
Argyll, Lady Mary (Figure 4.1) was pushed into an unhappy dynastic marriage in 1747, separated from her husband in 1750, and, after his death
in 1753, remained single for the rest of her life. The daughter of Charles
Lennox, 2nd Duke of Richmond, Lady Caroline (Figure 4.2) was the eldest
of the famous Lennox sisters (Sarah Lennox was more than twenty years
her junior); when she eloped with the politician Henry Fox in 1744 (and
thus became Lady Caroline Fox) she created a rift with her parents which
was not to be resolved until 1748; when she became a peer in her own right
in 1762 she signalled the attachment she felt to her home at Holland House
by taking the title Baroness Holland.

Given their close proximity and their shared social circles, Caroline Holland's misunderstanding of Mary Coke's retirement is striking; for, while
Lady Holland found the semi-retirement of Holland Park a welcome relief
from the world of her husband's politics, Lady Mary Coke's garden at Notting Hill was to be at once a distraction from, even as it was a demonstration
of, her social misery: the detailed accounts that Coke has left of her years at
Notting Hill record the life of a woman uneasy in her seclusion, resentful
that visits from London were few, and outraged that her hints of intimacy

Figure 4.1 Portrait of Lady Mary Coke (engraving by James McArdell; portrait by Allan Ramsay). ©The Trustees of the British Museum (1863,0110.165)
Based on Ramsay's 1762 portrait, Lady Mary was by this time already a widow. The lute (in fact a seventeenth-century theorbo) belonged to her friend Lady Ancram. Iconographically the lute could signify sexuality and fertility in marriage (an odd choice here); more likely is its association with sophisticated feeling and sensibility.

Figure 4.2 Lady Caroline Holland (by William Hoare of Bath) *c.* 1745. Courtesy of The Trustees of the Goodwood Collection / The Bridgeman Art Library
A portrait of Lady Caroline shortly after she had eloped with the politician Henry Fox. Holland House was leased in 1746; the pleasure of its gardens as a place of retirement would fill her letters for the next three decades.

with the Duke of York were dismissed by the fashionable world. A matter of yards away, Caroline Holland wrote letters to her sisters wishing for less company, longer periods of solitude, and greater distance from the bruising and consuming world of parliamentary politics.

In this chapter, then, my aim is to explore the role of the garden, and the need for retirement, in the lives of two women who were joined by their geographical location, by an emotional investment in the spaces they created, and by an acute awareness of landscaping fashion, but parted by the ways in which they inhabited the garden as a social and psychological space.

I. A less and more private way: Caroline Holland and Holland Park

Comprising around eleven acres of pasture, a flower garden, a kitchen garden, a courtyard, and an orchard, Mary Coke's estate at Notting Hill was relatively modest. Holland Park (Figure 4.3) was on a different scale: with its 200 acres of park, pleasure gardens, farms, and woodland and with its rambling Jacobean house, this was a country estate with a convenient capital city only a short ride away. In an importance sense, as a place of 'retirement' from town, this was not quite the 'country', with its implications of an abrupt break from London and a different set of pursuits brought on by a day or more's travel. Neither was it the *rus in urbe* of some of the larger aristocratic town gardens.[1] Close enough to town to have frequent city visitors, Holland House was often a place of entertainment, with the Fox family putting on their own private theatricals and hosting elaborate balls. Rooms were permanently set aside for Henry Fox's friends and family and more than this, as Stella Tillyard has noted, it became effectively an out-of-town club for Henry Fox's political associates.[2] However, in its early days at least, it could also be characterised as a place of retreat from city scandal-mongers and family outrage, and it is in this context, in part at least, that we should understand Caroline's repeated assertions of love for Holland House and its gardens. This was a large enough space to feel separate from London and its demands. Out of doors (and away from the increasing demands of Henry Fox's political coterie) it was also a space in which one could be solitary – a term striking in the eighteenth century for its extremes of both negative and positive connotations, its suggestions of release from insistent social incursions and its recognition of an oppressive and debilitating loneliness.

Figure 4.3 Holland House *c.* 1800. ©The British Library Board (Ktop XXVIII, image 10r)
A view from the 'Great Meadow' towards the south front (cf. Figure 1); the portico contained Caroline Holland's conservatory and aviary. After much pressure from Caroline the estate was finally bought in 1767.

Caroline and Henry Fox took out a lease on the Holland House estate in 1746, and eventually bought it in 1767. For Caroline, at least, it acted as a kind of partial retreat, not only from Henry Fox's all-consuming political life, but from Goodwood, the estate of her parents, the Duke and Duchess of Richmond, and the home from which she had eloped with Henry in 1744. Her choice of marriage for love caused the kind of scandal that Walpole wryly remarked could not have been greater had it been one of George II's daughters;[3] and Caroline was herself under no illusions about the nature of her conduct and its likely result, writing to Henry in 1744:

I know the step I am going to take is a wrong one and an undutifull one in regard to my parents; I shall be blam'd and abused by all the world, but I own the thought of your being so miserable (as you seem'd this morning) for seven, or eight, months together has got the better of all the reasons I could alledge against being in a so great a hurry... I am vastly fright'ned of what I am going to do I dare not reflect upon it I fear they will never forgive me.[4]

In these expectations she was largely correct: ministers spoke of their outrage, the King was consulted, and while her father secretly made enquiries about her over the coming years, in public he cast the Foxes off, refused to read the entreaties sent by both husband and wife, and demanded (with only partial success) that they should be shunned by society. Four years after their elopement, Caroline was still hearing stories of her parents' attempts to prevent people from visiting them,[5] and it was not until her younger sisters married that they were able again to write to her.[6] The Foxes were finally forgiven in 1748 and family relations were once again established. With that forgiveness came two archetypal acts by which aristocratic family ties were to be cemented: requests from the Duke of Richmond for political favours from Fox, and the gift of trees and shrubs from the Goodwood estate to be planted at Holland House.[7] By 1748 substantial improvements at Holland House had been under way for some years, though surviving documentary evidence of the work is limited.[8] Tillyard and others have noted that as a rambling old Jacobean structure Holland House itself was out of fashion when it was bought and remained so through Caroline and Henry's lifetimes.[9] The park and gardens, however, were a different matter. William Kent was brought in to advise on remodelling the terraces close to the house, the park was enclosed, and there was a sustained and well-funded period of planting and landscaping that began soon after they arrived and continued late into the 1760s.[10] Work on the estate received a major boost once Fox took up the post of Paymaster to the Forces in 1757, a position he held throughout the Seven Years' War and one which led to an immense leap in his income. Financial records for the period show more than half a million pounds a year going through his accounts, and it was during this period that 'Capability' Brown was paid a little over £200 for his advice at Holland House, though the form that advice took is now unclear.[11]

What descriptions there are of the early years of landscaping at Holland House make the usual gendered assumption that male landowners create landscape gardens. Two years after the Foxes arrived at Holland House, a tour guide recorded that: '. . . the present possessor has restored it, repaired and beautified it, embellished the gardens, enclosed the park . . . He is daily improving the delightful situation.'[12] In the same year Horace Walpole, with his characteristic stress on great men and great designers, wrote to their mutual friend Charles Hanbury Williams that Fox 'has made Holland House a very fine place; [but] Kent's death has rather put a stop to much farther improvement'.[13] And from the remaining correspondence between Henry Fox and the horticulturalist Peter Collinson this stress on the male landowner as creator would seem to be further confirmed. Throughout the 1750s and 1760s Henry Fox was writing to Collinson asking for his

Figure 4.4 Richard Bentley, Sketch for a three-sided Chinese House at Holland Park.
Courtesy of The Lewis Walpole Library, Yale University
Showing the side to face the flower garden, Bentley's sketch is labelled 'For Mr Fox'
though both the flower garden and the larger landscape of Holland Park were very
much Caroline's domain.

advice and for supplies of various kinds of plants and seeds.[14] A letter
of 1750 suggests a rather conventional gender divide: 'Lady Caroline has
a thousand Questions to ask You about Flowers, and I not much fewer
about Plants' (Figure 4.4).[15] A decade later he wrote to Collinson that he
required a thousand cedars of Lebanon at a cost of £75, and then continued in a tone almost comic in its masculine virility, 'Pray lett me have a
Prodigious Quantity of *good seed for sowing for I have Hundreds of acres* to
plant.'[16]

Much as Henry Fox delighted in sowing his seed, it was ultimately Caroline who became most closely associated with the Holland House estate,
and the brief hints we can derive from the Holland House Papers from the
1740s and 1750s along with the more sustained discussion of Caroline's
gardening activities in her letters to her sisters from the 1760s and 1770s
suggest a rather more complex picture of gardening at Holland House than
these opening accounts of male creativity imply. Collinson, Brown, and
Charles Hamilton – the last of these a family friend, subordinate to Fox

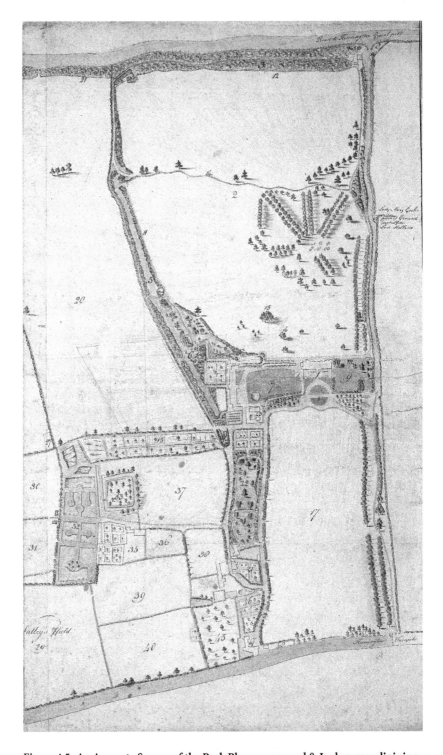

Figure 4.5 An Accurate Survey of the Park Pleasure ground & Inclosures adjoining
to Holland House in the County of Middlesex the Seat of the Right Honorable Lord
Holland Survey'd July A.D. 1770 By J[ohn] Haynes. ©The Trustees of the British
Museum (1880,1113.5568)

in the Pay Office, creator of Painshill in nearby Surrey, and debtor to Fox for a £10,000 mortgage – all played a part in advising on the laying out of the estate; but Caroline Fox's role was crucial, and it was sustained.[17] It is Caroline who seems to have been most closely involved in the making of views, in the siting of objects, but also in the actual use of the garden as a place of enjoyment (Figure 4.5).[18]

As early as 1750 she wrote to Henry, 'I have a vast deal more affection for [Holland House] than one should have for a Place', but by 1764 recognised that in this she was now alone.[19] Certainly throughout the 1760s, as her husband's attention turned to a newly purchased seaside residence in Kent, it was Caroline who directed the planting, the making of walks and the opening up of views within and beyond the estate. Henry Fox was undoubtedly in control of estate management, and it was to Henry that Charles Hamilton wrote his advice on how to keep the park and pleasure grounds in good order at a reasonable expense;[20] but it was Caroline who appears to have been responsible for the use of sheep and cattle to create movement in the park landscape, for placing benches around the estate to orchestrate particular views (including her favourite gothic bench near the Acton road), for continuing to plant trees and shrubs, for devising new plantations, and for making new walks around the pleasure grounds right up until her death in 1774.[21]

In 1759, looking back over the previous decade, Caroline makes clear in a series of letters to her sister Emily her active involvement in the creation of the gardens: 'I grow fonder every year of my pretty plantations and always routing the trees about, opening in this place and planting up in another, it's infinitely amusing.'[22] She also addresses, and quickly dismisses, those gendered assumptions about women and gardens which place them firmly within the confines of the flower garden:

I have been mighty busy planting and making a very pretty alteration in my pleasure ground. I have asked you forty times and you won't answer me, don't you delight in

←——————————————————————————————————————

The eastern half of the estate late in Caroline Holland's life; to the north the park (top), to the south the great meadow (bottom); west of the house (left) is the kitchen garden and stables, with the Green Walk (a major focus of gardening attention) running north-west. At the boundary with the Acton Road (top) Lady Holland was still siting benches and laying out gravel paths until her death in 1774. On the eastern boundary (far right), the lane separating Holland Park from Mary Coke's gardens, with annotation marking the small area of land she leased from her neighbours to improve her views.

scarlet oaks? Is it not charming to sit under shade of one's own planting? I'm fonder of plants and trees than ever I can rightly take to flowers. I love some excessively, particularly the spring ones, but I can't mind them enough to have 'em in great perfection; I should like a gardener that could.[23]

Quite conventionally she takes delight in the 'shade of one's own planting'. But if in 1750 Henry Fox chose to divide the horticultural world between women's flowers and men's woody growths, it was a distinction Caroline had learned to resist by 1759. Flowers here are the province of the gardener, the paid labourer; alterations, the choice of planting, and the act of design are what Caroline claims as her own. What is also important here is the stress on activity, on business, on action, rather than the relative passivity of reading; there is a stress on excitement here that isn't, for example, to be found when she records sitting down to her needlework. This surely comes from both a sense of creativity on a large scale, and – though this is only hinted at in the kinds of comments I have quoted above – a sense of treading on traditionally masculine terrain. Like her sister Emily (Countess of Kildare), who was heavily involved in the making of her gardens at Carton in Ireland, and her sister Sarah who designed her own house and had it built by their brother the Duke of Richmond, Caroline refused to be confined to the domestic world of flowers and took on instead the making of a ninety-acre park and pleasure ground. This is not to argue that Henry Fox played no role in the making of the Holland House landscape – of course he did – but it is to argue that Caroline Holland's role was at least as significant.

What marks the difference between husband and wife can be explained in part by the garden that took Henry Fox's attention away from Holland House. Since the early 1760s Henry Fox had been looking for a seaside residence that would be genuinely secluded from London life. His desire for a place away from London was made acute by two major factors: failing health meant that his doctors repeatedly advised sea bathing and a break from the unhealthy atmosphere of London; a failing political career and the loss of the lucrative Pay Office – looming in 1763 but held on to until 1765 – meant that, as the newly ennobled Lord Holland, Henry could indulge that classic activity of the ousted statesman: political retirement and moral outrage.[24] In this desire for an estate that would truly separate them from the world of politics he was joined by Caroline, but it is at this estate, Kingsgate in Kent, that the gendered nuances of retirement become most apparent.

In 1762 Caroline wrote to her sister Emily about a scheme for retirement. It would not be 'such absolute retirement as when we talked of it for six weeks; I want to stay in a place and that place to be fifty miles at least from London' and with room for 'one or two friends that choose to visit us'. The point of such a retreat would be to live a less grand life, a less public life, and a less political life:

What I wish is only to live one year in a less and more private way than we now do, just as many people of 2 or 3000 pounds a year do in the country, for Holland house, tho' I doat on the place, distracts me for the first two months I get there.[25]

Kingsgate was certainly much smaller than the Holland House estate, and, on the Isle of Thanet at the extreme north-eastern tip of Kent, it seemed to offer the kind of seclusion Caroline desired. In May 1762 she described it as a 'neat little habitation' with 'a neat little parlour ... a little comfortable drawing-room ... a little stable ... We are so quiet and pleasant here it's quite delightful'.[26] This stress on the delights of the little and the neat is inflected by that common fantasy of eighteenth-century literature – and all too apparent in Caroline's reading of Rousseau – the joys of cottage life. For Caroline, then, the search for a country retreat was recognisably a form of pastoral. It articulated the desire of a wealthy and public woman for a less complex life, a life away from the world of fine ladies and low politics, the desire for a life that Holland House was increasingly unable to offer. By September of the same year, still at Kingsgate, she wrote to Emily:

Nobody will agree with you more than I do that Holland House is one of the finest, most agreeable places in the world both within doors and without, and such is my fondness and partiality to it I should feel exceeding sorry not to pass the greatest part of my life there; but that I live so comfortable there as here, I will not allow. Health, spirits, solitude, and regularity, are things I enjoy here, the two first very much owing to the two last, which are not in my power to enjoy long together at Holland House; a sweet place to be sure, with pretty loitering and sauntering about, great pleasure in my plants and flowers, but even that I can seldom enjoy for a whole morning without interruption. Here, I confess, there is no amusement of that kind; but one's hours are one's own, very regular, and very early, not one visitor to come and prevent one taking a walk or a drive, both delightful in this place ... No people of business coming to Mr Fox; no dressing to go to Court, or any other stupid engagement; no loo, no great dinners, in short none of the things qui sont faits (as Martin says this world was) pour me faire enrager.[27]

These delights are pastoral because they are the delights of absence, and at least in the first year after they arrived at Kingsgate Caroline vied with Henry as to who enjoyed life away from London, from the court, and from company the most. At the end of their first summer in Kent she wrote in her journal that she had spent as 'Happy nine weeks as ever I passed we lived quite retired, our house too small for Company'.[28] In this desire for seclusion and the relish for a life of domestic retirement Henry appeared also to play his part, writing to Caroline in late 1763: 'Can you with truth say that you like Kingsgate Life better than I do? Indeed you cannot... Politicks, or political friendships, or rather Acquaintance, shall not take up one quarter of an Hour.'[29] A month later he wrote again: 'as to Kingsgate it will be endear'd to you by its difference from other Places... Indeed My Dear, Politicks will never more interfere with our Domestick Happiness.'[30] But in this he was wrong. Henry could not let go of politics or of political company, and Caroline's Kingsgate journal records the steady increase of both in life at Kingsgate: by 1764 their rural retreat was hosting dinner for nine; by 1768, and with the expansion of the house, Caroline ended her account of the year with the comment, 'unpleasant summer to me too many people in the house, latter season very wet, visiters'.[31]

More than all of this perhaps, while the gardens at Holland House were large enough to offer their own kind of retreat from political life, Kingsgate was rapidly becoming a political landscape in the tradition of Stowe and with this came the reassertion of a traditional gender divide. Caroline quickly set to work on a formally-arranged flower garden directly behind the villa and, as at Holland House, she was heavily involved in the interior decoration.[32] Beyond this, however, the landscape was the work of, and at times the obsession of, her husband. Henry bought the Kingsgate estate for £1880 in 1766 – more than a year before he finally agreed to his wife's long-standing wish to buy Holland House – a year earlier he had already spent over £2500 on buildings; a year later he spent another £1000; and finally in 1768 another £850 to complete the major phase of building work.[33] What he created was nothing if not quirky; it was also nothing if not political. Whereas at Holland House the great names of landscape design and horticulture had been brought in to advise, Kingsgate was for Henry Holland a much more personal affair. With the aid of amateur architects and friends – and rejecting at least some of the designs of Robert Adam in 1767 – the house was remodelled in the style of Cicero's Formian Villa and a series of frail flint and chalk gothic ruins were erected across the landscape (Figure 4.6).[34] The combination of classical and gothic architecture was in itself a convention of garden structures, a neat shorthand for the owner's claims to both a classical and patriotically British heritage. Joined together these styles were a reminder of the greatness of the classical past and of the frailty of empire, a means of claiming Saxon vigour as one's own and a celebration that such days of violence and superstition were now safely in Britain's past.

Figure 4.6 View in watercolour of Kingsgate Bay on the Isle of Thanet in Kent (1800). ©The British Library Board (Ktop vol. 18 image 30b)
Lady Holland's flower garden (largely hidden from view) was symmetrically arranged either side of a path leading from the back of the villa (centre) past the 'Convent' (top right). She wrote of the estate: 'My little garden there is soon done; flowers grow well, plants slowly if at all. Lord Holland's works don't amuse me; building old ruins and gateways I can't care about; they amuse him tho', which gives me great satisfaction.'

In these claims, Henry might of course align himself with any number of other landowners, Whig or Tory, in government or out. But they took on a particular significance because of the political moment at which they were erected and because of his own part in that moment. As Paymaster, and more particularly as a political fixer of great skill, Henry Fox played a crucial role in negotiating the peace at the end of the Seven Years' War. While he was also able to negotiate for himself a peerage, and became Lord Holland, he was ultimately removed from office for the part that he played. At Kingsgate, the combination of classical villa and gothic garden structures claimed for Lord Holland the role of Roman senator ousted by a corrupt administration, and reasserted his credentials as a patriot who held on to his country's ancient values and liberties. Again, such claims were not new – James Thomson's poem, *The Seasons*, claimed just such a role for Lord Lyttelton in retirement at Hagley in the 1740s – what was particular about them was that they were erected in the face of bitter invective and repeated claims in the press and from his erstwhile political allies that far from being patriotic he was, 'the public defaulter of unaccounted millions'.

Once he had left the Pay Office many of Lord Holland's one-time friends and more of his long-time enemies called for a public inquiry and prosecution over his alleged misuse of state funds. One of the few people who didn't was Thomas Harley, Lord Mayor of London. Henry chose to commemorate this support from an unknown man, along with his outrage that long friendships turned out to be no more than temporary expedients, in the form of Harley Tower. He wrote of this new Roman structure, 'My tower in honour of Mr Harley is built, I believe, more for my private amusement than from public spirit. But he is really almost the only man that has not been a coward. This gave me the thought, but I own the desire of making Kingsgate prettier than it is put it into execution.'[35] That shift between public and private motives, between earnest politics and aesthetic pleasures, captures neatly the problematic nature of many eighteenth-century garden structures. Kingsgate was certainly recognised by his contemporaries as a statement about Holland himself, and it became the opportunity for Thomas Gray's poem in which he characterised the buildings as an image of Holland's own corruption and ruin.[36] Indeed, for all that Holland appeared to dismiss Harley Tower as the pleasurable whim of a private man, it stood in the landscape as an expression of political outrage and as one further demonstration that the politician in retirement never leaves politics behind. We might add to this political outrage another motive for Henry Holland's building spree. Knowing that he was on his way out, Henry had made a deal to leave the ministry if he was in return given a peerage; the peerage was given, though not the earldom he had wanted. The monuments erected across the landscape at Kingsgate may also then have been an attempt to establish his own position in British history and to make concrete his passage from being the son of a lowly commoner, not fit for the daughter of the Duke of Richmond, to Lord Holland of Foxley.

In these architectural ripostes to Henry's political enemies, however, Caroline was resolutely uninterested. She wrote to Emily in 1764:

I agree with you I do think I have some taste in planting and laying out ground, which is very amusing work; I have none of that at Kingsgate. My little garden there is soon done; flowers grow well, plants slowly if at all. Lord Holland's works don't amuse me; building old ruins and gateways I can't care about; they amuse him tho', which gives me great satisfaction.[37]

One reason not to care for these new ruins was that they were building back into the landscape the political world from which Kingsgate had at first appeared to be a retreat. Moreover, while Caroline might plant her flower garden or build 'a little cover'd seat on the top of the cliff' at Kingsgate, alongside Henry's political monuments her activities seem to collapse back into those gendered stereotypes which confine women to a limited private world of temporary domestic pleasures while men engage in action, politics, and lasting endeavours.[38]

What, then, did retirement at Kingsgate mean for the Hollands? We might argue that Kingsgate illustrates a classic example of masculine political retirement to which women can make no claim: barred from public office, Caroline Holland was barred also from the stance of meditative ease after national labours. But we should also question this, for in crucial respects what Caroline Holland desired was also surely a form of political retirement. Perhaps the most striking aspect of the Lennox sisters' correspondence is the sheer quantity of politics that fills their letters. Caroline may not have held public office, but the all-consuming political world of Henry was undoubtedly also hers. From this perspective, then, we might argue that Caroline's desire for retirement to Kingsgate was also a desire for the kind of political retirement we usually associate with men. It was different, certainly, but the difference lay not least in Caroline's genuine desire to leave that world behind and Henry's inability to do so. Indeed, if we look to those classical models of the statesman's moral retirement, it is Caroline who characterised her life in terms we might recognise from Horace or Pliny – 'I read, work, write, walk, drive, live regularly and quietly, and consequently agreeably' – and Henry who built monuments as frail as his own health, and could not leave the world alone.[39]

Earlier I suggested that we could understand the attraction of Kingsgate in terms of pastoral precisely because those charms were about absence. In some ways this was also the case for Holland House, but here the absences multiply, and perhaps the most important of these was Caroline's own absence from Holland House. That is, we should also understand Holland House in terms of what it was not: it was not (quite) London, it was not the extended and often tiring periods of travel which increasingly took up the 1760s, and on the whole it was not for Caroline a place of illness in a way that was associated with all-too-regular convalescences at Bath. All of these cut down the amount of time that Caroline actually spent at Holland House; all also contributed to her experience of her gardens. Thus, another feature that we should recognise in the experience of the garden is its temporality. As with many aristocratic country estates, Holland House was used predominantly in the summer, but from the early 1760s on it had to compete not only with winter in London and Bath, but also with Kingsgate, the seaside, and continental travel in the summer. The result was that Holland House was a distinctly temporary experience for its inhabitants – it was a place of great beauty and delight for Caroline Holland but by the 1760s a place only seen briefly each year.

All of this may go some way to explaining the intensity with which Caroline wrote of Holland House when she was there. If by 1764 Kingsgate had lost some of its appeal for Caroline, Holland House still continued to exert its charm, and her shifting response to the two estates – always looking for a further temporary retreat from society – tells us much about what drove her both to garden, and into her garden. Indeed, one absence in which Caroline could only occasionally express delight was the absence of company. It was this, after all, that had initially made Kingsgate seem so appealing, and it was the crowding in of Henry's political 'friends' that had destroyed her enjoyment of it. This might suggest that Caroline's experience of the garden was driven by a dislike of company and by the need for solitude, but she was by no means a recluse in the manner of, say, Elizabeth Rowe, who actively shunned the company even of her friends in favour of pious retreat. In Paris both Caroline and Henry wrote of her enjoyment of the company she kept and the conversation that could be had. The problem was England, and more than this it was London. When in Paris, she wrote to Lady Susan Fox, 'you cant imagine how infinitely more agreeable our English Men make themselves . . . than they condescend to do in their own Country, they visit one and sit and chat with one continually in short are quite different creatures from what they are in London'.[40] At Holland House, the talk seemed to be only of politics and she wrote to Emily in 1761: 'Holland House life has not been an agreeable one these many years, and I regret that I can't lead a pleasant life in the place I love best at the season when it's most pleasant. I don't love a life of company in general, but that of Holland House is the worst sort of company.'[41]

Two things recur in the letters of women writing about their experience of the garden: the oppressiveness of solitude, and thoughts of absent friends which spring from that solitude; but in the case of Caroline Holland we find something of the reverse. Surrounded by her husband's political 'friends', brief moments in the garden are a flight from London, its politics, its fashion, and its impositions. They also offered something more positive, however. Not least they offered pleasure – one of those experiences so hard to pin down from the traces we are left of the past. To this we might add her claims of calm, peace, and health. Indeed, a striking feature of her account of her gardens is the sheer enjoyment she gained from them. While Elizabeth Montagu might use her gardens to rehearse her intellectual and financial status, and while as we will see in the coming pages, Mary Coke might stave off her anguish by insistent garden labour, for Caroline Holland the garden's combination of solitude and activity made it a place of pleasure. Thus, in 1764 she wrote with excitement to her sister:

I doat on this place, and lament I am the only one of the family that enjoys it. The evergreens are in the nighest beauty, the American trees you name I have been these ten years worrying you to admire, and at last you have had the sense to find out their beauty. Norway maple is a most beautiful tree, and don't come out very late; have you admired them yet?

I have been busy making some little alterations here which have amused me, and are done, as you may suppose, in a mighty good taste. My chief work is now clearing and cutting down trees to let in peeps here and there, and also to prevent the trees killing and over-running one another as they did at Goodwood. I have really cut down oaks that are quite timber.[42]

With intermittent poor health throughout her life, it was also in the gardens of Holland House that Caroline felt most healthy. Her belief in the healthiness of gardens was of course not unusual, but she sustained it throughout her life, whether in her hope that Holland House would revive her ailing son, or in the strict regimen she laid down for her husband at Kingsgate in his final years, or in the recognition that her own spirits – prone to depression – were lifted by the gardens she created.[43] At a time when she found, 'To be quite well above ten days at a time I never expect, when it comes to being very bad for a fortnight or three weeks together it wears me out, and I rather wish to be bad enough to have it over for good', the garden offered entertainment but it also offered a form of solitude that she found reviving. Looking forward to a summer at Holland House in 1759, she wrote to Emily:

living alone suits my disposition best, at least passing a great deal of my time so. I'm always in the best spirits when I do. I don't love work much, you know, nor do I vastly love being read to. I love to saunter about the gardens, looking at plants, flowers, etc., by myself, or being shut up in my own dressing room reading or writing; this is the way I love to pass my mornings.

By the end of the summer her view had not changed and she wrote to Emily of this period: 'Most part of my morning when I was alone here, indeed all that fine weather, I was employed in planting and alterations out of doors. My spirits are generally good when I live alone, which is odd I think.'[44] Despite Caroline's strong Christian beliefs, what is notably absent in this engagement with the garden – for all that it stresses solitude, quiet, and the state of one's spirits – is any insistent articulation of pious faith which looks forward to an afterlife and which we have already seen expressed by Elizabeth Montagu and more insistently by the reclusive Elizabeth Rowe. Indeed, the parallel, or rather the disparity, with Montagu is illuminating here. Montagu, as we have seen, also regularly styled herself as a woman alone in a garden, but what Montagu's letters make apparent is their own stylisation and careful literary self-representation. This is far less apparent in the words of Caroline Holland, and while Montagu fills her letters with carefully staged accounts of herself thinking in her garden, Caroline Holland makes much more limited claims. What she shares with Montagu, perhaps, is a nagging worry about leisure and about how time in one's garden should be justified; but where Montagu claimed thoughtfulness and expansive philosophical contemplation, Caroline Holland claimed for herself amusement, peace, and pleasure. Holland House offered the pleasure of seeing her plants, the pleasure of peace, of quiet, and of course the pleasure of leaving behind her husband's insistent political world.

What we see here, then, as with other women gardeners, is a confrontation of solitude which can lead either to a sense of release from the impositions of society or a reinforcement of one's sense of loneliness. What we can also see, however, is an insistence on those pleasures of the garden that are not simply abstract or intellectual. Unlike Montagu's account of Sandleford, Caroline Holland's garden at Holland House was not a paper-and-ink stage for a learned and literary self-representation. There is a pleasure here that extends from watching the growth of plants to the growth of a landscape; and there is a pleasure here in solitude. Though she appears not to have known it, it is the enjoyment of retirement and solitude that most clearly marks out the inhabitant of Holland House from her neighbour, Lady Mary Coke; and it is to Mary Coke that we should now turn, for, divided from Holland Park by only the narrowest of paths, her experience of her garden, of her solitude, and of the society she inhabited was altogether different.

II. I saw nobody: Mary Coke and Notting Hill

Mary Coke was convinced that people talked behind her back and treated her as a figure of fun. They did. She arrived at Notting Hill in 1767, more than twenty years after Caroline and Henry Fox took up residence at neighbouring Holland House. She had been a subject of their gossip for about as long. Mary Coke's experience of life at the rural edge of Kensington was undoubtedly different from that of her neighbours, despite their proximity, but this should not mask from us the strangely parallel trajectory that landed the two women in their respective gardens. Caroline Fox arrived at Holland House with the fashionable world still talking of her scandalous elopement and with her parents treating her estate as a place of banishment. Mary Coke likewise came to Notting Hill after a celebrated scandal, and, though hers had come many years before, she carried it with her, never forgot it, and lived out her periods of retirement all too aware of the society from which she felt separated. Both women's marriages had made them the talk of the town, both spent long periods travelling on the continent, both mixed with the highest in society despite their early discomfort, both suffered from a loss of 'spirits' that we might now recognise as a form of depression, and both, in strikingly different ways, chose solitude, retirement, and gardening.

Even more than her wealthy neighbour, Lady Mary Coke was the creator of the garden in which she spent so much time (Figure 4.7). She was also an avid writer: for most of her adult life she wrote extensive letter-journals to her sisters recording everything from social events to a poor night's sleep, and it is these letter-journals which give us such detailed access to her garden and her life.[45] From late in 1767 she embarked on an intense period of landscaping which coincided with a period of particular unhappiness in her life and which lasted for about three years. During that time she expanded the gardens by leasing land from the Hollands (Figure 4.5) and other neighbours; with the aid of the Hollands too (who cut down trees at her request), she created views to the villages around Notting Hill; a mount was constructed so that those views could be extended; gravel walks were laid out; her courtyard was redesigned; and, with the aid of Kennedy and Lee, the London nurserymen, she planted trees and shrubs, exotics and evergreens on a substantial scale (Figure 4.8).[46] More than this, if her neighbours at Holland House directed the labour of others, Mary Coke set to work on the gardens at Notting Hill with her own hands. She regularly reported on being out in her garden till late in the evening, planting out fifty plants for the new walk, weeding because her gardener would not do the work, and pruning for the same reason (in July 1768 she wrote, 'I worked hard all this Evening, tying up honeysuckles, sowing annuals, & weeding. I wish my Gardener took half as much pleasure as I do, for my garden wou'd then be kept better').[47] She could go through three sets of stockings a day if the weather was wet, and walked out of a morning with her dedicated gardening apron, her trowel, her shears, and her basket. This then, was a working garden rather than a pleasure ground maintained by the labour of others. Caroline Holland might characterise her time in the garden as sauntering: for Mary Coke it was always 'work'. That distinction is important because it marks a crucial difference in how these two women experienced the landscapes they created. Both women spent substantial periods away from their gardens while undertaking foreign travel, and both wrote intensely of them when they were home again; but what distinguishes

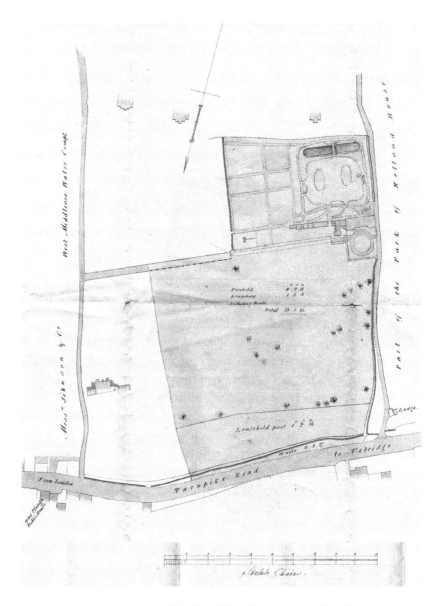

Figure 4.7 J. Osborn, Survey of Notting Hill, 1823. Courtesy of Royal Borough of Kensington & Chelsea, Family & Children's Service
The survey shows Mary Coke's garden much as it was in her time. To the south of the house are the more formal gardens and ponds (top right); to the north of the turning circle is the pasture which was home to Miss Pelham (bottom); to the west (far right) the lane marking the boundary with Holland Park, and the 'North Walk' where Lady Mary focussed much of her gardening attention (note that north is to the bottom of the map).

Figure 4.8 Notting Hill, view from the south, 1817. Courtesy of Royal Borough of Kensington & Chelsea, Family & Children's Service
The house and gardens were painted by Mrs Goldsmid several decades after Lady Mary's residence; while the gardens are likely to have been simplified after her departure Lady Mary's layout and planting remain much in evidence.

the two women most clearly is their experience of solitude. Certainly it is the concern with, and experience of, solitude that make Mary Coke's detailed journals from her time at Notting Hill such a rich source for us when we try to understand the role that the garden might play in the life of an individual.

In March 1748 Caroline Fox wrote to her husband for the second time in a month asking for news of the latest scandal buzzing around Bath:

When you have time do tell me about Lord and Lady Coke. There are various reports here about them. Sr C Windham tells me Lord Leicester first abused Lady M and forbid her seeing Lady Fane . . . Then begd pardon and that Lord Coke is at his (his Fathers) House I mean and Lady Mary with her Mother some people say they are both ill & dying some say Lord Coke is mad and shut up, pray tell me all you can learn about it.[48]

With no reply, she wrote again the following day:

I hear Mr OBrian is very much in love with Lady M Coke and interests himself exceedingly about her – does Lady M like him is her wrong behaviour Lord Hartington mention'd to you any thing of that sort? If tis I think her not much to blame surely to such a brute all is fair . . . I'm very curious to know about it because I hear so many different reports.[49]

Offering only a brief reply, Henry Fox claimed less interest, but from London to Bath, from East Anglia to Argyll, Lady Mary Coke had become the most scandalous figure of her day. As the unwilling but finally dutiful victim of the Campbell family's dynastic ambition she had been married to the notoriously libertine Viscount Coke, son of the equally libertine Lord Leicester. Married in 1747, and faced with Coke's continuingly riotous and threatening behaviour, she proved an unwilling wife. By 1748 she was desperate for a divorce and the subsequent proceedings caused a stir not only because divorce was relatively rare and made for salacious gossip, but because this was a divorce which eventually set two of the most powerful families and their allies against each other in a very public arena. Horace Walpole wrote to his friend Montagu that he had spent three days in London and had 'heard the history of Lord Coke three thousand different ways. I expect next winter to hear of no Whigs and Jacobites, no courtiers and patriots, but of the Cokes and the Campbells – I do assure you the violence is incredible with which this affair is talked over.'[50] Walpole's letter goes on to record tales of duels, wife beating, and attempted murder, but Mary Coke also left at least part of her own account, an account that goes some way towards explaining her life at Notting Hill twenty years later.

In a series of letters to Henrietta Howard, Lady Suffolk, Mary Coke bewailed her increasingly miserable life with Coke and her increasingly desperate attempts to get her family to remove her from her husband's house. Soon after her wedding, and already known by the servants as 'our Virgin Mary' because of her refusal to consummate the marriage, she wrote that Lord Coke had struck her on the arm and torn her ruffle to shreds, that she was being locked in a room, that her letters were being read or withheld, and that she feared for her life.[51] To her sister she wrote 'to implore your assistance for the most wretched Being in the World, for God Almighty's sake take compassion on your Unhappy Sister: something sure might be done to alleviate my Misery'.[52] And her sister in turn wrote to Lady Suffolk of Lord Coke's behaviour, 'about three days ago, as I left Lord Coke & Lady Mary together, while I went to finish a letter, he took that opportunity to abuse her in such a manner that notwithstanding all you know, I believe will surprise you'.[53] Faced with this behaviour the whole family rallied round in her support. But one of the most striking features of the letters that survive is her series of accusation that her family were not doing enough to help her escape from the marriage. She accused her sister, her brother-in-law, her parents, of having no love for her, of abandoning her in her hour of need, of showing her no friendship.[54] When Lady Suffolk suggested that not everything could be said in a letter that might be opened by the Leicesters, and counselled restraint, Mary read the letters again and then concluded:

those from my Sisters I cannot find any other intention they had in writing them (as circumstances are) but to afflict me. Tis true, tis a hard construction to put on the conduct of those who call themselves friends, and yet I know not what other interpretation to put on the contents of their letters. Is it my Dear Lady Suffolk consistent with friendship to add to ones distress? and have I deserved such treatment from them? O Dear Madam I find by this cruel experience that the unkindness of friends is infinitely more terrible, then all the injurious usage that can be inflicted on one by Enemies; and this I am a judge of, for tis certain that I have indured such hardships & misery, as I believe few besides myself have ever suffer'd. But I assure your Ladyship that tis you alone that shall ever learn from me this instance of their cruelty, and I will myself indeavour to forget it, and if possible never reproach them even in thought. But give me leave to say to Your Ladyship what I have just wrote to the Duke of Argyll. I told his grace that I fancy's the little assistance that I was like to receive from them, was occasion'd by their never having known what it was to be unhappy. But I told him that I was far from wishing that they might ever be brought to commiserate my condition by being made sensible of what I had suffer'd, for that cou'd not happen without their feeling an equal degree of misery, which God forbid they ever shou'd.[55]

Mary Coke's near contemporary and biographer, Lady Louisa Stuart, may have had the majority on her side when she characterised Lady Mary as 'invincibly wrong-headed' and as a woman whose 'understanding lay smothered under so much pride, self-conceit, prejudice, obstinacy, and violence of temper, that you knew not where to look for it'; and yet these letters – for all their threats and pride, delusions, and self-righteousness – recount a period of anguish and terror which we should not dismiss as mere eccentricity even if the judge at the divorce trial did.[56] Failing to provide any evidence of cruelty beyond her own peremptory assertions, the divorce proceedings inevitably failed. A separation was finally agreed, but this was itself another blow. According to Stuart, the triumphant Leicesters' price for the separation was an agreement that 'she should withdraw her suit, pay its expenses herself, never set her foot in town, and have no separate maintenance but her pin-money'.[57] Banned from London, the talk of the town, and in disgrace, Mary Coke went to live with her mother at Sudbrook in Surrey.

Five years later she was released from the marriage by the death of her husband; but twenty years later her own sense of the scandal, and more particularly her sense that she had been let down by her friends continued to weigh heavily on her. In the belief that scandal still hung about her she appears to have been almost entirely alone. While her theatrical performance in court had done little to gain the sympathy of the polite world – she appeared in rags and tears throughout – the Leicesters' behaviour towards her, and the passage of time, meant that whatever scandal has been attached to her in 1748 was largely forgotten by the time of her husband's death in 1753. Lady Mary seems to have clung to it, however, as a badge of shame, as a reason to avoid London, and as a reason to be suspicious of even her friends. This no doubt made her difficult to deal with, and it was in part what made her a figure of fun in the letters of her friends and family; it was also a crucial part of what drove her to an almost obsessive three-year period of gardening after her arrival at Notting Hill in 1767.

The move to Notting Hill in 1767 coincided almost exactly with the death of the Duke of York, with whom Lady Mary had formed a long-term intimacy.[58] Walpole's version of events is that she claimed a secret marriage and was outraged when her friends refused to believe her; her own diaries suggest not marriage but certainly a belief that he might at some point propose. When the Duke died, Lady Mary's very public grief found little sympathy (it was the occasion for the anecdote by Caroline Holland's sister with which I opened this chapter). As far away as Nice, Henry Holland was already dreading her appearance at Holland House: 'L[ad]y Mary Coke I hear continues inconsolable for the D[uke] of Y[ork], Princess A[melia] much lessens the dignity of L[ad]y Mary's sighs by calling it gaping, I dread her Ladys[hi]p sighing with me at H[olland] House I'm sure if she does she will make me Yawn.'[59]

Though she wrote to them almost daily in her letter-journals, Coke's sisters were hardly more sympathetic. Even before the Duke's death, Lady Dalkieth (later baroness Greenwich) had written to Lady Susan Stewart a wry account of Lady Mary's behaviour with the royal family and then continued, 'You see, my dear Lady Susan, what confidence I repose... by divulging the History of Mary. Consider the cross looks I should have if she ever knew it, and for my sake bury it deep in your own breast, but laugh and be amused yourself with it as much as I wish'.[60]

The lack of sympathy for her perceived loss seems to have recalled for Lady Mary that period in the late 1740s when she had once before felt completely abandoned by her friends. With the move to Notting Hill, the journals start to record both a deep-seated unhappiness in her solitary life and a recognition of the importance of gardening as an attempt to fend off depression. Long before this, Lady Mary had been a keen gardener. At her mother's estate at Sudbrook she had already got into the habit of working in the garden from morning till night, and not only giving directions to gardeners and carpenters, but taking an active role in planting, opening views, painting benches, and then painting them again after they had been spoiled by rain. She would hurry her breakfast and be late for her evening appointments so that she could spend more time in the garden.[61] What letters there are from the years before she arrived at Notting Hill suggest an ability to be happy in her garden, to enjoy it as a place of pleasure and absorption. But Notting Hill marked a change. The coincidence of living alone, the death of the Duke of York, and the sense once again of being let down and ridiculed by those closest to her made life at Notting Hill a quite different affair. Instead of being a place of welcome retreat from social demands, Notting Hill became the confirmation and the demonstration of a lonely solitude that no language of literary retirement could make pleasant.

Indeed, the cultural expectations surrounding the tradition of retirement was part of the problem: what might appear to be a supportive and enabling framework of meditative retirement could ultimately be oppressive because it represented another failure, an inability to do what one's culture insists one *should* do. Certainly when writing to her sister in 1768, Lady Mary questioned such complacent notions of female retirement:

You tell me that it is often said that happiness and contentment is to be found in retirement: I differ from the opinion, as I am persuaded retirement is never the effect of Choice; it may indeed be the best and most eligible thing for those who are disgusted with the World, by the sorrows and disappointments they may have mett with in it, but I fancy it is never accompanied with happiness, & in the case You mention, the poor Duchess of Grafton, who has brought all her distress upon herself, what chance has She for peace or contentment by having more time for reflection?[62]

The Duchess of Grafton was indeed a case in point, for, after separating from a husband who had taken to flaunting his mistress in public, the Duchess had tried the reclusive life, but been separated from her children, and, on giving birth to an illegitimate child by her future husband, the Earl of Upper Ossory, was finally divorced by the distinctly self-righteous Duke.[63] Walpole, who had become a close friend of the Duchess, thought her decision to separate from the Duke a mistake that arose from the poor advice

of other 'friends', and certainly, if the Duchess's flirtation with retirement
was intended to reclaim a wayward husband, it failed. In this account of the
Duchess and of the potential miseries of meditation brought on by scandal
Mary Coke undoubtedly saw something of herself. She saw, too, that easy
moral assumptions about the benefits of retirement could not adequately
encompass complex lives: if retirement could offer the opportunity for
reflection, such reflection could itself be deeply disabling: instead of an
opportunity to meditate instructively on one's past life or on futurity in
the way that, say, Elizabeth Montagu might claim, it could become instead
a means of dwelling on one's misery, a constant reminder of one's social
disgrace.[64]

In her account of the Duchess, Coke offers us a figure reminiscent of
the lonely impenitent women we have already met in Elizabeth Rowe's
moral tales. Insisting that the Duchess brought distress and punishment
upon herself, Coke clearly sought to distance herself from such archetypes;
and yet what complicates our understanding of retirement further is that
while Coke would hardly align herself with the shaky morals of impenitent
women, her experience of solitude was in some respects alarmingly similar.
Where Rowe's fallen heroines might exclaim from their country obscurity
that, 'thinking is my horror',[65] Coke's journals to her sister regularly record
a comparable loneliness and fear of thought:

I was out in my Garden till twelve O'clock, when it began raining, & it never held
up for any time after. It goes bad with me when I am confined almost the Whole
day to the House: so much time for thought when misery is all one has to think of
is very terrible. Mr Pope or somebody else said in their letters that the Unfortunate
were of all others the most unfit to be alone, yet the World generally took care they
shou'd be so; this observation I have experienced to be true, for tho' within the little
distance of two miles & a half from Town, 'tis very seldom that anybody ever comes
to me.[66]

Working in the garden – which for Caroline Holland could be an elegant
literary allusion to Rousseau, and an equally elegant means of justifying
her leisure – was for Mary Coke a necessity brought on by the very solitude her neighbour desired. Unlike reading – which could all too easily be
'interrupted by my miserable reflections on the sorrows of my life' – the
physicality of gardening, the concentration on finite, repetitive, and consuming tasks offered some kind of relief from thought, a means of blocking
it out, of holding melancholy at bay for at least as long as the labour continued. At Notting Hill, then, solitary retirement represented not that classical

or Christian ideal of pious and contemplative ease; rather it bore an uneasy resemblance to those traditions of eighteenth-century fiction which linked retirement with scandal and which forced women into country obscurity as a form of punishment. As I have also suggested, it bore an uneasy resemblance to Mary Coke's earlier life and to her sense of abandonment when most in need of aid. In 1748 she had written to her sister: 'I am sorry to say that after having been alone a twelve month in this place, and during the greater part of that time suffering under all the misery and hardship that could be inflicted on the greatest criminal, that I have the mortification to find, that my friends (or at least those that call themselves so) shou'd have attempted nothing in my favour.'[67] Twenty years later, the absence of friendship continued to dominate her life, and over the three-year period in which the gardens were first laid out, Coke's journals contain a singular refrain that we can best understand by a series of entries (my emphasis throughout):

November 1767

More rain fell in the night; my ground is so wet, it is very disagreeable walking, yet as it is my only amusement, I contrive to be out. *Nobody came to see me.* I worked in the Garden as usual, & at five O'clock settled to my Books... Thursday. – The Weather was clearer and warmer. I have had a hedge cut that has much improved my view. While it was light I amused my thoughts with working in my garden, but I have since been very bad. As *Nobody comes near me,* I wish I had some one person in the House, for I find the being intirely alone increases my dejection of spirits, & at times I am so melancholy that I know not what to do.

...I planted many flowers & some plants, *but saw Nobody the Whole day...* Wednesday. – I have planted a great many flowers, & been out in my grounds while it was light, *but have seen nobody.*

By spring of the following year, nothing had changed:

April 1768

Thursday. – The Wind is as high as ever; 'tis disagreeable Weather. The Garden cannot be kept in order, 'tis litter'd all over with bows from the trees; several of my new planted ones have been blown down... *Nobody has been here today.* Numbers talked of coming, but I fancy the amusements of the Town will prevent them.

And by the following winter Coke was again recording a life quite unlike that of *The Spectator*'s social solitude:

September 1768

I've done a good deal of work in my garden, *but have seen Nobody*... I'm sorry I am reduced to writing about myself, but 'tis so seldom that anybody visits me, that tho' within three miles of Town I am often very much behind hand in intelligence... Saturday... *I've seen no creature*, nor done anything worth mentioning'

October 1768

Saturday.–I have worked in my garden all morning, but *I have seen Nobody.*

What the writing of these journal entries demonstrates is an uneasy shifting from the concentrated oblivion of garden labour to uncomfortable moments of reflection as the journal is written: 'I was out in my grounds a great while, tho' it rained all the time a small rain, & excessively cold. I have no variety to tell you of. I cannot amuse myself, how then shou'd I be able to amuse you? I think I had better leave off my journals.'[68]

The journal is both an attempt to create social contact and a reminder of its absence. Unlike a letter, it was not to be sent immediately; only later would a journal be posted on to Coke's sisters. In the meantime entry after entry noting the absence of company accrued. Thus, as the journal is written, a pattern emerges in which day after day of gardening is recorded, but as it is recorded, so it becomes a reminder that gardening is not enough: the garden offers a temporary release from loneliness, which the journal can then only recognise and represent as a form of loneliness, a loneliness that is to be set against an absent but tantalisingly close world of amusement, pleasure, activity, and sociability just three miles away.

This longing for company in the records of its absence continued throughout Coke's years at Notting Hill, and it highlights the peculiar nature of gardens as spaces at once public and private. It is of course wholly conventional to introduce descriptions of gardens by apologising for a lack of social news – as Mary Coke's journals repeatedly do – but the insistent appearance of the garden in her correspondence of the late 1760s marks more than a polite topic of conversation. If she found the garden absorbing, that absorption required apology because it emphasised the private self over the public world and implicitly one's distance from that world. In this sense Notting Hill held an awkward cultural position as an object of sociability (the subject described and shared in a letter) and a marker of social absence. As a potentially sociable space the garden affirmed an emptiness and an absence which she could not ignore. It was an occasion for company, but it brought the recognition of failure; it was an occasion for sociable letters, but raised fears that no one cared.

For all its personal fascination, then, and for all Coke's detailed journals to her sisters, Notting Hill appears here as a place of social failings,
a place haunted by an absent society; even her pet cow (Miss Pelham),
'took a frisk ... and went near as far as London' which Coke concluded was
because, 'She thinks my Place too retired, for She was found among a great
herd of Cattle'.[69] But as these journal entries make clear, there was another
side to a seclusion so deep that even cows found it oppressive: as a place
of retirement Mary Coke's garden was also a place of wished-for public
display, it was an invitation to the public even if that public rarely arrived.
There is another complication too. When Sir Gilbert Elliot visited her in
December 1767 and 'wonder'd my friends did not endeavour to persuade
me to quit so melancholy & retired a life', Coke replied quite characteristically that she 'had some reason to think that Nobody interested themselves
about me, for that I have seen few people in almost four Months'.[70] In
doing so, however, she misrepresented those friends she had: Elliot was in
fact only reiterating the advice given by numerous others. It was Coke who
hung on to retirement, and it was that insistence on retirement that perhaps
in part drove society away. Moreover, the solitude of which Mary Coke
complained was far less total than these entries suggest. Alongside the journal's insistent sense of being abandoned by the world lie accounts of visits
to town, attendance at court, and increasingly long periods of continental
travel.[71]

There are accounts too of all those who did visit Notting Hill: Horace
Walpole was a regular, as were Coke's sisters; the Duchess of Grafton admired
the view from the mount; Lady Blandford praised the North Walk; the Por-
tuguese ambassador promised flowers from his home. Indeed, the journals
betray a desire for praise quite as strong as the desire for company; and once
guests had arrived, and offered their praise, Coke was happy for them to be
on their way. Characteristically Coke recorded that after she had shown Lord
March her house and gardens (Figure 4.9), 'which he admired extremely.
I then wished him gone', and indeed for brief periods Coke's garden could
even be a welcome relief from company.[72] In the summer of 1769 she wrote
in her journal, 'It has been a Charming day, & I have injoy'd it free from
Company or interruption of any kind: my hay is now began, which is an
addition to the beauty of the prospect. Was this weather to last I shou'd
want no amusement out of my small territory: my books & my garden are
all the pleasure I have left: you cannot imagine the aversion I now have for
those entertainments I was used so much to frequent'; while in 1770, after a
particularly disastrous evening of cards she resolved to give up play, writing,
'I refused a party at Lu this evening, instead of which I wattered my Garden,

Figure 4.9 North Front of Notting Hill House, 1817. Courtesy of Royal Borough of Kensington & Chelsea, Family & Children's Service
Goldsmid's view is taken from the gravel court, or carriage circle, in front of the house; the north walk started directly behind the viewer (but had been abandoned by the 1790s); the boundary with Holland Park is to the immediate right of the house (also out of view).

which was not near so expensive' (neither the resolution nor the pleasure was to last).[73]

Once again we are left with a paradox: I have characterised Mary Coke's garden labour as an activity aimed at blocking society from her view; but it was quite as much an attempt to make herself, and her retirement, the object of social attention. Coke saw herself not as a mere flower gardener, but as a worthy rival to the other great landscape designers of her day. She might not be able to bring in Brown or Hamilton as her neighbours had done, but she could intervene in the design of Holland Park to agree with her own vision of the landscape. And if she could not garden on the scale of her sister and brother-in-law's vast estate at Wentworth Castle in Yorkshire, she made no disjunction in her mind between their creations and her own, insisting soon after her arrival at Notting Hill that even they would have to admire the situation of her new estate. She slowly increased the size of her garden and transformed it from an overgrown and neglected plot into a landscape recognisably aligned with an English style and with an aesthetic she sharply divided from the mistaken formality of foreign design.[74] Trees were moved and removed to create views into the wider landscape, plantations were sown, large cedars were bought, new walks and driveways were laid out, benches were sited, planting of shrubs and flowers, evergreens and oaks was undertaken on a large scale, and all of this was done with the expectation of admiration and approval from the wider world.

This desire for public praise that we find in Mary Coke's journals is of course a claim to the cultural capital of taste in landscape, just as it was with Caroline Holland; but there is an important difference. At Holland Park, Lady Holland broke away from flowers and flower gardens to take increasing control of the kind of park landscape generally associated with men; on a smaller scale, Mary Coke did the same. Unlike flower gardens – which could be neatly assimilated as the domestic space of women – gardening on this scale claimed a more public dimension, it moved the designers beyond the private and domestic and into a world of national taste and national significance more usually the domain of men. However, while Caroline Holland's landscape placed her on the public stage, and then offered her a retreat from that stage, for Mary Coke gardening on such a scale proffered the entry of a public world from which she otherwise claimed to absent herself. That is, landscape design implicitly renegotiated the terms of Mary Coke's retirement: if gardening helped her to efface a sense of social misfortune by keeping it from her mind, it was also an attempt to re-engage with society on her own terms, and on her own ground. Her journals, then, make apparent the all-too-ambiguous experience of retirement. Retirement here is not simply a question of whether one is with or without company, in London or the country, rather, it signals a sense of oneself in the world.

Caroline Holland's retirement was formed from brief moments of solitude in a garden that shielded her from her husband's political world; Mary Coke's signalled an experience of loss which was not just of society but the scandalous loss of her place in that society. In her later years Coke became an inveterate traveller and was increasingly seen in the public world, but at Notting Hill in the final years of the 1760s Coke was thrust into the garden by a retirement both wished for and hated. Her garden, which might have offered solace, at best offered absence; and gardening, which promised relief from reflection and an end to solitude, enforced for Mary Coke an awareness of that solitude, an awareness too of false, absent, and careless friends.

5 | 'Can you not forgive?':

Henrietta Knight at Barrells Hall

In 1736 Henrietta Knight (1699–1756) was banned from London, from living within twenty miles of the Bath Road, and from corresponding with her closest friends. Sent to a rundown country estate in the Midlands, she spent the rest of her life cultivating a small circle of friends, and a garden. Born Henrietta St John (Figure 5.1), she married Robert Knight junior in 1727 and, on his elevation to the Irish peerage in 1745, she took the title of Lady Luxborough. Her father was the cantankerous Henry St. John of Lydiard Tregoze and Battersea, and while her brothers John and Holles would go on to make almost no impact in the world, her eldest brother, or rather half-brother, was the arch politician, arch-rival of Robert Walpole, figure of near adoration for Alexander Pope, and figurehead of Tory opposition politics in the early eighteenth century, Henry St. John, Viscount Bolingbroke. When the crisis of Henrietta's life arrived, it was Bolingbroke (1678–1751) who proved himself Henrietta's closest family ally, and it was Bolingbroke who continued to influence her life as she entered a world of enforced retirement at the neglected Knight estate of Barrells Hall in Warwickshire. Like her half-brother, Henrietta Knight would find herself ousted from a very public life and forced to live in the country; like her half-brother, too, she would take to gardening in the absence of that public world; unlike her half-brother, gardening would not be for her a means of self-justification and rehabilitation around which powerful public allies would gather in support.[1]

Knight's letters were published soon after her death, and almost as soon dismissed by Horace Walpole for their obsession with the everyday. That 'obsession', however, offers us richly detailed access to the life of a woman whose biography charts the now familiar trajectory from fashionable public life to country shame; a trajectory which turns on women's education, imaginative freedom, and the dangers of romance; a trajectory, too, which signals the shifting significance and the limits of the literary, as well as the damaging collisions between literary exercises and gender conventions, between romantic fantasies and rural realities.

Always close to her half-brother, Knight was acutely aware of Bolingbroke's stance as a politician in retirement; with the move to Barrells she

Figure 5.1 **Portrait of Henrietta Knight, Lady Luxborough (attributed to Maria Verelst). ©Lydiard House and Park**
Probably painted in the decade before the scandal and separation of 1736, this may be Knight's marriage portrait. After her death, her estranged husband took possession of Barrells, rebuilt the house, and swept away her landscape; almost no visual evidence of her work remains.

was increasingly influenced also by the poet and gardener William Shenstone (1714–63), whose unsettled retirement at the Leasowes became the subject of much of their correspondence. This awareness of male retreat was crucial to an equally acute understanding that for women retirement might bring altogether different burdens. It is the relationship between Knight and these two men, the shared circumstance but disparate experiences of unwelcome retirement, that is the subject of this chapter: Knight's life at Barrells offers us the opportunity to explore an idea of country life markedly different both from the retirement of the public man and from the cycles of temporary retreat we have encountered so far. A self-styled 'hermitess', Knight's retirement was much closer to banishment than to some elegant fantasy of pastoral seclusion, or even to Mary Coke's intense rounds of self-enforced retreat and expansive European travel. Central to this chapter, then, is that crucial question of how one interprets and lives with the dominant – or most immediate – models of retirement, of how the creation and inhabitation of a garden might allow one to mediate the public models of private life.

The crisis that led to Henrietta Knight's unsought retirement was an alleged love affair made all too public by her irate husband, Robert: choosing public shame rather than quiet negotiation, Robert Knight doomed his wife to a scandalous reputation and to a retired life with which she could never quite be reconciled. Scandal left her in the country and in shame, it dogged her for the rest of her life, and it is not too much to say that scandal came to Henrietta Knight because of her love of poetry and of pastoral romance. As a teenager, Henrietta St. John was the close friend of Frances Seymour, Lady Hertford, and both formed a circle of verse-writing friends with the more famous poet and pious recluse Elizabeth Rowe. Under the names of Marian, Renée, and Philomela, they circulated poems which styled them as the heroines of pastoral romance and which took as their subject the relationship between town and country, between fashion and retirement; Knight's favourite book, and the one she claimed to carry in her pocket while walking in the country, was Guarini's *Il Pastor Fido* ('The Faithful Shepherd').[2]

In the poems these friends wrote in the 1720s all three took delight in country life and in the idea of an idyllic country retreat that would separate them from the world of fashion and its false sophistication. Hertford would be teased by Knight over her position as a lady-in-waiting with, 'Your costly lace, your gems, and rare brocades, / Fin'ry unknown in these our lonely shades', and in return Hertford would stress her life away from the court as a mere country housewife, 'Contented with my lot in silent shades / To nurse my children and direct my maids'.[3] Glamorous but empty city life was not the only target of these exchanges, however. Writing to Hertford in 1736, perhaps only months before the unwished-for separation from her husband, Henrietta Knight described a life of country boredom quite different from the poetically inflected pastoral world created by the three friends in their exchange of letters. After a trip through the Hampshire countryside during which she saw 'nothing that pleased me', Knight found herself at a country house six miles from Andover but as far removed from a world of pastoral pleasures as she could image. Instead of the romantic prospects of her friend's estate at Marlborough she found the only view was the churchyard, the only walk the village street, the only book, *The Farrier's Guide*, the only pastime hunting: 'The gentlemen are booted at 5 in the morning and remain so all day; they hunt or set whilst 'tis light, stretch themselves and yawn when 'tis dark, sup at 9 and go to bed at 10 . . . I stay home out of complaisance and am idle through necessity.'[4] On telling the gentlemen that she had spent her time depicting the romantic tale of Antiochus and Stratonice on a fan, she first had to explain the story of the young prince's love for his step-mother and his determination to die if he could not have her, and then found one of the company exclaiming, 'What! A married woman employ herself in drawing love stories?' at which point she rapidly retreated into the conventionally domestic and 'changed the discourse to a pudding'.[5]

The recounting of this tale does not merely juxtapose romance narratives and country pursuits, rather, it goes out of its way to dramatise that clash and to set quotidian male experience of the rural against an imaginative – but for that very reason also unreal – female account. Knight's letter, then, is a demonstration of the trap in which women might find themselves: romantic models of country life may offer imaginative release from the quotidian and the dull, but they reinforce an account of women as neither robustly physical nor powerfully intellectual, and they stand to demonstrate the excesses of a femininity which must necessarily be contained within the confines of the domestic. Moreover, as Knight would find out for herself, such fantasies could also offer very real dangers, and the disjunction between an imagined country life and its realities was to become the problem with which she would struggle for the rest of her life.

Despite the reproofs of Andover, poems and letters modelled on pastoral romance circulated between the friends well into the 1730s, but while many continued to play off Hertford's position at court against Rowe's seclusion and Knight's less exalted social position, a new theme had appeared with the arrived of John Dalton, tutor to Hertford's son, and another aspiring poet. To Renée, Maria, and Philomela was now added Adonis, and the choice of name proved suitably unfortunate. In a series of poems of 1734 the four paid each other elaborate compliments in the language of romance. Dalton's brief return to Oxford led to Knight's verses entitled 'Venus in Town to Adonis at

Oxford' in which she claimed, 'No sooner was Adonis fled . . . / But I with sorrow dropp'd my head / And tore my platted hair'; Hertford on the same occasion argued that 'Lady's shd still have something new / Their wandring Fancy to delight'; and Dalton appears to have replied to a later poem by Knight, 'Give me the Friendship of my Fair, / Give me that something still more Dear – / In Love's light Plumes be others drest, / I ask no more – than to be blest'.[6] Suspicion about what form that blessing might take proved to be part of Knight's undoing. As Hertford's biographer, Helen Sard Hughes, has argued, however, while these poems make the rural landscape a place of love and suggest an intimacy between the authors, nothing was thought amiss by Elizabeth Rowe, who also engaged in the exchange; or by Lady Hertford, who copied the exchange of poems into her commonplace book; and indeed the poems were passed freely amongst their friends.[7]

Finally, however, it was less these poems of romance fantasy than Henrietta Knight's letters to Dalton that would push her into rural exile. During the visit to Hampshire, Knight had been asked by Lady Hertford to turn her hand to the translation of love letters, and while she concluded it would be impossible to do in the company of boorish squires shocked by married women's thoughts of love, Knight soon took up the effort. It was Dalton who became the object of the letters' address, and their discovery by Robert Knight would lead to her sudden separation and to a life of social disgrace that could only be lived in the country. The letters in question were either genuine love-letters to Dalton, or exercises in romantic letter-writing driven by what Knight herself called a 'silly but Platonick passion . . . ye only one I have ever had'.[8] Though the originals are now lost, one survives as a copy Knight sent to her husband. Begging to see Robert Knight so that she could ask his 'pardon on bended knees' and admitting that she had been guilty of conduct 'which I own is more then prudence or Decency allow', Knight ended her letter by wishing she would be punished 'in what way you please but there is nothing yt I can feel except that of not living wth you wch would be ye death of yr unfortunate wife' and asking in a postscript, 'Can you not forgive?' On the reverse of the letter she then copied out her 'literary exercise':

As soon as you were gone I employ'd myself (as it must ever be in something that regards you) in reading over yr letters, which I resolved to burn, but could not bring my heart or hand to execute what my reason told me was proper, for I found after having made a large bonfire, yt all remained which spoke your passion, & none were consumed but those which necessity had made cool and indifferent, these innocent victims are sacrificed whilst the guilty ones remain as cherished proofs of what were better be forgot at least, if not punished. but what do I say? they are perhaps already forgot by you or repented of. How different is your stile already even when security permit you to speak the dictates of your heart! pardon this reproach – perhaps my Fears belie you, but I can't help remembering the time when one hour or two brought me some publick or private token of your passionate tender sentiments wrote in your own hand, in one of the latter I find these words which I will repeat & answer

I love you still nay more I must ever do so unless you pour into my wounded soul the dear balm of your Compassion, & teach me by gentle means to conquer it.

pardon the present answer those words suggest to me. I have poured that balm & it has work'd its effect – for your passion is conquer'd.

I expect at least thanks for the cure, I might in vain ask the same Remedy in return for my self for alas 'Tis not in your power to give it. Since Virtue has not prevailed Death alone can work the Cure.

As an attempt to convince her husband of her innocence the transcription was a striking failure, despite her insistence that,

I am now more sure than ever, that I never wrote it as ye dictates of my own heart, & Little thinking that I should be thus accused, I was so imprudent as to translate & coppy over a large Bundle of such foolish Letters, 13 of wh. I burn'd last week to make room for things I was placing, & before God I swear not one was other than coppys & translations, I yet flatter my self I shall find ye original of this which I would have kept had I known it could ever be of consequence.[9]

Whether literary exercises inspired by Lady Hertford, or real love-letters inadvertently left on a table, what finally sealed Henrietta Knight's fate was the scandalous tales that had begun buzzing around London, and Robert Knight's willingness to confirm them by so sudden a break with his wife. Henrietta's duplicitous brother John was soon writing to her that he'd known of the affair, 'these 5 or 4 Months by all my friends and Acquaintances' and that while at first it was only a matter of speculation ignored by himself and their mother, 'yett of Late ye Whole World has agreed (I mean before Mr Kn. Spoke of it) on ye same story as to person & Circumstances' and reports 'came so thick so Well Authoriz'd, & so Exactly Agreeing yt indeed they left No room for doubt Even to the Most partial, of wch. I was One'.[10] John St. John's partiality appears to have tended another way, however, for a week before this letter to Henrietta, he had already written to his brother-in-law assuring him not only of a hearty welcome but that 'if I had been her husband by God I wd have dated my Ease & happiness from ye Hour she gave me a justifiable cause to part wth her, for I Know yt my temper & hers wd have hitt so ill yt I shou'd litterally have hanged My self if she wd not have play'd ye Whore & given me ye occasion of Separation she had done to you'.[11] So it was left to Henrietta Knight's exiled eldest brother, Henry Bolingbroke, to provide what support there would be from her family.

Bolingbroke was himself a close friend of Robert Knight, with shared political interests; he had also been trying to rid himself of his estate at Dawley in Middlesex by selling it to Knight's father, the disgraced South Sea Company Cashier, Robert Knight senior. The sale never happened, and though Dawley would play a role in Henrietta's life in other respects, in 1736 Bolingbroke was as keen as his brother John to remain on friendly terms with the wronged husband; he was also far away at Argeville in France, and news reached him long after advice would be of use. Exploring the circumstances of the love letters, he wrote to Robert Knight 'that ye First intimations of ye unfortunate affair you mention stunned me with surprise'. What seems to have shocked him most, however, was the thought that his sister could be involved with such a bad poet and that she would be foolish enough to leave love letters to be found on a table:

That a woman of quallity should prostitute herself to such a low fellow, and yt ye dullest Poet in christendom should turn her head, or warm her heart, seemed to me incredible. I thought it was not less so, yt any woman engaged in such a criminal commerce, should suffer a letter of this kind to lye loose about, for so I was informed it did. Such letters may be, and have been intercepted, but I never heard before of any yt were layed about in ye way to be found, as this was most neglectfully, according to ye information I have had. This circumstance weighs with me on one side, on ye other, the letter has not ye air of what it has been called, a jeu d'espirt. I confess it seems writ in good earnest, & on a particular occasion.[12]

Bolingbroke's response to the letter should alert us to the peculiar nature of letter-writing in the eighteenth century where the apparently personal or confessional could themselves be a literary trope styled on the models of other published letters.[13] Indeed, Bolingbroke could hardly be unaware of earlier letter-writers as models for contemporary correspondence, for his second wife was a niece of the famous Madame de Maintenon. What complicates this, of course, is that models and translations can serve a purpose beyond the explicit claims of a literary exercise, and Henrietta Knight's assertion that the most she 'ever granted to ye person I am suspected for was Compassion, which I have often accused my self of as a crime', alongside her admission that her 'silly but Platonick passion' led to compositions that were more than prudence and decency would allow, point to the erotic uncertainty created when literary exercises and shared sensibilities elide. More than this, Knight's problem was that her model was far from the pious Madame de Maintenon, and just as she was censured at the house near

Andover for depicting the tale of Antiochus and Stratonice, so she would be censured now for associating too closely with the conventions of romance and with a mode of writing not fit for married women. Certainly when faced with the evidence Bolingbroke concluded that, 'such a letter under a womans own hand cannot be excused by any pretence. I should not excuse it myself. I cannot therefore plead yt you should.'[14]

Where Bolingbroke differed strongly from Robert Knight and the rest of the St John family, however, was on how affairs should proceed. John St John wrote to his sister of her actions that 'Tis most Unhappy and I feel for you, but whats Blamable will be so' and counselled Robert Knight to make things public immediately.[15] As a born politician Bolingbroke's advice was instead to hush up the affair rather than make it public, to separate quietly some months later and thus, by not confirming the scandalous tales running round London (which now included not only Dalton, but Henrietta's physician, Dr Peters), to leave his sister's reputation intact.[16] By the time events came to Bolingbroke's attention in France, however, Robert Knight had already chosen a different route, and as Bolingbroke wrote to his sister some months after the separation: 'As to ye noise, that Burst out immediately, I am not at all surprised at it, for yr late mother talked ye whole matter over to servants, Besides whispering it in ye ears of twenty other persons. in short child, you all conducted your selves like people who wanted common sence.'[17] If Bolingbroke's response to events was driven by a desire to avoid 'any shocking Reflections in ye world', it was at least a response that would have saved his sister from public shame.[18] With that possibility lost, Henrietta's fate, and indeed the rest of her life, was to be haggled over and decided almost entirely by the men of the family.

What this episode demonstrates perhaps most clearly – in its flurry of letters between husband and wife, between brothers and sister, between brothers and husband – is just what might be at stake when women educated in the language of romance confront both the quotidian world of conventional gender politics and attempts to enforce the limits of female imagination. Charlotte Lennox would tell a much safer version of this story in her novel *The Female Quixote*, but as here in Knight's letters, she would point to the same problem of limiting female learning, of emphasising romance, and then of blaming women for their limited romantic pastimes. Mary Astell had argued at the turn of the century that women needed a language other than romance; but as Knight had found at Andover, the alternative might be nothing but puddings.

In the following months Henrietta continued to plead for forgiveness and to insist on her innocence; she begged Knight to think of the children, of their parents' outrage, of 'how terrible ye worlds censures are', and wrote, 'Try me for a little while & then if you have ye least complaint I'll not so much as endeavour to excuse myself'.[19] Instead, Robert Knight took his wife to Barrells Hall in Warwickshire, stayed there a night, and then left her in order to draw up an agreement of separation with Lord St John. Under that agreement, although the couple would not divorce, Henrietta was to live alone at Barrells. Lord St John proposed an income of £500 a year to be paid quarterly from the time she took up residence; Robert Knight agreed but insisted that he would be liable for no other debts she incurred; and it was also agreed that if she were to take up residence elsewhere, then the maintenance allowance would continue and she would be allowed to take with her the coach and a pair of coach horses as long as her new home 'be not out of England or within twenty miles of London or of the Bath Road'.[20] As Henrietta's letters go on to reveal, however, her situation was much worse than the agreement suggests: she was also banned from corresponding both with the friends whose letters had led to her problems and with close members of her family; added to this, her two children would remain under the care of her husband without any clear agreement as to when they might even visit their mother. She would not meet her daughter again for another thirteen years.

It was with this baggage that Henrietta Knight arrived at Barrells in 1736. Forced into retirement by her all-too-public disgrace, during the following twenty years, as she set about reconstructing her world, Henrietta Knight found herself repeatedly having to negotiate between her society's aspirational and punitive narratives of retirement. It was many years before she was to become an acceptable member of her local community and it was in part the creation of her garden which brought her visitors, which slowly began to change her status and which brought her some small degree of rehabilitation. Gardening, then, became the means by which Henrietta Knight could begin to re-establish a public life, but it was also a constant reminder of society's absence and of her over-solitary status.

The happy hermit: Bolingbroke and male retirement

As we have seen throughout this book, solitude and its uneasy engagement with society is at the centre of cultural ideas about retirement. Henrietta Knight did not have to look far to find those ideas being rehearsed, for both in the life and in the writings of her brother, Bolingbroke, retirement and its vicissitudes was a constant theme. While Knight had shared pleasant visions of pastoral romance with her friends Lady Hertford and Elizabeth Rowe, Bolingbroke too had held up to her idyllic notions of retirement when she was a teenager and, from the early 1720s, wrote to her regularly of his life as a happy hermit. Characteristically, however, it was Bolingbroke, too, who frequently found such retirement unsought, unwelcome, and unsustainable, and it is in some ways Bolingbroke who offers us an experience of retirement's aspirations and disappointments closest to his sister's. To make sense of Knight's disparate experiences of retirement, then, it is as well to look at the model most nearly to hand, a model offered both in personal letters and in the more public world of Bolingbroke's political publications.

We have already encountered traditions of male retirement and the relative ease with which the public man might slide into the classical pose of retreat, but Bolingbroke's insistently political and intellectual account of retirement is significant because it was so frequently offered, and at times so inappropriate.[21] In particular what Bolingbroke's various accounts of retirement make apparent is the gendered division of cultural resources he and his sister had available; indeed, as brother and sister, their correspondence makes clear just how far the language of retirement might mark both a sense of shared and of utterly disparate experience.

Bolingbroke's chequered political career had in fact made his life one of serial retirement, and each time his political aspirations collapsed he loudly if not always convincingly championed the life of the morally righteous recluse. In an essay that was not to be published till after his death, but which elaborated on the sentiments in his personal letters, Bolingbroke rehearsed the life of classical retirement and claimed it as his own. The essay, 'On the true Use of Retirement and Study', insists on the value of retirement as a means of casting off the fetters of the world, of abstracting 'ourselves from the prejudices, and habits, and pleasures, and business of the world', of dispelling the 'intoxicating fumes of philosophical presumption', and of teaching us 'to establish our peace of mind, where alone it can rest securely, in resignation: in short, such a view will render life more agreeable, and death less terrible'.[22] However, it also makes fundamental assumptions about those suited to such retirement, insisting that retirement can come only after a life of public ambition is over and that only those who have led a life of intellectual exertion can benefit: those who have 'trifled away youth, are reduced to the necessity of trifling away age'. While there should be time in one's retirement for amusements ("Dulce est desipere,' said Horace: 'Vive la Bagatelle!' says Swift'), 'I insist that a principal part of these amusements be the amusements of study and reflection, or reading and conversation'.[23] Although claiming to frame a general essay, Bolingbroke's account of intellectually rigorous retirement after a life in politics is quite obviously modelled on himself and as such it is not without its ironies. If in the essay he claims that 'in the midst of retreat, where ever it may be fixed, I may contribute to defend and preserve the British Constitution', his political desires were actually given up slowly and bitterly, his retirements were forced and unwelcome, and his claims to have left the world behind were far from compelling. By Bolingbroke, then, Henrietta Knight had been invited to think of retirement as a release from the cares of society, but, by Bolingbroke too, she was offered a model of retreat so clearly masculine in its conjunction of high politics and classical studies that it could be to her only of tangential aid. She was offered also, of course, in the life of her brother, an example of retirement that repeatedly found a disjunction between high ideals and disappointing realities, between intellectual aspirations and the stubborn emotional experience of disillusionment and loneliness.[24]

As early as 1716 Bolingbroke had already published a rather self-serving account of retirement, modelling himself on Seneca, entitled 'Reflections Upon Exile'. While exiled in France, he embraced the role of the retired politician and spent time and a substantial part of his wealth on adorning the Chateau de La Source, his estate near Orleans. But even in this first enforced retirement, for all that his letters claimed to welcome it and revelled in his life of hunting and study, what was created at La Source was nothing if not an address to the political world by which he had been rejected.[25] To the formal gardens that had been created in the late seventeenth century, Bolingbroke added an array of temples and inscriptions, all of which turned on his current state and gestured towards a political landscape from which he was now excluded. Close to the spring that gave the estate its name, Bolingbroke erected a small temple in the classical style and placed the statue of a river god close by to mark the source of the stream. On a tablet above this he placed an inscription that read:

By the frenzies of an outrageous faction,
On account of his unstained fidelity to his queen,
And his strenuous endeavour to accomplish a general peace
Having been forced to seek a new country
Here, at the source of this sacred fountain
                Henry of Bolingbroke,
                Unjustly banished,
                Lived pleasantly.

Closer to the house (now styled a 'villa') the effect was compounded by a further inscription that spoke again of his country's madness, claimed a happy mind and an immovable tranquillity brought on by this new life of retirement in France, but also of his desire to be restored to his native land. With their claims for rural happiness almost overbalanced by self-righteousness and political rancour, the sentiments are not only typical of Bolingbroke but mark out a characteristic we can recognise in later generations of ousted politicians who chose to relive their battles in their gardens. Henry Fox, Lord Holland, did much the same at Kingsgate; while most famously the Temples and the Grenvilles would pick up where Bolingbroke had left off by continuing their own opposition to Walpole with an ongoing programme of temple building and inscriptions at Stowe. What all of these politicians had at their disposal was a wealth of classical sources which allowed them to claim political failure as moral fortitude, and country obscurity as political virtue. This odd condition of claiming to have done with the world while planning a return to it is a further characteristic of Bolingbroke's political retirement: at different moments, he could be Horace or Seneca, a failed politician, or a man waiting to save his country from corruption.[26]

It was not literary resources, however, but a huge bribe to the King's mistress that finally enabled Bolingbroke to return to England in 1723 though even with this he was still kept out of the House of Lords through the machinations of Robert Walpole.[27] With his political ambitions thwarted almost as soon as they had been raised, Bolingbroke turned once again to the rhetoric of retirement, and this time claimed for himself the role of the patriotic farmer whose life at Dawley – his newly-purchased estate in Middlesex – would be a model for all true patriots.[28] As a 'farmer' Bolingbroke could once again claim a classical heritage – aligning himself with Cincinnatus, the unambitious leader who would leave his plough to save the nation – but he could also claim contemporary virtues of usefulness and productivity which might be set in opposition to the sudden grandeur of the great Whig estates that had been springing up since the accession of George I.

With the support of Pope and Swift, Dawley soon became a focus for cultural and political opposition to Walpole in the 1720s and early 1730s. It was Bolingbroke and Dawley Farm that Pope undoubtedly had in mind as the virtuous antithesis to his account of Timon's Villa, in the *Epistle to Burlington*, with its vulgar display of wealth, false taste, uselessness, and lack of proportion. However, as a farm and a farmer, Dawley and Bolingbroke were less than convincing. At Bolingbroke's *ferme ornée* it was ornament rather than agriculture that held sway and whatever income it produced seems to have been greatly outweighed by the huge sums spent on adorning the estate (£200 alone was said to have been spent on the paintings of agricultural implements in the great entrance hall). Knight certainly recognised the disjunctions, and gave her own account of Dawley when discussing William Shenstone's gardens at the Leasowes with her neighbour Lord Archer:

[I] told him it was what I had taken the liberty to call a *Ferme ornée*. 'And what' (said he) 'is more agreeable? It is the very thing one should choose; and what I have heard Lord Bolingbroke made Dawley.' But I told him, as to that, my Brother's calling it a Farm was only means as it really was one; for he then kept 700*l* per annum in hand: but that the house was much too fine and large to be called a Farm. But on the other side, its environs were not ornamented, nor its prospects good.[29]

The thrust of Bolingbroke's farming, then, was rhetorical and political rather than practical: the purpose of Dawley was not to be a place of endless retirement and unruffled social abstraction, rather it was to be a physical and ideological springboard from which Bolingbroke could launch himself back into the political world. Here, too, however, it was only a partial success; by the early 1730s he was in the dispiritingly unsuccessful throes of trying to sell the estate because it was such a drain on his resources; by the middle of the 1730s he had retired once again to France; and in his final years back in England he returned to his family home and cultivated an increasingly embittered role as the 'Hermit of Battersea'.

Sibling hermits

During all of this time Bolingbroke had kept in close – if not close enough – touch with his half-sister. While acting as a housekeeper to her father-in-law (also exiled in France for his part in the South Sea Bubble) she had visited Bolingbroke at La Source; soon after their marriage Bolingbroke was keen to find the couple a farm of their own so that they too could enjoy the rural life; and Henrietta was also a regular visitor at Dawley. When not visiting her brother, Henrietta received regular letters in which he continued to praise his rural life and to insist on the happiness of leaving the world behind: after a visit from the Duke and Duchess of Berwick he wrote to his sister, 'for you must know that those who are thought most happy in the world are glad to steal sometimes out of it, and to taste for moments those pleasures which happyer Hermits enjoy all the year'.[30]

Henrietta was not alone in receiving such eulogia – Bolingbroke wrote to both her husband and her father-in-law in similar terms at times – but with his sister there seems to have been a particular affection and concern for her happiness that Bolingbroke rarely expressed elsewhere. Unlike many of his political friends, she had continued to write to him during his first exile in France, and Bolingbroke's letters go out of their way to express an affection more than merely formal. Thus, in 1719 he wrote to Henrietta,

I have long taken it kindly of you yt I never found any variation in yr Sentiments for me, and I never will forget it, for it is an excellent Character as well as a rare one. I thank you for ye joy which you express att my good luck . . . if I can return to you, it will be a great satisfaction to me. if ye publick misfortunes, for such they are, hinder me att least you shall partake in my good fortune, for you was good natur'd enough to take a share in my bad.[31]

In 1720, urging her to marry – but not a man of 'narrow fortune, a mean birth, or a bad character' – Bolingbroke even joined her in the language of romance and wrote to Henrietta,

You seem so perfectly idle in England, that if I could send an enchanted boat, like that of Armida, to Battersea Stairs, you should sail down ye Thames, cross the seas, and up the Loire in a trice, & Land in my park, wherein the most beautiful place that ever Nature adorn'd you would find the tenderest welcome. This image flatters me so agreeably that I would dwell longer upon it if I could hope to think it into reallity & practice.[32]

After her public disgrace Bolingbroke no longer turned to the world of romance when he wrote to his sister; instead, he shared with her the role of hermit, and as hermit siblings they continued to write to each other until Bolingbroke's death. As late as July 1751, Bolingbroke concluded a letter to his sister by writing, 'All I can say is that if I am able to share your Hermitage with you, it will be the greatest comfort I can have'. A month later, taking treatment for a cancer in his face that would cause his death by the end of the year, he wrote again, 'One way or other we will try to be mutual comforts, to ease our infirmitys, and to soften our afflications'.[33] This sense of a shared fate seems to have provided them both with some kind of solace. Certainly both were forced into an unlooked-for retreat from the world, and as 'hermits', part of what they shared was their gardens.

Soon after her arrival at Barrells in 1736, Bolingbroke wrote that he was 'rejoyced to hear that yr books and your gardens amuse you so well in your Solitude' and he appears to have sent her a steady supply of seeds and plants. As we will see, Henrietta carefully modelled aspects of Barrells on

what Bolingbroke had done at Dawley, and his bust was put alongside that
of Pope in her library. Yet, for all this, their situations were quite different.
For Bolingbroke, even if it failed to satisfy his political ambitions, there was
a ready-made role as the great statesman in retreat, and he could convince
himself at times, as he wrote to Henrietta's estranged husband in 1738,
that:

I have been fond of power, and as they were necessary to that, desirous, but not
fond, of Riches ... I have never valued power any further than I retained ye liberty
of applying it to those purposes to which my opinion & my Sentiments led me to
apply it. There has not been these thirty years a point of time, where the greatest
degree of power, and ye highst Elevation in honour & dignity in an Administration
whose conduct I disapproved, or despised, & could not hope to alter, would have
tempted me. a man of this temper cannot expect to please long any court, nor
any Party, and this experience should make him content to retire from business
to amusement, & from ye government of state to the government of himself. in
this Retreat I am at last ... nothing shall draw me out of it again. My study and ye
woods of Fontainbleau divide all ye time yt can be spared from ye necessary dutys
of friendship and private life.[34]

As in his formal essays on retirement, so in this letter to Robert Knight, Bolingbroke could rehearse a classical account of male retirement that suited
his own needs. Retirement here marks the change from business to amusement, from affairs of state to the studious good government of oneself, but
as the preserve of a male political elite, Bolingbroke's account of retirement
represents a model almost wholly unavailable to women. This was only one
of several disparities between the siblings as they wrote of their shared sense
of retreat, however, and if political retirement based on classical models
was not something Henrietta Knight could share with her brother, neither
was that element of retirement with which we are now most familiar: age.[35]
Writing to his sister in 1751 he asserted that:

The World, dear sister, may very well spare a man as useless in it as I am, and I
do assure you, I can as easily spare the World; I can do it so easily that I think not
only of retreating from it, and of excluding it from my Retreat which is to die civilly
before I die naturally; but that this thought gives me more comfort than any other,
and that I hasten to put it in execution.[36]

It still remained the case, however, that for Bolingbroke, retirement – welcome or otherwise – could be claimed after a life of labour, and even its
serial nature could, at a pinch, be likened to the temporary but repeated
retreats of classical politicians; for his sister retirement came early in life (she
was in her mid thirties), it was to be permanent, and, rather than classical

precedents, it brought with it the unwelcome association of popular fiction and tales of scandal. Moreover, while Bolingbroke always had Horace, or Seneca, or Cincinnatus, or Epictetus to hand, faced with the prospect of being banished to the country, when Henrietta Knight set out her initial response to being sent to the county, the first model to which she turned was once again that of the heroine of romance, claiming 'Liberty is so sweet that it is more natural for me to chuse to be in a remote cottage Free, than at home a Prisoner; But as it appears to My Friends that ye latter will be best for my familly & as to ye world, I will consent to it'.[37] However, when she then attempted to negotiate the details of this retirement, the income she would receive, and the requirement that she should be able to move to another house if it did not suit her, she was swiftly reprimanded by her own father for her impertinence and recognised that she must submit to the will of her family and the dictates of 'ye world'. Her problem, then, was that she and her brother were implicated in quite different cultural narratives and narratives that allowed them different degrees of agency: where Bolingbroke could assert himself as the saviour of the nation even in defeat, Henrietta Knight was manoeuvred into a role far more restrictive and far less valued by her society.

A damned wet ditch: Barrells

The agreement that had been reached between father, half-brother, and son-in-law – as well as the geographical location in which she found herself – confirmed Henrietta Knight's status as a woman in disgrace and abruptly dislodged her from the sociable world in which she had moved. Indeed, where once she had written poems that made her the heroine of romance she now found herself far too closely associated with an altogether different, but highly influential, narrative of shameful retreat. Just as Sarah Lennox's family reiterated popular narratives of disgrace in the 1760s by insisting on the punishment of rural seclusion, so in the 1730s Henrietta Knight was being pushed into a landscape that would insist on her shame. If romance had been part of her trajectory towards scandal, and if popular scandal narratives could all too easily lead others to think of her country life as a form of endless disgrace, when she set about reshaping Barrells as a space that might resist such stereotypes, the stakes for Henrietta Knight as a gardener were very high indeed.

On her arrival in Warwickshire, Barrells was less than impressive. Her relations, the Cholmondleys referred to the place as a 'damned wet ditch' into which she had been unceremoniously thrown, and, like Knight some years later, claimed that 'when she was sent, there were not half the windows up, no doors to the house, and the roof uncovered'.[38] Knight's letters soon expressed her desire to leave. What prevented her at first were the needs of her family to keep her out of sight, and she reluctantly agreed to stay for a year. It soon became apparent, however, that Robert Knight had no intention of letting her return from what both her friends and family recognised as banishment.[39] When she did try to leave, he threatened to stop paying her allowance and took advice from lawyers on the legality of the separation agreement. On Henrietta's behalf, Bolingbroke did the same. Each was advised that they would lose in court, both therefore settled for the status quo, and thus conflicting legal advice was also to play its part in ensuring that Henrietta Knight would remain trapped in a life of rural seclusion.

Faced with this life in the country, Henrietta Knight set about the wholesale remodelling of the house and gardens at Barrells. Though there is little evidence of her activities in her first few years at Barrells because of the ban placed on her writing letters, by the early 1740s she was not only corresponding regularly with her friend Lady Hertford about her garden, but had made an important new acquaintance, the poet and landscape gardener William Shenstone. Indeed, by the late 1740s she appears to have spent most of her time either designing these gardens or writing to Shenstone of them; and Shenstone for his part was not backward in proffering both books and suggestions. Along with other female members of her household, Knight spent a great amount of time designing not simply within the confines of a flower garden or shrubbery but, like her contemporaries Mary Coke and Caroline Holland, creating an entire landscape garden. And if she relied on Shenstone for advice – as did many – she was nevertheless the prime mover both in the details and in the broader design of the estate.

Over the course of about twenty years, Knight established a fifty-acre garden consisting of bowling green and shrubbery, coppice and grove, with both straight and serpentine walks leading out beyond the ha-ha and through the pleasure grounds. Close to the house were the kitchen garden to the east and the terrace and lower garden to the south. Further east of the house, between the coppice and the shrubbery, was a service walk the contrasting roughness of which, she proudly reported, was much admired by the local artist Thomas Smith; to the west was a grotto which would become the Temple of Venus. To the north was the aviary garden, and in the north-east corner, beyond the coppice, was a thatched hermitage. Further structures included a pedimented pavilion and summer house, while a marl-pit was heavily planted to add further variety to the scene; elsewhere shell urns, an obelisk, root seats, and a piping fawn were – after much discussion – placed (and re-placed) at various points to catch the eye.[40] In all of this Knight took an active and physical role and was regularly to be found out in her gardens shaping new paths, marking out vistas and arranging the planting. Just as her brother had taken to his garden when excluded from public life, so now Henrietta Knight made gardening a central part of her world; it filled her days and her letters even as it emptied her coffers and ran her into debt.

In fact, the example of her brother seems never to have been far from Knight's mind, and if his self-fashioning as a hermit presented her with a rather ambiguous model, his designs at La Source and Dawley offered more concrete examples. Knight's use of stucco in the library undoubtedly echoed Bolingbroke's use of the same effect in his great hall at Dawley: she wrote of the effect, 'When my brother Bolingbroke built Dawley, which he chose to call a Farm, he had his hall painted in stone-colours, with all the implements of husbandry placed in the manner one sees or might see arms and trophies in some General's hall; and it had an effect that pleased every body'.[41]

But Bolingbroke's influence stretched far beyond painted effects: an early visitor to La Source, Henrietta Knight had grown up with gardens that addressed the public even from a rural seclusion, gardens that assumed an audience both for themselves and for their owner. However, if like her brother, Knight would draw on busts, inscriptions, memorials, and architecture to establish her as much in the social as the physical landscape, these were landscapes over which she could only have partial control. Bolingbroke of course had the likes of Pope to help him insist on the legitimacy of his vision; such public support was strikingly absent for Knight. But if Horace Walpole was characteristically quick to damn Knight's letters when they appeared in print, they have nevertheless left us with a peculiarly detailed record of the decisions and discussions driving the creation of a landscape. Certainly her gardens embodied Knight's recognition of the cultural capital achieved by a display of taste, but they also embodied her recognition that any such capital could only be achieved as part of a cultural conversation, a conversation in which – as Walpole knew – others might have their say. What that conversation might be becomes apparent if we explore some of the features of Knight's garden in more detail.

Knight's summer house is a good place to begin both because it seems to fit easily within a conventional account of iconography in gardens, of former models and ongoing traditions, and because setting Knight's garden in such a context reveals the limits of that approach. At Barrells, the busts and iconography found within the house were mirrored in the garden by their appearance in Knight's summer house. Certainly they were linked in Knight's mind: in the summer of 1742, with their friendship only recently re-established by letter, Knight wrote to Lady Hertford describing the work she had been doing at Barrells since her arrival there six years earlier, describing first the library, complete with its portraits of her friends, and then the summer house with its stucco busts of Pope, Dryden, Shakespeare, Milton, Newton, Locke, and of course her own brother, Bolingbroke. As David Coffin has noted, Knight's array of busts in her summer house is likely to have been influenced by William Kent's designs for Queen Caroline at Richmond.[42] Since the early 1730s Richmond gardens had been famous for the highly emblematic – and quickly ridiculed – designs of William Kent for Queen Caroline. It was here that Kent produced 'Merlin's Cave' as a residence for Stephen Duck the Thresher Poet, complete with life-size wax statues, including Merlin and his secretary, and here also was a hermitage containing busts of Newton and Locke, Wollaston and Boyle. Kent's designs for Caroline were part of the game of high politics in the 1720s and 1730s, an attempt to link the Hanoverian with the Tudor court, and an attempt swiftly met by deliberate misinterpretation of the iconography from those in opposition to the Walpole administration.[43] With Bolingbroke very much in the wrong political camp, straightforward emulation of Richmond seems unlikely on Knight's part: rather, it may be that, like Bolingbroke's Dawley, Knight's summer house was not simply influenced by Richmond but rather was a riposte to a political vision in which her brother was so unwelcome. In this it may have been a riposte to something else too. Given Richmond's overtly political and public agenda, we must surely ask why a woman so obviously set apart from public life set out to engage with a work defined by high politics.

One answer at least is that it represents a claim for that seriousness of retirement Bolingbroke thought open only to the masculine world of the political elite. The riposte, then, may also be to Bolingbroke. During her time at Barrells, Knight gathered about herself a group of poets and versifiers, chief amongst whom was William Shenstone. Though Shenstone undoubtedly took the lead, as a group they offered advice on inscriptions for the garden, and, with the aid of Robert Dodsley, their work appeared in that most characteristic of mid-century literary publications, Dodsley's *Miscellanies*. Certainly, then, Knight was excluded from retirement after political endeavours, but the creation of both a garden and a circle of literary friends was nevertheless an attempt to claim relation to a culture of male poets extending from minor writers to national icons. One might say that the agenda here remains carefully domestic in that Knight's letters stress the moral quite as much as the poetical or political merits of her authors, but the clear gesture towards Richmond's iconography nevertheless places her in a larger cultural conversation not only about taste but also about national worth.

In this she was not in fact alone: perhaps inevitably, Queen Caroline's garden buildings at Richmond became the focus not only for men and politics, but also for women writers who recognised and lamented the absence of women from this emblem of national greatness. Jane Brereton's, 'On the Bustoes in the Royal Hermitage', and, more notably (with its assertion that women should lay claim to popular science and philosophy), Mrs Cockburn's 'A Poem, Occasioned by the Busts set up in the Queen's Hermitage' both took up the theme.[44] Few women, however, could claim such a sustained response as Knight's in the creation of her summer house.

Income, aspiration, and the influence of William Shenstone

What complicated any claim for Knight's garden buildings as a gendered riposte both to Bolingbroke's studiously masculine retirement and to Queen Caroline's equally masculine national heritage is an alternative strand of thinking which runs throughout Knight's correspondence with William Shenstone, a strand of thinking which at once admits to the lack of seriousness Bolingbroke found so wanting in others, challenges the value of such seriousness by offering instead the pleasure of trifles, but which cannot quite rescue itself from a fear that money underpins taste, and that lack of money must inevitably produce questionable taste.

Knight's limited finances were fundamental to her status as a woman separated and alone. It is not that she was poor, rather, her income seemed constantly to have been outstripped by her aspirations, a problem she shared both with Bolingbroke and with Shenstone. But what made Knight's sudden retirement so hard was not least the stark mismatch between the fantasy of romantic retirement she had shared with her friends and the reality of a rundown country estate in Warwickshire. Now that she was no longer the pastoral heroine of her own romance, country life and the drudgery of estate management appeared far from glamorous. Six years after her forced move to Barrells, the role still rankled, and she wrote to her old friend Lady Hertford:

The thing in life I am least accustomed to, the thing I most detest, has filled a great part of my time. Imagine me letting leases, receiving rents, paying parish dues, and anxious lest a shower of rain should spoil my hay. I fear I shall have given you such a description as would make you ashamed to correspond with me.[45]

While the hugely wealthy Elizabeth Montagu, or even her impecunious sister Sarah Scott, might find a way of idealising economic relations in a country estate (and in so doing justifying their own aspirations to spend), Knight was frequently accused – by her estranged husband at least – of reckless spending on foolish adornments to her estate: certainly the later letters between husband and wife made money their predominant theme. From the £500 a year of her initial settlement, Henrietta Knight's income grew substantially over the years. On the death of her brother Holles she gained a further £110 per annum (along with shares in the Covent Garden Playhouse); and with the death of her father her yearly income increased with a further £100 per annum from a house in Albermarle Street and the interest from £10,000 capital.[46] Notwithstanding, by 1750, she was writing to her husband suggesting that she spend some of the capital on which her yearly income depended in order to pay off the debts she had incurred in remodelling the estate. Knight attempted to justify her expenditure on the house and gardens, as did many men and women, by claiming it as an addition to her children's inheritance;[47] but there was another account of women's spending with which she had to contend, an account far less flattering, and one which linked women in particular with the weaknesses of luxury and excess.[48] This kind of attack on the fashionable excess of women at home was to be expressed perhaps most famously some twenty years after Knight's death in Smollett's *Humphry Clinker*, where the misguided Mr Baynard has allowed his wife to create a showy but impractical landscape garden. Things start badly – if characteristically, for the representation of a fine lady – with Mrs Baynard exclaiming, 'So (she said) I am to be buried in the country' and soon become worse, with a lake that will not hold water, and a burden of expense that can only be removed by returning the estate to its proper use as farmland.[49] Even without Smollett's example, however, it was all too easy for Robert Knight to align his wife's activities not with patrimonial investment but with selfish luxury. Bolingbroke could overspend at Dawley and still have the greatest poet of the day justify his actions; Henrietta Knight had no such recourse. Instead, right until the end of her life she found herself in an ongoing battle with her estranged husband over her expenses; and his self-serving and wildly inaccurate calculations about her likely wealth served only to reinforce his comfortable outrage over a woman whose spending was beyond control.[50]

The unaccountable gulf between income and aspirations undoubtedly drew Knight closer to Shenstone; indeed, we can understand what was a shared worry about expense as itself central to their experience of retirement, of their behaviour in a state of retirement, and of their sense of a public reaction to that retirement. Shenstone himself was constantly concerned with the restricted scale of his estate, and his equally restricted ability to remodel it. In 1749 he wrote to Knight of his wealthy neighbours' garden-building programme at Hagley:

Two hundred Pounds expended in a Rotunda at *Hagley*, on Ionic Pillars! The Dome of Stone, with thin Lead underneath, to keep out wet. While *I* propose, or *fancy* I propose to build a piece of Gothic Architecture, at Sight of which, all modern Castles near shall bow their Heads abased, like the other Sheaves to JOSEPH's. I send you the Plan; 'tis for a Seat on the Bank above my Hermitage, and will amount, on a moderate Computation, to the Sum of fifteen Shillings.[51]

Such comments fill the pages of their letters and Shenstone in particular appeared to revel in the cheapness with which taste could be achieved. Indeed, in the face of inevitable comparisons between Hagley and the Leasowes – the one huge and the other moderate at best – Shenstone shared in his correspondence with Henrietta Knight an aesthetic of littleness which he at once championed and found to be deeply unsettling, even embarrassing. If the great estate of his neighbour Lord Lyttelton at Hagley presented grand public gestures which appeared to belittle the aspirations of the Leasowes, Shenstone offered an account of his garden which valourised the small scale, littleness, cheapness, the personal and the private; and yet the nervousness that littleness of scale implied littleness of taste was never wholly absent in his letters to Barrells.[52] Taking up the theme, Knight wrote to complain of a Mr. Meredith's detrimental comparison of the Leasowes with Hagley in just these terms, arguing that Meredith should have 'left structures out of the question' when talking of the beauties of the two estates, for they are 'owing to the purse more than to the taste: and with which you never intended to vye'. Instead of Lyttelton's mock castles, Knight claimed for Shenstone 'the force of truth, exemplified by that of proportion' and championed this in the design of the Leasowes irrespective of scale.[53] Money – or its lack – could not, however, be so easily sidestepped. With limited incomes, the problem for both Shenstone and Knight remained that the expensive 'structures' Knight sought to dismiss had become part of the public language of taste, a language they both found themselves unable wholly to reject: while wealth might easily be recognised as different from taste, taste could not so easily be dissociated from wealth.

Rivalry between, or at the very least awareness of, other estates should highlight for us once again the social networks in which retirement was enmeshed. Both Shenstone and Knight had an acute awareness not only of public taste but that a demonstration of taste could give them a place in the public eye they might not otherwise attain. Gaining that place, however, came with its own risks, risks made all the greater because, by its very nature, a claim to retirement invited the moral judgement of the world beyond. In Shenstone's case, soon after his death he was famously, and influentially, criticised by Samuel Johnson for his choice of retirement and for the economic frailty of his aspirations to taste. In Johnson's view, Shenstone had chosen wrongly by abandoning the usefulness of a productive farm for the elegant inactivity of a garden: the determination to live in retirement while hankering for fame made him a figure not of admiration but of pity.[54] For Johnson, then, any grounds Shenstone might have for his claims to taste were simply cut from under his feet because he lacked the wealth to sustain them and the moral of his life was that of a man who effeminised himself by foolish spending on adornment. Knight's husband, of course, turned with alacrity to just such a moral criticism of his wife for her misplaced spending, when attempting to renege on his own financial commitments; but even without this, Henrietta Knight was all too aware of the need to establish public justifications for a private life. At issue was not least the purpose of retirement, and it formed a major part of the correspondence between the small group of friends she slowly rebuilt after her earlier disgrace. Knight's emphasis on the domestic scale of her own (and Shenstone's) garden might remove her from Lyttelton's world of high politics, but it did so only to set her firmly within that other acutely politicised argument surrounding the proper place of women in retirement and their significance as icons of pious virtue and domestic accomplishments. That argument was of course about knowing one's place, and just as Shenstone was feminised and trivialised by Johnson for failing to recognise his place in the world, so Knight's garden iconography marks the fracture in cultural expectations not simply about the structures she had created but about her proper role as a woman in retirement. We have already seen Bolingbroke elaborate an account of retirement by turns abstractly studious and politically outraged, and we have seen also how neither model could serve his sister as it did him. Indeed, for Bolingbroke anyone outside his world of male politics and classical learning was effectively doomed to carry the frivolous desires of their youth into the disquietude of an unhappy retreat. Knight, then, had to look elsewhere, and she looked not least to frivolity and to the apparently trivial.

Writing to Shenstone in the summer of 1749, Knight described a journey across her garden from the pavilion and the bowling green to the coppice and the shrubbery. She records the 'great variety of cowslips, primroses, ragged-robins, wild hyacinths both white and blue, violets, &c. &c.', as well as the whitsun roses, the syringa, and the sweet-briar, the shrubs that are past their best and the flowers that now droop to the ground. As the letter continues, however, she turns to another kind of flower. After transcribing some of her verses, she writes:

Those persons who cannot find pleasure in trifles, are generally wise in their own opinions, and fools in the opinions of the wise, as they neglect the opportunities of amusement, without which the rugged road of life would be insupportably tedious. I think the French are the best philosophers, who make the most they can of the pleasures, and the least they can of the pains of life; and are ever strewing flowers among the thorns all mortals are obliged to walk through; whereas, by much reflection, the English contrive to see and feel the thorns double, and never see the flowers at all, but to despise them; expecting their happiness from things more solid and durable, as they imagine: but how seldom do they find them! One meets indeed with disappointments in trifles; but they are easier borne.[55]

For Knight, as for Shenstone, the physical garden constantly merges with its moral counterpart and the one becomes an invitation to consider the other: physical and metaphysical flowers become indistinguishable. What Knight argues for, here, is a philosophy of gardens that sets itself in opposition to the larger public claims of such figures as the Lytteltons at Hagley. A deliberate interest in trifles – flowers, gardens, domestic husbandry – is set against grander concerns. Her correspondence comes back to the issue again and again, arguing for a domestic scale of design and expenditure which seeks philosophical validation both of her own estate and that of Shenstone. This may well be some kind of riposte to her brother's studious retreat; but it is also surely a reaction to, and reversal of, that common association made between effeminacy and luxury (that is, a philosophical argument for the virtue of ephemeral pleasures implicitly addresses the problem confronted by well-to-do women of adopting feminine pastimes and then being damned for the triviality of those pastimes).[56] Thus, we should understand Knight's insistence on trifles not only as a riposte to her brother, but as an attempt – if perhaps a flawed one – to recuperate for women (or at least for herself) the garden as a place of pleasure potentially untroubled by the insistent moralising of others.[57] We should also understand it, perhaps, as betraying a nervousness about the small scale and an awareness of alternative – less favourable – interpretations. It is to those more difficult interpretations that we should now turn.

I would ward against the foolish and the censorious

Just as Bolingbroke had used Dawley, so Barrells was imagined as a means of propelling Knight back into the public world: it gathered about her a group of men and women, and thus helped in the creation of her own literary circle; it resulted in a garden that would be visited by the wider world; and just as Dawley was championed by Pope as an image of its owner, so the garden Knight created would be recognised as an account of the woman herself. It is here, however, that Knight's status as a woman in disgrace sees any positive aspects of that analogy break down, and it was Knight's acute sense of a public audience which would arguably prove most troublesome to her: not only was it public shame which had pushed her into obscure retirement, but any attempt to return from that obscurity could all too easily be met by a distinctly unforgiving public judgement. Knight's problem remained that, from the perspective of society, quiet disgrace appeared to be the only proper option. That Knight knew this, and that she saw how vital would be the interpretation of her garden's design, is made apparent not least by the sheer volume of correspondence on individual elements of the garden, their design, location, effect, and cost.

Certainly if we ask what visitors might see when they viewed Knight's landscape, one of the more alarming answers for Knight herself was that – rather than the carefully negotiated meanings of a personal iconography – they saw the much blunter images created by a public predisposed to judge landscape by gender expectations and by easy narratives of scandal and disgrace. It is important to keep this in mind as we explore Knight's garden, because it remains a subtext – and often more than that – in both design decisions and in the experience of retirement. Here, too, the longevity of Knight's public shame should not be underestimated. In the last decade of life her reputation was still thought questionable, and potentially dangerous to others, even as she remained a figure of gossip and fun. Travelling to the country for the health of her children, Delany's sister, Ann Dewes, wrote to Bernard Granville of an encounter with Knight (now Lady Luxborough) late in the summer of 1750:

We *were obliged* to ask leave of Lady Luxborough to come through her grounds, the roads being so bad the other way a coach *cannot come.* She was at the door to receive us, and obliged me to go in, was most profoundly civil, and comes to see me this week; I am not vastly fond of her acquaintance, though she is entertaining, and has made her house and garden very pretty.[58]

Hearing of the encounter, Delany soon replied:

Your journal, the account of Lady Luxborough, your farm-house, and all matters relating to you, entertained me extremely...

Now for Lady Luxborough. I am vastly entertained at your being acquainted with her in spite of your prudence; but I really see no reason why her acquaintance is to be declined. If she leads a discreet life, and does generous and charitable things, she ought to be taken notice of, as an encouragement to go on in the right path, and your conversation and example may be of infinite service to her.[59]

Two years later, Knight's notoriety continued to be a matter of amusement and concern, with Delany once again offering Knight as a figure of only half-reclaimed virtue, and writing in April 1752:

I am really diverted at your difficulties about Lady Luxborough... *Your* character is *too well* established to be hurt by an acquaintance with her, and Bath acquaintance are said to pass *with the waters*, and as people of fashion *and reputation* do not shun her I see no reason why you should do so in any *remarkable* way.[60]

What the Delany–Dewes exchange misses, of course, is the personal reso-nances of a landscape and the negotiations over an iconographic language at once public and private. Iconography in the form of busts and inscriptions assumes a certain kind of willing and to some extent intellectually sympa-thetic audience; Knight's problem, as these letters show, is that for the likes of Anne Dewes the experience of Barrells is not of a summer house, or an inscription, or any specific part of the garden, rather, it is an encounter with a disgraced woman. For Delany and Dewes the iconography is not in the detailed design of a landscape referred to simply as 'very pretty', instead, the icon is Knight and – irrespective of the design – her landscape signals a place of retired disgrace, or worse, a bodying forth of the unrepentant epicure. In some sense, of course, Delany and Dewes hardly need the physical geog-raphy of Barrells at all in order to see a landscape of shame; but if Knight remained unaware of Dewes' distinctly blunted moralising vision of her situation (they remained on visiting terms for some time to come), she was certainly aware that the designed features of a garden might lead to a clash of expectations. Just as for Shenstone, part of Knight's problem in designing and inhabiting a landscape was the ready conflation and confusion of pub-lic and private visions of landscape. In Shenstone's case that might mean no more than the locals picking his flowers and destroying his hedges, or, more challengingly, his fear that the great would laugh at the littleness of his designs. For Knight, however, it could be far more damaging, and we can see what is at stake by turning to some of the key features of Barrells ignored by Dewes: the statue of Venus, the hermitage, and the memorial urn to the poet William Somervile.

As the Delany–Dewes exchange suggests, any amount of iconography could fade from view when confronted by a moralising vision at once sweeping and bland; but for Knight, the choices involved in creating a landscape to be both inhabited by oneself and seen by others, were amongst the most important concerns of her last years. Of these, the most obviously curious – because the most apparently inappropriate – is also the least discussed in her remaining correspondence. As at the Leasowes, Knight had erected a statue of Venus in her garden.[61] At Barrells, however, the statue represents something of a conundrum, for as we have seen – most notoriously at West Wycombe – while Venus is the goddess of gardens, her erotic potential was hardly forgotten by those who chose to place her in their landscapes. Given Knight's history, we might wish to claim the choice of Venus therefore as a deliberate attempt to recover an earlier, less troubled landscape of pastoral romance, shared not only by Knight and Hertford and Rowe, but by women writers as disparate as the two Montagus, Elizabeth and Lady Mary. Conversely, and with the far safer figure of Diana apparently absent, we might also see the appearance of the Barrells Venus as an implicit attempt to resist or even ignore public opinion about a woman forced into retirement by sexual scandal.

Neither possibility seems quite adequate, if only because the remorseless gendering of nature as female and the equally remorseless, if casual, language of male erotics with which it was associated could hardly be unknown to Knight. What complicates matters further is that Knight was not wholly in control of the statue's more public meanings if only because the Latin inscriptions in her garden were selected and decided upon by men. In the case of Venus it was her friend Mr Outing who appears to have had the last word, placing the opening line of Horace's Ode I.30 – O Venus Regina Cnidi – above her 'Shrine' in the new pavilion and in doing so inviting not only Venus but Cupid to visit the garden (in Horace's original ode they are invited to leave Cyrus and visit Glycera – in the hopes that they will aid Horace to woo the latter – thus Outing's Latin tag invites at least a male audience to think of seduction).[62]

Without further evidence we cannot finally know Knight's agenda; however, where we have been left detailed letters a far more anxious account of garden iconography emerges, and we can trace this most easily with the aid of two quite different features of Knight's garden, the memorial urn to the poet William Somervile, and the hermitage.

William Somervile's only real claim to fame was a poem of 1735 entitled *The Chace*. A near neighbour of Knight's, Somervile lived at Edstone Hall in Warwickshire, and while he had published a series of poems on the theme of country sports, it was *The Chace* that made his name and that would be republished throughout the eighteenth century. By the time Knight arrived at Barrels in 1736, Somervile – known for his generous hospitality and sociability – was already an old man; he died six years later at the age of sixty six. Over a period of about a year, Knight wrote constantly to Shenstone on the question of a memorial urn for Somervile which she wanted to place in her grounds. While much of the letters was taken up with a discussion of the appropriate location for the urn, other major issues were the form the urn should take, its iconography, and the possible interpretation of that iconography. So, in a letter of late 1749, she told Shenstone, '[I] could wish it could be executed quite plain; and yet something expressive of him as a poet should be too. – Would not the laurel-wreath encircling the inscription be sufficient?', but tellingly she then continues, 'A thing much ornamented would be no proper expression of friendship from me, nor would it become the place: which is exposed a good deal to the licentiousness of our mob, which is not near so decent as yours'.[63] What starts to emerge here is an anxiety which becomes recurrent: Knight is all too aware of her own past, of the scandal which has forced her into retirement, and of the continuing influence of that scandal when she uses her garden to address the world beyond her own domestic space.

Some days after this letter, Knight wrote again on 'the inexhaustible topic of Urns', this time considering whether the motto should be in Latin or English. Deciding for the moment on English, she wrote:

It may be uncustomary; but a woman may be privileged to swerve from such rules as she may be supposed not to understand: and it will better please the generality of his and my common acquaintance, as well as the mob whom you call your friends. There will be less affectation in it, and will more become me. As also, to have the whole seem plain, and not costly. And also, the reason of my erecting it, to be plainly understood to mean no more than my esteem for him as a worthy Man and a good Poet, who had honoured me with his friendship: but I would ward against the *foolish* and the *censorious*, who might be capable of forging several such ridiculous reasons (notwithstanding his age and every other circumstance) that might draw on a reproach upon me for paying this tribute to his memory; and although I am in no sort afraid of unjust censure, yet I have suffered too much by it not to be cautious.[64]

What follows is another long discussion of the shape of the urn and its cost, along with a decision not to include garlands of flowers 'exclusive of the reason above-mentioned', and a further reiteration of her motivation as one of friendship and no more. The whole episode of the urn demonstrates not only the cultural depth of an eight-word inscription but the particular problems for women when 'speaking' in gardens. While Knight can exclaim at one point, 'Why don't I understand the beauties of Latin? or why have I not somebody to point them to me?' when discussing the appropriate language for the inscription, and so recognises herself as being embroiled in a far broader debate over male and female spheres of learning, she is also acutely aware that her actions are open to a specifically sexual misinterpretation which is unlikely to be at issue for men.[65] She shares with Shenstone a concern that the urn should be 'plainly understood', but she shares also an awareness that the garden and its design invite a potentially difficult range of response. Finally, then, while this long series of long letters about appropriate ornament and expression may be understood as an attempt to control the iconographic significance of a garden scene, the very length of the letters and their constant repetition point to an anxiety that this kind of control is not possible.[66] For all that she desires her urn to be 'plainly understood', Knight remains acutely aware that much of the language available to her (whether written words or decorative ornamentation) is open to a kind of sleazy or ribald interpretation beyond her control.

God knows I am as much alone as an hermit

One effect of public insistence on Knight's 'scandal' was that it was an insistence also that Knight should have no public life beyond the memory of that scandal. Banished to rural Warwickshire, she found herself publicly positioned as private because of an unsuitable public identity, and it was with this dilemma that both her garden and her correspondence had to contend. Nowhere was this more the case than in her relationship with the last of the garden structures I want to explore, the thatched hermitage she had constructed in the north-eastern corner of her garden.

The popularity of the hermitage in English landscape gardens was in no way confined to women, and Knight was only one of many who included a grotto or hermitage as part of the garden scene; but it is perhaps the hermitage more than any other structure in the garden which highlights a radical disjunction between easy public judgements and a more difficult world of private reflection. As David Coffin has shown, Knight's hermitage – like

Shenstone's – is part of a much larger gardening tradition with structures
ranging from mere root-houses (like Shenstone's) to much grander structures like those built for Queen Caroline at Richmond, or by Lord Orrery
at Caledon, his estate in County Tyrone.[67] Mary Delany's description of the
latter provides us with a good sense of just how elaborate such structures
might be. Writing to Anne Dewes of the ongoing work at Orrery's gardens
in 1748 she notes:

Nothing is completed yet but an *hermitage*, which is about an acre of ground – an
island, planted with all the variety of trees, shrubs, and flowers that will grow in this
country, abundance of little winding walks, differently embellished with little seats
and banks; in the midst is placed an hermit's cell, made of the roots of trees, the floor
is paved with pebbles, there is a couch made of matting, and little wooden stools, a
table with a manuscript on it, a pair of spectacles, a leathern bottle; and hung up in
different parts, an hourglass, a weatherglass and several mathematical instruments,
a shelf of books, another of wooden platters and bowls, another of earthen ones, in
short everything that you might imagine necessary for a recluse. *Four little gardens
surround his house* – an orchard, a flower-garden, a physick-garden, and a kitchen-
garden, with a kitchen to boil a teakettle or so: I never saw so pretty *a whim* so
thoroughly well executed.[68]

In part what Delany recognises here – not least in that claim for the whim-
sicality of Orrery's designs – is the public nature of an apparently private
gesture towards meditation and reflection. Such structures, whether large or
small, work as emblems: they speak to the idea of meditation – 'everything
that you might imagine necessary for a recluse' – rather than being spaces
in which one might actually meditate; they offer a public gesture, but have
little to say about the private experience of being alone; and they affirm
a set of normative values in this case assuming the importance of pious
meditation when retired from public life.

   This sense of the hermitage as at once public and private, and, more
than this, that it might signal a disjunction between public expectation and
private experience, finds its close companion in those eighteenth-century
discussions of pleasurable melancholy and debilitating low spirits already
encountered. In the letters of Elizabeth Montagu and Elizabeth Carter,
in those of Lady Mary Wortley Montagu, of Anna Seward, and of Frances
Burney, the hermitage becomes an easy shorthand for the simple life, for the
contemplative and private, rather than the fashionable and public. Montagu
might invite Frances Boscawen to visit Sandleford and style this large house
and garden as 'my hermitage, where you shall be entertained with the
wholesome fare of brown bread, sincerity, and red cow's milk, which afford

good nourishment to the mind and body; and far away be the poison of ragouts and flattery'; Carter might find in Bath that, 'in spite of all the infection of the Pump-room, and my very little care to prevent catching it, I remain as wise, and as sober, and as dull, as if I dwelt opposite to it, in some hermitage on the side of the rock'; and Seward might enjoy the natural style of Mrs Mompessan's garden, where 'Instead of arbours, that looked like green wigs, we sit at noon in root-houses, and in the rocky hermitage';[69] but just as Carter recognised the pleasures of melancholy were pleasures only with the knowledge that they could be left behind, so the hermitage appears as a feature to be seen, or visited, or imagined, rather than one to be physically or psychologically inhabited when alone.[70]

For Knight, things were quite different: they were different because of the contradictory ways in which female retirement might be imagined, and different too because she inhabited a landscape which she could not leave. We have already seen how Knight was excluded from her brother Bolingbroke's insistently masculine vision of retirement even as their letters shared the language of the reclusive hermit. We have seen, too, that Knight shared with the melancholic Shenstone the urge to create a garden inviting and supporting a sociability which might move its owner beyond the reclusive state.[71] But the easy language of the happy hermit – with its reliance on pleasurable moral choice – could at times be hard to sustain, and indeed could find itself most strained when confronted by the very garden structure apparently signifying the pleasures of that choice. Knight's hermitage, like Shenstone's, was far from the grand designs of Lord Orrery or Queen Caroline, but if it did not contain the wealth of emblematic features of either of these earlier models, it nevertheless held an iconic place within her landscape precisely because it was an invitation to think upon one's situation.

Delany's judgement on the whimsical hermitage of Lord Orrery is driven in part by the recognition that the sheer emphasis on detail, the physical creation of an emblematic design, implicitly undermines its other-worldly claims. Just as at Richings Lady Hertford could laughed at Lord Bathurst's obsessive garden-making and set it against her own ability to enjoy that garden as a place of use, so, here, Orrery's hermitage can be figured as no more than an expensive object of desire, an icon of consumerism masquerading as an invitation to pious retreat. Many years after she had written that poem, it was Hertford, too, perhaps more than any other, who reminded Knight of an alternative – and unwelcome – mode of inhabiting retirement. After the death first of her son and then of her husband, Hertford (by this time Duchess of Somerset) had retreated almost entirely from public life, maintaining a small household and a pious disposition. That disposition, while undoubtedly devout, did little to assuage Knight's own sense of retirement as a form of loss; it did, however, make apparent two quite different experiences of female retirement.

What Knight and Hertford undoubtedly shared was a sense that the way in which one inhabits retirement cannot be divorced from a sense of one's place in the world. But we can see the split between the two friends perhaps most clearly when we turn to their reactions to the same book, James Hervey's *Meditations on a Flower Garden in a Letter to a Lady* (1746).[72] Hervey's title page included the following quotation from *The Spectator* no. 477:

I look upon the Pleasure, which we take in a Garden, as one of the most innocent Delights in human Life. A Garden was the Habitation of our first Parents before the Fall. It is naturally apt to fill the Mind with Calmness and Tranquillity, and to lay all its turbulent Passions at Rest. It gives us a great Insight into the Contrivances and Wisdom of Providence, and suggests innumerable Subjects for Meditation.

In the essay which followed Hervey took quite literally the suggestion that gardens furnish innumerable subjects for meditation: each element of the garden is either, by analogy, a representation of God's wondrousness, or is actually a demonstration of God's beneficence. Thus, according to Hervey:

One can scarce be melancholy with the *Atmosphere* of Flowers: Such lively Hues, and delicious Odours, not only address themselves agreeably to the Senses, but touch, with a surprising Delicacy, the sweetest Movements of the Mind . . . How often have I felt them *dissipate* the *Gloom* of *Thought*, and transfuse a sudden Gaiety through the dejected Spirit . . . But if this be so pleasing, what transporting Pleasures must arise, from the Fruition of uncreated Excellency! O, what *unknown Delights*, to enter into thy *immediate Presence*, most Blessed Lord God. (pp. 48–9)

More than this, a right understanding of the garden, a recognition that it is full of 'sacred hints', and that to 'an attentive Mind the *Garden* turns *Preacher*' (p. 94), leads Hervey to insist on the acceptance of one's lot, however miserable that lot may be:

What a striking Argument is here for *Resignation*, unfeigned acceptance, to all the Disposals of Providence! Too often are our dissatisfied Thoughts apt to find Fault with Divine Dispensations: We tacitly arraign our Maker's Conduct, or question His Kindness with regard to ourselves: We fancy our Lot not so commodiously situate, or our Condition not so happily circumstanced, as if we had been placed in some other Station of Life. – But let us behold this exquisitely nice *Regulation* of the *minutest Plants*, and be ashamed of our repining Folly. (pp. 74–5)

Hertford admired the book greatly and had recommended it to Knight in 1748.[73] Knight in turn wrote of it to Shenstone, but with far less admiration.[74] Having collected flower seeds for Shenstone's hermitage, including star of Bethlehem and passion flower, she wryly claimed this would make 'your Hermitage more proper for the reception of Mr. James Hervey, should he travel your way' (2 November 1748). Hervey's insistence that one see past the physical creation to the greater creation beyond it clearly appealed to Hertford, and in many ways reiterated the views of her old friend and mentor Elizabeth Rowe; conversely, the playfulness of Knight's letter – the implicit urge to treat the hermitage as an amusement, a trifle – surely demonstrates a resistance both to Hervey's claims and to Hertford's way of life. In describing that life, Hertford wrote to Knight of a typical day:

> I rise at seven, but do not go down till nine, when the Bell rings, and my whole Family meet me at Chapel; after Prayers, we go down to Breakfast; any Friend who happens to be there, myself, and my Chaplain, have ours in the little Library ... About eleven, if the Weather permits, we go to walk in the Park, or take the Air in the Coach: but if it be too bad for either, we return to our various Occupations. At three we dine; sit perhaps near an Hour afterwards; then separate, till we meet at eight for Prayers; after which we adjourn again to the Library, where somebody reads aloud, unless some Stranger comes who chuses Cards, until Half an Hour past nine, when we sup, and always part before eleven. This to the fine World would sound a melancholy monastic Life; and I cannot be supposed to have chosen it from my Ignorance of the Splendour and Gaiety of a Court, but from a thorough Experience that they can give no solid Happiness; and I find myself more calmly pleased in my present Way of Living, and more truly contented, than I ever was in the Bloom and Pomp of my Youth. I am no longer dubious what Point to pursue. There is but one proper for the Decline of Life, and indeed the only one worth the Anxiety of a rational Creature at any Age: but how do the Fire of Youth and Flattery of the World, blind our Eyes, and mislead our Fancies, after a Thousand imaginary Pleasures which are sure to disappoint us in the End![75]

But this emphasis on pious domestic seclusion held less and less appeal for Knight. A year before her death she wrote to Shenstone: 'My correspondents are few: the Duchess of Somerset is too much retired to hear what passes, and is too wrapt up in religion and moral reflection to admit of other subjects in her letters.'[76]

The friends' division over Hervey's *Meditations*, and the lack of welcome with which these last letters from Hertford were received, points not only to Hertford's distinctly conventional choice of a pious retirement but to Knight's quite different understanding of her situation. Indeed, despite

Hertford's last letters to Knight continuing to record her pleasure in the joys of the garden, her focus on domestic piety, the unwelcome sense of contentment they express for the small-scale society of the household, and their insistent lack of expectation in earthly pleasures, should highlight for us Knight's desire for something beyond this, a desire for that larger and more public world that Anne Dewes and her like were so unwilling to allow a woman in disgrace.

By the winter of 1753–4 Knight no longer embraced the role of the hermit as she had once claimed to do, writing to Shenstone on the departure of her friend Mrs Davies that she has been left:

to horrid solitude . . . You will, methinks, stare at the epithet *horrid* which I have annexed to *solitude*; as that used to please me, and be called *sweet* at least; but changes of one kind bring changes of another, even without being owing to fickleness, as my life has proved to me; yet my tastes are the same; and I had rather now deck a rural bower than glitter on a birthnight at court; but as we are all made for society, the loss of neighbours and of limbs, makes these bowers more irksome than inviting.

Two months later she wrote again to Shenstone, 'God knows I am as much alone as an hermit'.[77] But even before this, the idea of pleasurable solitude to which the hermitage so insistently gestured was capable of sparking uneasy sensations.[78] Writing to Hertford in 1742, soon after their correspondence had been re-established, Knight took up the theme, and, to Hertford's suggestion that studious reading must make solitude pleasurable, Knight countered with the following confession:

The time was that well you know I preferred reading to all the gaieties of the town . . . consequently you'd have thought it would have been my greatest comfort in solitude, but I have fatally experienced that my anxious thoughts have been so far from relieved by it, that I could not settle to it, or know what I have read . . . for some ungrateful friend or low-minded enemy has generally furnished me with disagreeable reflections, which other more agreeable ones could not put out of my mind. For what one meets with in books, though pleasing to the imagination, are not realities, which the mortifications of life are . . . in short I have found that books are of the least use when most wanted.[79]

What is most striking here is just how far Knight finds herself both from Hertford and from Bolingbroke. With Hertford she had shared that early delight in pastoral romance, with Bolingbroke she shared the language of the happy hermit. In his essay on the true use of retirement, Bolingbroke, like Hertford, had insisted on the importance of 'study and reflection, or reading and conversation', for Knight, however, disgrace – and her acute

awareness of that disgrace – distanced her from those things claimed both
by her friend and by her brother to make solitude admirable or bearable.
While the solitary act of reading is set against the false pleasures of public life,
an equally false vision of retirement as easy pastoral pleasure is set against –
and shown unable to resist – the unromantic realities of life. As Knight
had found, that world of books, of *Pastor Fido* and of pastoral romance,
not only failed to relate to 'realities' but in its failure to do so was actively
dangerous; the imagined pleasures of solitary meditation are set against the
false pleasures of the town, but here solitude ultimately invites bitterness
and misery because it allows 'disagreeable reflections' to flood in, and offers
nothing to resist them.

What could resist such 'disagreeable reflections', however, was gardening
itself. Just as Mary Coke would immerse herself in the activity of planting
and weeding in order to ward off misery, so Knight would use the garden
to waylay an overwhelming sense of loneliness. In 1749, complaining to
Shenstone that all her friends have left the country at the same time, she
wrote: 'Nothing is so terrible as parting from friends: and to have taken
leave and then have gone to bed, had been such an image of death, that I
avoided it as much as possible, and endeavoured to banish them all from
my mind.' She then continued:

luckily a man came to fell some trees, just as they were setting out: and immediately
looking upon him as upon a tutelar angel sent to my assistance, I never returned to
the house, but walked, under his protection, all over my grounds, and particularly
to the farther end of the Long Avenue; where I ordered a crooked row of scrub
trees to be fallen, and a strait row of elms to be planted, and other views to be
opened, by felling and transplanting about the Old Summer-house; as also near the
Grove-Pool, to shew the winding of the walk from the Coppice and other points;
and several roots to be stocked up for future root-houses.[80]

What then of the hermitage, its invitation to reflect on one's situation, and
its implicit invitation, also, to accept one's lot? As Elizabeth Carter was
aware, for visitors to a landscape garden, the hermitage and other such
signals of melancholia may be a pleasant invitation to private thought, but
that invitation becomes unwelcome – even destructive – if the scene cannot
be left behind: the pleasures of melancholy are pleasures only when they are
momentary indulgences, to be abandoned with the scene itself. For Carter
(as for Anne Grant, who begged a friend in Plympton not to 'wed yourself
too much to your hermitage. Too much ease, convenience, and dominion,
breed either apathy, or peevishness, just as people are formed'), the danger

of the hermitage was that one would come out of it just as one went in, or worse, its invitation to reflection could merely amplify one's sense of misery. As Carter wrote in a letter to Elizabeth Montagu: 'I know not what other virtues a hermitage may be capable of producing, but I am not absolutely of your mind that it is a soil for charity. The faults (for faults there will be in every state) which arise in solitude, are of a restrained and solitary kind, and not likely to give us the fellow feeling which we should naturally experience in society.'[81]

For Knight, too – trapped in her enforced retirement at Barrells – the hermitage signalled a disjunction between the casually viewed and the constantly inhabited, between the social expectations of quiet retreat and the debilitating experience of depression. It is not that Knight was unable to feel contentment in retreat, indeed her letters continue to gesture towards the pleasures of solitude. We can even find brief moments in which she can enjoy an experience close to classic pastoral retirement, as in a letter from the summer of 1751, where she writes,

I sat last night agreeably though alone, looking at the neighbouring hills, hearing my mowers whet their scythes, seeing the troop-horses scamper about my avenue, and hearing one of the Grass-Guard Dragoons play on his German Flute.[82]

But more often, that ability to live the literary fails her, and her hermitage – the classic site for solitary meditation – stays uninhabited. Writing to Shenstone of her hermitage, she concludes, 'you will say, it is just a proper place for indulging melancholy thoughts; which is true; but therefore I ought to shun it'.[83] Part of Knight's problem then, is that the private space of the hermitage, with its claim for the garden as a place of meditative retirement, is also a sign of public expectations, a sign of one's place in the world, and a sign by which one might be judged.

Thus, by the 1750s, while Knight acknowledges her position as a recluse, that position is hardly comfortable and we find her writing of her situation:

The stagnation of the commodity *Scandal*, I am *not* sorry for; but *that* of the currency of wit, humour, or indeed the mere occurrences of the day, we suffer by: for when *they* circulate, *we* give less way to melancholy thoughts, which are too apt to prey upon the minds of us recluse people, and do us as much hurt in one sense, as the people of the world's having no thought at all does them in another.[84]

Faced with this absence of society, faced too with the knowledge of a scandal-loving public quite willing to remember her shame, Knight's experience of retirement left the hermitage a troubling reminder of a life she failed to lead. It was an invitation to meditate, certainly, but an invitation which implicitly assumed the kind of pious quietude embraced by her friend Lady Hertford, or worse, the necessity of retreat as the continuing punishment for a scandalous past.

Knight's teenage letters were full of youthful imaginings of pastoral solitude; her letters to Bolingbroke and to Shenstone attempted to share the tenuous happiness of the recluse; but by her forties the role of the hermitess is increasingly recognised as damaging and dangerous because it reinforces a sense of loneliness, abandonment, and failure. Where the politically disgraced Bolingbroke could place righteous inscriptions around his estates, flattering his own self-worth, and finding their champion in Alexander Pope, Knight had to contend with a kind of gendered scandal that made recuperation almost impossible: her disgrace set her apart, and her retirement offered neither rehabilitation nor quiet ease. Disappearing from public view, she remained a figure of scandal in the public imagination.[85] Despite the attempts to create a new circle of friends, and despite a few brief trips beyond Warwickshire, her life of retirement was as much enforced as it was a choice, and those old stories of scandal remained acutely present. The effect of this can be seen in the long anxieties over Somervile's urn, but it can be seen, too, in Knight's ambiguous response to a life she was expected to embrace. Outside of the *Spectator*'s complacent fiction of domesticity, that is, solitude, meditation, and retirement could become alarmingly oppressive, and the knowledge of literary traditions, or of pious friends, could only make them weigh more heavily.

Confronting a melancholy more than merely literary, and with a situation from which one could not simply walk away, Knight's letters from Barrells may yearn for the pleasure of retirement but they also register its impossibility. In this, then, she shares much with Elizabeth Montagu and with Elizabeth Carter, with Caroline Holland and with Mary Coke. If meditation offers the literary ideal of pleasing melancholy, it also offers the risk of debilitation and depression. And solitude – so much vaunted by Addison as part of a domestic idyll – becomes something quite different when one feels genuinely abandoned and alone. Knight's small pleasures, and the need to define such pleasures as trifles, found itself echoed in her friend Shenstone's uncomfortable retreat; so too did her need for the garden to be a place of immediate pleasures rather than a reminder of joys to come.[86] More than this, Knight's 'disagreeable reflections' would find their echo in Mary Coke's 'miserable reflections on the sorrows of my life', and, as for Coke, it would not be the opportunity for meditation but the activity of gardening, the busy work of planning, and the laborious work of planting, which offered any release there might be from the experience of retirement as punishment, loneliness, and shame.

6 | 'Though very retired, I am very happy'

The case studies in the second half of this book offer no neat narratives of formal change in garden design, nor do they claim a form of garden characteristic of women. Rather, in constructing an account of how individual women wrote of themselves and their gardens throughout the century, they seek to explore some of the ways in which the garden might be inhabited and imagined. That imagining and habitation at times has little to do with the formalities of design; but it has much to do with the activity of gardening and with the experience of retirement – however they might be defined.

At the beginning of this book I suggested that women's experience of retirement was affected by the peculiar nature of retirement itself, at once an invitation to pleasure and to resignation, to suffering and to delight. I suggested another peculiarity, too, which is that eighteenth-century archives offer us only limited access to the experience of most women who spent their time in gardens: we must move some way up the social scale if we are to find sustained accounts of women's gardening life. It is with one such account, by a woman from the lower reaches of the middling sort, that we can conclude.

In the early years of the nineteenth century, the young governess Ellen Weeton wrote letters in which she recorded the experience of working in gardens she did not own.[1] Even here, references to gardening are hardly extensive, but I turn to them because these glancing references offer us so much of what has been important, so many of the tropes and figures of gardening that we have encountered throughout this book, and so clear a demonstration of what might be shared by women when they find themselves in the physical and imaginative space of the garden.

In her early letters, Weeton, at this point a young governess, records both the strangeness and the delight of planting, weeding, and digging new beds in her employers' vegetable gardens; in later letters, with more confidence in her skill, and with more room to work, she tells also of her attempts to replant an arbour and to cut new views. Perhaps most striking in the brief glimpses of Weeton's gardening life, for all the obvious differences, is just how much she shares with other far more wealthy women. It is not simply the record of events or actions that is important here, it is that the language on which she can draw in order to make sense of, and at times make tolerable, a life of often uncomfortable servitude is also a language shared by women of much higher status and with much larger gardens.

In the summer of 1808, working on the vegetable plot of her neighbours the Braithwaites at Up Holland (near Wigan), Weeton wrote with pride to her brother of the seven hours spent 'weeding, scuttling, raking and sweeping', of a garden 'almost like a wilderness' and of earning her dinner 'by the sweat of our brows'.[2] A year after this early encounter with gardening she wrote to Catherine Braithwaite that: 'Sewing occupies a very small portion [of my time]. It never was an amusement with me. I always consider it as work. I am a great deal in the garden, working – or according to my ideas, playing with the spade, the fork, and the rake, delving, planting potatoes, cabbages, and beans.'[3] Distanced from the 'work' of the needle – so closely aligned both with responsible femininity and with the leisured status of the lady – the value of garden labour appears as a form of release from domestic life inside the house; the early nod to Genesis, to turning a wilderness into paradise through labour, is of course a commonplace of garden writing, while planting potatoes or using a rake are nothing if not quotidian; but the ubiquity of these ideas and actions should not hide from us the importance of the garden as a space in which to articulate a gendered sense of self in terms of leisure and of labour, of pleasure and of virtue. Indeed, Weeton's easy elision of labour and pleasure – again so characteristic of garden writing – is characteristic also, of course, of pastoral, and highlights for us the peculiar ability of the garden to take the gardener elsewhere, to release them from the everyday even in the performance of everyday activities. But as Weeton's letters also suggest, that release is rarely complete. Writing to her brother again, she records coming from the garden one morning with spade and rake in hand, and confesses 'I all on a sudden grew frolicksome, and began to dance and jump over various back-yard utensils'. The sense of sheer pleasure is important here, certainly, but as she describes her 'elegant' and 'graceful agility' and her stout landlady's good-natured but clumsy caricature of her actions (which end with the latter falling and 'sprawling like – a frog in a ditch'), so too is Weeton's awareness of nuanced class distinction and of the need to conjure up vulgarity if only in order to distance oneself from it ('Now only imagine you saw two lone women, God help 'em! going on as I tell you we did – Surely the innocence of our amusements were equal to their vulgarity').[4]

Five years later – writing from High Royd, near Huddersfield – the uncertainty of a governess's social status is no less keenly felt when she writes of her unhappiness in the household of Mr and Mrs Armitage, of the latter vindictively preventing her from buying a bonnet (and thus from going to church), of 'The little wood I began cutting some walks in last Autumn, [which] has again become the scene of my daily labours this Spring', of 'laborious, though agreeable employment . . . cutting brambles, hollins, brackins, and broom, and planting flowers', and of her acute sense of dismay that her employers 'have not once thanked me, either directly or indirectly'.

Thanked or not, Weeton found in this garden of her own creation (and re-creation) a place both of pleasure and of escape; she found, too, a happy image of the moral failures of 'fine ladies' and of her own sense of worth: where 'Mrs A[rmitage] had suffered it to be neglected', Weeton 'went into a little overgrown wood, where once had been a pretty walk', and 'Here, with a pair of great hedge-clippers, I worked for an hour before dinner, literally cutting my way'. The literal here is of course also metaphorical, and garden labour offers a powerful image of Christian fortitude. But it also offers less comfortable realisations, a sense that one's desires may be foolish or excessive ('Should I remain here, this wood would become my hobby horse'), and that the pleasure one takes in nature will naturally be thwarted:

Mr A[rmitage] has given me leave to have a few trees cut down, to open a view, and to plant an arbour in their place; this will occupy my leisure hours next Spring, and my little ones please themselves with thinking what a delightful place the wood will be, for playing in at hide-and-seek. In the evening, we took a walk. But now that Winter has arrived, all these little amusements are put a stop to. I wish . . . I wish Winter was over![5]

That the odious Mrs Armitage went on to place a summer house in this wood, and enjoyed its pleasures (but not its labours) as her own, was a further cause of rancour for Miss Weeton; but it should alert us once again to the ways in which the shared physical location of the garden might be inhabited by two individuals as fundamentally different spaces.

This sense that the physical location of the garden can mark other kinds of dislocation – whether social, emotional, spiritual, or imaginative – has been at the centre of this study and has found itself most frequently articulated in the troubled language of retirement. In my opening chapters I aimed to set out some of those troubles in some detail, and in the case studies which followed I attempted to map out that complex of ideas which makes retirement a place of pleasure and of punishment, a welcome solitude and a lonely ordeal; but Weeton can help us here too. Like many other women, Weeton claims the language of retirement as her own, but in doing so she signals an uncertainty about its value which is not just characteristic of women's garden writing, but characteristic of the position in which women find themselves when confronted by the complex and often contradictory conventions and narratives of female retirement.

In an early letter from the outskirts of Liverpool, Weeton frames her stay at a house called Beacon Gutter ('a fine elegant sounding name, is it not?') in terms of retirement from the city and from the sophistications of public life: 'Though only two miles from Liverpool, I am as retired here as possible, few people passing or coming in.' As we have seen, that awareness of the city, even in the claim for retirement, is hardly unique to Weeton; neither is the pairing of phrases in the same letter to her friend Mrs Whitehead, where she writes, 'though very retired, I am very happy'.[6] Rather, Weeton reiterates a long tradition of women's writing from the country which makes a troubled claim for the pleasures of retirement even as it recognises the desire for something else, or something more, and even as it recognises a predominating cultural weight which insists such female desires are wrong.

At the very end of our period, Weeton's letters offer us the perspective of a woman who did not own the gardens in which she laboured. But they offer us also a gendered and hierarchically nuanced sense of identity; an awareness of how one will be seen and positioned by others; a turn to the language of retirement and to gendered models of labour and virtue; an urge to find in the garden a space which allows one to leave one's social position behind, and an equally strong sense that this is impossible. Above all, Weeton's letters demonstrate an acute sense that the garden offers peculiar pleasures and a peculiar opportunity to represent the complexities of the social self. Though their experiences were radically different, and though they gardened on an altogether different scale, this complex of concerns was as pressing for Elizabeth Montagu as it was for Caroline Holland, Mary Coke, and Henrietta Knight. Those case studies have sought to tease out the nuances of understanding and self-representation – of what is different as well as what is shared – and in so doing they have sought also to recover at least some sense of what the garden might mean for individual women, whether that garden was owned, or visited, or imagined.

Gardens reiterate the obsessions of eighteenth-century culture, but most particularly in the language of reward and punishment, of desire, delight, and danger, they highlight the problem for women of attempting to do retirement by the book. As we have seen, those books are so many and so various that one single account of retirement is impossible, and one easy experience of it impossible also; but, those divisions and dichotomies of pious retirement and disgraced retreat which we have seen repeated throughout this volume nevertheless remain central to women's understandings of their gardens throughout the century and they are central too, therefore, to our own understanding of the eighteenth-century garden as a space to be inhabited, used, and imagined, a space in which to understand oneself.

Notes

Introduction

1. But for this last see Mary Delany's letter to Anne Dewes, December 21 1753 in which she records the death of Mr Osborn (brother-in-law to Lord Halifax) who hanged himself in the garden with his pocket handkerchief, in Delany, *Autobiography and Correspondence*, vol. 1, pp. 189–90.
2. For this, see Hudson, *Holland House*, p. 26; and for Sarah Lennox's life, and that of her sisters, see Tillyard, *Aristocrats*.
3. She had also, of course, swapped her name firstly to Bunbury, then on her divorce in 1776 she returned to Lennox, and later, with her remarriage in 1781, to Napier.
4. Strong, *Artist and the Garden*, p. 15.
5. See Longstaffe-Gowan, *London Town Garden*.
6. For what remains a useful overview of solitude in the eighteenth century, see Havens, 'Solitude and the Neoclassicists'; the theme is central also to Spacks, *Privacy*; and for an account of solitude in Mary Wollstonecraft's writing which is also an account of solitude and self in the western tradition, see especially Taylor, 'Separations of Soul'.
7. Williamson, *Polite Landscapes*.
8. Recent work has begun to set this right. See Bell, 'Women Create Gardens in Male Landscapes'; Bennett, *Five Centuries of Women and Gardens*; Way, *Virgins, Weeders, and Queens*; for the early modern period, and especially for the gendered division of labour, see Bushnell, *Green Desire*, and Munroe, *Gender and the Garden*; for the beginning of the nineteenth century, Schenker, 'Women, Gardens, and the English Middle Class', and for the late eighteenth to the mid-nineteenth century see Page and Smith, *Women, Literature, and the Domesticated Landscape*.
9. While he concentrates largely on the French context, I have found Daniel Brewer's formulation of 'space' (via Lefebvre) particularly helpful: 'Space is not neutral or objective; nor is it fixed, transparent, innocent or indifferent. Instead, it is wilfully produced, a product resulting from the transformation of matter, the application of knowledge, of technology, and of labor. Space is a social product, moreover, generated by a social subject, be it an individual subject, or just as likely, a collective one. In either case that subject's reality results from and depends upon its ability to occupy and master space', Brewer, 'Lights in Space', pp. 179–80.

10. See Røstvig, *The Happy-Man*, E. M. W. Tillyard, *Some Mythical Elements in English Literature*.

11. For the most recent account of Luxborough's life, see Brown, *My Darling Herriot*.

12. For models of classical male retirement, see Røstvig, *The Happy Man*.

13. See, for example, Clark, *English Landscape Garden*; Hussey, *English Gardens*; Hunt, *Figure in the Landscape*; Brownell, *Alexander Pope and the Arts*, ch. 5.

14. See Clark, *English Landscape Garden*; Hussey, *English Gardens and Landscapes*; Hunt, *Figure in the Landscape*; Brownell, *Alexander Pope*; Hadfield, *History of British Gardening*; Paulson, *Emblem and Expression*; Williams, 'Making Places'; Williamson, *Polite Landscapes*; Harwood, 'Personal Identity'.

15. Quaintance, 'Walpole's Whig Interpretation of Landscaping History'; Bending, 'Horace Walpole and Eighteenth-Century Garden History'; Leslie, 'History and Historiography in the English Landscape Garden'.

16. Snell, *Annals of the Labouring Poor*; Bermingham, *Landscape and Ideology*; Williamson, *Transformation of Rural England*; Williamson & Bellamy, *Property and Landscape*; Neeson, *Commoners*.

17. Williamson, *Polite Landscapes*.

18. See Wilson (ed.), *Country House Kitchen Garden*; Campbell, *History of Kitchen Gardening*; Laird, *Flowering of the Landscape Garden*; Longstaffe-Gowan, *London Town Garden*.

19. Hunt, *Greater Perfections*, p. 81.

20. Cosgrove, *Social Formation and Symbolic Landscape*, ch. 1; Andrews, *Landscape and Western Art*, ch. 3.

21. Hunt, *Afterlife of Gardens*.

22. See, for example, Ousby, *Englishman's England*; Bending, 'One among the Many'; Calder (ed.), *Experiencing the Garden*.

23. See also Ross's exploration of the problems in *What Gardens Mean*, ch. 6.

24. See, for example, Daniels' careful accounts of the exchanges between Repton and his clients, in *Humphry Repton*.

25. Lady Caroline Damer to Lady Caroline Dawson, Countess of Portarlington, 28 April 1785, in Clark (ed.), *Gleanings from an Old Portfolio*, vol. 2.

26. Laird, *Flowering of the Landscape Garden*.

27. Young, *Six Week Tour*, pp. 40–1.

28. But see Lewis's account of Sarah, Duchess of Marlborough, at Blenheim, Frances, Viscountess Irwin at Temple Newsam, and Frances Talbot at Saltram, 'When Is a House Not a Home'; see also Halpern, 'The Duke of Kent's Garden at Wrest Park' which argues that because Wrest retained a formal layout it hasn't been deemed important by garden historians looking at the development of the English style; as she demonstrates, it featured in numerous tours and was not seen as old-fashioned by contemporaries.

29. Way, *Virgins Weeders and Queens*, p. 7.

30. Journal entry, Notting Hill, 26 September 1767, in James A. Home (ed.), *The Letters and Journals of Lady Mary Coke*, 4 vols. (Edinburgh: David Douglas, 1889).

31. Elizabeth Montagu to Elizabeth Carter, Sandleford 22 June 1786, and Montagu to Elizabeth Vesey Sandleford 26 July 1786 (Huntington Library Ms, MO6129, and MO6610).

32. The Wotton estate papers are at the Huntington Library: Wotton account book, 1757–70 (STG Accounts Box 24) Brown was paid £100 on 2 December 1757, and the same again on 3 June and 16 November 1758; a further bill for plants and seeds was paid to 'Brown and Williamson' in October 1766; Garden Accounts 1771–75 (ST vol. 236); Wotton Accounts 1780–99 (STG Accounts Box 25), containing the associated payment vouchers quoted here.

33. Shaftesbury, *Life, Unpublished Letters and Philosophical Regimen*, p. 251.

34. Coffin, *English Garden*, ch. 2; Bowerbank, *Speaking for Nature*. And, for a mid-century example of this, see the accounts of the Honourable Mrs Monk and Catherine Bovey's lives of retirement in Ballard, *Memoirs of Several Ladies of Great Britain*.

35. As Hunt has argued, for example, Stephen Switzer's work makes far more sense in the context of later seventeenth-century understandings of the garden's intimate and intertwined relations with the agricultural and horticultural world of which it was a part rather than as anomalous prophecy. See Hunt, *Greater Perfections*, p. 181.

36. Switzer, *Ichnographia Rustica*, vol. 1, pp. 73–4.

37. Indeed, while garden history has always had a place for royal patrons, as the mass of writing surrounding Kew suggests, women's involvement still tends to be figured in terms of sexuality, domesticity, and piety. For the politics of Kew, see especially, 'Kew Gardens: A Controversial Georgian Landscape', *New Arcadian Journal*, and Bending, 'A Natural Revolution?'.

38. Thus, while garden writing of all kinds might be addressed to men, an overt address to women tends to be confined to publications on flowers and flower or kitchen gardening, as, for example, *The Flower-Garden Displayed ... To which is added, A Flower-Garden for Gentlemen and Ladies...* (1734); *The Complete Florist; or, the Lady and Gentleman's Recreation in the Flower Garden* (1775); *The Garden-Companion, for Gentlemen and Ladies; or, a Calendar, pointing out what should be done every month in the Green-House, Flower, Fruit and Kitchen Garden ... (c. 1795)*; or the numerous drawing books aimed specifically at women, such as Heckle, *The Lady's Drawing Book: Consisting of about an Hundred Different Sorts of Flowers, all drawn after Nature ... the whole adapted to engage the Fair Sex to a Profitable Improvement of their Leisure Hours* (1755). As Shteir's work demonstrates, by late in the century women were becoming more firmly associated also with the scientific discourse of botany, for which see Shteir, *Cultivating Women, Cultivating Science*; see also Page and Smith, *Women, Literature, and the Domesticated Landscape*.

39. Evelyn, *The Lady's Recreation*, p. 1.

40. Hervey, *Reflections on a Flower Garden in a Letter to a Lady*; the title page motto is a quotation from *The Spectator*, no. 477, 'I look upon the Pleasure, which we take in a Garden, as one of the most innocent Delights in human Life. A Garden

was the Habitation of our first Parents before the Fall. It is naturally apt to fill the Mind with Calmness and Tranquillity, and to lay all its turbulent Passions at Rest. It gives a great Insight into the Contrivances and Wisdom of Providence, and *Suggests innumerable Subjects for Meditation.*'

41. See Mason, *The English Garden*, Book IV, and in particular the sentimental tale of Nerina (in turn reminiscent of James Thomson's Amelia, Lavinia, and Musidora).
42. Anon, *Letters to Honoria and Marianne*, vol. 1, p. 57.
43. But for a knowing, and delighted, reversal of these gendered assumptions about flower gardens, see Frances Burney to Charles Burney, Bookham, October 1796, one of the many letters in which she describes her husband's dedication to, and pleasure in, the vegetable and flower garden, in Burney, *Diary and Letters*, vol. 3, p. 592.
44. Letter from Lady Mary Wortley Montagu to Mary Wortley Montagu Stuart, Countess of Bute, 6 March 1753 in Montagu, *Letters and Works*, vol. 3, pp. 52–3.
45. Carter, *Letters to Mrs. Montagu*, vol. 3, p. 358.
46. Usher, *Letters of Elizabeth, Lucy, and Judith Ussher*, Letter XVI.
47. British Museum Satires 5442. A husband and wife venture, the Darlys' satirical prints appear to have been designed by Mary and engraved by Matthew. For further satirical prints on this theme, see Donald, *Age of Caricature*, ch. 3; and for the image in the context of town gardens, see Longstaffe-Gowan, *London Town Gardens*, p. 7.
48. Coffin, 'Venus in the Eighteenth-Century English Garden'; Frith, 'Sexuality and Politics in the Gardens at West Wycombe and Medmenham Abbey'.
49. For the ubiquity of this language in garden writing, see Fabricant, 'Binding and Dressing Nature's Loose Tresses'.
50. The temple was substantially remodelled in the 1770s, and renamed as the Queen's Temple in 1789. Lady Fane's shellwork grotto was similarly famous, so too was the Duchess of Richmond's at Goodwood, while Lady Walpole's grotto became the subject of a satirical poem on the fashionable luxuries of the great and not so great (for which see *Gentleman's Magazine*, 1734, p. 697).
51. The best account of Stowe's political iconography remains 'The Political Temples of Stowe' a special issue of the *New Arcadian Journal*.
52. All of these translations appear under the relevant temples in Seeley, *Stow. A Description*.
53. Recorded by Joseph Spence in his *Observations*, vol. 1, p. 303.
54. See, for example, George Bickham and Benton Seeley's guides to Stowe.
55. For an insistence on which, see Fabricant, 'Binding and Dressing'; Frith, 'Castle Howard: Dynastic and Sexual Politics'.
56. Morgan, *Tour to Milford Haven*, pp. 83–5.
57. Lady Caroline Dawson, Countess of Portarlington's to Lady Louisa Stuart, 7 July 1781, in Clark (ed.), *Gleanings*, vol. 1.

58. For the development of that voice, see Bowerbank, *Speaking for Nature*, p. 89.
59. For a detailed account of Bathurst's garden, see Martin, *Pursuing Innocent Pleasures*, pp. 66–78.
60. Hertford to Pomfret, London, Feb 19 OS 1741, *Correspondence*, vol. 3.
61. The standard account of Hertford's life remains, Hughes, *The Gentle Hertford*; for a further account of Hertford and representations of country life, see Hill, 'Genre and Social Order in Country House Poems of the Eighteenth Century'; and for Bathurst's various estates, see Martin, *Pursuing Innocent Pleasures*, ch. 3.
62. Hertford to Pomfret, London, Feb 26 OS 1741, *Correspondence*, vol. 3.
63. Letter from Elizabeth Sheridan Lefanu to Alicia Sheridan Lefanu, Bath, 28 June 1786, in *Betsy Sheridan's Journal*, pp. 89–90.
64. But for the value of this approach, see Shteir, *Cultivating Women* and for the early nineteenth century, Page and Smith, *Women, Literature, and the Domesticated Landscape*; for the increasing number of late eighteenth-century botanical drawing books intended for women to copy or colour, see Henrey, *British Botanical and Horticultural Literature*, vol. 2, ch. 20.

1 'Gladly I leave the town': retirement

1. See also Caroline Holland's description of Lady Gray twenty years later: 'The old Lady is now in her eighty-fourth year, as lively and full of spirits as people are at fifty, able to walk about her garden, which is all her own making, and planting and taking to the full as much pleasure as ever in it . . . she says she has not time to be melancholy at her age. She is indeed a most amazing old woman', Caroline Holland to Emily, Countess of Kildare, Kingsgate, 3 September 1767, in Fitzgerald (ed.), *Correspondence of Duchess of Leinster*, vol. 1, p. 519.
2. Røstvig, *The Happy-Man*; Kenny, *Country-House Ethos*.
3. Pomfret, *The Choice*, ll.5–18
4. Johnson, *Lives of the English poets*, vol. 1, p. 432.
5. Sitter, *Literary Loneliness*, p. 131; and Doody, 'Women poets of the eighteenth century', p. 230; but see also Williamson, *Raising their Voices*, for an exploration of Katherine Philips' use of the Horatian retirement theme.
6. Anna Williams, 'The Happy Solitude, or the Wished Retirement', in *Miscellanies in Prose and Verse*, p. 71.
7. The oddly nebulous conclusion to *Candide*, that we must cultivate the garden, articulates an uncertainty at the heart of retirement which is that unresolved tension between the active and passive moral life, between the public and the private, between complacency and rigour.
8. Dorothy Wordsworth to Jane Pollard, 25 January 1790, in Hill (ed.), *Letters of Dorothy Wordsworth*.
9. [Wright (ed.)], *Pleasing Reflections on Life and Manners*, pp. 117–19.

10. See, for example, Mary Chandler, 'My Wish', in her *The Description of Bath. A Poem*, p. 65.

11. See Guest, *Small Change*, p. 14; for the problematic relationship between the terms private and domestic, see Bannet, *Domestic Revolution*, ch. 4; Clery, *Feminization Debate*.

12. Røstvig, *The Happy-Man*, p. 17.

13. For the continuing influence of the *Spectator*'s advice, see, for example, Mary Davys, *The Reform'd Coquet* (1724), where the heroine repeats Addison almost verbatim: 'My Lord, said *Amoranda*, I retire sometimes from Company, to make it more acceptable to me when I come into it again; and this, I think, I may do as often as I please without a Breach in either Good-nature or Good-manners', p. 41 (the novel had reached its 7th edition by 1760).

14. Rostvig aptly refers to this as the 'belief in regeneration through rural retirement', *The Happy-Man*, p. 47.

15. According to Aristotle, 'He who is unable to live in society, or who has no need because he is sufficient for himself, must be either a beast or a god' Aristotle, *Politics*, Book 1, Part 2; in our period we might point to the apparently opposed views of Thomas Browne and William Blackstone, the former arguing, 'Be able to be alone. Lose not the advantage, and the society of thyself', *Christian Morals*, p. 98, and the latter asserting that 'Man was formed for society and is neither capable of living alone, nor has the courage to do it', *Commentaries of the Laws of England*, vol. 1, p. 43.

16. Sung by the character of Sylvia, the song appears in More's, *The Search after Happiness. A Pastoral Drama* (1773); the play had reached its twelfth edition by 1800.

17. Thus, the 'sweet retired solitude' of Milton's *Comus*; 'numquam minus solus, quam cum solus' (never less alone, than when alone) the quotation from Scipio which is the focus for Cowley's essay, 'Of Solitude'; numerous lines from Pope's 'Solitude', and more problematically from 'Eloisa to Abelard' are frequently cited in letters and echoed in poetry.

18. Chudleigh, *Poems on Several Occasions*, ll.1–9.

19. See Scodel, 'Lyric Forms', p. 133.

20. Henry Fielding, *History of Tom Jones*, vol. 3, p. 255.

21. Empson, *Some Versions of Pastoral*, p. 35.

22. See Hardin, *Love in a Green Shade*.

23. Alpers, *What Is Pastoral?*, p. 68.

24. Spacks, *Desire and Truth*, pp. 18–19.

25. Quoted in Sahil, *Judith Butler*, pp. 122–3.

26. A repeated theme in her work, but see especially Butler, *Bodies that Matter*, ch. 3.

27. Winchilsea, *Miscellany Poems*, p. 33.

28. Robinson, *Poems* (1791).

29. Robinson, *Poems by Mrs Robinson* (1774).

30. Cowper, *The Task*, Book I, pp. 12–14.

31. Though as Guest argues throughout *Small Change* such neat divisions are undermined by the increasing recognition and national importance of the learned lady.

32. Elizabeth Montagu to Edward Montagu, 8 [June] 1753), *Letters of Elizabeth Montagu*, vol. 3, p. 235.

33. Lady Mary Wortley Montagu, 'A Summary of Lord Lyttelton's Advice to a Lady' in Montagu, *Letters and Works*, vol. 2, p. 494.

34. Letter from Elizabeth Montagu, 25 October 1757, in *Letters of Elizabeth Montagu*, vol. 4, p. 72; notably, she suggests that young women would also benefit from retirement and late marriage, see Montagu to Lord Lyttelton, Newcastle, 22 November 1763: 'Poor girls are sadly deceived by the words *House of their own, being their own Mistress*, &c. Alas their house & they have a master; I know the being call'd an old maid is terrible to them; but a woman of merit, family, & fortune, may marry at eight & twenty; she will then have gather'd the flowers in the primrose path of gayety & pleasure; may without self denial live a retired domestick life, her character will be more respectable, her understanding more improved, her conduct more uniform, & she will be more likely to gain the esteem of her Husband, & is much fitter to educate her children' (Huntington Library MO1428).

35. See Guest, *Small Change*, and in particular her account of Carter's 'Ode to Wisdom' in which she notes 'the difficult and ambiguous continuity between the "silent Joys" and virtues of retirement and domesticity and the more absolute public virtues appropriate to the poet, patriot, and hero', p. 149.

36. My account of Thomson's poem is – inevitably, one feels – heavily reliant on John Barrell's reading of *The Seasons* in *English Literature in History* 1730–1780, ch. 1, and, with Harriet Guest, 'On the Uses of Contradiction'.

37. George Lord Lyttelton, 'To the Memory of a Lady lately Deceased', in Lyttelton, *Works* (1775), pp. 471–8.

38. For a reworking of Lyttelton's poem as a series of sonnets which largely reiterate these gendered norms, and for at least two admiring female readers, see Anna Seward's letter to Sophia Weston Simmons, 20 March 1787, in Seward, *Letters*, vol. 1, pp. 259–63.

39. See, for example, the two mid-century collections, *Christian Biography: or, a collection of the lives of several excellent persons eminent for faith and piety, from the works of the Rev. Mr Baxter, and Dr Bates . . . viz. Mrs Elizabeth Baker . . . Mrs Mary Hanmer . . . Mrs Mary Coxe . . .* (1768), and Thomas Amory's, *Memoirs: containing the lives of several ladies of great Britain . . .* (1769), as well as the wider-ranging, *Biographium Faeminium. The Female Worthies: or, Memoirs of the most illustrious ladies, of all ages and nation* (1755). More broadly, of course, poetry on the death of aristocratic women inevitably celebrates Christian and domestic virtues rather than metropolitan sociability. For the mid-century

phenomenon of memorialising learned and pious women, see Guest, *Small Change*, ch. 2, and O'Brien, *Women and Enlightenment*, ch. 2 & 3.

40. For women's wider reactions to and use of Pope's poetry, see Thomas, *Alexander Pope and Women Readers*.

41. Rousseau, *Eloisa: or, a series of original letters collected and published by J. J. Rousseau. Translated from the French* (1761).

42. Bannet, *Domestic Revolution*, p. 163.

43. Fitzgerald (ed.), *Correspondence of Duchess of Leinster*, vol. 1, p. 533.

44. Astell, ed. Springborg, *A Serious Proposal to the Ladies*, pp. 19–20.

45. See Perry, *Celebrated Mary Astell*; Hill (ed.), *First English Feminist*; on Astell's *Proposal* as a riposte to the gender politics of *Paradise Lost* see Macey, Jr., 'Eden Revisited'.

46. On the crucial role of Bluestocking women in the changing structures of capitalism, see Kelly, 'Bluestocking Feminism', in Eger et al. (eds), *Women, Writing and the Public Sphere*, pp. 163–80.

47. Jones (ed.), *Women and Literature*, p. 10; and notably Guest, *Small Change*.

48. In Jones (ed.), *Women and Literature*, p. 34.

49. Montagu to Edward Bridgen, Sandleford, 16 June 1777 (Huntington Library, MO689).

50. Montagu, *Letters of Elizabeth Montagu*, vol. 2, p. 40, to Freind, Dec 29 [1741]; see also, for example, her comment in a letter to her cousin Gilbert West of 3 July 1755 that 'I will amuse myself with books and such pleasures as the country affords, and in November, most willingly return to London...after five months of the most serious retirement, I shall be glad to return to the cheerful joys of society, and if you add, to the idle dissipations of town in some degree, I acquiesce', vol. 3, p. 302.

51. Talbot to Carter, 28 December 1747, and 13 January 1746, both in *Letters between Carter and Talbot*.

52. Cf. Anne MacVicar Grant's letter to her friend Mrs Smith in Glasgow, 3 September, 1791, 'In return for these reveries of solitude [of mine], you owe me something from the busy haunts of men', *Letters from the Mountains*, vol. 1, Letter XL.

53. D'Monté and Pohl (eds), *Female Communities 1600–1800*.

54. See Dolan, *Ladies of the Grand Tour*, pp. 169–70, 175–6; and Chedgzoy, '"For Virgin Buildings Oft Brought Forth": Fantasies of Convent Sexuality'.

55. Carter to Talbot, 30 October 1763, *Letters between Carter and Talbot*, vol. 3; Thrale, *The French Journals*, pp. 91, 110.

56. Hertford and Pomfret, *Correspondence*, vol. 2, pp. 127–8; for an account of this correspondence as itself a form of retreat, or in his own words a 'redoubt', see How, *Epistolary Spaces*, ch. 4.

57. For a similar desire expressed by a later generation, see Grant's *Letters from the Mountains*, vol. 1, pp. 3–4, where she writes, 'I think, if there was such a thing allowable...a nunnery (a protestant one, remember) might be very agreeably

situated here . . . as an asylum from the levity and dissipation of the age; where we might . . . enjoy the tranquil pleasures of a rural retirement'. See also Isabella Kelly 'Extempore in the garden of a convent' which praises religious retirement not as death in life but as a place where heaven resides, *Poems and Fables on several occasions* (1807). For the ongoing debates about Protestant nunneries, see Hill, 'A Refuge from Men: the Idea of a Protestant Nunnery'.

58. Hertford and Pomfret, *Correspondence*, vol. 1, p. 130.
59. Hertford and Pomfret, *Correspondence*, vol. 1, pp. 149–50.
60. Hughes, *The Gentle Hertford*, p. 90 Hertford claimed to have recovered quite suddenly from these bouts of depression by the sacrament of Holy Unction in 1728; for the political context of Hertford and Pomfret's retirement from public life see How, *Epistolary Spaces*, ch. 4.
61. Pomfret to Hertford, Brussels, 5 August 1744, *Correspondence*, vol. 3, pp. 348–54.
62. Hertford to Pomfret, Marlborough, 1 August 1741, *Correspondence*, vol. 3, pp. 366–8.
63. At the end of the century, see, for example, Melesina Trench: 'I arrived on the 1st at Lady Buckingham's. La Trappe itself could not be more solitary than her habitation. The house is convenient, the walks retired and shady. She does not encourage visits, which pleases me, as solitude is preferable to the casual uninteresting society to be obtained in a villa near London. Lady Buckingham has engaged me for a month's *tête-à-tête*. If our friendship survives this ordeal, it may be immortal', Diary of Melesina Chevenix St. George Trench, October 1798, in *Remains of the Late Mrs. Trench*.
64. See Hughes, *The Gentle Hertford*; Prescott, 'Provincial Networks, Dissenting Connections, and Noble Friends: Elizabeth Singer Rowe'; Bigold, 'Elizabeth Rowe's Fictional and Familiar Letters'; and for the position of the woman writer as at once famous and retired, see Guest, *Small Change*.
65. Rowe, *Devout Exercises of the Heart in Meditation and Soliloquy, Prayer and Praise* (1738).
66. See, for example, John Wesley's notes on the great show gardens of the eighteenth century, including Piercefield, in south Wales, after a description of which he concludes, 'And must all these be burned up? What will become of us then, if we set our hearts upon them?', in *Journal of the Rev. John Wesley*, entry for Friday, 25 August 1769. And for wider dissenting context of which Rowe was a part, see Morris, *Religious Sublime*, and Keeble, *Literary Culture of Nonconformity*.
67. On the role of charismatic women in Quaker institutions, see Plant, "Subjective Testimonies': Women Quaker Ministers and Spiritual Authority in England'.
68. Waring, *Diary of the Religious Experience of Mary Waring* (1809), p. vi.
69. Woods, *Journal*, p. 14.
70. 'Letters from Margaret Althans', in *The Christian Character Exemplified*, p. 156.
71. For a detailed account of how Carter's career as an author situates her as both an archetypally domestic *and* public figure, see Guest, *Small Change*.
72. Montagu to Lyttelton, 7 October 1765 (MO1443).

73. Carter, *All the Works of Epictetus*, ch. 13.
74. Though as Guest argues, its significance lies also in the fact that Carter is translating a work 'central to the most exclusively masculinist and Shaftesburian forms of civic humanism', *Small Change*, p. 129.
75. For Carter's merging of virtuous retirement with the heroic, and for her use of Epictetus as a bulwark against 'the luxurious state of modern society', see Guest, pp. 145–51, 114–15.
76. O'Brien, *Women and Enlightenment*, pp. 56–65.
77. Carter to Vesey, 25 July 1779, in *Letters between Carter and Talbot*, vol. 4, p. 227.
78. Talbot to Carter, Cuddesden, 8 June 1751, in *Letters between Carter and Talbot*, vol. 2, p. 33.
79. For Talbot, again see O'Brien, *Women and Enlightenment*, who argues that, 'Talbot's *Reflections* offered its readers not a set of prescriptions for a holy life, but the inner voice of someone going through the often difficult process of making her life fit those prescriptions. Both the *Reflections* and the *Essays* are haunted by an acute sense of the pointlessness of the writer's constricted female existence. Yet Talbot often manages to render that sense of pointlessness emblematic of the wider Christian condition . . . ', p. 64.
80. Talbot to Carter, Wrest, 24 October 1751, and Carter to Talbot, Deal, 2 November 1751, in *Letters between Carter and Talbot*, vol. 2, pp. 58–60.
81. O'Brien, *Women and Enlightenment*, p. 65.
82. Talbot to Carter, Piccadilly, 29 February 1751, *Letters between Carter and Talbot*, vol. 2, p. 7.
83. Carter to Talbot, 4 March 1751, *Letters between Carter and Talbot*, vol. 2, p. 14.
84. *Works of Catharine Talbot*, Essay XXIV, p. 195.
85. Talbot to Carter [n.d., July–August 1752?], *Letters between Carter and Talbot*, vol. 2, p. 89.
86. Talbot to Carter, 13 November 1752, *Letters between Carter and Talbot*, vol. 2. See also Frances Burney's diary record of an exchange in January 1788 with 'Mr Turbulent' (her fictious name for the queen's French reader, La Guiffardière): '"No, ma'am, no!– 'tis a fruitless struggle. I know myself too well– I can do nothing so right as to retire– to turn monk– hermit." "I have no respect," cried I, "for these selfish seclusions. I can never suppose we were created in the midst of society, in order to run away to a useless solitude."'
87. See Carter to Talbot, 13 July 1748, and Talbot's reply, 26 August 1748, *Letters between Carter and Talbot*, vol. 1, pp. 274–5.
88. It is an experience recounted by numerous women who found themselves without their friends in London: see, for example, Mary Delany's letter to Mary Port from St. James' Palace, 15 April 1776, 'at present I am in as quiet a solitude (excepting London cries) as if on the top of Bunster or pinnacle of Thorp Cloud, for all the world, great and *small*, are gone to Westminster *Hall*', Delany, *Autobiography and Correspondence*, vol. 2, p. 280.

89. See, for example, Mary Ann Arundell, Baroness Arundell to Anne Elizabeth Granville, Duchess of Buckingham and Chandos, 27 November 1818, who, after a visit from her brother and sister-in-law wrote, 'It required all my philosophy... & a whole morning pass'd in my Green house to stop a hearty cry when you had fairly driven off, but such a week is worth purchasing by a good crying fit', Huntington Library manuscript, STG Box 6 (2).

90. Carter to Montagu, Deal, 20 December 1777, *Letters to Mrs. Montagu*, vol. 3, Letter CCVII.

91. For valuable speculation on Johnson's understanding of Carter as both a domestic and intellectual woman, see Thomas, 'Samuel Johnson and Elizabeth Carter'.

92. Hervey, *Letters of Mary Lepel, Lady Hervey*, Letter XCII, Chevening, 21 October 1761, pp. 284–5.

93. Brant, *Eighteenth-Century Letters*, p. 22.

94. Hertford to Pomfret, Marlborough, 25 June 1741, *Correspondence*, vol. 3, p. 358.

95. Carter to Vesey, 12 October 1784, *Letters between Carter and Talbot*, vol. 4, p. 351.

96. For the significance of the conventional but also the significance of departure from 'models' in letter writing, see Brant, *Eighteenth-Century Letters*.

97. Mary Wortley Montagu to Lady Mar [June 1726], in *Complete Letters*, vol. 2, p. 66; and again in May 1727, p. 75.

98. Mary Wortley Montagu to Lady Bute 20 July 1754, *Complete Letters*, vol. 3, p. 62.

99. Lennox to the Duchess of Leinster, Goodwood, 28 November 1778, in, Fitzgerald (ed.), *Correspondence of Duchess of Leinster*, vol. 2, p. 262.

100. Hertford to Pomfret, Marlborough, 10 June 1739, *Correspondence*. For her admiration of Sévigné, see her letter to Henrietta Knight BL Add.Ms.23728.f.8 Percy Lodge, 7 October 1742.

101. Though as Brant argues, the trope of apology is endemic in letter writing, see *Eighteenth-Century Letters*.

102. Mary Delany's letter to Swift, 2 September 1736, is characteristic: 'I would not tell you so much about myself, if I had anything to tell you of other people', Delany, *Autobiography and Correspondence*, vol. 1, p. 151; notably, it is a refrain to be found through the journal-letters of Mary Coke.

103. Letter from Livry, March 1671, in Sévigné *Letters* (1727), vol. 2, Letter VII. Cf. Hertford to Pomfret, 25 June 1741, *Correspondence*.

104. Cf. Pomfret to Somerset [Hertford], 1740[?], 'For my own part, I do not dislike this solitude; since I am of an age and complexion to love being alone sometimes: I am only in pain for my young people, and for the additional dulness with which you are likely, in consequence, to be troubled'. *Correspondence*, vol. 2, p. 336.

105. Grundy, *Lady Mary Wortley Montagu*, p. 489.

106. Montagu, *Complete Letters*, vol. 2, p. 402; Grundy, *Lady Mary Wortley Montagu*, p. 493.
107. Montagu to the Countess of Bute, 26 July 1753, *Complete Letters*.
108. See Grundy, *Lady Mary Wortley Montagu*, ch. 26.
109. See Grundy, *Lady Mary Wortley Montagu*, pp. 508, 554.

2 'No way qualified for retirement': disgrace

1. 'A Short, But True Novel', *Weekly Journal or British Gazette*, 2 July 1720.
2. For the powerful influence of the Roman matron as a model for modern British culture later in the century, see O'Brien, *Women and Enlightenment*, pp. 113–21, and Hicks, 'The Roman Matron in Britain'.
3. For self-fashioning and the domestic interior, see Girouard, *Life in the English Country House*; Smith, *Eighteenth-century Decoration*; Scott, *The Rococo Interior*; West, 'The public nature of private life: the conversation piece and the fragmented family'; Vickery, *Gentleman's Daughter*; Arnold (ed.), *Georgian Country House*; K. Sharpe, 'Women's Creativity and Display in the Eighteenth-Century British Domestic Interior'; Aynsley and Grant (eds), *Imagined Interiors*; Styles and Vickery (eds), *Gender, Taste and Material Culture*; Ponsonby, *Stories from Home*.
4. See Fabricant, 'Binding and Dressing'; Frith, 'Sexuality and Politics'.
5. See also Lloyd, 'Amour in the Shrubbery'.
6. Ballaster, *Seductive Forms*; Bowers, 'Representing Resistance: British Seduction Stories, 1660–1800'.
7. Smith, *Emmeline*, vol. 4, pp. 1–2.
8. Anon, *Female Gamester*, vol. 1, p. 45.
9. Montagu to Gilbert West, Sandleford, 25 October 1753, *Letters of Elizabeth Montagu*, vol. 3, p. 259.
10. Anne Dewes to Catherine Collingwood (Lady Throckmorton), 17 June 1736, Delany, *Autobiography and Correspondence*, vol. 1, p. 148.
11. Lady Louisa Stuart to Lady Caroline Dawson, Countess of Portarlington, 15 July 1778, in Clark (ed.), *Gleanings from an old Portfolio*, vol. 1, p. 18.
12. Grierson, in *Poems by Eminent Ladies*, vol. 1, pp. 211–13.
13. For an account of the decline of romance, of its possibilities as a mode of resisting gender norms, and of the ambivalence of Lennox's response, see Ross, *Excellence of Falsehood*; Langbauer, *Women and Romance*, ch. 2; on *The Female Quixote*, see Spacks, *Desire and Truth*, ch. 1.
14. Quoted from the approving review in the *St. James' Chronicle*, 6 June 1761.
15. Grant to Mrs Brown, Laggan, 9 March 1789, *Letters from the Mountains*, vol. 1, Letter XXVIII.
16. Carter to Talbot, London, 13 July 1748, *Letters between Carter and Talbot*, vol. 2, p. 274.

17. Baroness Elizabeth Berkeley Craven to Christian Friederich Carl Alexander, Margrave of Brandenburg, Anspach and Bayreuth, 21 June 1785, in *A Journey through the Crimea to Constantinople*, p. 14.

18. Masters, *Familiar Letters and Poems* (1755).

19. Hearne, *The Lover's Week* (1718); nothing is known of her, but these two novels and the name may be a pseudonym.

20. Hearne, *The Female Deserters. A Novel. By the author of The Lover's Week* (1719[1718]), p. 6.

21. For a slightly earlier use of the country estate as a convenient location for sexual intrigue, see, for example, the brief narrative of an adulterous relationship, 'Memoirs of Lady L – R and Count A – TI', in which we find, 'This retirement to the country was planned for no other purpose than to carry on an infamous amour, commenced long before this, which *duty* and *gratitude* should forbid on her side, *honour* and the laws of *hospitality* on his', *Middlesex Journal*, 7 May 1771.

22. Based on Massinger and Field's 1632 *The Fatal Dowry*, Rowe's *The Fair Penitent* (1703) continued to be produced throughout the century, notably starring Sarah Siddons in the 1770s.

23. For the ongoing popularity of the seduction narrative and its politicised uses, see Bowers, 'Representing Resistance'; and for its use in early eighteenth-century fiction, see Ballaster, *Seductive Forms*; Doody, *A Natural Passion*; Kern, 'The Fallen Woman, from the perspective of Five Early Eighteenth-Century Women Novelists'; Spencer, *Rise of the Woman Novelist*; and Staves, 'British Seduced Maidens'.

24. For the argument that Haywood's fiction offers women readers both an image of their exploitation by men and a fantasy of escape, see Ballaster, *Seductive Forms*, ch. 5.

25. For an analysis of garden structures, their significance and their dangers in *Clarissa*, see Lipsedge, 'A Place of Refuge, Seduction or Danger?'.

26. All quotations are from Rowe, *Friendship in Death . . . To which are added, Letters Moral and Entertaining, in Prose and Verse. In Three Parts* (1733).

27. As for example, Rowe's letter to Lady Hertford, Alnwick MS 110, p. 60 (quoted in Stecher, *Elizabeth Singer Rowe*) in which she writes, 'I am certainly dead and buried according to your notions of life, interred in the silence and obscurity of a country retreat . . . '; and for Rowe's acute awareness of the uncomfortably overlapping worlds of religious and sexual desire, see Achinstein, 'Romance of the Spirit'.

28. Alnwick MS 11, 154, quoted in Stecher, *Elizabeth Singer Rowe*, pp. 128–9.

29. Boswell, *Life of Johnson*, p. 222; Rowe, *Letters Moral and Entertaining*, pp. xxxiv–xxxv.

30. The poem appeared in Yearsley's second collection, *Poems on Various Subjects* (1787).

31. 'A true Story for the Use of Young Ladies', in, *The New Pleasant Instructor* (1781), pp. 151–6.

32. Stecher, *Elizabeth Rowe*, p. 193.

33. E. M. W. Tillyard's claim in, *Some Mythical Elements in English Literature*, pp. 102–7.

34. For an excellent teasing out of Cowper's relationship with the world beyond rural Olney, see Goodman, 'The Loophole in the Retreat'.

35. For the complex relation between Carter's 'private' life and public fame, see Guest, *Small Change*, ch. 6.

36. Guest, *Small Change*, ch. 6; O'Brien, *Women and Enlightenment*, p. 59.

37. Most notably Henry Home, Lord Kames, *Elements of Criticism*, (1762); William Shenstone, 'Unconnected Thoughts on Gardening', in *The Works in Verse and Prose* (1764); Thomas Whately, *Observations on Modern Gardening* (1770); William Mason, *The English Garden*; and see Coffin, *The English Garden*, esp. pp. 2–6, and 59–60.

38. Carter to Vesey, South Lodge, 11 September 1781, *Letters between Carter and Talbot*, vol. 4, Letter CXLIV.

39. Carter to Montagu, 21 October 1763, *Letters to Mrs Montagu*, vol. 1, Letter LVI.

40. Carter to Vesey, Deal, 1 October 1781, *Letters between Carter and Talbot*, vol. 4, Letter CXLV; Carter continues, 'sublime enthusiasm and poetic melancholy are too high an exertion of our intellectual powers to be long continued without pain and languor, and are quite inconsistent with the general temper that qualifies us for social life, and therefore are better fitted for an occasional exercise of the faculties of the soul than for a constant habitation'. For Mary Sharpe's own views during this period, see her manuscript letters (1779–82) in the John Rylands Library, HAM/1/22.

41. Carter to Montagu, Deal 6, October 1776, *Letters to Mrs Montagu*, vol. 3, Letter CXCVIII.

42. Carter to Montagu, Bristol, 22 August 1759, *Letters to Mrs Montagu*, vol. 1, Letter XII.

43. Carter to Montagu, Deal, 23 November 1776, *Letters to Mrs Montagu*, vol. 3, Letter CC; or see her letter to Montagu of 1784, 'I dined once at Stoke with Lord Bottetourt; and was carried there once merely to see it, by Mrs. Anne Pitt. It is certainly a very fine place; but if the Duchess of Beaufort lives there quite alone, I should think she would find it rather too melancholy for her spirits, which have suffered so many, and such grievous trials', Deal, 1 October 1784, *Letters to Mrs Montagu*, vol. 3, Letter CCLI.

44. Carter to Montagu, Deal, 21 June 1783, *Letters to Mrs Montagu*, vol. 3, Letter CCXLII.

45. 'Parliamentary Intelligence. House of Lords. Friday May 23', *London Packet or New Lloyd's Evening Post*, 23 May 1800.

46. 'Parliamentary Intelligence. House of Lords. Wednesday, March 13', *Morning Post*, 14 March 1799.

47. And see Lloyd, 'Amour in the Shrubbery'.
48. For which see Malcomson, *The Pursuit of the Heiress*, pp. 102–3.
49. Mary Wortley Montagu to Edward Wortley Montagu, 2 February, 1747, *Complete Letters*.
50. Elizabeth Montagu to Anne Donnellan, 1741[?], *Letters of Elizabeth Montagu*, vol. 1, p. 163.
51. Carter to Montagu, 20 July 1788, *Letters to Mrs Montagu*, vol. 3, Letter CCLXIX.

3 Bluestocking gardens: Elizabeth Montagu at Sandleford

1. Huntington Library MO4533.
2. Montagu in, Lyttelton, *Dialogues of the Dead*, p. 301.
3. As O'Brien has argued in *Women and Enlightenment*, pp. 56–9, Montagu and the Bluestockings were heavily influenced by the works of Joseph Butler; for Butler's account of limited human understanding when confronting the vastness of the Universe and the need to accept those limits, see, for example, his *Analogy of Religion, Natural and Revealed* (1736), I.vii.
4. Notably, for example, in *The Mysteries of Udolpho*, and *The Romance of the Forest*.
5. Rousseau, *The Reveries of the Solitary Walker*.
6. Penny, *The Birth-Day*, in *Poems* (1780), p. 189.
7. See, for example, Goldsmith's *The Lady's Magazine*, vol. 1 (1759–60), pp. 257–61.
8. Along with Milton, Akenside was a favourite source of quotations for Montagu's letters from the country.
9. See, for example, *The Works of the Most Reverend Dr. John Tillotson* (1717), vol. 1, Sermon LXXXIII, 'The Wisdom of God in the Creation of the World'; John Ray, *The Wisdom of God Manifested in the Works of the Creation* (London: Samuel Smith, 1691) and *Three Physico-Theological Discourses* (1692); Thomas Burnet, *Sacred Theory of the Earth* (London, 1681); amongst aristocratic women writers at the beginning of our period we could add the likes of Lady Anne Clifford, and Mary Rich, Countess of Warwick (for which see Coffin, *The English Garden*, pp. 59–66); and of course the tradition continued, see, for example, in the Huntington Library's *c.* 1811–32 commonplace book of Anne Grenville, Duchess of Chandos, in which she copied, 'Lines Written by the late Elizabeth Lee in a Bower called by her name at St. Leonard's Hill', which begins, 'This peaceful shade – this green roofed Bower / Great Maker! all are full of Thee' and ends, 'The bower, the shade, retired[?], serene, / The grateful Heart may most affect, / Here, God in every leaf is seen / And Man has leisure to reflect'.
10. Althans, *Diary*, 17 February 1783 (pp. 89–90).
11. Cf. Althans, *Diary*, who writes, 'Oh haste my beloved and remove me from a land in which I never can be happy!' 29 September 1783 (p. 93); and see O'Brien, *Women and Enlightenment*, pp. 56–9.

12. The *Critical Review* November 1803 disapproved of their publication, especially by a minister of the established church.

13. Blunt records Montagu's account of the various assemblies and gatherings she had been to in the Spring of 1787, 'I have, indeed, declined some assemblies, but I think my Journal on the whole may rival that of the fine lady in the Spectator, only I have not worked a tulip, but as Betty Tull has done it for me, I think it quite as well . . . ', Blunt (ed.), *Mrs. Montagu*, vol. 2, p. 210; Montagu presumably has in mind, *Spectator* 606 (13 October 1714).

14. Delaney to Port, St J[ames] P[alace], 19 January 1775, in Delaney *Autobiography and Correspondence*, vol. 5, p. 97.

15. Boscawen to Delany, Glan Villa, 18 October 1775, in Delany, *Autobiography and Correspondence*, vol. 5, p. 165.

16. Elizabeth Montagu to Leonard Smelt, Sandleford, 28 October 1776, quoted in Blunt (ed.), *Mrs Montagu*, vol. 1, p. 339.

17. Montagu to Anne Donnellan, 5 July 1741[?], in *Letters of Elizabeth Montagu*, vol. 1, p. 229; for Montagu's building projects and business activities, see Schnorrenberg, 'Mrs. Montagu and the Architects', and Child, 'Elizabeth Montagu, Bluestocking Businesswoman'; brief accounts of the 'Capability' Brown landscape at Sandleford can be found in Hyams, *Capability Brown*; Stroud, *Capability Brown*; Turner, *Capability Brown*; Hinde, *Capability Brown*; and Baird, *Mistress of the House*, but the most detailed account remains Wade's unpublished *Sandleford Priory: The Historic Landscape of St. Gabriel's School* (1997).

18. Montagu to Thomas Lyttelton, Carville [near Newcastle upon Tyne], 20 October 1758 (MO1499).

19. Cf. Montagu to Elizabeth Vesey, Sandleford, 20 May 1778, which offers an account of easy sauntering much closer to those characteristics which led to Vesey's nickname, 'the Sylph': 'My present situation in the quiet tranquillity of the Country, with all the gayety of the rural scenery around me, contents my mind, & I pass my hours in a sauntering reverie so agreeably, that far from agreeing with those who say one should be merry & wise, I assert one may be happy without being either' (MO6518); and by the 1790s, with far less at stake, Montagu to Matthew Montagu, Sandleford 3 October 1790, 'I have lately pass'd every morning in sauntering on foot or lolling in my Whiskey, taking pleasure & improving my health this fine weather, but the life of a butterfly cannot be more idle, or insignificant. I hardly ever remember to have seen Autumn wear a more delightfull character, & I cannot at my age expect to see many returns of that sweet & tranquill season, so I hope I am more excusable in my intemperate enjoyment' (MO3677).

20. The Huntington Library dates the letter 1760–62, but given its closeness to the letter to the Earl of Bath (MO4533) it is likely also to be from August 1762.

21. See, for example, Shaftesbury (notably in his *Philosophical Regimen*) and indeed Montagu's close friend Elizabeth Carter, but also the more radical challenge to

all sublunary things that appears in the strand of Christian writing associated with Elizabeth Rowe and John Wesley.

22. Montagu to the Earl of Bath, Sandleford, 20 May 1764 (MO4632); characteristically, this comes as part of a larger claim to be able to entertain herself in solitude, and which thus, implicitly, distinguishes her once again from the 'fine lady'.

23. The house at Sandleford was eventually to be remodelled by Wyatt.

24. Elizabeth Montagu to Edward Montagu, September 1751, *Letters of Elizabeth Montagu*, vol. 3, p. 168.

25. Sévigné, *Letters*, 2nd edition (1763–8), vol. 2, pp. 9, 43, vol. 9, p. 228; Montagu to Elizabeth Vesey, Sandleford, 5 June 1764 (MO6376); Montagu to Gilbert West, 26 June 1755, in *Letters of Elizabeth Montagu*, vol. 3, pp. 294–5.

26. *Letters of Elizabeth Montagu*, vol. 3, pp. 338–9; and cf. Haywood, *Epistles for Ladies* (1756), vol. 1, Epistle XLIX, pp. 188–91.

27. Elizabeth Montagu to Edward Montagu, Sandleford, 28 June 1757 (MO2332). However, a reading of the letters from the 1740s to the end of the eighteenth century also makes it apparent that Elizabeth Montagu often wished to be in the country when she was in town and vice versa and thus that both country and city acted as objects of desire depending upon her location.

28. Montagu to Lord Lyttelton, Sandleford, 24 May 1764 (MO1430); Montagu repeats this last passage verbatim in a letter of the same date to the Earl of Bath (MO4635); see also her letter to Bath two days earlier, in which she writes, 'I have not felt one moments ennui in my solitude since I came. It is a great blessing to be able to live alone, & no one is truly independent that cannot do so, for daily amusement is as necessary as daily bread, & if one cannot get it for oneself, one must ask it of others. I wish often for the company of those I love & esteem, but I prefer thinking of them in my solitary walk to the conversation of persons indifferent to me.' Montagu to the Earl of Bath, Sandleford, 22 May 1764 (MO4633).

29. Montagu to Lord Lyttelton, 21 October 1760 (MO1403); the letter continues, by way of supporting Lyttelton's pastoral landscape at Hagley, 'vacant minds love a spectacle that fills them, but a philosopher would prefer the more gentle scene which Assists his contemplation and does not press to be the object of it'; similarly, in letters written from Spa, Germany, in 1763, Montagu makes explicit the value of poetic allusion in the encounter with landscape: 'I think one of the greatest pleasures poetry now gives me, is, when the objects before me bring to my mind some fine passage; for one recollects it with the same spirit with which it was written by the author', Montagu to Lyttelton, Spa, 27 July 1763 (MO1425); and in a letter to Benjamin Stillingfleet, Spa, 9 August 1763 (MO5119) she writes of, 'how much amusement I can make to myself in my lonely walks from memory and imagination'; for similar sentiments expressed to the Earl of Bath, see her letter of 20 May 1764 (MO4632).

30. Elizabeth to Edward Montagu, Sandleford, May[?] 1764[?] (MO2514).

31. Montagu to the Earl of Bath, London, 9 June 1762 (MO4524). This in itself is a conventional move for those who seek to distance themselves from agriculture and labour: the Earl of Bath was equally careful to point out that while he enjoyed the retirement of the country, he knew nothing about farming, see Earl of Bath to Montagu, Shrewsbury, 8 June 1762 (MO4258).

32. Montagu to Mrs Donnellan, 20 April 1741, *Letters of Elizabeth Montagu*, vol. 1, p. 159.

33. Cf. her account of quotidian rural life in a letter to Gilbert West, Sandleford, 21 January 1753, where she writes of Sandleford, 'you [should] not consider Sandleford as a place so remote; it is certain . . . that we cannot receive so frequent visits from those we like, nor so short ones from person we do not. The rules of civility and hospitality regulate our intercourse with our neighbours, rather than choice. As to our fireside, it is under the protection of that serious goddess of dullness, who passes in all the country firesides in England, for the true Minerva', *Letters of Elizabeth Montagu*, vol. 3, pp. 224–5.

34. See in particular, Ballaster, *Seductive Forms*, Langbauer, *Women and Romance*, and Deborah Ross, *The Excellence of Falsehood*.

35. Montagu to Freind, Bulstrode, 29 December [1741], *Letters of Elizabeth Montagu*, vol. 2, p. 40.

36. Kermode, *English Pastoral Poetry*, p. xiv.

37. Montagu to the Earl of Bath, London, 9 & 10 June 1762 (MO4524).

38. Rizzo, 'Two Versions of Community: Montagu and Scott'.

39. For an account of Montagu's charitable activities, see Larson, 'A Measure of Power: The Personal Charity of Elizabeth Montagu'.

40. On the unglamorous nature of Scott's life, see, for example, Montagu to Gilbert West, Sandleford, 16 October 1755, in which she describes a typical and very worthy day in the life of Scott and her companion Lady Bab Montagu, where they lived, 'a manner of life which most people will approve, but very few will commend'. *Letters of Elizabeth Montagu*, vol. 3, p. 336; but see also her defence of Scott in a letter to the Earl of Bath, 26 April 1762 in which she writes of Scott, 'I believe she has more than common talents, & I am sure she has uncommon virtues. Disappointments, poverty, ill health, retirement, & perhaps worse than all, a degree of ridicule thrown upon her situation has not dejected or chagrin'd her she is cheerful, contented, & in spite of fortune which seems to have destined her to beg assistance, ready to give it wherever real want requires it' (MO4250).

41. See Myers, *Bluestocking Circle*, who suggests that Carter did not enjoy this attempt at literary fame and that, 'her own admiration for Mrs Rowe may have suggested that she could function better as a virtuous woman poet in Deal rather than in London' p. 59. See also Guest, *Small Change*, ch. 4.

42. See, for example, Carter to Montagu, Deal, 3 October 1770, in which she writes of her current illness, 'I regret the loss of this fine season, as much as the finest of all fine ladies could the loss of a masquerade or a ball at court', Montagu Pennington (ed.), *Letters from Elizabeth Carter*, vol. 2, Letter CXXIX.

43. Carter to Montagu, Deal, 30 April 1763, *Letters from Elizabeth Carter*, vol. 1, Letter L; Montagu's rather hazy knowledge of Carter's garden in Deal is suggested by her comment, 'I can not even allow you to venture ye length of your own Garden, tho I believe it does not extend many acres', Montagu to Carter, 28 May 1783 (MO3543).
44. Carter to Montagu, Deal, 25 August 1777, *Letters from Elizabeth Carter*, vol. 3, Letter CCIII.
45. Elizabeth to Edward Montagu 10 May 1764 (MO2506).
46. Carter to Montagu, Deal, 29 July 1770, *Letters from Elizabeth Carter*, vol. 2, Letter CXXVII.
47. Carter to Montagu, Broome, 31 October 1760, *Letters from Elizabeth Carter*, vol 1, Letter XXXIII.
48. Carter to Montagu, Langton, 31 July 1781, *Letters from Elizabeth Carter*, vol. 3, Letter CCXXXIII.
49. Montagu to Carter, Sandleford, 5 June 1764 (MO3122); characteristically, the letter continues: 'This careless sauntering mightily repair'd my shatter'd health & fatigued spirits. I was too agreeably amused even to want to read much, and what can one read so agreeably as the great volume of infinite wisdom in this fair creation . . . When one considers the majesty of his power in his great works, the tenderness of his mercies in his lesser, all other things fade in ones esteem, & can have no part of ones admiration.'
50. Carter to Montagu, Deal, 12 June 1764, *Letters from Elizabeth Carter*, vol. 1, Letter LXII; see also Carter's letter to Vesey on having visited Montagu later that summer, in which she moves characteristically from the sublime to the beautiful and the domestic character of Sandleford and concludes, 'Great and sublime views afford a noble and striking entertainment, and are at proper intervals very useful to elevate the mind beyond the pitch of ordinary life: but the cultivated and good-humoured and familiar scenes of nature, are best suited to the general state, and to the purposes of social duty', Deal, 29 September 1764, *Letters between Carter and Talbot*, Letter IX.
51. On Carter and Talbot's admiration for Rowe as a role model, see Myers, *Bluestocking Circle*, pp. 153–4; Spencer, *Rise of the Woman Novelist*, pp. 81–6.
52. Drawn to think of her own married life when discussing the love poetry of Cowley, Montagu wrote to Carter, 'I agree with you that his love verses are insufferable; I think you and I, who have never been in love, could describe it better, were we asked *what is it like?*', Montagu to Carter, Sandleford, 23 June 1761, *Letters of Elizabeth Montagu*, vol. 4, p. 349.
53. See, for example, Talbot to Carter, Cuddesden, 26 July 1748, 'I have even sometimes thought our favourite Mrs Rowe went a good deal too far in shunning the cheerful engagements of life, and nourishing a disgust and hatred of it', *Letters between Carter and Talbot*, vol. 1, pp. 290–1.
54. Montagu continued to write letters which would place her in her garden, participating 'in the joys of the whole Creation' and looking up to their author, as

late as the 1790s, as, for example, Montagu to Carter, Sandleford, 6 November 1793 (MO3723).

55. Even in her early life Montagu was not averse to playing on Rowe's writing in letters to friends; in an elaborate account of how she died because she has not received an expected letter from the Duchess of Portland she writes, 'I thought it proper to acquaint you with my misfortune, & so call'd for the pen & ink Mrs Rowe had made use of to write her letters from the Dead to the Living', Montagu to the Duchess of Portland, 1739 (MO287).

56. See Myers, *Bluestocking Circle*, p. 19. On Sarah Scott's use of pastoral allusion to destabilise the assumptions of patriarchal marriage, see Macey, Jr., 'Eden Revisited'.

57. See Earl of Bath to Montagu, St Ives Place, *c.* 1762 (MO4328); he expected Montagu to reply in kind.

58. Lord Lyttelton to Montagu, 14 October 1761 (MO1297).

59. Lord Lyttelton to Montagu, Ebrington, Glouc., 21 May 21 1764 (MO1321).

60. Montagu to Lord Lyttelton, 21 October 1760 (MO1403).

61. Montagu to Elizabeth Carter, Sandleford, 11 July 1782 (MO3530).

62. Quoted in Evelyn Elizabeth Myers, *A History of Sandleford Priory*, p. 34.

63. See Fabricant's account of gendered landscape aesthetics, 'Binding and Dressing Nature's Loose Tresses'.

64. Montagu to Scott, Sandleford, 15 June 1778 (MO6036).

65. Montagu to Carter, Sandleford, 5 June 1775 (MO3361).

66. Edward to Elizabeth Montagu, Sandleford, 1 August 1756 (MO1882); 3 August 1756 (MO1883); 1 November 1757 (MO1891); 8 November 1762 (MO1945).

67. Montagu to Lord Lyttelton, Sandleford, 7 October 1765 (MO1443).

68. On the early history of the site, see Wade, *Sandleford Priory*, and Myers, *History of Sandleford*.

69. Scott to Montagu, 15 October 1762 (MO5928).

70. Montagu to the Earl of Bath, Hill Street [London], 9 July 1762 (MO4527).

71. Elizabeth to Edward Montagu, 25 November 1762 (MO2464).

72. For the exchange of letters between Brown and Montagu, see Stroud, *Capability Brown*, pp. 195–7, and Hyams, *Capability Brown*, pp. 102–6.

73. Montagu to Vesey, London, 5 March 1778 (MO6514).

74. Elizabeth Montagu to Elizabeth [Charlton] Montagu, Sandleford, 23 July 1786 (MO2959); and to Carter and Scott, Sandleford, 26 July 1786 (MO3607 & MO6132).

75. Stroud, *Capability Brown*; Hinde, *Capability Brown*; Turner, *Capability Brown*; Baird, *Mistress of the House*; Wade, *Sandleford Priory*.

76. Montagu to Vesey, Sandleford, 31 July 1781 (MO6565).

77. Montagu to Carter, Sandleford, 16 September 1781 (MO3516).

78. Elizabeth Montagu to Scott, Shooters Hill, 9 July 1790 (MO6200); Elizabeth Montagu to Matthew Montagu, Sandleford, 3 October 1790 (MO3944);

Elizabeth [Charlton] Montagu to Matthew Montagu Sandleford, 27 October 1790 (MO2859); Elizabeth Montagu to Carter, Sandleford, 5 July 1792 (MO3700).

79. For an early reading of the novel's conservative agenda, see Todd, *The Sign of Angelica woman*, p. 202, a claim to some extent reiterated by Gary Kelly in his Broadview edition of the novel; for Scott's use of sentimental tropes in order to justify aristocratic philanthropy, see Elliott, 'Sarah Scott's Millenium Hall and Female Philanthropy'; for claims of the novel's more radical credentials, see Woodward, ' "My Heart so Wrapt": Lesbian Disruptions in Eighteenth-Century British Fiction'; Bannet, 'The Bluestocking Sisters' and also her, *Domestic Revolution*, pp. 166ff. See also, Pohl, 'Sweet Place, Where Virtue Then Did Rest'.

80. Notably, Scott wrote to Montagu shortly before the publication of *Millenium Hall*, 'Nabob making is a better trade than King making, the earl of Warwick was nothing to our East India Conquerors. This conquest of Pondicherry I find is to make more Clivenian Fortunes. I fear the Nation will find in time no small detriment from such immense property in the possession of persons so little qualified by education for them.' Scott to Montagu, 2 August 1761 (MO5386).

81. For the park aesthetic as a conversation between landowners at the expense of establish land use and the language of moral economy, see Harwood, 'Personal Identity'. On Montagu as a mine owner, see Child, 'Elizabeth Montagu, Bluestocking Businesswoman'.

82. For Montagu's anger with her father, rather than her sister, over claims that Lady Brumpton's 'character was designed for me', see Montagu to Sarah Scott, 7 April 1764 (MO5807), in which she also writes, 'For my part I shd not have been ye least concernd if any other person had written ye book, if ye character had been ascribed to me.... With some pretensions to admiration as a pretty Woman I left ye gay World much younger than I need to have done, which is not a sign vanity was predominant, with some little pretensions of other kinds I believe there is as little conceit, affectation, or presumption in my conversation as in most peoples. As to wearing good Cloaths, & having good furniture, I think if one means to live in ye World upon a certain establishment there is not any thing ill judged in it, & to avoid ye character of a witt & a pedant, it is more necessary for me than for others. Lady Brampton outshines me most prodigiously, & she has a rage of shining which makes all lustre ridiculous, & she is at ye bottom without principles...'.

83. See, for example, MO4639 (1764); but note also her willingness to enclose common land and thus to join in that long-term destruction of an independent peasantry: 'I am very desirous, anxious, ambitious, avaricious, to obtain what will enable me to compleat Mr Browns plan, for ye lines he drew were the lines of beauty & grace, but *what is one Will when many Wills rebel*? If my neighbours will not allow me what I desire, I must be content with what they

will grant, but if I offer a handsome compensation for what I would enclose why should they refuse it?' Elizabeth Montagu to Matthew Montagu, [April?] [1778?] (MO3889).

84. Montagu to the Earl of Bath, Sandleford, 2 June 1764 (MO4639).
85. Montagu to Scott, Sandleford, 4 November 1789 (MO6194).
86. Montagu to Carter, Sandleford, 25 September 1781 (MO3517).
87. December 1782, quoted in Stroud, *Capability Brown*, p. 196.
88. Montagu to Gilbert West, 27 September 1753, *Letters of Elizabeth Montagu*, vol. 3, p. 247.
89. For Montagu's acute awareness of her stance as an 'Englishwoman' in relation to a British empire and to ideas of liberty, see Major, 'Femininity and National Identity: Elizabeth Montagu's Trip to France'.
90. Montagu to Benjamin Stillingfleet, Sandleford, July 1761 (MO5118).
91. Montagu to the Earl of Bath, 12 October 1762 (MO4545).
92. Elizabeth Montagu to Edward Montagu, Sandleford, 17 June 1762 (MO2454).
93. Montagu to Frances Boscawen, Sandleford, 22 July 1794 (MO582).
94. Montagu to Lord Lyttelton, Sandleford, 12 August 1765 (MO1440).
95. Morgan, *A Tour of Milford Haven*, pp. 31–49.

4 Neighbours in retreat: Lady Mary Coke and the Hollands

1. See Longstaffe-Gowan, *London Town Garden*.
2. Stella Tillyard, *Aristocrats*, p. 48.
3. Horace Walpole to Horace Mann, 29 May 1744, OS, *Walpole Correspondence*, vol. 18, pp. 450–1; and see Liechtenstein, *Holland House*, vol. 1, 59–63.
4. The Holland House Papers are at the British Library Add.51408–51445. Vast as this archive is it provides only limited references to the actual landscaping of the Holland House estate though it does include more detailed documentation of the Hollands' second country retreat at Kingsgate in Kent. Caroline Lennox to Henry Fox, 28 April 1744, BL Add.51414.f.1.
5. See BL Add.51414.f.88 Caroline to Henry Fox [Thursday, 4 February 1748?], 'a queerish Woman called Lady Meath a sister of Sir Thomas Predergasts is here and has been to see me. She said Lady Albermarle had told her she was not allow'd to see me but that truly she had no notion of asking any body leave to Visit who she pleased . . .'.
6. The story of Caroline's courtship and elopement is recounted by Stella Tillyard, *Aristocrats*, pp. 20–9.
7. See Add.51424.f.68, Duke of Richmond to Henry Fox, 8 November 1749, 'You shall have all the beeches you want by next Wednesday, if the Carryer does not aske an unreasonable price for carriage . . . [P.S.] There was butt very little beech [?] this season & what little was gathered in sown. And as for chesnuts I have but few trees that bear them, & they are eat by the Deer as they fall. Butt Miller sayes if you will lett him know what quantities you want he can supply you'; and f.70,

10 November 1749, which details the 20 beeches 13 foot high, 3 beeches 20 foot high and a note that Richmond has 'added half a dozen very pretty Acacias' all of which he suggests should be planted the morning after they arrive.

8. For general histories of Holland House and its inhabitants, see Liechtenstein, *Holland House*; Ilchester, *The Home of the Hollands*; and Hudson, *Holland House*.

9. See Stella Tillyard, *Aristocrats*, p. 133, and Baird, *Mistresses of the House*, ch. 7.

10. Ilchester, *The Home of the Hollands*, vol. 1, p. 175; none of the recent studies of Kent's work (Wilson, *William Kent, Architect, Designer, Painter, Gardener*; Hunt, *William Kent: Landscape Garden Designer*; Mowl, *William Kent: Architect, Designer, Opportunist*) has found any evidence of this however.

11. For Fox's vast financial turnover – arising largely from the contemporary practice of the army's funds being paid directly into the account of the paymaster – see Add.51413, and for the payment to Brown in 1758, see f.35.

12. *A Tour through England* (1748) quoted in Ilchester, *Henry Fox, First Lord Holland*, vol. 1, p. 142.

13. Horace Walpole to Charles Hanbury Williams, 27 June 1748, *Walpole Correspondence*, vol. 30, p. 114.

14. See, for example, a receipt from Peter Collinson of 'money laid out for Mr Fox' for the purchase of chestnuts, cypress sees, &c, dated 5 December 1751, Add.51413.f.16.

15. Henry Fox to Peter Collinson, quoted in Liechtenstein, *Holland House*, vol. 2, p. 214.

16. Add.28727. f.77 Henry Fox to Peter Collinson, 14 September 1760.

17. For the important role played by Hamilton, see especially Symes, 'The Hon. Charles Hamilton at Holland Park'.

18. See, for example, Caroline to Henry Fox, February 1751, where she gives detailed instructions on the construction, painting, and siting on a gothic bench near the Acton road which must be made ready in time for her return to Holland House, Add.51415.f.7.

19. See Fitzgerald (ed.), *Correspondence of Duchess of Leinster*, vol. 1, p. 412.

20. See Add.51408.f.108–10, discussed by Symes, 'Preparation of a Landscape Garden: Charles Hamilton's Sowing of Grass at Painshill'.

21. See, for example, Add.51444.f.34–40 which record between 1772 and 1773 the making of 'my new little Gravel path on the outside of my pleasure ground', 'my Gravel path . . . near the Acton road finishd', and 'My favourite Bench at Mrs Daniels allterd and inlarged'. See also Caroline's correspondence with Emily in Fitzgerald (ed.), *Correspondence of Duchess of Leinster*; and Stella Tillyard, *Aristocrats*, p. 147.

22. Lady Caroline Holland to Emily, Countess of Kildare, undated letter, summer 1759, in Fitzgerald (ed.), *Correspondence of Duchess of Leinster*, vol. 1, p. 255.

23. Lady Caroline Holland to Emily, Countess of Kildare, 9 October 1759, in Fitzgerald (ed.), *Correspondence of Duchess of Leinster*, vol. 1, p. 259.

24. Fox took the title of Lord Holland of Foxley in 1763.

25. Lady Caroline Holland to Emily, Countess of Kildare, undated letter 1762, in Fitzgerald (ed.), *Correspondence of Duchess of Leinster*, vol. 1, p. 319.

26. Lady Caroline Holland to Emily, Countess of Kildare, 23 May 1762, in Fitzgerald (ed.), *Correspondence of Duchess of Leinster*, vol. 1, p. 326.

27. Lady Caroline Holland to Emily, Countess of Kildare, 5 September 1762, in Fitzgerald (ed.), *Correspondence of Duchess of Leinster*, vol. 1, p. 338.

28. Kingsgate Book, after October 1762, Add.51444.

29. Add.514146.f.124 Henry to Caroline, 29 November 1763.

30. Add.51416.f.139 Henry to Caroline, [23 December 1763].

31. Add.51444.f.9.

32. On her work at Holland House, see Baird, *Mistress of the House*, ch. 7.

33. Add.51413.f.97, f.99, f.113, f.123. Negotiations to buy Holland house went back at least to 1765 but stalled because its owner wanted much more than Henry Fox was initially willing to pay, see Add.51409.f.161.

34. A decade after Holland's death, Walpole wrote of Kingsgate, '... it is certainly singular and in no light disagreeable. Its situation is uncommon and cheerful, and the buildings and erections so odd, and so little resembling any one ever saw, that a view might to those who were never there, be passed for a prospect in some half-civilized island discovered by Capt. Cook...'. Walpole to Lady Ossory, 19 August 1784, *Walpole Correspondence*, vol. 33, p. 437. For a more supportive contemporary account of the buildings at Kingsgate, see T. Fisher, *The Kentish Traveller's Companion* (1776), pp. 124ff.; a more recent account, itself heavily reliant of Fisher, is Jessup, 'The Follies of Kingsgate' (1957), but this has been wholly superseded by Michael Cousin's two-part account of Holland's building work at Kingsgate, 'As for Paradise which is but another Name for Kingsgate'.

35. Letter to J. Campbell, 26 August 1768, quoted in Ilchester, *Henry Fox*, vol. 2, p. 327.

36. See Thomas Gray, 'Suggested by a view, in 1766, of the seat and ruins of a deceased nobleman, at Kingsgate, Kent'.

37. Lady Caroline Holland to Emily, Countess of Kildare, 4 September 1764, in Fitzgerald (ed.), *Correspondence of Duchess of Leinster*, vol. 1, p. 408.

38. Lady Caroline Holland to Emily, Countess of Kildare, 28 September 1762, in Fitzgerald (ed.), *Correspondence of Duchess of Leinster*, vol. 1, p. 341.

39. Lady Caroline Holland to Emily, Countess of Kildare, Kingsgate, 16 July 1766, in Fitzgerald (ed.), *Correspondence of Duchess of Leinster*, vol. 1, p. 459.

40. Lady Caroline Holland to Lady Susan Fox, [Paris], 29 November 1763, Add.51352.f.78–9.

41. Lady Caroline Holland to Emily, Countess of Kildare, 1761, in Fitzgerald (ed.), *Correspondence of Duchess of Leinster*, vol. 1, p. 306.

42. Lady Caroline Holland to Emily, Countess of Kildare, Holland House, 20 September 1764, in Fitzgerald (ed.), *Correspondence of Duchess of Leinster*, vol. 1, p. 412.

43. See Add.51434.f.17, 'Lord Holland's Hours, Exercises & Diet', Kingsgate, July 8 1766, which includes a report that after breakfast, 'Lady Holland makes Him walk in the Garden, & he hears, He is to encrease that Fatigue every Day'.

44. Lady Caroline Holland to Emily, Countess of Kildare, Holland House, 8 May 1759, and October 1759, in Fitzgerald (ed.), *Correspondence of Duchess of Leinster*, vol. 1, pp. 219, 260.

45. Lady Mary Coke wrote detailed letter-journals to her sisters during the whole of her time at Notting Hill and beyond; much of this was published in Coke, *Letters and Journals*.

46. For a detailed account of the garden's genesis, see Knox, 'Lady Mary Coke's Garden at Notting Hill'. For a brief history of the house and its owners, see Gladstone, *Aubrey House, Kensington*.

47. Coke, *Letters and Journals*, July 1768, vol. 2, p. 332.

48. Caroline to Henry Fox, [8 March 1748], Add.51414.f.145.

49. Caroline to Henry Fox, [Bath], [9 March 1748], Add.51414.f.147–8.

50. Walpole to Montagu, 14 July 1748, *Walpole Correspondence*, vol. 9, p. 59; the story of the duel also appears in Fanny Boscawen's journal, see Aspinall-Oglander, *Admiral's Wife*, pp. 89–91; in the same journal, p. 70, Boscawen refers to Coke as Lady Mary's 'worthless Lord, who games and drinks and stays out till 8 in the morning'.

51. Add.22629.

52. Mary Coke to Elizabeth Mackenzie, [no date], Add.22629.f.92.

53. Lady Elizabeth Campbell to Lady Suffolk, 15 June 1748, Add.Ms.22629.f.87.

54. On the crucial role played by 'friends' when women sought separation from their husbands, see Stone, *Road to Divorce*; and Tadmor, *Family and Friends*.

55. Mary Coke to Lady Suffolk, 12 July 1748, Add.Ms.22629.f.93.

56. Lady Louisa Stuart, 'Some Account of John Duke of Argyll and his Family' (1827), privately printed 1863; reprinted in Coke, *Letters and Journals*, vol. 1, pp. xv–cxxii.

57. Stuart, 'Some Account', in Coke, *Letters and Journals*, vol. 1, p. lvii.

58. For her dreams of the Duke's death, see *Letters and Journals*, vol. 2, p. 145, where she writes 'My mind was so distrub'd that I rose early & went into my Garden: stay'd out till twelve O'clock'.

59. Add.51408.f.216 Henry Holland to Richard Bateman, Nice[?], 22 March [1768].

60. Lady Dalkieth to Lady Susan Stewart, 20 [after September] 1764, in Argyll (ed.), *Intimate Society Letters of the Eighteenth Century*, vol. 1.

61. See, for example, Coke, *Letters and Journals*, vol. 1, pp. 43–5.

62. Coke, *Letters and Journals*, vol. 2, p. 332. Coke's letters had been stressing the necessary but unhappy nature of retirement since her arrival at Notting Hill.

63. For the Countess of Upper Ossory, see *Walpole Correspondence*, vols. 32–4, though only Walpole's letters survive. An account of the events leading up to the divorce proceedings appears in, *Trials for Adultery* (1779–80), vol. 4. For Grafton, see Stone, *Divorce*, p. 341.

64. At least some remembered the 'disgrace' long after the event: see, for example, the letter from Gilly Williams to George Selwyn, Tuesday, 4 December 1764, in which he associates Coke with the recent case of Grafton, in Jesse, *George Selwyn and his Contemporaries*, vol. 1, p. 326.
65. Rowe *Letters Moral and Entertaining* Part III, Letter XV.
66. Coke, *Letters and Journals*, vol. 2, p. 148.
67. Mary Coke to Elizabeth Mackenzie, 16 July 1748, Add.Ms.22629.f.96.
68. Coke, *Letters and Journals*, vol. 2, p. 136.
69. Coke, *Letters and Journals*, vol. 2, p. 362.
70. Coke, *Letters and Journals*, vol. 2, p. 171.
71. For Coke as a Grand Tourist, see Dolan, *Women of the Grand Tour*, pp. 75–85.
72. Coke, *Letters and Journals*, vol. 2, p. 282.
73. Coke, *Letters and Journals*, vol. 3, pp. 105–6, 268.
74. On her numerous continental tours Coke was regularly withering about the false taste of foreign gardens, though she admired the picturesque landscapes of the Rhine.

5 'Can you not forgive?': Henrietta Knight at Barrells Hall

1. For Knight's life, see Hughes, *The Gentle Hertford*; Sichel, *Bolingbroke*; and Brown, *My Darling Herriot*.
2. On this early correspondence between Knight and Lady Hertford, see Hughes, *The Gentle Hertford*.
3. The poems are reproduced in Hughes, *The Gentle Hertford*, ch. 5.
4. Hughes, *The Gentle Hertford*, p. 142.
5. The story had been popularised in *The Spectator*, Thursday, 15 June 1710, and appeared again in Lewis Theobald's *The History of the Loves of Antiochus and Stratonice* (1717); engravings of the scene in which Antiochus's doctor realises the cause of his illness had been circulating from at least the 1690s.
6. Hughes, *The Gentle Hertford*, pp. 170–81.
7. The practice was hardly unusual: cf. Montagu's styling of herself as 'Pastorella' in Chapter 4; or Grierson's playful transformation of country lawyers into pastoral swains in 'To Miss Laetitia Van Lewen . . . at a Country Assize'.
8. Henrietta Knight to Robert Knight, Junior, no date, but before April 1736, Luxborough Papers, British Library Add.MS.45889.f.9–10. Slightly wayward transcripts of these letters appear in *The Knights of Barrells*, compiled by Arthur E Carden (privately printed, 1993) [British Library YK.1994 b.9783].
9. Add.MS.45889.f.7–8.
10. John St. John to Henrietta Knight, 26 July, Add.MS.45889.f.28–9.
11. John St. John to Robert Knight Junior, Tuesday, 29 June, Add.MS.45889.f.26.
12. Bolingbroke to Robert Knight, Argeville, 30 August 1736, Add.MS.45889.f.32–3.
13. For which, see Brant, *Eighteenth-Century Letters*.
14. Bolingbroke to Robert Knight, Argeville, 30 August 1736, Add.MS.45889.f.32–3.

15. John St John to Henrietta Knight, Chipping Warden, 6 July 1736, Add.MS.45889. f.28–9.
16. See Bolingbroke to Robert Knight, Argeville, 30 August 1736, Add.MS.45889. f.32–3.
17. Bolingbroke to Henrietta Knight, Argeville, 7 December 1736, Add.MS.45889. f.38.
18. Bolingbroke to Robert Knight, Argeville, 30 August 1736, Add.MS.45889.f.32–3.
19. Henrietta Knight to Robert Knight, Junior, no date, but before April 1736, Add.MS.45889.f.9–10.
20. For the terms of the agreement, Add.MS.45889.f.137–42; reproduced in both Sichel, *Bolingbroke*, and Brown, *My Darling Herriot.*
21. Notably, too, while Bolingbroke follows quite closely in the footsteps of Cowley, he distances himself from the much easier-going accounts of retired life popularised on the one hand by Pomfret in *The Choice* (1700), and on the other by the more scholarly Robert Castell in his *Villas of the Ancients* (1728).
22. But see the judgement of one of Bolingbroke's admirers, Lord Chesterfield, 'Though nobody spoke and wrote better philosophy than his lordship, no man in the world had less share of philosophy than himself. The least trifle, such as the over-roasting of a leg of mutton, would strangely disturb and ruffle his temper; and his passions constantly got the better of his judgement', quoted in Hopkinson, *Married to Mercury*, p. 212.
23. Bolingbroke, 'Of the true Use of Retirement and Study', in *Works*, vol. 2, pp. 512–27.
24. See, for example, Bolingbroke's letter to his friend William Wyndham, February 1725: 'If the Marquise [his wife] and one or two other friends did not attach me to life, I should grow tired of the world, as one grows tired of bad company, and wish to be out of it . . .', quoted in Hopkinson, *Married to Mercury*, p. 164.
25. For the inscriptions at La Source, see Hopkinson, *Married to Mercury*, p. 149.
26. That conundrum is of course repeated by James Thomson in his account of Lord Lyttelton at the centre of *The Seasons*, for which see Barrell, *An Equal Wide Survey*, ch. 1.
27. Hopkinson, *Married to Mercury*, p. 157.
28. For a detailed account of Bolingbroke, Pope, and Dawley, see Martin, *Pursuing Innocent Pleasures*, ch. 5.
29. Luxborough, *Letters to William Shenstone*, Letter XLI nd 1749, p. 170.
30. Bolingbroke to Henrietta Knight, 24 June 1722, Add.Ms.34196.f.19.
31. Bolingbroke to Henrietta St. John, 20 December 1719, Add.Ms.34196. f.9; see also 23 July 1720, 'I am too just, my dear Girl, not to be persuaded of your sincerity, and therefore I take all the expressions which flow from yr pen to flow from yr heart. be just in your turn, and be persuaded yt I love you entirely', Add.Ms.34196.f.11.
32. Bolingbroke to Henrietta St John, [France], 23 July 1720, Add.Ms.34196.f.14–15.

33. Bolingbroke to Lady Luxborough, Battersea, 9 July 1751 & 16 August 1751, Add.Ms.34196.f.153, f.155.

34. Bolingbroke to Robert Knight, 12 June 1738, Add.Ms.34196.f.136.

35. Replying to a letter from Bolingbroke suggesting that he should buy Dawley for Henrietta and her husband, Robert Knight senior (Henrietta's father in law) wrote: 'If his and his Lady's Turn was for a Country Life, and that he understood and rellished the management of Country affairs, the difference would not be very great between living there and living in the Town, but a young man should be in the world, and only old men, or incapable men, retire into the Country; and to live in so great a House during the Summer, is not only expensive but will take him from amongst those whom he should converse with to establish an interest . . . ' Robert Knight senior to Henry Bolingbroke, nd (but summer 1736), reproduced in Carden, *The Knights of Barrells*, p. 114.

36. Bolingbroke to Henrietta Knight London, 11 April 1751, Add.Ms.34196.f.151.

37. Henrietta Knight to Robert Knight (husband) [nd] Add.MS.45889. f.11–12 (reproduced in Carden, *The Knights of Barrells*, p. 108).

38. Hughes, *The Gentle Hertford*, p. 145.

39. Hughes, *The Gentle Hertford*, p. 145.

40. For the genesis of the garden, see Percy, 'Lady Luxborough'; and Brown, *My Darling Herriot*, p. 196, with a reconstructed map, pp. 162–3.

41. Henrietta Knight, 28 April 1748, *Letters by Lady Luxborough*.

42. Coffin, *The English Garden*, p. 158.

43. See Colton, 'Merlin's Cave and Queen Caroline'; for Chambers at Kew, see Harris, *Sir William Chambers*, ch. 3; see also King, *Royal Kew*.

44. Jane Brereton, 'On the Bustoes in the Royal Hermitage', in *Poems on Several Occasions* (1744); Mrs Cockburn, 'A Poem, Occasioned by the Busts set up in the Queen's Hermitage', in *Poems by Eminent Ladies*, vol. 1, pp. 234–8.

45. Henrietta Knight to Lady Hertford, 19 July 1742, in Hughes, *The Gentle Hertford*, p. 157.

46. According to Add.Ms.34196.f.137–42.

47. Hertford too made just this claim: 'The Satisfaction I take in adding either Beauty of Convenience to my Habitation, is greatly enhanced by the Reflection, that while I am adorning it, I at the same Time can shew my Value for the Gift, and my Gratitude to the lamented Giver.' Duchess of Somerset to Lady Luxborough, Percy Lodge, 31 December, 1751, Hull (ed.), *Selected Letters*, Letter XLIII.

48. This finds its echo of course in Elizabeth Montagu's insistence that she only ever paid for her (extensive) building projects from annual income rather than capital; for what is now the standard account of luxury as effeminacy, see Clery, *The Feminization Debate*.

49. Smollett, *The Expedition of Humphry Clinker* (1771), Matthew Bramble to Dr Lewis, 30 September 30.

50. See Robert Knight, now Lord Luxborough, to Henrietta Knight, now Lady Luxborough, 19 February 1750/1, Add.MS.45889.f.62–3.
51. Shenstone to Henrietta Knight, Lady Luxborough, 2 June 1749, in Hull (ed.), *Selected Letters*, vol. 1, pp. 93–4.
52. See Bending, 'Uneasy Sensations: Shenstone, Retirement and Fame'.
53. Henrietta Knight to Shenstone, 28 December 1749, in *Letters by Lady Luxborough*, pp. 173–4.
54. In the 'Life on Shenstone' he writes: 'In time his expenses brought clamours about him, that overpowered the lamb's bleat and the linnet's song; and his groves were haunted by beings very different from fauns and fairies. He spent his estate in adorning it, and his death was probably hastened by his anxieties.' Johnson, *Prefaces, Biographical and Critical, to the Works of the English Poets* (1781), p. 9 (separate pagination for each preface); but cf. also Pope's championing of Knight's brother Bolingbroke and his distinctly over-ambitious spending at Dawley.
55. Henrietta Knight to Shenstone, 4 June 1749, *Letters by Lady Luxborough*, pp. 99–100.
56. Certainly Horace Walpole damned Knight's correspondence on just these grounds of triviality and mere domesticity.
57. Cf. Caroline Holland to her sister Emily, Holland House, 6 October 1768: 'I agree with you a taste for trifling amusements is a great happiness. Perhaps I go farther; I think when one is no more young, nothing is so rational, nothing else is worth while . . . Lord Holland, besides his other buildings at Kingsgate, is going to make a portico, and improve the house there. It is to be an Italian villa, *cela amuse*, does good to the poor people by employing them, and consequently when one can afford it is a rational amusement.' Fitzgerald (ed.), *Correspondence of Duchess of Leinster*, vol. 1, p. 546.
58. Anne Dewes to Bernard Granville, Mapleburrough Green, 12 August 1750, Delany, *Autobiography and Correspondence*, vol. 2, p. 577.
59. Mary Delany to Anne Dewes, Mount Panther, 24 August 1750, Delany *Autobiography and Correspondence*, vol. 2, pp. 585–6; see also same to same Delville, 8 November 1750, where Delany's brief comment that, 'I was much diverted with Pauline's account of Lady Luxborough' suggests that Knight remained the subject of gossip and amusement for those outside her local circle (vol. 2, p. 611).
60. Mary Delany to Anne Dewes, Delville, 7 April 1752, in Delany, *Autobiography and Correspondence*, vol. 3, p. 109.
61. Wendy Frith, 'Sexuality and Politics in the Gardens at West Wycombe'.
62. See Henrietta Knight to Shenstone, 29 August 1749, *Letters by Lady Luxborough*, p. 121.
63. Letter XLI (nd), *Letters by Lady Luxborough*, p. 169.
64. Henrietta Knight to Shenstone, 28 December 1749, *Letters by Lady Luxborough*, p. 176.

65. Henrietta Knight to Shenstone, 13 Sunday [May?] 1750, *Letters by Lady Luxborough*, p. 205.

66. Even within her own circles this obsessive concern over urnary inscriptions was not beyond satire. See, for example, the 'Receipt for a modern Urn. By Parson Allen; Extempore' in, *Shenstone's Miscellany 1759–1763*, p. 34.

67. Coffin, *The English Garden*, ch. 3

68. Mary Delany to Anne Dewes, 2 August 1748, in Delany, *Autobiography and Correspondence*, vol. 1, pp. 357–8.

69. Montagu to Frances Boscawen, 1749, *Letters of Mrs Elizabeth Montagu*, vol. 3, p. 106; Carter to Montagu, 20 June 1759, *Letters from Carter to Montagu*, vol. 1, p. 46; Anna Seward to Humphry Repton, 1 June 1791, in *Letters of Anna Seward*, vol. 3, p. 63.

70. Famously, the hermitage at Painshill was said to be intended for a paid 'hermit' and not for the owner, Charles Hamilton. As Michael Symes has demonstrated, the story appears to be apocryphal, but he provides useful evidence of the hermitage being used – in passing – for moments of meditation. For this, and for the best account of Painshill to date, see Symes, *Mr Hamilton's Elysium*, pp. 92–5.

71. Shenstone wrote to Knight of the genesis of the Leasowes' paths and views: 'At First I meant them merely as Melancholy Amusements for a Person whose circumstances required a solitary Life. They *were* so; but I ever found the solitude too deep to be agreeable. Of *late* . . . I began to covet to have my Place *esteem'd* agreeable in its way; to have it *frequented*; to meet now and then an human Face unawares – to enjoy even the Gape and Stare of the Mob', 27 June 1750, in Williams (ed.), *Letters of Williams Shenstone*, p. 282.

72. Hertford was in fact reading his collection of essays, *Meditations and Contemplations* (1748), a volume which went through dozens of editions by the end of the century.

73. Hertford to Henrietta Knight, Percy Lodge, 15 May 1748, in Hughes, *The Gentle Hertford*, p. 164.

74. Hearing of Knight's views, Hertford replied, 'I am sorry yu find any defects in Mr Hervey, for both the design & manner of his Writing pleases me extreamly', Percy Lodge 20 November 1748, Hertford to Henrietta Knight, Add.Ms.23728.f.27–8 (reproduced in Hull (ed.), *Selected Letters*, p. 81).

75. Duchess of Somerset [Hertford] to Lady Luxborough [Knight], Percy Lodge, 31 December 1751, in Hull (ed.), *Selected Letters*, Letter XLIII, pp. 166–7.

76. Knight to Shenstone, Barrells, 2 February 1753, *Letters by Lady Luxborough*, Letter XCII.

77. Henrietta Knight to Shenstone, 12 November 1753, and 20 January 1754, *Letters by Lady Luxborough*.

78. In Hertford's letters, that clash between pleasurable ease and proper religious meditation can be seen in an early response to Knight's hermitage, made soon after a visit in 1742. To Knight's request for advice she writes: 'It is impossible

not to approve of yr Hermitage which must be delightfull by its situation, & when improved by yr good Taste I dare say will be the prettiest thing of its kind in England – Yet as y^u ask my Opinion I must Object to the Cross . . . tho' I am not a Roman Catholick I think it cannot be properly placed any where but upon Buildings which are really set apart for Worship.' Hertford to Henrietta Knight, Percy Lodge, 7 October [1742], Add.Ms.23728. f.8.

79. Henrietta Knight to Hertford, Barrels Green, 19 July 1742, quoted in Hughes, *The Gentle Hertford*, p. 157.
80. Henrietta Knight to Shenstone, nd 1749, *Letter by Lady Luxborough*, Letter XLI, pp. 162–3.
81. Anne Grant, 9 May 1800, in *Letters from the Mountains*, vol. 3, p. 90; Carter to Montagu, 21 October 1763, in *Letters from Carter to Montagu*, vol. 1.
82. Henrietta Knight to Shenstone, 10 July 1751, *Letter by Lady Luxborough*, p. 277.
83. Henrietta Knight to Shenstone, 1 August 1751, *Letter by Lady Luxborough*, p. 284.
84. Henrietta Knight to Shenstone, 27 May 1751, *Letter by Lady Luxborough*, p. 263.
85. Walpole was still happy to peddle tales of excess – now alcoholic rather than sexual – well after her death. See his letter to Mary Berry, 4 September 1789, in which he writes: 'I have talked scandal from Richmond like its gossip, and now by your queries after Lady L. you are drawing me into more, which I do not love . . . Lady Loughborough . . . retired to the country, corresponded, as you see by her letters, with the small poets of that time, but having no Theseus amongst them, consoled herself, as it is said, like Ariadne, with Bacchus.' *Walpole Correspondence*, vol. 11, pp. 64–6.
86. See her letter to Shenstone in which she agrees with his sentiment, 'an absent pleasure is equivalent to present pain', 28 April 1748, *Luxborough Letters*, p. 18.

6 'Though very retired, I am very happy'

1. Hall (ed.), *Miss Weeton*. For a discussion of Weeton's later (unhappy) married life, see Vickery, *The Gentleman's Daughter*, p. 77.
2. To her Brother, Up-Holland, 13 July 1808, Hall (ed.), *Miss Weeton*, vol. 1, p. 98.
3. To Miss Catherine Braithwaite, Up-Holland, 2 March 1809, Hall (ed.), *Miss Weeton*, vol. 1, p. 151.
4. To her Brother, Beacon's Gutter, 6 February 1809, Hall (ed.), *Miss Weeton*, vol. 1, p. 147.
5. October–November 1813, Hall (ed.), *Miss Weeton*, vol. 2, pp. 104–5.
6. To Mrs. Whitehead, Beacon's Gutter, 3 January 1809, Hall (ed.), *Miss Weeton*, vol. 1, pp. 140–1.

Bibliography

Manuscripts

British Library: Holland House Papers Add.51408–51445; 'Letters of Lord Bolingbroke 1716–1751' Add.Ms.34196; Letters of Frances, Countess of Hertford to Henrietta Knight Add.Ms.23728; Luxborough Papers, Add.Ms.45889; Suffolk Papers (relative to Lady Mary Coke) Add.Ms.22629

Huntington Library: Montagu papers; Wotton estate papers STG Accounts Box 24–5, ST vol. 164, 236

John Rylands Library: Mary Sharpe letters (1779–82) HAM/1/22

Books and Articles

Achinstein, Sharon, 'Romance of the Spirit: Female Sexuality and Religious Desire in Early Modern England', *ELH*, 69 (2002), 413–38

Allen, David, *The Naturalist in Britain: A Social History* (London: Allen Lane, 1976)

Alpers, Paul, *What Is Pastoral?* (Chicago University Press, 1995)

Althans, Margaret, 'Letters from Margaret Magdalen Jasper Althans to Henry Andrew Althans, William Althans and George Althans, 1789', in *The Christian Character Exemplified from the papers of Mrs Frederick Charles A–s of Goodman's Fields* (Hartford CT, 1804)

Amory, Thomas, *Memoirs: containing the lives of several ladies of great Britain...*, 2 vols. (London: John Noon, 1755)

Andrews, Malcolm, *Landscape and Western Art*, Oxford History of Western Art (Oxford University Press, 1999)

Anon, *Christian Biography: or, a collection of the lives of several excellent persons eminent for faith and piety, from the works of the Rev. Mr Baxter, and Dr Bates... viz. Mrs Elizabeth Baker... Mrs Mary Hanmer... Mrs Mary Coxe*, 2 vols. (London: W. Harris, 1768)

Anon, *Letters to Honoria and Marianne, on Various Subjects*, 3 vols. (London: J. Dodsley, 1784)

Anon, *The Berwick Museum, or, Monthly Literary Intelligencer. Forming an Universal Repository of Amusement and Instruction*, 3 vols. (Berwick, 1785–7)

Anon, *The Complete Florist; or, the Lady and Gentleman's Recreation in the Flower Garden* (London: R. Snagg, 1775)

Anon, *The Female Gamester: or, the pupil of fashion*, 2 vols. (London: Vernor and Hood, 1796)

Anon, *The Flower-Garden Displayed... To which is added, A Flower-Garden for Gentlemen and Ladies...* 2nd edition (London, 1734)

Anon, *The Kentish Traveller's Companion, in a descriptive view of the towns, villages, remarkable buildings, and antiquities, situated on or near the road from London to Margate, Dover and Canterbury* (Rochester: T. Fisher, 1776)

Anon, *The New Pleasant Instructor. Containing a Variety of Pathetic Eastern Tales, Entertaining Histories, &c... Taken from the Most Celebrated Authors* (Perth: J.Taylor, 1781)

Anon, *Trials for Adultery* (London: S. Bladon, 1779–80)

Argyll, John, Duke of (ed.), *Intimate Society Letters of the Eighteenth Century*, 2 vols. (London: Stanley Paul & Co, 1910)

Arnold, Dana (ed.), *The Georgian Country House: Architecture, Landscape and Society* (Stroud: Sutton, 1998)

Aspinall-Oglander, Cecil, *Admiral's Wife: Being the life and letters of the Hon. Mrs. Edward Boscawen from 1719 to 1761* (London: Longmans, 1940)

Astell, Mary, *A Serious Proposal to the Ladies*, Parts I & II (1694–7) (ed.) Patricia Springborg (Peterborough, Ontario: Broadview, 2002)

Aynsley, J. & C. Grant (eds), *Imagined Interiors: Representing the Domestic Interior since the Renaissance* (London: V&A Publications, 2006)

Baird, Rosemary, *Mistress of the House: Great Ladies and Grand Houses, 1670–1830* (London: Weidenfeld & Nicolson, 2003)

Ballard, George, *Memoirs of several ladies of Great Britain, who have been celebrated for their writings or skill in the learned languages arts and sciences...* (Oxford: For the Author, 1752)

Ballaster, Ros, *Seductive Forms: Women's Amatory Fiction from 1684–1740* (Oxford: Clarendon Press, 1992)

Bannet, Eve Tavor, *The Domestic Revolution: Enlightenment Feminisms and the Novel* (Baltimore and London: Johns Hopkins University Press, 2000)

Bannet, Eve Tavor, 'The Bluestocking Sisters: Women's Patronage, *Millenium Hall*, and "The Visible Providence of a Country"', *Eighteenth-Century Life*, 30:1 (Winter 2005), 25–55

Barrell, John, *English Literature in History 1730–1780: An Equal, Wide Survey* (London: Hutchinson, and New York: St Martin's, 1983)

Barrell, John & Harriet Guest, "On the Uses of Contradiction: Economics and Morality in the Eighteenth-Century Long Poem', in Felicity Nussbaum & Laura Brown (eds), *The New Eighteenth Century: Theory, Politics, English Literature* (London: Methuen, 1987)

Burney, Frances, *The Diary and Letters of Madame D'Arblay (1798–1840)*, (ed.) Charlotte Frances Barrett, 3 vols. (London: Frederick, 1892)

Bell, Susan Groag, 'Women Create Gardens in Male Landscapes: A Revisionist Approach to Eighteenth-Century English Garden History', *Feminist Studies*, 16:3 (1990), 471–91

Bending, Stephen, 'Horace Walpole and Eighteenth-Century Garden History', *Journal of the Warburg and Courtauld Institute*, 57 (1994), 209–226

Bending, Stephen, 'A Natural Revolution? Garden Politics in Eighteenth-Century England', in Kevin Sharpe & Steven Zwicker (eds), *Refiguring Revolutions: British Politics and Aesthetics, 1642–1789* (Berkeley & London: University of California Press, 1998)

Bending, Stephen, 'One Among the Many: Popular Aesthetics, Polite Culture and the Country House Landscape', in Dana Arnold (ed.), *The Country House in Georgian England* (Stroud: Sutton, 1998), pp. 61–78

Bending, Stephen, 'Uneasy Sensations: Shenstone, Retirement and Fame', *New Arcadian Journal*: 'The Leasowes, Hagley, Enville, Little Sparta', 53/4 (2002), 20–40

Bennett, Sue, *Five Centuries of Women and Gardens* (London: National Portrait Gallery, 2000)

Bermingham, Ann, *Landscape and Ideology. The English Rustic Tradition, 1740–1860* (London: University of California Press, 1987)

Bigold, Melanie, 'Elizabeth Rowe's Fictional and Familiar Letters: Exemplarity, Enthusiasm and the Production of Posthumous Meaning,' *British Journal for Eighteenth-Century Studies* 29/1 (2006), 1–14

Blackstone, William, *Commentaries of the Laws of England*, 4 vols. (London, 1765–9)

Blunt, Reginald (ed.), *Mrs. Montagu 'Queen of the Blues': Her Life and Friendships from 1762 to 1800*, 2 vols. (London: Constable & Co., 1923)

Bolingbroke, Henry St. John, Viscount, *The Works of the late Right Honourable Henry St. John, Lord Viscount Bolingbroke*, 5 vols. (London: David Mallet, 1754)

Boswell, James, *Life of Johnson*, R. W. Chapman (ed.), introduced by Pat Rogers (Oxford: World's Classics, 1980)

Bowerbank, Sylvia, *Speaking for Nature: Women and Ecologies of Early Modern England* (Baltimore & London: Johns Hopkins University Press, 2004)

Brant, Clare, *Eighteenth-Century Letters and British Culture* (Houndmills, Basingstoke: Palgrave Macmillan, 2006)

Brereton, Jane, *Poems on Several Occasions, with letters to her friends, and an account of her life* (London: Edward Cave, 1744)

Brewer, Daniel, 'Lights in Space', *Eighteenth-Century Studies*, 37:2 (2004), 171–86

Brown, Jane, *My Darling Herriot: Henrietta Luxborough, Poetic Gardener and Irrepressible Exile* (London: Harper Press, 2006)

Browne, Thomas, *Christian Morals* (Cambridge University Press, 1716)

Brownell, Morris, *Alexander Pope and the Arts of Georgian England* (Oxford: Clarendon Press, 1978)

Burnet, Thomas, *The Theory of the Earth Containing an Account of the Original of the Earth . . .* (London: R. Norton, 1684)

Bushnell, Rebecca, *Green Desire: Imagining Early Modern English Gardens* (Ithaca: Cornell University Press, 2003)

Butler, Joseph, *Analogy of Religion, Natural and Revealed* (London: Knapton, 1736)

Butler, Judith, *Bodies that Matter: On the Discursive Limits of "Sex"* (London: Routledge, 1993)

Calder, Martin (ed.), *Experiencing the Garden in the Eighteenth Century* (Bern: Peter Lang, 2006)

Campbell, Susan, *A History of Kitchen Gardening* (London: Frances Lincoln, 2005)

Carden, Arthur E., *The Knights of Barrells*, compiled by Arthur E. Carden (privately printed, 1993) [British Library YK.1994 b.9783]

Carter, Elizabeth, *All the Works of Epictetus, which are now Extant; Consisting of his Discourses, preserved by Arrian, in four books, the Enchiridion, and Fragments* (London: Millar, Rivington and Dodsley, 1758)

Carter, Elizabeth & Catherine Talbot, *A Series of Letters between Mrs. Elizabeth Carter and Miss Catherine Talbot from the Year 1741 to 1770: To Which are Added Letters from Mrs. Carter to Mrs. [Elizabeth] Vesey between the Years 1767 and 1787*, 4 vols. (London: Rivington, 1809)

Carter, Elizabeth, *Letters from Mrs. Elizabeth Carter to Mrs. Montagu between the Years 1755 and 1800* (ed.) Montagu Pennington, 4 vols. (London: F. C. & J. Rivington, 1817)

Castell, Robert, *The Villas of the Ancients, Illustrated* (London: Printed for the Author, 1728)

Chandler, Mary, *The Description of Bath. A Poem . . . To which are added, several poems by the same author*, 3rd edition (London: James Leake, 1736)

Chedgzoy, Kate, '"For Virgin Buildings Oft Brought Forth": Fantasies of Convent Sexuality', in D'Monté and Pohl, *Female Communities*, pp. 53–75

Child, Elizabeth, 'Elizabeth Montagu, Bluestocking Businesswoman', in Nicole Pohl and Betty A. Schellenberg (eds), *Reconsidering the Bluestockings* (San Marino: Huntington Library, 2003)

Chudleigh, Mary Lee, Lady, *Poems on several occasions. Together with the song of the three children paraphras'd. By the Lady Chudleigh* (London: Bernard Lintot, 1703)

Clark, Alice (ed.), *Gleanings from an Old Portfolio, containing some correspondence between Lady Louisa Stuart and her sister Caroline, Countess of Portarlington, and other friends and relations*, 3 vols. (Edinburgh: Privately Printed for David Douglas, 1895)

Clark, H. F., *The English Landscape Garden* (London: Pleiades Books, 1948)

Clery, Emma, *The Feminization Debate in Eighteenth-Century England: Literature, Commerce and Luxury* (Basingstoke: Palgrave, 2004)

Coffin, David R., *The English Garden: Meditation and Memorial* (Princeton University Press, 1994)

Coffin, David R., 'Venus in the Eighteenth-Century English Garden', *Garden History*, 28:2 (Winter, 2000), 173–93

Cogan, Thomas, *John Buncle, Junior*, 2 vols. (London: J. Johnson, 1776–8)

Coke, Lady Mary, *The Letters and Journals of Lady Mary Coke* (ed.) James A. Home, 4 vols. (Edinburgh: David Douglas, 1889)

Colton, Judith, 'Merlin's Cave and Queen Caroline: Garden Art as Political Propaganda', *Eighteenth Century Studies*, 10 (Fall 1976), 1–20

Hertford, Frances Seymour, Countess of, and Henrietta Louisa Fermor, Countess of Pomfret, *Correspondence between Frances, Countess of Hartford (afterwards Duchess of Somerset) and Henrietta Louisa, Countess of Pomfret, Between the years 1738 and 1741*, 3 vols. (London: R. Phillips, 1805)

Cosgrove, Denis, *Social Formation and Symbolic Landscape* (London: Croom Helm, 1984)

Cousins, Michael, 'As for Paradise which is but another Name for Kingsgate', *Follies Magazine* 12:2 (2000), 7–14, and 12:3 (2000), 5–10

Cowper, William, *The Task* (London: J. Johnson, 1785)

Craven, Elizabeth, *A Journey through the Crimea to Constantinople in a Series of Letters . . . to his Serene Highness, the Margrave of Brandenbourg, Ansbach, and Bayreuth* (London: G. G. J. & J. Robinson, 1789)

Daniels, Stephen, *Humphry Repton: Landscape Gardening and the Geography of Georgian England* (New Haven & London: Yale University Press, 1999)

Davys, Mary, *The Reform'd Coquet* (London: Printed for the Author, 1724)

Delany, Mary, *The Autobiography and Correspondence of Mrs. Delany, Revised from Lady Llanover's edition* (ed.) Sarah Chauncey Woolsey, 6 vols. (Boston: Roberts Brothers, 1879)

D'Monté, Rebecca & Nicole Pohl (eds), *Female Communities 1600–1800: Literary Visions and Cultural Realities* (Houndmills, Basingstoke: Macmillan, 2000)

Dolan, Brian, *Ladies of the Grand Tour* (London: HarperCollins, 2001)

Donald, Diana, *The Age of Caricature: Satirical Prints in the Reign of George III* (New Haven & London: Yale University Press, 1996)

Doody, Margaret Anne, *A Natural Passion, A Study of the Novels of Samuel Richardson* (Oxford: Clarendon Press, 1974)

Doody, Margaret Anne, 'Women poets of the eighteenth century', in Vivien Jones (ed.), *Women and Literature in Britain, 1700–1800* (Cambridge University Press, 2000)

Eger, Elizabeth, *Bluestockings: Women of Reason from Enlightenment to Romanticism* (Basingstoke: Palgrave Macmillan, 2010)

Elliott, Dorice Williams, 'Sarah Scott's Millenium Hall and Female Philanthropy', *Studies in English Literature*, 35:3 (Summer, 1995), 535–53

Empson, William, *Some Versions of Pastoral* (London: Chatto and Windus, 1935)

Evelyn, Charles, *The Lady's Recreation, or, The Third and Last Part of Gardening Improv'd* (London, 1717)

Fabricant, Carole, 'Binding and Dressing Nature's Loose Tresses: The Ideology of Augustan Landscape Design', in R. Runte (ed.), *Studies in Eighteenth-Century Culture*, 8 (Madison: Wisconsin University Press, 1979)

Fielding, Henry, *The History of Tom Jones, a Foundling*, 6 vols. (London: A. Millar, 1749)

Fitzgerald, Brian (ed.), *Correspondence of Emily, Duchess of Leinster*, 3 vols. (Dublin: Stationery Office, 1949–67)

Frith, Wendy, 'Castle Howard: Dynastic and Sexual Politics', *New Arcadian Journal*, 29/30 (1990), 66–99

Frith, Wendy, 'When Frankie met Johnny: Sexuality and Politics in the Gardens at West Wycombe and Medmenham Abbey', *New Arcadian Journal*, 49/50 (2000), 62–104

Frith, Wendy, 'Sexuality and Politics in the Gardens at West Wycombe and Medmenham Abbey', in Michel Conan (ed.), *Bourgeois and Aristocratic Cultural Encounters in Garden Art, 1550–1850*, Dumbarton Oaks Colloquium of the History of Landscape Architecture (Washington D.C.: Dumbarton Oaks, 2002), pp. 285–309

Girouard, Mark, *Life in the English Country House* (New Haven and London: Yale University Press, 1978)

Gladstone, Florence M., *Aubrey House, Kensington, 1698–1920* (London: A. L. Humphreys, 1922)

Goldsmith, Oliver, *The Lady's Magazine. Or Polite Companion for the Fair Sex* (1759–60)

Goodman, Kevis, 'The Loophole in the Retreat: The Culture of News and the Early Life of Romantic Self-Consciousness', *The South Atlantic Quarterly*, 102:1 (Winter, 2003), 25–52

Grant, Anne MacVicar, *Letters from the Mountains: Being the First Real Correspondence of a Lady, Between the Years 1773 and 1807*, 3 vols. (London: Longman, 1807)

Grundy, Isobel, *Lady Mary Wortley Montagu* (Oxford University Press, 1999)

Guest, Harriet, *Small Change : Women, Learning, Patriotism, 1750–1810* (University of Chicago Press, 2000)

Hadfield, Miles, *A History of British Gardening* (Harmondsworth: Penguin, 1960)

Weeton, Ellen, *Miss Weeton, Journal of a Governess 1807–1821*, (ed.) Edward Hall, 2 vols. (London: Oxford University Press, 1936)

Halpern, L. C., 'The Duke of Kent's Garden at Wrest Park', *Journal of Garden History*, 15:3 (1995), 149–78

Hardin, Richard F., *Love in a Green Shade: Idyllic Romances Ancient to Modern* (Lincoln: University of Nebraska Press, 2000)

Harris, John, *Sir William Chambers, Knight of the Polar Star* (London: Zwemmer, 1970)

Harwood, Edward, 'Personal Identity and the Eighteenth-Century Garden', *Journal of Garden History*, 13:1 & 2 (1993), 36–48

Havens, Raymond D., 'Solitude and the Neoclassicists', *ELH*, 21:4 (December, 1954), 251–73

Haywood, Eliza, *The British Recluse* (London: D. Brown et al., 1722)

Hearne, Mary, *The Lover's Week or, The Six Days Adventures of Philander and Amaryllis* (London: E. Curl, 1718)

Hearne, Mary, *The Female Deserters. A Novel. By the author of The Lover's Week* (London: J. Roberts, 1719[1718])

Heckle, Augustin, *The Lady's Drawing Book: Consisting of about an Hundred Different Sorts of Flowers, all drawn after Nature . . . the whole adapted to engage the Fair Sex to a Profitable Improvement of their Leisure Hours* (London: T. Bowles, 1755)

Henrey, Blanche, *British Botanical and Horticultural Literature before 1800*, 3 vols. (Oxford University Press, 1975)

Hervey, James, *Reflections on a Flower Garden in a Letter to a Lady* (London: J. Rivington, 1746)

Hervey, James, *Meditations and Contemplations* (London: J. Rivington, 1748)

Hervey, Mary Lepel, Lady, *Letters of Mary Lepel, Lady Hervey, with a Memoir and Illustrative Notes* (London, 1821)

Hicks, Philip, 'The Roman Matron in Britain: Female Political Influence and Political Response, *ca.* 1750–1800', *The Journal of Modern History*, 77 (2005), 35–69

Hill, Bridget (ed.), *The First English Feminist: Reflections upon Marriage and other Writings by Mary Astell* (Aldershot: Gower/Maurice Temple Smith, 1986)

Hill, Bridget, 'A Refuge from Men: the Idea of a Protestant Nunnery', *Past and Present*, 117 (1987), 107–30

Hinde, Thomas, *Capability Brown, The Story of a Master Gardener* (London: Hutchinson, 1986)

Hopkinson, M. R., *Married to Mercury: A Sketch of Lord Bolingbroke and his Wives* (London: Constable & Co, 1936)

How, James, *Epistolary Spaces: English Letter Writing from the Foundation of the Post Office to Richardson's Clarissa* (Aldershot: Ashgate, 2003)

Hudson, Derek, *Holland House in Kensington* (London: Peter Davies, 1967)

Hughes, Helen Sard, *The Gentle Hertford: Her Life and Letters* (New York: Macmillan, 1940)

Hull, Thomas (ed.), *Selected Letters between the late Duchess of Somerset, Lady Luxborough, Mr. Whistler, Miss Dolman, Mr. R. Dodsley, William Shenstone, Esq. and others; including a Sketch of the Manners, Laws, &c. of the Republic of Venice, and some Poetical Pieces; the whole now first published from Original Copies*, 2 vols. (London, 1778)

Hunt, John Dixon, *The Figure in the Landscape: Poetry, Painting, and Gardening in the Eighteenth Century* (Baltimore and London: Johns Hopkins University Press, 1976)

Hunt, John Dixon, *William Kent: Landscape Garden Designer* (London: Zwemmer, 1987)

Hunt, John Dixon, *Greater Perfections: The Practice of Garden Theory* (Philadelphia and London: University of Pennsylvania Press, 1999)

Hunt, John Dixon, *The Afterlife of Gardens* (London: Reaktion, 2004)

Hussey, Christopher, *English Gardens and Landscapes, 1700–1750* (London: Country Life, 1967)

Hyams, Edward, *Capability Brown & Humphry Repton* (London: Dent, 1971)

Ilchester, Earl of, *Henry Fox, First Lord Holland: His Family and Relations*, 2 vols. (London: John Murray, 1920)

Ilchester, Earl of, *The Home of the Hollands 1605–1820* (London: John Murray, 1937)

Johnson, Samuel, *The lives of the most eminent English poets; with critical observations on their works*, 4 vols. (London: Bathurst, Buckland et al., 1781)

Johnson, Samuel, *Prefaces, Biographical and Critical, to the Works of the English Poets*, 10 vols. (London: J. Nichols, 1779)

Jesse, John Heneage, *George Selwyn and his Contemporaries; with memoirs and notes*, 4 vols. (London: Richard Bentley, 1843–4)

Jessup, Ronald, 'The Follies of Kingsgate', *Archaeologia Cantiana*, 71 (1957), 1–13

Kames, Henry Home, Lord, *Elements of Criticism*, 3 vols. (Edinburgh: Millar, Kincaid and Bell, 1762)

Keeble, N. H., *The Literary Culture of Nonconformity in Later Seventeenth-Century England* (Leicester University Press, 1987)

Kelly, Gary, 'Bluestocking Feminism', in Elizabeth Eger, Charlotte Grant, Cliona O Gallchoir, Penny Warburton (eds), *Women, Writing and the Public Sphere, 1700–1830* (Cambridge University Press, 2001)

Kelly, Isabella, *Poems and Fables on several occasions* (Chelsea, 1807)

Kenny, Virginia C., *The Country-House Ethos in English Literature, 1688–1750: Themes of personal retreat and national expansion* (New York & Brighton: Harvester, 1984)

Kermode, Frank, *English Pastoral Poetry from the Beginnings to Marvell: An Anthology* (New York: Norton, 1972)

Kern, Jean B., 'The Fallen Woman, from the perspective of Five Early Eighteenth-Century Women Novelists', *Studies in Eighteenth-Century Culture*, 10 (1981), 457–68

Kew Gardens: A Controversial Georgian Landscape', *New Arcadian Journal*, 51/2 (2001)

King, Ronald, *Royal Kew* (London: Constable, 1985)

Knox, Tim, 'Lady Mary Coke's Garden at Notting Hill', *The London Gardener, or The Gardener's Intelligencer*, 4 (1998–9), 52–63

Laird, Mark, *The Flowering of the Landscape Garden 1720–1800* (Philadelphia: University of Pennsylvania Press, 1999)

Laird, Mark & Alicia Weisberg-Roberts (eds), *Mrs Delany and her Circle* (New Haven and London: Yale University Press, 2010)

Langbauer, Laurie, *Women and Romance: The Consolations of Gender in the English Novel* (Ithaca and London: Cornell University Press, 1990)

Larson, Edith Sedgwick, 'A Measure of Power: The Personal Charity of Elizabeth Montagu', *Studies in Eighteenth-Century Culture* 16 (1986), 197–210

Leapor, Mary, *Poems* (London: J. Roberts, 1751)

Lennox, Charlotte, *The Female Quixote; or The Adventures of Arabella*, 2 vols. (London: Millar, 1752)

Leslie, Michael, 'History and Historiography in the English Landscape Garden', in, Michel Conan (ed.), *Perspectives on Garden Histories* (Washington D.C.: Dumbarton Oaks, 1999), pp. 91–106

Lewis, Judith S., 'When Is a House Not a Home: Elite English Women and the Eighteenth-Century Country House', *Journal of British Studies* (April 2009), 48:2, 336–63

Liechtenstein, Princess Marie, *Holland House*, 2 vols. (London: Macmillan and Co., 1874)

Lipsedge, Karen, 'A Place of Refuge, Seduction or Danger? The Representation of the Ivy Summer-House in Samuel Richardson's *Clarissa*', *Journal of Design History*, 19:3 (2006), 185–96

Lloyd, Sarah, 'Amour in the Shrubbery: Reading the Detail of English Adultery Trial Publications of the 1780s', *Eighteenth-Century Studies*, 39:4 (2006), 421–42

London Packet or New Lloyd's Evening Post

Longstaffe-Gowan, Todd, *The London Town Garden 1740–1840* (New Haven and London: Yale University Press, 2001)

Luxborough, Henrietta Knight, Lady, *Letters Written by the Late Right Honourable Lady Luxborough, to William Shenstone, Esq.* (London: J. Dodsley, 1775)

Lyttelton, George, Lord, *Advice to a Lady* (London: Lawton Gilliver, 1733)

Lyttelton, George, Lord, *Dialogues of the Dead* (London: W. Sandby, 1760)

Lyttelton, George Lord, *The Works of George Lord Lyttleton; formerly printed separately, and now collected together: with some other pieces, never before printed* (London: J. Dodsley, 1775)

Macey David J., Jr., 'Eden Revisited: Re-visions of the Garden of Eden in Astell's *Serious Proposal*, Scott's *Millenium Hall*, and Graffigny's *Lettres d'une péruvienne*', *Eighteenth-Century Fiction*, 9:2 (January 1997), 161–82

Major, Emma, 'Femininity and National Identity: Elizabeth Montagu's Trip to France', *ELH*, 72 (2005), 901–18

Malcomson, A. P. W., *The Pursuit of the Heiress: Aristocratic Marriage in Ireland 1740–1840* (Belfast: Ulster Historical Foundation, 2006)

Martin, Peter, *Pursuing Innocent Pleasures: The Gardening World of Alexander Pope* (Hamden, CT: Archon Books, 1984)

Mason, William, *The English Garden; A Poem* (York: Dodsley et al., 1783)

Masters, Mary, *Familiar Letters and Poems on Several Occasions* (London: Printed for the Author, 1755)

The Middlesex Journal

Montagu, Elizabeth, *The Letters of Elizabeth Montagu, with some of the letters of her correspondents*, 4 vols. (London: Cadell and Davies, 1809–13)

Montagu, Mary Wortley, *The Complete Letters of Lady Mary Wortley Montagu* (ed.) Robert Halsband, 3 vols. (Oxford: Clarendon Press, 1965–67)

More, Hannah, *The Search After Happiness. A Pastoral Drama* (Bristol: S. Farley, 1773)

Morgan, Mary, *A Tour to Milford Haven, in the year 1791* (London: John Stockdale, 1795)

The Morning Post

Morris, David B., *The Religious Sublime: Christian Poetry and Critical Tradition in Eighteenth-Century England* (Lexington: University of Kentucky Press, 1972)

Mowl, Timothy, *William Kent: Architect, Designer, Opportunist* (London: Jonathan Cape, 2006)

Munroe, Jennifer, *Gender and the Garden in Early Modern English Literature* (Aldershot: Ashgate, 2008)

Myers, Evelyn Elizabeth, *A History of Sandleford Priory*, Newbury District Field Club, Special Publication no.1 (Newbury, 1931)

Myers, Sylvia Harcstark, *The Bluestocking Circle* (Oxford: Clarendon Press, 1990)

Neeson, J. M., *Commoners: Common Rights, Enclosure and Social Change in England 1700–1820* (Cambridge University Press, 1993)

Nourse, Timothy *Campania Foelix; or, a Discourse of the benefits and improvements of Husbandry* (London: Thomas Bennet, 1700)

O'Brien, Karen, *Women and Enlightenment in Eighteenth-Century Britain* (Cambridge University Press, 2009)

Ousby, Ian, *The Englishman's England: Taste, Travel, and the Rise of Tourism* (Cambridge University Press, 1990)

Page, Judith W. & Elise L. Smith, *Women, Literature, and the Domesticated Landscape: England's Disciplines of Flora* (Cambridge University Press, 2011)

Paulson, Ronald, *Emblem and Expression: Meaning in English Art of the Eighteenth Century* (London: Thames & Hudson, 1975)

Penny, Anne, *Poems* (London: J. Dodsley, 1780)

Percy, Joan, 'Lady Luxborough (1700?–1756), Farmeress and her lost ferme ornee', *Hortus*, 14 (Summer 1990), 90–8

Perry, Ruth, *The Celebrated Mary Astell: An Early English Feminist* (University of Chicago Press, 1986)

Plant, Helen, ''Subjective Testimonies': Women Quaker Ministers and Spiritual Authority in England: 1750–1825', *Gender and History*, 15:2 (2003), 296–318

Poems by Eminent Ladies. Particularly, Mrs. Barber, Mrs. Behn, Miss Carter . . . to which is prefixed, A Short Account of each Writer, 2 vols. (Dublin: Sarah Cotter, 1757)

Pohl, Nicole, "Sweet Place, Where Virtue Then Did Rest'; The Appropriation of the Country House Ethos in Sarah Scott's *Millenium Hall*', *Utopian Studies* 7 (1996), 49–59

'The Political Temples of Stowe', *New Arcadian Journal*, vols. 43–4 (1997)

Pomfret, John, *The Choice* (London: J. Nutt, 1700)

Ponsonby, Margaret, *Stories from Home: English Domestic Interiors 1750–1850* (Aldershot: Ashgate, 2007)

Porter, Katherine Harriet, *Margaret Duchess of Portland. A Thesis Presented to the Faculty of the Graduate School of Cornell University for the degree of Doctor of Philosophy*, June 1930

Prescott, Sarah, 'Provincial Networks, Dissenting Connections, and Noble Friends: Elizabeth Singer Rowe and Female Authorship in Early Eighteenth-Century England', *Eighteenth-Century Life*, 25 (Winter, 2001), 29–42

Quaintance, Richard E., 'Walpole's Whig Interpretation of Landscaping History', *Studies in Eighteenth-Century Culture*, 9 (1979), 285–300

Radcliffe Hill, David, 'Genre and Social Order in Country House Poems of the Eighteenth Century: Four Views of Percy Lodge', *Studies in English Literature*, 30:3 (Summer, 1990), 445–65

Ray, John, *The Wisdom of God Manifested in the Works of the Creation* (London: Samuel Smith, 1691)

Rizzo, Betty, 'Two Versions of Community: Montagu and Scott', in Nicole Pohl and Betty A. Schellenberg (eds), *Reconsidering the Bluestockings* (San Marino: Huntington Library, 2003)

Robinson, Mary, *Poems by Mrs Robinson* (London: C. Parker, 1775)

Robinson, Mary, *Poems* (London: J. Bell, 1791)

Ross, Deborah, *The Excellence of Falsehood: Romance, Realism, and Women's Contribution to the Novel* (Lexington: University Press of Kentucky, 1991)

Ross, Stephanie, *What Gardens Mean* (University of Chicago Press, 1998)

Røstvig, Maren-Sofie, *The Happy-Man: Studies in the Metamorphoses of a Classical Ideal 1600–1700* (Oxford: Basil Blackwell, 1954)

Rousseau, Jean-Jacques, *Eloisa: or, a series of original letters collected and published by J. J. Rousseau. Translated from the French. In four volumes*, 2nd edn, 4 vols. (London, 1761)

Rousseau, Jean-Jacques, *The Reveries of the Solitary Walker* translated, with preface, notes, and an Interpretative Essay, by Charles E. Butterworth (New York University Press, 1979)

Rowe, Elizabeth, *Friendship in Death: in Twenty Letters from the Dead to the Living. To which are added, Letters Moral and Entertaining, in Prose and Verse. In Three Parts* (London: T. Worrall, 1733)

Rowe, Elizabeth, *Devout Exercises of the Heart in Meditation and Soliloquy, Prayer and Praise. By the late Pious and Ingenious Mrs. Rowe. Review'd and Published at her Request, by I. Watts, D.D.* (London: R. Hett, 1738)

Rowe, Nicholas, *The Fair Penitent* (London: J. Tonson, 1703)

Sahil, Sara, *Judith Butler* (London: Routledge, 2002)

Saumarez Smith, Charles, *Eighteenth-century Decoration : Design and the Domestic Interior in England* (New York: H. N. Abrams, 1993)

Schenker, Heather, 'Women, Gardens, and the English Middle Class in the Early Nineteenth Century', in, Michel Conan (ed.), *Bourgeois and Aristocratic Cultural Encounters in Garden Art, 1550–1850* (Washington, D.C.: Dumbarton Oaks, 2002), pp. 337–60

Schnorrenberg, Barbara Brandon, 'Mrs. Montagu and the Architects', in Linda Troost (ed.), *Eighteenth-Century Women: Studies in their Lives, Work, and Culture*, 4 (September 2006), 287–312

Scodel, Joshua, 'Lyric Forms', in Steven N. Zwicker (ed.), *The Cambridge Companion to English Literature, 1650–1740* (Cambridge University Press, 1998)

Scott, Katie, *The Rococo Interior: Decoration and Social Spaces in early Eighteenth-Century Paris* (New Haven and London: Yale University Press, 1995)

Seeley, Benjamin, *Stow. A Description of the Magnificent Gardens of the Right Honourable Richard, Earl Temple, Viscount and Baron Cobham. With a Plan of the House and Gardens* (London: J. Rivington, 1756)

Sévigné, Marie de Rabutin-Chantal, Marquise de, *Letters of Madame de Rabutin Chantal, Marchioness de Sévigné, to the Comtess* [sic] *de Grignan, her daughter... Translated from the French*, 2 vols. (London: N. Blandford, 1727)

Sévigné, Marie de Rabutin-Chantal, Marquise de, *Letters from the Marchioness de Sévigné, to her daughter the Countess de Grignan. Translated from the French of the last Paris edition*, 2nd edn, 10 vols. (London: J. Coote, 1763–8)

Seward, Anna, *Letters of Anna Seward: Written between the Years 1784 and 1807*, (ed.) A. Constable (Edinburgh: A. Constable and Co., 1811)

Shaftesbury, Anthony Ashley Cooper, Third Earl of, *The Life, unpublished Letters and Philosophical Regimen* (ed.) Benjamin Rand (London: Macmillan, 1900)

Sharpe, K., 'Women's Creativity and Display in the Eighteenth-Century British Domestic Interior', in S. McKellar & P. Sparke (eds), *Interior Design and Identity* (Manchester: Manchester University Press, 2004)

Shenstone, William, *The Works in Verse and Prose of William Shenstone* (London: R. & J. Dodsley, 1764)

Shenstone, William, *The Letters of Williams Shenstone* (ed.) Marjorie Williams, (Oxford: Basil Blackwell, 1939)

Shenstone, William, *Shenstone's Miscellany 1759–1763, now first edited from the manuscript* (ed.) Ian A. Gordon (Oxford: Clarendon Press, 1952)

Sheridan, Betsy, *Betsy Sheridan's Journal: Letters from Sheridan's Sister, 1784–1786 and 1788–1790* (ed.) William LeFanu (Oxford University Press, 1986)

Shteir, Ann B., *Cultivating Women, Cultivating Science: Flora's Daughters and Botany in England 1760–1860* (Baltimore and London: Johns Hopkins University Press, 1996)

Sichel, Walter, *Bolingbroke and his Times*, 2 vols. (New York and London: J. Nisbet & Co, 1901–2)

Sitter, John, *Literary Loneliness in Mid-Eighteenth-Century England* (Ithaca and London: Cornell University Press, 1982)

Smith, Charlotte, *Emmeline, the Orphan of the Castle*, 4 vols. (London: T. Cadell, 1788)

Smollett, Tobias, *The Expedition of Humphry Clinker* (London: W. Johnson, 1771)

Snell, K. D. M., *Annals of the Labouring Poor: Social Change and Agrarian England, 1660–1900* (Cambridge University Press, 1985)

Spacks, Patricia Meyer, *Desire and Truth: Functions of Plot in Eighteenth-Century English Novels* (University of Chicago Press, 1990)

Spacks, Patricia Meyer, *Privacy: Concealing the Eighteenth-century Self* (University of Chicago Press, 2003)

Spence, Joseph, *Observations, Anecdotes and Characters of Books and Men* (ed.) James M. Osborn, 2 vols. (Oxford: Clarendon Press, 1966)

Spencer, Jane, *The Rise of the Woman Novelist: From Aphra Behn to Jane Austen* (Oxford: Blackwell, 1986)

Staves, Susan, 'British Seduced Maidens', *Eighteenth-Century Studies*, 14 (1981), 109–34

Stecher, Henry F., *Elizabeth Singer Rowe, the Poetess of Frome. A Study in Eighteenth-Century Pietism* (Bern & Frankfurt: Herbert Lang, 1973)

Stone, Lawrence, *The Road to Divorce: England 1530–1987* (Oxford: Clarendon Press, 1990)

Strong, Roy, *The Artist and the Garden* (New Haven and London: Yale University Press, 2000)

Stroud, Dorothy, *Capability Brown*, 2nd ed. (London, 1975)

Styles, John & Amanda Vickery (eds.), *Gender, Taste and Material Culture in Britain and American 1700–1830* (New Haven and London: Yale University Press, 2007)

Switzer, Stephen, *Ichnographia Rustica: or, the Nobleman, gentleman, and gardener's recreation. Containing directions for the general distribution of a country seat, into rural and extensive gardens, parks, paddocks, &c* . . . 3 vols. (London, 1741–2)

Symes, Michael, 'The Hon. Charles Hamilton at Holland Park', *Journal of Garden History*, 3 (1983), 130–3

Symes, Michael, 'Preparation of a Landscape Garden: Charles Hamilton's Sowing of Grass at Painshill', *Garden History*, 13:1 (Spring, 1985), 4–8

Symes, Michael, *Mr Hamilton's Elysium: The Gardens of Painshill* (London: Frances Lincoln, 2010)

Tadmor, Naomi, *Family and Friends in Eighteenth-Century England* (Cambridge University Press, 2001)

Talbot, Catherine, *The Works of Catharine Talbot. A new edition* (London: Rivington, 1780)

Taylor, Barbara, 'Separations of Soul: Solitude, Biography, History', *The American Historical Review* (June 2009), 114:3, 640–51

Theobald, Lewis, *The History of the Loves of Antiochus and Stratonice, in which are interspers'd some accounts relating to Greece and Syria* (London: Jonas Browne, 1717)

Thomas, Claudia, 'Samuel Johnson and Elizabeth Carter: Pudding, Epictetus, and the Accomplished Woman', *South Central Review*, 9:4 (Winter, 1992), 18–30

Thomas, Claudia, *Alexander Pope and His Eighteenth-Century Women Readers* (Carbondale: Southern Illinois University Press, 1994)

Tillotson, John, *The Works of the Most Reverend Dr. John Tillotson, Late Archbishop of Canterbury: containing two hundred sermons and discourses, on several occasions...published from the originals by Ralph Barker*, 2 vols. (London: Timothy Goodwin et al., 1717)

Tillyard, E. M. W., *Some Mythical Elements in English Literature* (London: Chatto & Windus, 1961)

Tillyard, Stella, *Aristocrats: Caroline, Emily, Louisa, and Sarah Lennox, 1740–1832* (London: Chatto & Windus, 1994)

Todd, Janet, *The Sign of Angelica: Woman, Writing and Fiction 1660–1800* (London: Virago, 1989)

Trench, Melesina, 'Diary of Melesina Chevenix St. George Trench', in Richard Trench (ed.), *The Remains of the Late Mrs. Trench, Being Selections from her Journals, Letters and Other Papers* (London: Parker, Son & Bourn, 1862)

Trusler, John, *The Garden-Companion, for Gentlemen and Ladies; or, a Calendar, pointing out what should be done every month in the Green-House, Flower, Fruit and Kitchen Garden...* (London: John Trusler, 1795)

Turner, Roger, *Capability Brown and the Eighteenth-Century English Landscape* (London: Weidenfeld & Nicolson, 1985)

Tyson, Moses & Henry Guppy (eds), *The French journals of Mrs. Thrale and Doctor Johnson: edited from the original manuscripts in the John Rylands Library and the British Museum*, (Manchester University Press, 1932)

Way, Twigs, *Virgins, Weeders, and Queens: A History of Women in the Garden* (Stroud: Alan Sutton, 2006)

Ussher, Elizabeth, Lucy & Judith, *Extracts from the Letters of Elizabeth, Lucy, and Judith Ussher, late of the city of Waterford, Ireland* (Philadelphia, 1871)

Vickery, Amanda, *The Gentleman's Daughter: Women's Lives in Georgian England* (New Haven and London: Yale University Press, 1998)

Vulliamy, C. E., *Aspasia: The Life and Letters of Mary Granville, Mrs Delany (1700–1788)* (London: Geoffrey Bles, 1935)

Wade, Sybil, *Sandleford Priory: The Historic Landscape of St. Gabriel's School* (unpublished report, April, 1997).

Walpole, Horace, The Yale Edition of the Correspondence of Horace *Walpole Correspondence* (ed.) W. S. Lewis et al., 48 vols. (New Haven: Yale University Press, 1937–83)

Waring, Mary, *Diary of the Religious Experience of Mary Waring . . . of Godalming* (London: W. Phillips, 1809)

Weekly Journal or British Gazette

Wesley, John, *The Journal of the Rev. John Wesley, A.M., sometime fellow of Lincoln College, Oxford, enlarged from original mss., with notes from unpublished diaries, annotations, maps, and illustrations* (ed.) Nehemiah Curnock, 8 vols. (London: Robert Culley, 1909–16)

West, Shearer, 'The public nature of private life: the conversation piece and the fragmented family', *British Journal for Eighteenth-Century Studies*, 18 (1995) 156–8

Wortley Montagu, Lady Mary, *The Letters and Works of Lady Mary Wortley Montagu* (ed.) Lord Wharncliffe, 2 vols. (London: Bell, 1837)

Whately, Thomas, *Observations on Modern Gardening* (London: T. Payne, 1770)

Williams, Anna, in *Miscellanies in Prose and Verse* (London: T. Davies, 1766)

Williams, Robert, 'Making Places: Garden-Mastery and English Brown', *Journal of Garden History*, 3:4 (1983), 382–5

Williamson, Marilyn L., *Raising their Voices: British Women Writers, 1650–1750* (Detroit: Wayne State University Press, 1990)

Williamson, Tom, *Polite Landscapes: Gardens and Society in Eighteenth-Century England* (Stroud: Alan Sutton, 1995)

Williamson, Tom, *The Transformation of Rural England: Farming and the Landscape 1700–1870* (University of Exeter Press, 2002)

Williamson, Tom & Liz Bellamy, *Property and Landscape: A Social History of Land Ownership and the English Countryside* (London: George Philip, 1987)

Wilson, C. A. (ed.), *The Country House Kitchen Garden, 1600–1950*, Stroud: Sutton, 1998)

Wilson, Michael I., *William Kent, Architect, Designer, Painter, Gardener, 1685–1748* (London: Routledge & Kegan Paul, 1984)

Winchilsea, Anne Kingsmill Finch, Countess of, *Miscellany poems, on several occasions. Written by a lady* (London: John Barber, 1713)

Woodhouse, Rev. R. I. (ed.), *The Life and Poetical Works of James Woodhouse (1735–1820)* (London, 1896)

Woods, Margaret Hoare, *Extracts from the Journal of the Late Margaret Woods, From the Year 1771 to 1821* (London: H. Longstreth, 1850)

Woodward, Carolyn, "My Heart so Wrapt': Lesbian Disruptions in Eighteenth-Century British Fiction', *Signs*, 18:4 (Summer, 1993), 838–65

Wordsworth, Dorothy, *Letters of Dorothy Wordsworth* (ed.) Alan G. Hill (Oxford University Press, 1981)

Wright, George (ed.), *Pleasing Reflections on Life and Manners with essays, characters and poems, moral and entertaining, principally selected from fugitive publications* (London: S. Hooper, 1787)

Yearsley, Ann, *Poems on Various Subjects* (London: G. G. J. & J. Robinson, 1787)

Young, Arthur, *A Six Week Tour, through the Southern Counties of England and Wales* (London: W. Nicoll, 1768)

Index

and scandal, 93

and seduction, 106, 107, 110, 111, 112, 121, 230

and self-cultivation, 93

and self-fashioning, 93, 186, 204, 243, 245

and self-reflection, 5

and sensuality, 32, 35

and shame, 108, 130

and sociability, 83, 86, 200, 202, 234

and social rehabilitation, 61, 212

and solitude, 4, 132, 145, 146, 153, 188, 189, 190, 191, 203, 212

and space, 8, 176

  gendered, 156, 179, 181, 182, 184, 186, 203, 243

  imagined, 242

  liminal, 93

  shared, 5, 7, 37, 38, 111, 113, 217, 221

and surveillance, 108, 110

and taste, 223, 225

and temporality, 187

and temptation, 93, 153

and transgression, 108

and visiting, 12, 30, 31, 33, 37, 38, 121, 127, 160, 162, 201, 228, 238, 239

as abnegation of responsibility, 153

as aesthetic commodities, 166

as dangerous spaces, 32, 38, 108, 153, 154

as dirt-pies, 20

as domestic and decadent, 27

as emblems, 29, 49, 227, 235, 243

as erotic space, 11, 27, 30, 29–32, 43, 93, 98, 102–3, 105, 111, 113, 155, 158, 230, 232

as false paradise, 153, 155

as metaphor, 4, 10, 23, 25

as microcosm, 1, 12, 93

as naturalisation of wealth, 116

as paradise, 93, 143, 153, 155, 243

as political landscapes, 184–6, 214, 216, 222

as product of liberty, 9

as public and private, 3, 7, 13, 20, 24, 35, 38, 170, 186, 200, 201, 203, 206, 214, 221, 226, 228, 229, 231, 239

as public identity, 7, 172, 228, 232, 239

as representations of nature, 12

as wilderness, 93, 243

in women's fiction, 93–5

indistinguishable in Yorkshire, 33

labourers

  women, 16–19

public, 160

range of uses, 1, 4, 12, 13, 33, 38

shaped by use, 15

town, 162, 176

urns, 230–2

women's presence in, 15

gender, constructions of, 5, 7, 8, 14, 15, 25–7, 31, 32, 33, 35, 36, 38, 40, 43, 68, 93, 94, 97, 155, 157, 158, 178, 181, 186, 204, 211, 213, 226, 227, 228, 230, 232, 240, 243, 245

George II, 177

George III, 1, 2

Gessner, Salomon

  La Mort d'Abel, 96

Giaccomini, Teresa, 72–3

Gilpin, William

  A Dialogue on the Gardens at Stowe, 31

Goldsmith, Oliver

  The Lady's Magazine, 136

Goodwood, viii, 1, 175, 177, 178, 189, 250

Gordon, Lord William, 5

Gower, Dowager Countess of, 163

Grafton, Anne Fitzroy, Duchess of

  and Coke, 201

  scandal and retirement, 197–8

Grant, Anne MacVicar, 100

  on hermitages, 238

  on protestant nunneries, 254

  romances destroy retirement, 99

Gray, Lady Hester, 43, 251

  garden at Denhill, 43

Gray, Thomas

  on Lord Holland and Kingsgate, 186

greenhouses, 23

Greenwich, Caroline Townshend, Baroness

  and Coke, 196

Grenville, Lord

  on solitude and repentance, 131

Grierson, Constantia, 101

  'To Miss Laetitia Van Lewen', 96

  'To the Same', 97

Grimsthorpe, 22

Guarini, Giovanni Battista, 55

  Il Pastor Fido, 206, 238

Guest, Harriet

  on Carter, 126

guidebooks, 30, 31, 40

Hagley, 61, 62, 63, 64, 155, 156, 157, 159, 168, 170, 185, 225, 227

  as pastoral, 263

Hamilton, Charles, 9, 202, 276, 290

  advice on pleasure grounds, 181

  and Holland House, 179

  and Painshill, 181

Mulgrave, Lord
  on adultery and repentance, 131
Myers, Sylvia
  on the Bluestockings and the erotic,
    156

nature, 47
  and culture, 12
  and desire, 113
  and ideology, 9
  and representation, 12
  and retirement, 50
  and Sandleford, 159
  and sexuality, 28
  and the garden, 93
  and wealth, 117
  as feminine, 8, 230
  as wild, 98
  Bluestockings on human, 79
  contemplation of, 79
  gendered accounts of, 13
  god of, 75
  ideas of, 25, 27, 32, 33
  in Berkshire, 167
  in Rousseau, 66
  works of, 103
needlework, 29, 73, 182, 243
New Pleasant Instructor, The
  tale of Henrietta, 123
Newton, Isaac, 222
nightingales, 16, 63, 107, 112, 113, 147, 148
Notting Hill, 191
Notting Hill House, ix, 16, 38, 39, 173, 176,
    190, 191, 193, 194, 196, 197, 198, 200,
    201, 202, 203
  visitors, 201
Nuneham, 23

O'Brien, Karen
  on Carter, 126
  on Talbot's *Reflections*, 256
  on the Bluestockings, 79, 80, 139, 261
Orrery, John Boyle, Earl of Cork and
  hermitage at Caledon, 233, 234
Osterley Park, 13
Oxenden, George, 43

Painshill, 9, 276
painting, 29
  erotic, 29, 30
Paradise, 93, 96, 122, 123, 145, 153
passion, 24, 30, 63, 89, 109, 110, 112, 119, 132,
    153, 209, 235, 273

pastoral, 5, 6, 17, 19, 148, 243
  an urban product, 149, 150
  and desire, 54, 183, 207
  and fantasy, 66, 102
  and fine ladies, 117
  and happiness, 56
  and leisure, 54
  and location, 53–4, 55, 58
  and melancholy, 124
  and moral responsibility, 168
  and otium, 54
  and pleasure, 121, 122, 149
  and retirement, 183
  and romance, 1, 2, 5, 55, 92, 95–123, 147,
    149, 150, 157, 204, 206, 207, 208, 217,
    219, 237
    in women's letters, 100
  and sexuality, 55, 122
  and sociability, 53
  and solitude, 206
  and the city, 81
  and transgression, 101
  appeal for women, 56, 57
  as a city vision, 51
  as absence, 168, 183, 187
  as absence of location, 53
  as articulation of longing, 54
  as beyond reach, 54
  as deception, 104
  as desire for simplicity, 54, 183
  as erotic space, 97
  as fantasy, 97
  as idyll, 16, 53, 54, 58, 96, 116, 206, 238, 239
  as loss, 54, 58
  as nostalgia, 150
  as resistance and acceptance, 56
  as suspension between states, 81
  as transformative, 55
  attractions of, 148
  conflicting accounts of, 155
  decline of in the eighteenth century, 56
  epic and romance, 55
  expectations, 54
  experience of, 54
  Frank Kermode on, 149
  in Shakespeare's romances, 55
  models, 96
  modes and definitions, 56, 149
  Paul Alpers on, 55
  Samuel Johnson on, 56
  William Empson on, 54
pastourelles, 54
penitence, 1, 5, 39

For EU product safety concerns, contact us at Calle de José Abascal, 56–1°,
28003 Madrid, Spain or eugpsr@cambridge.org.